The Saturdays of my childhood were spent in Jay Sebring's studio watching him cut my father's hair. But even if I wasn't privileged to possess such a fond memory, I'd still have been moved by this biography. In telling the story of Jay's glamorous life and brutal demise, Anthony DiMaria and Marshall Terrill also share a horror as terrible as the Manson killings themselves: They expose an industry of hucksters who write books that prefer sensation over fact, with inaccuracies so egregious they seem to murder the people on Cielo Drive all over again. They even take us to a convention of subculture ghouls who sell these books, as well as T-shirts, coffee mugs, and any imaginable merchandise glorifying the homicides on August 8, 1969, a night that brought pain to so very many families. The only solace they might find is that the authors penned a book that finally educates the public not only about who Jay Sebring was, but on the truth of what really happened on Cielo Drive and the pitiless aftermath the surviving families faced afterwards.

Griffin Dunne
Actor, Director and Producer

OPENING - AUGUST 1969

Hi, my name is Jay Sebring and I'm thirty-five years old.

The purpose of the [book you are about to read], is to pass on to you the findings and the knowledge that I have acquired over the years. As time goes on, styles will change as they have in the past. But the basic concept will remain the same. And that is what we are endeavoring to present to you here in its simplest form.

You will best benefit yourself by keeping an open mind and forgetting most of what you have learned in the past. Because after all, the usefulness of a bowl is in its emptiness.

And now we will begin with some basic fundamentals....

JAY SEBRING....

CUTTING TO THE TRUTH

THE BIRTH OF COOL, THE DEATH OF THE SIXTIES, AND THE MURDERS THAT SHOCKED A NATION

MARSHALL TERRILL

ANTHONY DIMARIA

Genius
Book Publishing

Published by:
Genius Book Publishing
PO Box 250380
Milwaukee Wisconsin 53225 USA
GeniusBookPublishing.com

Paperback ISBN: 978-1-958727-76-8
Hardcover ISBN: 978-1-958727-77-5

250904 Trade
Approved

CONTENTS

Introduction   xi

Prologue   1
1. Tom from Michigan   5
2. Oh, a Sailor's Life is Not for Me   16
3. A Gap Year   29
4. The Mirage Factory   41
   Photos   49
5. Reinvention and Revolution   67
6. The Ball Has Started Its Roll   78
7. Piece by Piece   89
8. A Jack in Vegas   102
9. A Slave to Fashion   112
10. Demand and Supply   122
11. To Have and to Hold for One Hell of a Ride   133
12. The Cost of Success   146
13. Friends to the End   158
14. Enter the Dragon   171
15. The Go-Go Generation   187
16. Exquisite Beauty   197
   Photos   215
17. Expand the Brand   239
18. The Tastemaker   250
19. London Calling   260
20. The Beautiful People   273
21. Trial and Error   284
22. You've Come a Long Way, Baby   296
23. The Family   308
24. Exposed   326
25. Hot August Night   342
26. A Weird Homicide   357

27. Live Freaky, Die Freaky 370
28. The Family Shit-Show 388
29. The Spaghetti Defense 403
30. Damaged Dynasty 415
31. Parole Purgatory 429
32. Politics, Policies, and Pernicious Precedents 445
33. Distortion, Distraction and Deflection 457
   Epilogue 480

   Photos 483
   Afterword 507
   Closing 509
   Acknowledgments 511
   Source Notes 515
   Selected Bibliography 559

This book is dedicated to the memories of Gary Hinman, Steven Parent, Jay Sebring, Wojciech Frykowski, Abigail Folger, Sharon Tate, Paul Richard Polanski, Rosemary LaBianca, Leno LaBianca, Donald Shea and their families.

Also, to the memory of Scott Seckel, who started this book with us but unfortunately could not finish. However, his spirit, unwavering enthusiasm and booming inner voice stayed with us for the entire journey.

Marshall Terrill and Anthony DiMaria

I'd like to dedicate this book to Jay Sebring, a pioneering figure, a true visionary and once in a millennia artist. I hope we have made you proud wherever you are.

To my co-author, Anthony DiMaria. I could not have asked for a more dedicated writing partner than you, pal.

And to my wife Zoe, who allows me time and space to create and write without complaint.

Marshall Terrill

I am so grateful to Bernard and Margarette Kummer, Jay Sebring, and Peggy and Tony DiMaria for their abounding love, support and resource shared in this endeavor. This is also extended to Christy and

Mishele DiMaria, Fred and Mary Kummer, Geraldine Kummer O'Connor and Ed O'Connor, Tracy Rowland, and nephews Brody and Blake. Thanks to them, this book contains the detail and quality Jay's story demands.

And to my significant better half, Maria Alicia Rogers, who reminds me every day the miracles of beauty, courage, intelligence, humor and generosity. Sadly, on June 18, 2025, Maria succumbed to her decade-long battle with pseudomyxoma peritonei. If only....

In 1977, my sixth-grade teacher pulled me aside during a lunch break. She pointed at me and said, "You are a writer." I was confused as she apparently was unaware of my future plans to play in the National Football League. Later, during a written class exam, that same teacher would slip to me, on the sly, a small hardcover book titled *The Elements of Style*, which I still have. Sister Joseph Therese, it's taken nearly fifty years to prove you right, so thank you, for inspiring me and stoking the fires within.

Anthony DiMaria

INTRODUCTION

We're going to start off like Jay would: this is about you.

His story is about you because you look the way you do thanks to Jay (this is directed at male readers, obviously).

Before Jay, men went to a barbershop and pointed to a poster on a wall. It had photos usually of nine haircuts, almost all a variation of the flattop. There was the "Butch," the "Flattop," "Flattop Boogie," the "Forward Combed Boogie," the "Crew," and the "Hollywood." There were also three versions of the "Contour." They were the "College," the "Executive," and the "Professional." Those were your options.

The barber wore a white coat with short sleeves, usually betraying a tattoo. Forget tribals and inspirational quotes; this guy had an anchor, a mermaid, or a hula dancer. There were ashtrays (lots of them) and side tables stacked with magazines—auto, hunting, true crime, plus a few *Playboys* (if you were under fifteen and dared sneak a peek you could expect to hear, "Those aren't for you, son," from the barber). He shaved your neck with hot foam and a straight razor, then he dabbed on potions with "Jockey" or "Prince" in the name until you smelled like him.

And you looked like shit.

Every guy did because every guy got one haircut: a variation of the same haircut.

That is until Jay came along. He made you the best-looking version of you. Before Jim Morrison was Jim Morrison, Elektra Records sent him to Jay's salon sometime in late 1966.

"What can I do for you?" Jay asked.

"I wanna look like this," Morrison said.

He pulled out a picture of a statue of Alexander the Great. The iconic image of Jim Morrison that is plastered on T-shirts and posters to this day is what Jay created.

Jay Sebring was the first superstar hairstylist (though he often corrected people and referred to himself as a "hair designer"). He was Vidal Sassoon before Vidal Sassoon. He was Gene Shacove before Gene Shacove. In the 1960s, he charged the equivalent of $1,000 in today's dollars for one of his cuts. He introduced concepts like privacy and exclusivity, which salons, restaurants, and nightclubs embrace today. His client list read like the essential Hollywood power structure, circa 1965. Steve McQueen once demanded that Metro-Goldwyn-Mayer studio fly in Jay for an on-location cut in New Orleans at $2,500 a per day for the stylist's services, but it was really an opportunity for them to hang out, smoke pot, and chase women. Jay jetted in on a Friday, partied with McQueen for two days, cut his hair on the third, and a few hours later was back at his trendy Fairfax salon, tending to his Hollywood clientele of icons, movie stars, A-listers, moguls, titans of industry, entertainment executives, and power players who queued in line for hours to experience Jay's magic.

This is the story of an American entrepreneur and visionary who left his modest Midwestern home in a car that had to be push started and went to seek his fortune in Southern California—a place that often doesn't get the credit due for the profound cultural changes happening there at that time. The old Hollywood, ruled by the studios, with its carefully curated stars and pearlescent publicity photos, was giving way to a grittier, more rebellious aesthetic by the time Jay arrived.

Music, architecture, movies, art, graphic design, cuisine, and fashion were all being remade in Southern California. While San Francisco gets credit to this day for dominating 1960s popular culture, anyone there at the time who became someone later on eventually went to L.A.

In Los Angeles, there was no six degrees of separation in this era. It was more like two. There was a palpable intimacy in L.A.'s Thirty Mile Zone. Common dreams were stoked up by the vibe of the times and those cool sounding street names: Hollywood Boulevard, the Sunset Strip, Santa Monica Boulevard, Melrose Avenue, Rodeo Drive, La Cienega, and the ones that ran through the canyons: Laurel, Benedict, and Topanga. It's where Neil Young, Bruce Palmer, Richie Furay, and Stephen Stills spotted each other going in opposite directions one afternoon on Sunset Boulevard. Young was hard to miss: He was driving a '53 Pontiac hearse with Palmer riding shotgun. They pulled a U-turn, stopped their cars, greeted each other, and created Buffalo Springfield on the spot. This was also the same roadway where Steve McQueen would cruise in one of his high-end sports cars and troll for young women and hitchhikers. His pickup was crude but highly effective: "Get in. Shut the door. You know who I am, right? I don't like to talk—you can see me talk in the movies. But if you're up for a little fun and games...."

In Hidden Hills at a record producer's private retreat, Janis Joplin cracked Jim Morrison over the head with a bottle of Southern Comfort to fend off his sloppy and drunken advances. It had the opposite effect: it turned him on, and he *begged* for her phone number. Up in Laurel Canyon, David Crosby and Joni Mitchell performed acoustic sets in living rooms together while appreciative guests swayed their heads, sipped on wine, and passed a roach around. In Beverly Hills, Brian Wilson composed the Beach

Boys' next wave of classic songs on a piano sitting in a bed of sand because he liked to wiggle his toes in it while he was working.

Meanwhile, the scene in his brother's Pacific Palisades mansion was a crowd of freeloading hippies and drifters, including a creepy ex-con trying to wheedle his way into the music business with a load of hipster patter and a bevy of unwashed nymphs. L.A. in the 1960s was a place where things like this happened all the time.

Two degrees of separation.

All those elements and lives intersected here. And nothing would ever be the same.

PROLOGUE

Jay Sebring had two lives: his rise to become a cultural icon and, later, as a victim of one of the most barbarous crimes in American history. The second overshadowed the first in what should have been a triumphant legacy—the legacy of someone who earned everything the American dream offers: fame, fortune, respect and being the very best in his field.

All of that was firmly in his grasp. Before the zenith of his success, Sebring's true fate and destiny was obliterated. His name garnered immense respect in the entertainment and hair care industries. His legend had spread beyond Hollywood. His hair cutting and styling technique cross pollinated acting, music, sports, business, and society's elite. Having conquered those worlds, he was breaking ground with a chain of salons, a complete line of products bearing his name, and wealth and fame that would guarantee him a dynasty at age thirty-five.

He had all the trappings that come with that—a cozy, historic chalet in Benedict Canyon (once owned by film star Jean Harlow), luxury sports cars, tailored clothes, and a string of beautiful women. His phone rang with calls from movie, television, and recording stars, as well as producers and industry tycoons who wanted his company as much as they wanted his cuts. The interest in his companionship developed because of his keen eye for exquisite quality, defining the best look for personal style and hell-bent-for-leather lifestyle.

He also could be counted on for honesty and sincerity, the two rarest Hollywood virtues. Jay's Midwestern values, humility, and candor made him stand out in this regard.

Jay was intense in the way driven men usually are. His eye was always on the ball, always on the cutting edge, light years ahead of societal norms. There was no guile or insecurity with him. He didn't need approval or to be coddled. He didn't have a weak ego in constant need of being fed or stroked. He had a Solomonic mind with great insight, reasonableness, and discretion. If his clients had personal or professional issues, Jay was the guy to talk to. He was the perfect insider and confidante. Having people spill their guts to him was part of the job, like a bartender or therapist, but much deeper and more expensive.

Most of this book is about that Jay Sebring. Enough ink has been spilled about his second life, and far too little about his first.

Since his murder, Jay's reputation has been as mutilated as his body. The press—and a few backstabbing Hollywood associates—played a huge part in that. Printing rumor, innuendo, and outright falsehoods in an era when the Fifth Estate had practiced restraint but was now on its way out. A story as lurid and twisted as the Manson murders got a lot of attention. To get more attention, journalists had to be more salacious than the rest. Jay was caught in that crossfire. More than a half-century after the crimes, he is still caught in that crossfire.

Jay's story and the historical context surrounding these notorious murders needs to be corrected. He was a man who led an extraordinary life in an extraordinary time and, until now, that's a tale that hasn't been told.

While the second Jay Sebring remains silent in his grave, the first Jay Sebring—the man who lived—has more to share....[1]

---

1. For this book, the authors have opted to use four dots whenever an ellipsis appears in the text. Jay Sebring intentionally used four throughout his life in his personal correspondence, letters, and most notably on his Fairfax shop front signage, "SEBRING...." The added touch, literally and figuratively, embodied Sebring's constitution of thinking outside the box and gravitation into the beyond.

CHAPTER 1
TOM FROM MICHIGAN

Jay Sebring was not born Jay Sebring. He was born Thomas John Kummer. Jay was much bigger than Tom. He had to be created, not born. Stars are like that.

Just as Cherilyn Sarkisian, Stefani Germanotta, and John Joseph Nicholson are different people from Cher, Lady Gaga, and Jack Nicholson respectively, Tom Kummer had to reinvent himself to get where he wanted to be.

Whether it's being deemed a star among stars, dating Hollywood's most beautiful women, driving high-end sports cars like Jaguars and Cobras, flying across the globe in private jets, or living in historic Benedict Canyon chalets, this lifestyle is not available to the average person. It is in another atmosphere altogether. You need to escape gravity to get there.

Tom Kummer wasn't going to be able to do that.

But Jay Sebring could. And did.

This is his story, presented in its entirety for the very first time.

It begins with fire and ice—his mother and father.

Jay's father, Bernard, was born in Michigan, the son of German immigrant, Kurt Frederick Kummer, and his wife, Ottilia "Tillie" Marie Burk.

Kurt Kummer abandoned his family when Bernard was three, so Tillie took her two sons with her to live with her parents. She earned a living hand-painting porcelain and teaching the same. Her mentor and uncle, master painter George Leykauf, said she could put the breeze in flowers on a tureen. Leykauf porcelain is highly valued today.

She might have passed her artistic abilities on to her oldest son, but Bernard felt he had to become the man of the house during harsh, difficult times. He had to step up and help his mother provide for their family, according to Jay's sister, Peggy DiMaria. She said of her father:

> He needed to have this strength and always be determined and always think outside of himself and what is good for the family and what needs to be done. He worked during the day and went to school at night. There was no childhood in between. It wasn't that he didn't want to take chances. He wasn't allowed.

Bernard and his brother were Jesuit educated in grade school, high school, and college. Bernard graduated from the University of Detroit. His upbringing, moral code, and thinking revolved around regimentation. Restrict yourself. Tell the truth. Always do the right thing. After graduation, he worked for Deloitte and Touche, one of the Big Four accounting firms in the United States.

Jay's mother, Margarette ("Peg"), was the sixth of eleven children of Scottish immigrant Thomas Wilson Gibb, and Lavona McLain, an Alabama native.

Raised in Pratt City, Alabama, a small town outside Birmingham, she was a coal miner's daughter from a large family.

"Raising eleven children in Alabama, I would have to conclude they were poor," said Fred Kummer, Jay's younger brother. "I think they had a pretty tough time with it."

One of Peg's sisters once confided to their mother that classmates made fun of her and she was ashamed of being poor.

"You should never be ashamed of being poor," Lavona said. "You should only be ashamed of being dirty." Though often poverty stricken, the Gibb family was wealthy with pride.

Peg strongly believed these two things: soap doesn't cost much, and it doesn't cost anything to keep yourself clean. The youngest children in the family only had shoes when they were old enough to go to school, where shoes were required. The shoes were passed down from the older siblings, holes patched with cardboard.

Her father, a small, slight man, worked in the mines. After years down in the pit he developed black lung. Unable to go underground anymore, he turned a room in their house into a barber shop. He set up a chair, saw clients, and made a living cutting hair.

When one of her sisters, Beth, moved to New Orleans, Peg soon followed, working as a switchboard operator.

As a junior accountant, Bernard was often on the road tending to clients. (He later earned his CPA through night school.) On a trip to Louisiana, he met his future wife.

"My parents met in New Orleans," Peggy DiMaria said. "My dad was there on business and my mother was visiting her sister. It was Mardi Gras. They went out a lot."

With its distinct blend of French, Spanish, Creole, and American architecture, festive spirit, music-filled culture, bustling nightlife, and relaxed adherence to Prohibition restrictions, the iconic city at the foot of the Mississippi River was catnip for lovers.

It's unclear how long the two dated or where they spent most of their time courting, but on August 14, 1932, Bernard and Peg were married. Bernard relocated to Memphis, regularly commuting to Pratt City to spend time with his newlywed.

In no time, Thomas, their first child (later known to the world as Jay Sebring), was born on October 10, 1933, in Fairfield,

Alabama, at Lloyd Nolan Hospital. Thomas was close with his parents, although he talked to them differently. Everyone did.

Having been raised in a single-parent household with the strains of the Depression indelibly etched in his psyche, Bernard was strict, accurate, regimented, and blunt. He was a no-nonsense, old-school parent, and there was no room for debate or thinking outside the box, especially when it came to his children. Peggy DiMaria said her father had a sharp tongue and equally sharp mind:

> He could shoot you down with the English language and really put you in your place when you thought you had it all figured out. He would always come from a different angle than what you were discussing when you wanted to do something or when you wanted to get your way.

In Bernard's worldview, ambiguity did not exist. You did not go out on a school night. You did not come home after curfew. You did not do a shoddy job on a chore. And you did not dare to ask for an exemption to any of the above. If you did, you knew what the answer was going to be.

Often, Thomas did know what the answer was going to be, but he poked the bear as often as he could, according to his brother.

"I think their personalities conflicted in a very big way," Fred Kummer said. "Tom pretty much wanted to do what he wanted to do, and Dad was an authoritarian. And the two mixed like oil and water."

Peg was a listener. When her children came home from school, she wanted to hear all their stories about what happened that day. She had a way of being encouraging, of making the kids feel good about their ideas. She wanted them to have ideas.

"It doesn't matter to me what you decide to be," she told them. "What I would like to know is that you be the best you can be at whatever you choose to be."

It was a far cry from Bernard's mantra of "Be the best you can be every minute of your life." Her youngest son Fred Kummer called her the "heart of the family."

There would be four children: After Thomas ("Tom") came Geraldine ("Gerry"), then Frederic ("Fred"), and finally Margaret ("Peggy"). Tom was the rugged individualist. Peggy was like Tom, but quieter. Fred and Gerry were well-behaved.

Life in the Kummer household was strict, but certainly not by the standards of the time. If you were supposed to do something and didn't do it, you were in trouble.

One day Tom was in trouble (again). He hadn't waxed the stairs properly or had to be told to clean out the fireplace. Punishment was painting the metal fence in the backyard. Bernard was gone for the day; he went into the office a lot on Saturdays, especially during tax season. Before he left, he gave detailed instructions on how he wanted the fence painted.

Peg glanced out the window. Tom was not painting. He was sitting on a rock. The next time she looked out, she couldn't see him. She grew concerned. Six, six-thirty that night Bernard was going to be home. He was going to want dinner and a fully painted fence when he got there. He could be a little stricter than he needed to be, in her mind, and she gave the kids a little more leverage, but it was all good in the end to her.

She went outside. Tom was sitting on a step directing a group of his friends as they painted the fence.

"Your father's going to be home soon," Peg told Tom, her tone hinting that he might be in further trouble if the chore wasn't finished at day's end.

He looked up and smiled without saying a word.

The fence got painted. Saint Benedict classmate Jerry Mullin recalls that memorable spring Saturday afternoon.

"I was one of the four guys painting the fence," Mullin said.

"Some people did ceilings, you know, Michelangelo and so forth. I did the fence. Tom was behind the whole thing directing us."

"He was the leader of the pack," Peggy said. "He was the one with the idea and he was the one who got everything going."

Their house had a screened-in back porch. Jay told his parents he wanted to spend the summer sleeping out there because he liked the fresh air and wanted a change of pace. What he did not tell them was that sneaking out of the house at night from the back porch was easier. He would head to his buddies' houses in the middle of the night.

Tom was usually awake most nights. Like many artists, he was a nocturnal creature.

"He was at his best at night," his sister Peggy said. "It was like he didn't want to lose the time when you normally sleep. He would want to spend that living life as well."

Childhood chum Jim Graham described Jay's adventurous spirit as a young lad:

I heard a stone at my window. And it was Tom. I went downstairs. My parents were sleeping, and he said, "C'mon let's go down the street, go out and do something." I said, "Tom, man, it's the middle of the night!"' I wasn't gonna go out there.

Jim complained the stone might wake his parents to which Tom suggested, "If you tie a string to your foot or hand then put it out the window, I can just pull on it." Tom was a mischievous guy and marched to a different beat.

The problem was as much as Tom loved the night, he hated mornings—a trait that lasted well into adulthood. His sleeping patterns resulted in frequent exchanges between Tom and his father.

❧

In the 1940s, Detroit was hardly a sleepy town but a bustling company city that "put the world on wheels." Grand Boulevard was plastered with ads for Ford, Cadillac, and Firestone. J.L. Hudson's was the big department store downtown. The last of the passenger steamers cruised Lake Erie and two giant ferries took passengers across the river to the amusement park on Boblo Island.

The Tigers played at Briggs Stadium. For coffee, Qwikee Donut and Coffee Shop had three downtown locations. This was the city's golden era. The population peaked in 1950 at just under 1.9 million people.

It is true auto workers were the highest paid manufacturing employees in the country, but what's less well known is that it wasn't steady work because of material shortages after World War II. It was unhealthy work, too. The plants were filthy, with bad air quality and oil swirling all around. Men contracted black lung disease, cancer, and a variety of musculoskeletal disorders in these plants, not to mention punctures, cuts, burns, electrocution, and other non-fatal injuries that amputated various body parts. "Horror stories," one Detroiter of the period called them.

After the war, many smaller auto companies went bust. Most auto workers had side jobs. Civic leaders were dismayed that after the war all the people who had flocked there for jobs didn't return home. Housing was scarce. Highland Park, where the Kummers lived, was a working-class neighborhood at the time. The Ford Highland Park plant employed thousands of people.

Even still, kids in Tom's neighborhood had idyllic childhoods. They walked everywhere because few people had cars. They knew everyone and who lived in every house. In winter they ice skated on Ford Field and sledded off the roof of Tom's garage. In summer they rented ponies at Palmer Park and played pickup games of baseball and basketball. Tom directed his friends in skits they put on in the garage, with singing, dancing, and comedic bits.

"He was very friendly, and he had a charisma," said Jim

Graham, who first met Jay in grade school at Saint Benedict's and knew him into adulthood. "He was always upbeat, but I could see where people might have thought he was a little introspective."

That introspection was most likely inherent. After all, he came from a lineage of creative individuals.

At his grandmother Tillie's house, Tom was exposed to jars of porcelain paint, the tang of turpentine, and the glow of creation. George Leykauf had Tillie paint the gold leaf scrolling on the rims of dishes and platters. He only wanted the real thing. He believed raised paste ornamentation detracted from the artistry of the pieces. Leykauf's work is noted for never repeating a theme. Tillie explained this to Jay. He was exposed to exacting standards of artistry, beauty, and quality at a young age, the very qualities he would incorporate into his salons decades later.

Tom was not a particularly dedicated student. He wasn't a wise guy, creating problems in class. He just wasn't present mentally. He drew—cars, ships, movie stars, pinup girls—and dreamed. Big. For grade school he went to Saint Benedict's, a Catholic school. His mother was called in to speak with Tom's teacher because he spent his time in the classroom staring out the window with a smile on his face, oblivious to what was being taught. Peg knew Tom was wired differently than the other children.

"You know, once they lost him, they lost him, and they probably lost him as soon as they started talking, quite honestly," his sister said.

Perhaps, if Saint Benedict's had had an art program or a subject that remotely appealed to Tom, they might not have lost him. Schools didn't have anything like music or art programs back then. Public schools had shop classes, but they didn't have arts programs.

Once he sat behind Jerry Mullin at a schoolyard lunch table, intensely drawing on the inside fold of his beige raincoat collar. "Whatever you do, don't put your collar up," Tom said when he was done. When they went to chapel, Tom's buddy flipped his collar up, only to have it seized by an angry nun who hauled the boy outside. Tom had drawn a naked woman. In ballpoint ink.

Tom was a creative powerhouse. He just knew what looked good.

Very Best Candies on Hamilton Avenue in Highland Park had window waxing contests every year at Halloween and Tom won the competition twice.

From time to time, Peggy would do their mother's hair, and Tom would walk in the kitchen, watch for a moment, and then make suggestions.

"You could try this," he would say. "Or you could do it like that, that way."

His friends remember him as being a fastidious dresser whose shoes gleamed. Sartorially he was put together, even in eighth grade.

"He was very good looking and presented himself nicely," Jim Graham said. "And that really worked well in his business obviously, styling."

After he graduated from St. Benedict's, Tom attended the University of Detroit Jesuit High School. A Jesuit education is strict and academically and intellectually rigorous. In other words, a disaster for Tom. He was kicked out after his freshman year for bad grades. In his yearbook, he appears in his class photo, kneeling and squinting into the sun, but that's his only appearance. No glee club, camera club, science club, or sports teams. His report card for June 1949 stated the reason for withdrawal in one word: "Failure."

Tom's extracurricular activities as a teenager included joyriding with his friend Jerry Johnson. The two often ventured to a used car lot on Woodward Street—Detroit's Main Street. The dealer made the mistake of leaving the keys in the cars, and they would "borrow" a car, drive it around all weekend, and bring it back on Sunday night.

The older Tom got, the more tensions rose in the Kummer home in classic father-son clashes.

"It's the little things that count," Bernard told Tom. "Be on time or earlier. Do what you say, no matter what. I'd like to compliment you some time and not always correct you." (It was more than a little ironic since Bernard also liked to stay up at night. "He was the only CPA that I ever knew of that went to work at 10:00 a.m.," his daughter said.)

A letter Tom wrote to his father in 1949, a year before he left home, revealed the general shape of what was an ongoing conflict.

"Instead of being smart and snippy when you speak to me, I should take the right attitude and not scowl and make smart remarks," Tom wrote in what strongly smacks of a mandated apology letter. "When I have done something wrong, I should not only say, 'I'm sorry' but I should also prove myself."

A pillar in the Catholic community, Bernard lobbied to enroll his expelled son into Catholic Central, a parochial all boys school—and Tom was admitted. Bernard had high hopes but should have known better. It wasn't as strict but his grades were still not up to par and Tom didn't last long—about a month, with Tom doodling, staring out the window and flunking a majority of his classes.

Months after Tom started at Catholic Central, Peg and Bernard received a phone call. The United States Navy was on the line. On October 10, 1950, Thomas John Kummer personally submitted his enlistment form on his seventeenth birthday to the local naval office. The authorities found the parental consent signature of Bernard John Kummer suspicious. For good reason. The teen had forged his father's signature in the absence of both parents. As Tom happily waited to be recruited in the armed forces, his plot was foiled when naval officers notified the Kummers.

Bernard was shocked. They sat down after dinner—the time reserved for anything serious in the Kummer home—and there was a long conversation.

"I want to see the world," Tom said, pleading his case. "I *need* to see the world."

They contemplated his words. Maybe this is what Tom needs, they thought. Maybe he should go in the service. It might be good for him. School certainly wasn't. After much contemplation, Bernard reluctantly signed.

"He [Tom] was probably thinking, *I'm out!*" Peggy said. "*I'm out of the house. No more rules, no more school.* And of course, what he found out was that the navy was a whole lot of rules."

Tom was about to discover his father's regimentation paled in comparison to life in the American military. Living under Bernard Kummer's roof was a frolic contrasted with a regiment of commanding officers and serving on a destroyer during war time.

In time, he would understand this.

CHAPTER 2

OH, A SAILOR'S LIFE IS NOT FOR ME

I n the fall of 1950, Tom Kummer reported to basic training at Naval Training Station Great Lakes on the southwestern shore of Lake Michigan in Illinois, an hour's drive north of Chicago.

The Great Lakes seems an odd choice for training a blue water navy—it's 1,000 miles from any ocean—but after the Spanish American War, navy leaders noticed 43 percent of their recruits came from the Midwest. So it made sense to train them there.

World famous band leader and composer John Philip Sousa was Bandmaster of Great Lakes during World War I. Other famous alums include the Fighting Sullivans, five brothers from Iowa who were all killed in the Pacific during the Naval Battle of Guadalcanal. (Their deaths caused all branches of the military to restrict siblings serving together.) In all global battles fought by the U.S. Navy, one in four of its enlisted sailors came from the Great Lakes. (It's now called Recruit Training Command, Great Lakes.)

When Tom arrived, the Cold War was in full swing. On June 25, 1950, North Korea attacked South Korea, and President Harry Truman ordered American forces to help save its ally from the clutches of communism.

Great Lakes was on a war footing, cranking out sailors as fast as it had during World War II. A year after Tom's training, instructors graduated ninety-eight companies of recruits in one week, matching records from the 1940s.

Tom was assigned to Company 372, according to *The Keel*, the station's cruise book (what is elsewhere called a yearbook), which numbered 129 young men.

Boot camp was eleven weeks long in the 1950s, but it roughly followed the tenets of basic training today. After being examined medically, dentally, and administratively, recruits received inoculations, an initial issue of uniforms, and their first military haircut. Tom's close navy buddy Larry Longlott described that and all other subsequent military haircuts: "Disaster. It was disaster. Especially for Tom."

They were taught basic grooming standards, the Uniform Code of Military Justice, and standards of conduct. The first week was devoted to general orders, the core values of the navy, basics of watch standing, and learning to organize equipment. (The Sailor's Creed didn't exist yet.) The second week was physical conditioning, which was not an issue for Tom. After that it was laws of armed conflict, basic seamanship, shipboard communication, navy ship and aircraft identification, the chain of command, custom and courtesies, weapons training, shipboard damage control and fire-fighting, skills.

Tom was taught how to swim and studied *The Bluejacket's Manual*, a reference book for sailors of all ranks. It includes chapters on ships and aircraft, uniforms, weapons, damage control, communications, naval customs and ceremonies, security, leadership, pay and benefits, naval missions, military fundamentals, and seamanship.

A photo of Tom on the rifle range squinting down the barrel of an M1 Garand made it into *The Keel*, his navy yearbook. In his class photo, he looks exactly like what he was: a newly minted seventeen-year-old with a goofy grin.

But marksmanship and firefighting weren't all he would learn over the next four years. Jay Sebring was born in the navy.

After graduation, Tom was assigned to his duty station, Guam, a 210-square-mile island in the western Pacific. It was not a dream assignment or ideal locale, according to Larry Longlott.

"In the States, there was a navy yard in Norfolk, Virginia, and we were not happy," Longlott said. "We were going to Guam versus the States."

The two were stationed in Guam approximately five years after the end of World War II. The island wasn't covered in high-rise hotels stuffed with Japanese tourists like it is now. Twenty-nine percent of the U.S. territory is devoted to military bases, surrounded by the kind of questionable bars bases everywhere attract. It was a sleepy backwater island with amazing beaches. The Chamorros—the native people of Guam—didn't like American servicemen and spat at them. When military sports teams traveled around the island in big trucks for games, the Chamorros pelted the trucks with rocks and whatever else was at hand. When not being hassled by the natives, Marines and sailors brawled like clockwork.

Tom was placed in a barracks with Larry Longlott from Philadelphia. The two became fast and notorious friends.

"Through the two years we became buddies," Longlott said. "We went everywhere on Guam."

They became adept at getting out of work details and making the best of their military service.

"We would sneak out, went to some bars. We were always having fun," Longlott said. "We would come back to the barracks and people would think, *Here they come again, Larry and Tom.*"

Horrified by navy barbers whose dome chops were messing with their love lives, Tom started cutting his own hair (or doing as much as he could while still staying within regulations). Sister Peggy DiMaria described Tom's rude awakening in the service.

My brother, from grade school to high school, wanted his own identity. He wanted to look different; he wanted to look special. And now he looked like everybody else. That really bothered him. He felt like his identity was stripped from him. So that was the beginning for him. He was telling his buddies what he was doing, and some said, "Would you cut *my* hair?" So that was the beginning, and he had everybody having somewhat of a style.… as much as he could within the navy rules.

About the only thing Tom liked in the navy were denim shirts and pants. More than ten years later, he would share the same navy garb aesthetic with Hollywood designer Fred Segal when creating the look for his staff in what later became the uniform for his future business.

Larry Longlott said Tom's sense of style stood out among his fellow servicemen, and many didn't approve.

He was sharp.… real sharp. And he got me to start being sharp. I was his first customer, actually. And some of the guys laughed at us because they didn't like the haircut he gave me. We called 'em duck's asses. They laughed at us because they didn't like it. "Shit kickers." Yeah, that's what we called them. We got in a couple of fights with them, too. Some of the guys thought he was too sharp. They thought he was a little cocky.

But not all of them. Many GIs on the base sidled up to him and asked if he could do the same thing for them. Tom assured them he could.

"I'll make you look a lot better than *that* guy," Tom said. He was already a style setter, according to Longlott.

He would look for something different than the rest. Like if we had these black things on, he would want his farther up than the other ones. Things like that. And I would follow him as well. He was cool. He was sharper than any of the other people. And some of 'em liked it.

By now Tom had acquired a nickname: "TJ."

Life on Guam fell into a routine of chores, carousing, fighting, cutting hair, sneaking out, and avoiding work. In other words, a normal seventeen-year-old life.

He found time to write his sister Peggy a charming letter in 1951, with a drawing of himself straight out of Andy Capp by Reg Smythe.

"I wish I could grow as fast as you, but I'm almost the same I was when you saw me last," he wrote with a sweet and sentimental tone.

For Father's Day, Tom also dropped his father a hand-made postcard featuring a picture of the navy rascal proudly standing at the base on the card's cover with the title "FOR YOU DAD On Father's Day." He inscribed on the photo: "To the best dad a guy could have, Tom." The postcard not only demonstrated a newfound respect for Bernard, but must have melted his old man's heart:

Though I say it too seldom
I hope by now you've guessed....
That I think the world
Of you, DAD
And I wish you all the best
Your loving son always,
All ways
Tom
"1951"
Guam

There was plenty of that love to go around, too. One night at a bar, Tom and other guys bet Larry he couldn't get a dance. He looked around and pointed to the best-looking female in the place.

"I'm gonna get that girl to dance with me," Larry said with more than a touch of confidence.

"And I stood up and she's sitting down. I said, 'How about a dance?' And she said, 'Alright,'" Larry related.

She happened to come with a date, who punched Larry in the eye. Larry countered and began hitting him on the head, breaking his watch as the barroom erupted into a brawl. The paramour took off. Larry, TJ, and the other guys frantically searched several island watering holes looking for him and his shitkickers.

"We never did find the guy," Longlott said years later. "That was a fun night."

Another night Tom and a buddy named Terry Lanfear, a child-hood friend also from Detroit, came across some marijuana in a bar. He talked Larry into taking a puff or two, which was considered taboo by almost all Americans, except for perhaps the jazz crowd.

I told them I'll try it, but I couldn't handle it. TJ (Tom) could. He was having a ball. They were laughing like crazy, Terry and him. And I'm just sitting there waiting for it to stop. I didn't get to the happy part. I don't even know where he got it. But he would be the one that would find it.

It may have been life on a tropical island with crystal waters and white sand beaches, but it was still life in the military. One day it came to a head when Tom got into an argument with an officer.

The officer punched Tom in the mouth. Something hit the deck. Tom looked down.

"That's my tooth!" he said.

Tom picked it up and stuck it back in his mouth. Surprisingly, it took and remained in his upper gum but with ongoing effort.

TJ's determination to keep that tooth would nag him for the remainder of his life, resulting in numerous dental procedures and surgeries.

Back home, Christmas in the Kummer household could be a muted affair during Tom's navy years. Peg played carols in the kitchen with her daughters as they each shed a tear while making Christmas sugar cookies as "I'll be home for Christmas" played on the radio. She missed her son terribly and worried about his safety.

Late one holiday evening the doorbell rang, around midnight, way past the time anyone would visit. Bernard, the night owl, was up and opened the door.

"Oh my gosh!" he said.

"Surprise!" Tom said. "I'm home for Christmas!"

"My mother was thrilled to death," Peggy said. "We were so excited."

It wasn't until later they found out Tom had gone away without leave and upon his return was tossed in the stockade. Though he felt it was worth it, Tom was assigned to the Pacific Northwest as a disciplinary lesson, creating a massive geographical expanse between him and his family.

The days of swanning around Guam's pristine beaches and seedy dives ended when Tom was ordered to report to a ship repair unit at the naval station at Tongue Point in Astoria, Oregon, in February 1953, after a short stop in San Diego.

To say Tom's sojourn in Astoria was not a raging military success is an understatement. He was constantly in trouble. He was written up once in March (failure to muster with duty section), twice in July (failure to obey an order and wearing mutilated clothing—someone didn't care for the way he had styled his hat, apparently), and three times in August (unauthorized absence, "intentions unknown"; unauthorized absence for 11 days, 18 hours, and 45 minutes, apprehended by Seattle City Police; and violation for failure to go to an appointed place of duty). His superiors had

had it with him by this point, recommending a court martial. But on August 28, 1953, he was transferred to the USS *Uhlmann* in San Diego, and skirted serious consequences. The assignment would further Tom's ambitions as he described to his sister Peggy, "I wanted to see the world. I REALLY wanted to see the world. But not through a porthole."

The *Uhlmann* was a 376-foot-long destroyer bristling with three types of guns, torpedoes, and depth charges, capable of speeds up to 35 knots (40 miles per hour). It was a Fletcher class destroyer, the first to be outfitted with radar. During Tom's time aboard, the ship was part of Task Force 77, a fast carrier force operating in the Sea of Japan. Because it was wartime, ship's company numbered 329 personnel. (A peacetime crew usually numbered around 250.) A crew that big allowed around the clock manning of gun mounts, repair parties, and watch stations. "Manpower was cheaper than technology" was the navy's philosophy at the time.

Life aboard the ship was by no means easy duty. Sailors slept in canvas bunk tiers stacked four high. There were no portholes or air conditioning. The galley was on the main deck, but food had to be carried on trays down to the mess deck. There was no fore and aft passage inside the ship. In bad weather, when it was unsafe to go on deck, the two ends of the ship could be cut off from each other. Luckily for Tom, the ship had its own barber station (where he would hone his skills) and a medical facility (where he received an emergency appendectomy).

In those days a Pacific Fleet destroyer operated on a two-year cycle. The cycle started at the end of a shipyard overhaul. After the yard period there would be a stint at the Fleet Training Group in San Diego for refresher training followed by a workup for deployment to the Far East. Deployments were six months long followed by a six-month period in the U.S., about half of which was spent underway in various fleet exercises off the West Coast.

On Tom's tour, following exercises off the West Coast, the

Uhlmann was again deployed to the western Pacific. She sailed via the Hawaiian Islands and arrived at Yokosuka on November 20, 1953. During this seven-month tour, the destroyer patrolled waters off Japan and Korea and engaged in training and operations out of Yokosuka and Sasebo with Task Force 77. The year before Tom walked up the *Uhlmann's* gangplank, the ship saw serious action in the Korean War, destroying gun emplacements onshore, dropping off spies, and suffering thirteen wounded in one engagement.

Tom's naval job was provisions as storekeeper in the commissary. He liked it and, in a letter home, called it a "good job."

At one point in January of 1953, Tom had what he called "the scare of his life." "General Quarters" sounded, followed by the announcement "This is not a drill!"

"I never moved so fast in my life," Tom wrote.

For twenty minutes he waited, poised by the gun mount that was his battle station.

Nothing happened.

The word to stand down and secure was announced. Shortly afterward, the captain announced some MIG fighters had been spotted on radar rapidly approaching the task force, but they turned around.

"I just hope they stay back for about five more months," Tom noted in his letter.

When not being terrified by enemy aircraft, Tom spent time on board studying for his GED. He made plans to take the exam his next time in port. The GED meant entry to higher education. Exactly what that meant he didn't know in that moment.

"I have much reason to believe I will past [*sic*] it," he said. Academics were easier for Tom when there was nowhere to sneak out to at night.

Entertainment was, to say the least, limited. Sailors had a rating system for the evening movies. It was usually inscribed on the movie folders:

GF—Good Flick

GFF—Good Fxxxing Flick

GDGFF—God Dxxx Good Fxxxing Flick

Other than books, movies were the only entertainment on board ship. The 2000–2400-hour watch was the most hated because it meant missing the wardroom movie. Tom was among the faces beaming at the screen. He paid special attention to how the stars looked. He had no idea then, but cinema was going to play a huge role in his life in a few years.

While the food was better in the officers' mess, they 1) had to pay for it, and 2) had to eat with the commanding officer. Three forbidden topics at the table were women, politics, and religion. If the CO was a hard-ass or cantankerous, meals degenerated into ass-chewing sessions.

In July 1953, United Nations forces, led by America, came to a cease-fire agreement with North Korea. A peace treaty has, to this day, never been signed, but the four-year "conflict" was finally over.

A few months later in October 1953, Tom penned a letter to his parents while at sea. In the correspondence, Jay Sebring is beginning to eclipse Tom Kummer. The man who would befriend most of Hollywood and much of Los Angeles by making them look amazing didn't start off small. He dated a young lady in Seattle who was well-connected in the music scene up and down the West Coast. Together they went to shows, concerts, parties, clubs, and dinners.

She took him to a party at saxophonist Earl Bostic's house. In a letter to his family, Tom describes his indelible encounter with the jazz legend and icon.

You mentioned the "September Song" by Earl Bostic. He invited us up to his place. Man, what a party. When Joanna introduced me to him, he said, "Well, I've heard a lot about you. I'm very pleased to meet you." Wow, he thinks he's heard a lot about me?!

Tom told Bostic that he had been a fan since he was fifteen. They went to a late dinner with pop singer Joni James after her show. It was an intimate affair where he also met jazz artists Stan Kenton and Lionel Hampton at the same dinner, which no doubt left a deep and lasting impression on the Michigan native.

On a trip to L.A., they saw jazz drummer and composer Max Roach, a pioneer of bebop, who incorporated many other styles of music in his work and is generally considered one of the most important drummers in history. He also saw Shelly Manne, an American jazz drummer most frequently associated with West Coast jazz, at The Lighthouse in Hermosa Beach.

They also heard Ray Anthony, an American bandleader, trumpeter, songwriter, actor, and the last surviving member of the Glenn Miller Orchestra at the Hollywood Palladium on Sunset Boulevard. They saw and later met jazz vocalist King Pleasure, and James Moody, jazz saxophone and flute player and very occasional vocalist, at the famed 5-4 Ballroom. The two-story brick building was to South-Central Los Angeles what the Apollo Theatre was to Harlem and was the center of the hipster scene for many years. Tom was also introduced to Woody Herman, the famed jazz clarinetist, saxophonist, singer, and big band leader.

It wasn't all musical acts. These red-blooded All-American boys made sure to take in Lili St. Cyr at the Follies Theatre in the heart of downtown Los Angeles. The burlesque star was a tall, blond beauty who left almost nothing to the imagination when she stepped dripping wet out of her signature onstage bubble bath.[1]

---

1. The Follies were raided, closed, and reopened at least half a dozen times according to historian Andy Davis. They finally shuttered its doors in 1974 when a wrecking ball razed the building.

Now, after four years in the navy, TJ Kummer, who had left Detroit a seventeen-year-old high school sophomore, was hobnobbing with some of the most revolutionary jazz artists on the West Coast. All of this was a far cry from sneaking out of the house to joyride in cars in Detroit or raising havoc in military bars on a distant island. This was a different world with a real night life filled with sophisticated people, and Tom's eyes opened wide. You can almost see the wheels spinning in his head. This was something he hadn't seen before, and he knew he wanted it. Tom wrote a letter to his parents, detailing his adventures:

I guess you could say I met a lot of people in the past year. I guess there were a lot more, but those were the ones I met through different friends of mine. These people offered me small jobs, and they all seemed to like me quite a bit, but at least I know what I want to do when I get out. Don't laugh but I want to be a beautician.

He didn't have a pseudonym, alter ego, or persona yet, but that short sentence was the birth of "Jay Sebring." Tom saw his future. America didn't know it yet, but it was about to look a whole lot better. For now, only a small band of smelly sailors on a ship in the middle of the Pacific Ocean sported styles the Hollywood elite were soon going to pay dearly for. One day while sitting on the deck of the USS *Uhlmann*, Tom contemplated his future. With his honorable discharge in sight, he took a deep drag of his cigarette, staring at the ocean horizon, and deeply pondered.

What does the world need that does not already exist?

Those navy cuts amplified Tom Kummer's ultimate nexus.

"Every time I have my hair cut, I come out looking like the village idiot," he said. "But women have everything to make them beautiful—hair, makeup, clothing, style. But men have nothing."

Getting there required some strategy and a lot of discipline on

Tom's part. His plan was to go to barber college on the GI Bill, followed by beautician school, according to a letter he penned to Bernard and Peg.

> Then I know that I can get a good job that I like, and it pays very well. That will be good enough for a while anyway.... I figure that while I am going to beautician school, I can make money on the side cutting hair. Of course, I'll cut the families [*sic*] hair for a cheaper rate. HA HA.

His immediate plan was to become the ship's barber. He befriended the ship servicemen who ran the laundry, ship's store, and barber shop. He had three months left before he went home.

Tom Kummer went into the navy, but a glimpse of embryonic Jay Sebring exited the other side. The name, the salon, the A-list clientele, the glamour, the cut, and the acclaim had yet to be realized, but the foundation had been laid.

His next ship would ultimately take him back to Los Angeles. But first he needed to make a brief detour in Detroit.

CHAPTER 3
A GAP YEAR

Downtown Detroit in 1954 was humming with people, big department stores, fancy restaurants, lunch counters, and a vibe that came from one of America's linchpins of industry.

Cars, car accessories, and cigars were featured on nearly every available billboard that filled the sky. Down on the street, everyone was dressed their best. Going downtown was an event, and there was nothing casual about it. People dressed sharply. Men wore suits, ties, monogrammed hankies, and shined shoes. Women wore dresses, trendy hats, gloves, and heels. They lived in nice homes. Church attendance on weekends was more the norm than a rarity, and manners seemed to matter.

Detroit was one of America's greatest cities and helped transform the country, leading the way in manufacturing, diversity, and culture. The downtown area was almost always bustling, filled with street cars, large automobiles, and pedestrian traffic. It was home to tall buildings, bridges, plazas, statues, ornate churches, department stores, mansions, an opera house, a progressive transit system, and an Italian Renaissance-style city hall that stood three stories tall and took a decade to build. Canada was just a fifteen-minute drive via bridge or underwater tunnel a mile long surrounded by 80,000 cubic yards of concrete and 750 tons of reinforced steel and requiring 1.5 million cubic feet of fresh air pumped into the tunnel every minute.

That was the Detroit that Thomas Kummer experienced growing up and into his early adulthood. A few decades before, the city was a shell of itself. Because Detroit had been so closely linked to the automobile industry, the economic pendulum swung between boom and bust. The Great Depression flipped this once bustling, glamorous metropolis filled with nightclubs, gambling, and backroom speakeasies[1] into a blue-collar town with widespread unemployment, soup kitchens, vacant storefronts, and empty warehouses. Detroit historian, engineer, and author Paul R. Kavieff had this to offer:

> The auto companies absolutely refused to accept unions, especially before 1935. I think they had come to the realization they were either going to go out of business or were going to have to unionize. That brought labor unions, organized crime, and racketeering. A lot of the unions were mobbed up. The major auto companies—Chrysler, General Motors, Ford—managed to make it through. World War II pulled Detroit and the whole country out of the Great Depression.

Detroit not only had a major mafia presence, but also produced another underworld gang of bootleggers, armed robbers, hijackers, and extortionists known as The Purple Gang. This loose confederation of criminals were the American-born children of Jewish immi-

---

1. Michigan was the first state to pass a prohibition law and the first one to ratify the act that finally ended it on April 3, 1933.

grants from Russia and Poland who were tough and tainted delinquents.

"The Purple Gang was a lot of hard guys, so tough they made Capone's playmates look like a Kindergarten class," said Milton "Mezz" Mezzrow, a jazz clarinetist and saxophone player from Chicago who played in a lot of clubs and roadhouses owned by Al Capone.

They were led by Abe Axler, the four Bernstein Brothers (Abe, Joe, Raymond, and Isadore "Izzie"), and Harry Millman, an erratic and brutal enforcer with a pathological hatred of Italian criminals. The Bernsteins moved in their youth from New York to Detroit's Lower East Side in 1902. As they grew older, their movements weren't restricted to Detroit, and their crimes escalated to gambling, loansharking, liquor sales, drug trafficking, kidnapping, arson, and murder. They had been labeled the bloodiest and most sinister gang(s) of that era, with estimates of rivals killed during the bootleg wars reaching more than 500.[2] "The Purples" were tagged as Al Capone's main supplier of Canadian liquor and used as spotters in the 1929 St. Valentine's Day Massacre in Chicago. Decades later (after he had become Jay Sebring), Tom called upon the "Junior Purples," descendants of the original gang,[3] when he was embroiled in a barber's union dispute in Los Angeles, California.

Like many big cities in America throughout the 1950s, Detroit offered two different sets of rules: one for Whites and the other for minorities.

The Motor City experienced its first race riot in June 1943. Rumor spread quickly that a group of White sailors tossed a Black

---

2. One of the Purple Gang members, Zigmund "Ziggie" Selbin, once cut off a man's finger because he fancied his ring.
3. By 1935, The Purple Gang's dominance in Detroit had ended. Attrition had sent at least eighteen of its members to prison or early graves. Surviving members splintered into other gangs and continued with their criminal activity.

lady and her child off the Bell Isle Bridge,[4] a concrete and steel structure that spans high above the Detroit River. The riot lasted several days and thirty-four people were killed—twenty-five of them Black. The United States Army brought in 3,500 troops in jeeps, personnel armored and armed with automatic weapons—to restore the peace. More than 1,800 rioters were arrested, and the protest resulted in an estimated two million dollars in property damage.

The same decade saw the start of the Great Migration, during which more than six million Blacks left their rural homes in the Deep South for jobs and a new start in the Northeast, Midwest, and West.

Detroit offered plenty of work in the auto industry and "Black bombed" the city's Lower East Side where everybody with dark skin was forced to live. Many Whites who had historically held those jobs felt their new neighbors were taking money out of their pockets and food off their tables. If that wasn't enough to chap their hides, the new recruits were making just as much money as their veteran co-workers, causing a great deal of tension during and after World War II.

After Tom Kummer left Detroit in 1955, the city experienced approximately 150 riots from 1965 to 1968 as the municipality was in an entire state of economic and social strife. It also hit close to home to the Kummers and their extended family. Tony DiMaria, Jay's brother-in-law, remembers more than a few close calls:

I grew up in the east side of Detroit, which was a histori-cally Italian neighborhood but over time transitioned to a Black neighborhood. Our family was not racial or preju-diced at all. I grew up amongst Black children and Black families. They would come over to my house for a snack or

---

4. Today it's known as the Douglas MacArthur Bridge.

dinner and I would go to theirs. I had a lot of Black friends that were good friends and good people. Once I started going to Mackenzie High School[5] in 1960, race relations grew very tense. The second week of school there was a riot, and it got a full response—police, fire trucks, hoses, the whole business. It was a very divided and very racial time. A lot of angry people on both sides—White and Black.

Cars may have been the skeleton and muscles of the city, but music was the pulse. The 1950s was the final decade in which jazz flourished as a broad youth culture. It was just as popular as rock 'n' roll and doo-wop in its heyday but required a more sophisticated and informed ear. Chet Baker, Billie Holiday, Charlie Parker, Miles Davis, John Coltrane, Charles Mingus, Dizzy Gillespie, Thelonious Monk, and Sonny Rollins were considered America's premier artists —but they were also the epitome of cool among audiences that vibed to rawer and uncharted notes. Tom, with his instinctive eye for anything chic or stylish, naturally gravitated toward that sound.

The city's "Black Bottom" neighborhood, home to more than 100,000 African Americans, boasted approximately 300 Black-owned businesses and offered some of the best jazz, blues, and R & B clubs as well as backdoor speakeasies in the country. Hastings Street, which ran north-south through the area, was a hub for musicians and home to such entertainment establishments as Jake's, the Paradise Theater, the Graystone Ballroom, the Tropicana, Club Harlem, the Flame Show Bar, Sportee's Lounge, and the Horseshoe Bar. These legendary places drew mixed-race audiences.

But Detroit's real musical heart lay in Grinnell Brothers Music House, a downtown mega emporium on Woodard Avenue, which sold everything from pianos and organs to drumsticks, sheet music,

---

5. Famous alumnus includes actor Tom Skerritt and NFL Hall of Fame running back Jerome Bettis. The school was demolished in 2007.

and records. By the mid-1950s, Grinnell's was the largest piano distributor in the country, and every Detroit musician, whether they played the saxophone or the organ, ended up there. Since childhood, authentic jazz had been a passion of Tom's. It was only natural that the young Detroiter would end up at the seminal music institution after his four-year enlistment in the navy. In the same letter announcing his vision to be a "beautician," Tom mentioned to his parents a potential secondary career in music.

Lacking any specific plans, Tom came home and got a job that best suited his personality given the limited number of options an uneducated serviceman had at that time. The job at Grinnell's was simply a waystation until Tom figured out how to get back to California and realize his dream. He needed time and money to figure out how to do both.

It was his gap year.

Free from the confines of a uniform, Tom showed up every day to work looking sharp, according to his sister Peggy. "He went to Grinnell's like he was going out on the weekend. He came home, and his suits would look great. They looked better than the other guys' suits. He always looked special."

In a 1955 black and white photo, Tom is in the store, one arm draped on the counter near the cash register, and the other on his hip. The smiling record store clerk looks resplendent in a black suit and tie, folded handkerchief, and free flowing hair. He could easily pass for crooner Eddie Fisher at his peak, except Jay was even more handsome.

Tom told his mother about his idea of moving to California and opening a shop. She listened intently. She wanted him to do it and encouraged him to pursue this dream. Bernard, on the other hand, had a different reaction. He didn't know why Tom wanted to move to California. He was out of the navy. He had a steady job at Grinnell's where he could go to work every day. He was getting promoted (probably because he knew the latest songs and was familiar with cutting edge artists, but his sister suspected it was because he was the best-looking guy in the place and sold a lot of products), and Bernard likely felt there was no need to rock the boat.

Tom's list of admirers included clients and co-workers. One of them was Judith Jumisko, a local fashionista and part-time jazz singer. Her son, Christopher Barson, a Washington DC-based interior designer and contractor, said his mother often talked about Tom Kummer's great style.

> My mother was really into fashion and dressing beautifully, and so was Tom. He was the first person my mom ever knew who did not have cuffs on the bottom of his pants, which was really cutting-edge at the time. My mom also told me that he would arrive at work with a coat hanging over his shoulders instead of wearing a topcoat. And when he got off the elevator to his department, all the women would swoon.

Jumisko was also into fashion and looking her best, doing most of her shopping on Livernois, affectionately referred to as the "Avenue of Fashion," a regional destination for couture. It was home to one of the largest shopping districts in the country and was filled with trendy boutiques, dress shops, and restaurants.

"My mom would buy cashmere sweaters, dresses, and skirts on sale, so she always looked fabulous at work," said Christopher Barson.

Tom and Jumisko developed a close friendship, and he bestowed on her a nickname that stuck for the rest of her life.

"She loved Chris Connor, who was an American jazz singer. So, Jay nicknamed my mother 'Chris,'" Barson said. "And my mother went by that name until the day she died."

Barson suspects his mother's friendship with Tom had become

intimate even though she was seeing his father, James Barson, a pitcher who was pegged to play for the Chicago White Sox. James Barson and Tom were classmates at the University of Detroit High School, with Barson a few years ahead of him. They definitely knew each other. Everyone, in their own way, was hard to miss. Barson ended up ditching a life in professional baseball in favor of law school and later became a powerful attorney who was well-known throughout Detroit. He said their parents shared an interesting history with Tom.

> My dad never spoke of Tom Kummer or Jay Sebring or even hinted that he knew him until one day in August 1969. My dad was painting the kitchen when we moved to Bloomfield Hills, a suburb of Detroit, after the 1968 riots. He was listening to a transistor radio while painting and the news broke that Jay Sebring, Sharon Tate, Abigail Folger, Wojciech Frykowski, and Steven Parent were all killed. My father almost fell off the ladder because he knew Tom and the Kummer family, and later he was contacted by Bernard to settle some things for his son's estate. So, my mom and father realized at that point they both knew Tom because they had never spoken about him.

Which leads Christopher Barson back to the idea that Tom and his mother were more than just work associates.

> One night in the Seventies when she was drunk, she said something about Tom/Jay that made me wonder if they had fooled around or something. He gave her a shirt with French cuffs and a beautiful set of 22-carat gold and enamel cuff links by Victoria Fleming, which I still have.... And he gave her a gun.

The gun evolved from an incident when Bernard hired a laborer to do some work on the family porch. Peggy was twelve years old at the time and remembered certain details about that day.

> My dad walked off our porch to meet this worker to give him some instruction. For some reason, this guy was giving my dad a hard time. They went back and forth, and the guy knocked my father down. My dad's head was bleeding. I was in the house and my brother heard the scuffle and came out. Tom had words with the guy and the guy backed off.

That may be because Tom was packing heat[6] and most likely brandished the weapon. He brought home a gun from his time in the service and certainly knew how and when to use it. The police were called, Bernard went to the hospital, the worker was hauled off to jail, and Jay hid the gun. Most likely, it's the same pistol that ended up in Barson's possession.

Christopher Barson said his parents never explained why they had a gun or if they were holding it for someone. He said his father disposed of it sometime in the 1980s after they were divorced. But, before their parting, the Barsons were drawn back into Tom's life in the aftermath of his murder.

~

JIM GRAHAM, WHO ATTENDED GRADE SCHOOL WITH TOM AT St. Benedict's and, later, University of Detroit High, visited with his

---

6. When Jay Sebring made his mark in Hollywood, many friends and associates often spoke of him carrying a gun. The night of the Manson murders the Los Angeles Police Department found a gun in the glove compartment of Jay's car. He did not bring the gun inside because he was among friends and could not possibly anticipate the horror of that night.

friend at Grinnell's. He sensed Tom's restlessness and longing for another place that could fulfill his dreams.

"I remember him telling me that he didn't feel the Detroit area was, you know, something that was good for him," Graham recalled. "He said he was thinking of putting everything in his older car and driving to California."

Whenever Tom brought up dreams he wanted to accomplish, Peg patiently and with intent listened to him describe what he wanted to do. Bernard grilled him.

What are you going to do about this?

How are you going to take care of that?

Where will you live?

What if something happens? What will you do then?

Peggy said Tom often dreamed about his future, and Detroit wasn't a part of the equation.

"My dad tried to talk Tom into staying. He felt he was doing good," she recalled. "I believe he received a few promotions because they really liked him at Grinnell's.[7] But it wasn't his dream."

Bernard often played devil's advocate, and a good one at that. Where his younger brother Fred and sister Gerry were compliant, Tom was prepared with answers, and if necessary, willing to go toe-to-toe.[8] And he was prepared to take further steps, which he finally did in late 1955 when he felt he had enough money saved up to sustain himself for a few months while he got on his feet.

The night before he left, he visited with Judith Jumisko and gave her the shirt, cufflinks, and gun. Two months later, he called her from Southern California, according to Christopher Barson.

---

7. In April 1981, Grinnell's, once called the world's largest music merchandiser, was forced to declare bankruptcy by a federal bankruptcy judge after it defaulted on a plan to pay back $2.3 million to its creditors.

8. Tom's sister Peggy was also fiercely independent, marrying at eighteen, moving to Las Vegas, and getting pregnant by nineteen.

Tom/Jay said that he had gotten himself involved in the Hollywood scene and that she should come out if she really wanted to be a jazz singer. My mom told me [about the call] in a conversation around 1976… around the time the TV movie *Helter Skelter* first aired… [she told Tom] that she was pregnant with my older brother and was going to marry Jim Barson. And then he burst out laughing. My mom always thought that was strange—that he laughed about that. So, they hung up and my mom married my father. She kinda regretted not going out there to California.

Barson often wondered about what went on between Tom and his mother, but it has never been fully explored. He said, "It was a sensitive subject for my mom, and I rarely brought it up."

Tom left behind the safety of his Midwestern home and his friends to seek his fortune in Southern California. And he did it in a beater car that had to be push started by a couple of buddies to get out of the driveway. Martin Halloran, Tom's Saint Benedict's classmate, remembered his humble exit from Michigan.

He was going to California. He called me up and the old Cadillac wouldn't start. So, he says, "Can you give me a push?" Those were the days when all cars had clutches, all you had to do was put it in gear and let the clutch out going about twenty miles an hour. So, I push him on to Six Mile. He gives me the wave like, "Let me go." And the car starts spitting and spattering and conks out. So anyway, this happened three or four times. We get down to the freeway and it's still spitting and sputtering. He makes a turn to Service Drive, I give him a big push, down he went on the ramp to the large freeway. He's waving to me, and the car is going. And that's the last time I saw him.

It was an inauspicious start for someone who would end up transforming men's style, infiltrating the Hollywood industry, and leaving an indelible mark on popular culture. With Tom laser focused on his quest in the West Coast, his parents would languish in concern for their first born. The Kummers, including Tom, would be anxious for what lay ahead. For them, it was the great unknown.

The main question on all their minds was, "Would it be worth it?"

CHAPTER 4
THE MIRAGE FACTORY

Tom Kummer was not the first man to cut hair in Los Angeles.

The first barber shop in the city was opened in 1852 by a Black man named Peter Biggs. Biggs was a former slave from Liberty, Missouri, and "belonged" to an Army officer name J.A. Smith who was posted back to the states after the Mexican American War. The officer offered Biggs his freedom if he stayed behind in California, saving him the cost of taking him back to the Midwest.

Biggs was more than fine with this option. Like many Angelenos, he loved the idea of reinvention (his real name was Reuben Middleton and changed it when he became a California resident). He opened the New Orleans Shaving Saloon on the ground floor of the Bella Union Hotel, site of innumerable shootouts and the birthplace of several lynchings in frontier Los Angeles.

He knew almost everyone in Los Angeles (which was not a stretch given the city's tiny population at the time). The *Californios* affectionately called him "Don Pedro." Americans called him "Nigger Pete."

Most of his clientele were White Southern men who migrated

to the City of Angels after the Civil War. Biggs also thought of himself as a proper Southern gentleman and prided himself on his impeccable manners, refined vocabulary, and worldly charm. He got along famously with these Dixie ex-pats who also admired his hard work ethic (his shop was open from sunrise to 9:00 p.m.) and agreeable manner. This ability to navigate these worlds was a big part of Biggs' success, which stretched to a chain of barbershops after a few years—almost unheard of for a Black man in this era.

Biggs had a long and successful run until a senseless act of violence claimed his life. He was stabbed to death by a Mexican waiter, Victor Lamorie, in a Main Street restaurant on May 5, 1869. Some memoirists have claimed that Biggs was highly critical of Lamorie's serving skills, and Lamorie was later acquitted by a Spanish majority jury.

Twenty to thirty years before towns like Dodge City and Tombstone became notorious, Los Angeles was one of the most violent places in the country. In 1850, the population was approximately 6,000, with more than 100 homicides. In comparison, the L.A. murder rate was fifty times greater than New York City, which had a population of 600,000 and only forty-eight murders. And that doesn't include assault, battery, rape, and other mayhem that plagued Los Angeles during this era.

This was the L.A. romanticized in later generations as the Eden of sunshine, orange groves, bougainvillea, ranchos, and pretty *señoritas*. John A. Lewis, a newspaper editor for the *Los Angeles Star*, couldn't understand the carnage in such an idyllic setting. He mused in an 1853 op-ed:

> There is no brighter sun, no milder clime, no more equable temperature, no scenes more picturesque, no greener valleys, no fairer plains in the wide world, than those we may look upon here. There is no country where nature is more lavish of her exuberant fullness; and yet, with all our

Humphrey Bogart, Frank Sinatra, Elizabeth Taylor, Spencer Tracy, Sophia Loren, Clark Gable, Joan Crawford, Zsa Zsa Gabor, and Burt Lancaster were all out and about, dining at Romanoff's, Perino's, Musso & Frank's, Tail o' the Cock, or Chasen's, on lobster thermidor, trout amandine, Waldorf salad, and tomatoes stuffed with crab. Everyone smoked or tippled alcohol and dressed to the nines in white tie and diamonds and looked amazing.

The Brown Derby and the Ambassador Hotel were still going strong, the latter hosting six Oscar ceremonies. Some of the stars didn't have to walk far. The Cocoanut Grove on Wilshire Boulevard hosted performers including Bing Crosby, Nat King Cole, Little Richard, Liberace, Judy Garland, and Lena Horne beneath palm trees where stuffed monkeys blinked with electrified amber eyes.

On the Sunset Strip, Ciro's, the Mocambo, and Crescendo were gleaming supper clubs with cigarette girls, in-house photographers, and star-studded clientele. ("You had to hit all three in an evening," Andy Williams once said.) There was sure to be some spectacle or another any time you were there. Film star Sonia Henie once rode in on an elephant. An FBI agent, fishing for commies, left a tape recorder in a heat duct in the men's room and got so drunk he forgot it. And businessman and movie mogul Howard Hughes once tried to reserve an entire front row of banquettes at Ciro's and was refused because the owner had a "three fist fights and you're permanently out" rule. However, he waived this rule for crooner Frank Sinatra, reasoning, "He didn't hit him on the jaw."

But the furs, pearls, and tuxedos night life was on the wane. While it shone brightly in 1955—the year Tom arrived—it was the light of a dying star that shone. Ciro's closed that year, a victim of the Internal Revenue Service. The big-name acts that once packed the Sunset Strip were migrating to Las Vegas, including The Rat Pack in 1957, lured by generous fees the supper clubs couldn't match. Rock 'n' roll was coming in, and it didn't wear white tie and order Oysters Rockefeller.

natural beauties and resources and advantages, there i
country where human life is of so little account. Men l
one another to pieces with pistols and other cutlery :
God's image were of no more worth than the life of on
the two or three thousand ownerless dogs that prowl ak
our streets and make night hideous.

By 1955, that version of Los Angeles was long in the pas
least far below the surface. The movie business arrived witl
Griffith in 1910, driven west by New York's miserable v
Three years later the Los Angeles Aqueduct, under the supe
of Chief Engineer William Mulholland, opened in 1913.
floodgates brought not only water, but plenty of people, h
and industries. The 1920s saw 350 people arriving daily. Su
sions were built by the dozen. The population hit one milli
1924.

With a sprawling city came cars—160,000 of them by
Downtown congestion was so bad the city council banned pa
there at peak hours. But businesses complained trade was dov
to 50 percent, so the ordinance was hastily repealed. Histo
pinpoint this as the birth of L.A.'s legendarily bad traffic.

A Santa Fe railroad promotional video from 1953—"Wel(
to Southern California"—showed near-empty freeways along
fair-haired women wearing hats and carrying purses, perusing
Hollywood Walk of Fame, polo matches, baseball games, museu
the Griffith Observatory, golf courses, sailing, and the beaches
drenched in sun and skies so blue it hurt to look at.

"There is no other area holding such charm, beauty, and
good things in life than southern California," the narrator drean
intones. Los Angeles had grown "from a sleepy pueblo to a v
metropolitan city" with "a day-to-day influx from people from
over the world."

This was still the Golden Age of Hollywood. Marilyn Monr

And neither did "TJ" Kummer[1] in this period. He was certainly aware of this world of klieg lights and film premieres; but for the millions of people like TJ, who weren't movie stars, Southern California was no less of a paradise. Unlike the thousands before, and following him, TJ Kummer sought not fame on the silver screen or fortune from the Gold Rush. He marched to a different drumbeat and grooved to the notes of his own trumpet, vibes, and whistles. The biggest clue to why young TJ gravitated to Southern California exists in the pervasive themes throughout the art and sketches of his youth—beautiful women, pioneering ships piercing ocean expanse, Wild West settings, muscle cars, and iconic Hollywood actors.

TJ held no interest in Hollywood screen time or credits—his desire was to originate his instinctive intuitions that did not exist in L.A. or anywhere else on the planet.

Perhaps TJ did not have a clear vision for how his dream would manifest until he discovered his destination, but he knew he was meant for big things. To many, TJ's adventure seemed reckless, foolish, or silly, but as American film critic and *Los Angeles Times* writer Charles Champlin[2] once opined: "He was just always his own self, like a snail. He carried his own house with him all the time. He was an original."

TJ Kummer did not arrive in Hollywood to reinvent himself; he would bring his inventions to Hollywood. And they showered him with attention during his lifetime but turned their back on him in death.

Life then, as now, revolved around cars. General Motors, Ford, and Chrysler all had huge assembly plants. Derricks pumping

---

1. "TJ" Kummer was the moniker Tom adopted when he first arrived in Los Angeles; a few years later he adopted another name – Jay Sebring.
2. Charles Champlin was a well-respected film critic, editor, and columnist for the *Los Angeles Times* from 1967 to 1980. He also wrote for *LIFE* and *TIME* magazines as well as teaching film criticism at Loyola Marymount University and the University of Southern California, UC Irvine and the American Film Institute Conservatory.

around the clock fed cars and industry with diesel, oil, and gas, almost all of which was consumed locally.

Southern California adapted to the car like nowhere else on Earth, as if the culture were trying to turn the population into auto centaurs. Dairies, dry cleaners, banks, and burger stands began offering drive-through service. Drive-in movie theaters sprung up wherever there was a piece of available land. And if you could pull up to see a movie or deposit a check, why not hear the gospel too? Robert Schuller began preaching from the roof of the Orange Drive-in snack bar on Sunday mornings in 1955. Vacation trailers (the first RVs) came on the market and were wildly popular. People, especially snowbirds, quickly began staying in them in trailer parks and stops along America's highways.

The region's freeways were built stretch by stretch during this period. The four-way, four-level stack interchange opened in 1953 and the Hollywood Freeway brought the suburbs to the city in 1959.

The fifties were the glory days of the suburb. Everyone wanted cheap, spacious houses with big yards, and developers razed orange groves and cotton fields to supply them. Lakewood is the perfect example. On the first day of sales in March 1950, an estimated 30,000 people lined up to walk through model houses. By the end of the next month, more than 1,000 families had purchased homes. (Thirty per day on average, and on one occasion, 107 homes were sold in just one hour.) There was a nursery next to the sales office where parents could leave their kids while they toured homes.

Space age architecture—picture the iconic Theme Building at the Los Angeles International Airport—was in vogue. If something didn't have a space theme, then it was Old West (Knotts Berry Farm) or exotic, as in tiki bars and luau gardens. Animals were popular and well-attended attractions. A Pomona appliance store held a well-attended in-store promotion where a midget boxed a kangaroo.

Aerospace outfits like Boeing, McDonnell Douglas, Rockwell, Hughes, Northrop, Lockheed, and General Dynamics were the area's biggest employers, but not the only game in town. Southern California was also the world's second-largest clothing manufacturer.

The Garment District (later known as the Los Angeles Fashion District) in the downtown area was established in the early 20th century and flourished in the 1920s and 1930s, becoming the West Coast nexus of the clothing, accessories, and fabric industry. By the 1950s, the area became a center for sportswear, women's clothing, and iconic swimwear thanks in large part to the contributions of Jewish entrepreneurs who migrated from New York City and felt a new beginning just might set them apart.

While the fashion industry took its cues from the Big Apple, Hollywood set the trends for Middle America. Designers wanted to dress movie stars and starlets, and apparel manufacturers quickly followed. The Cooper Building on 9th and Los Angeles Streets was the first multi-level retail building in the district and became L.A.'s premier address for fashion industry showrooms into the 1940s and 1950s, while Santee Alley off Olympic Boulevard introduced to the area the first open air bazaar where customers could get cheap goods and bargain deals.

Los Angeles dripped with style and glamour in the 1950s, and with style came accessories, accoutrements, and other developing cottage industries under this umbrella, including men's hair, paving the way for an up-and-coming arbiter of men's style.

TJ Kummer—soon to christen himself Jay Sebring—would become a leading player in the "Mirage Factory" of Los Angeles where life was beautiful and serene…. at least from a distance.

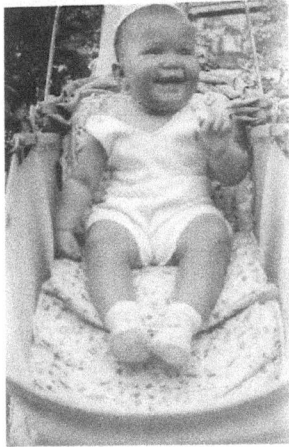

Earliest known photos of Thomas John Kummer
(known to the world as Jay Sebring), who was born on
October 10, 1933, in Fairfield, Alabama at Lloyd Nolan
Hospital. These baby photos show a happy and
healthy child at the Kummer's Alabama residence.
*Courtesy of Jay Sebring Collections/The DiMaria
Family.*

Jay's father, Bernard Kummer, in his early twenties.
An accountant by trade, he was described by loved
ones as strict, exacting, regimented, and blunt. He
was also a no-nonsense, old-school parent who left
no room for debate when it came to his children.
*Courtesy of Jay Sebring Collections/The DiMaria
Family.*

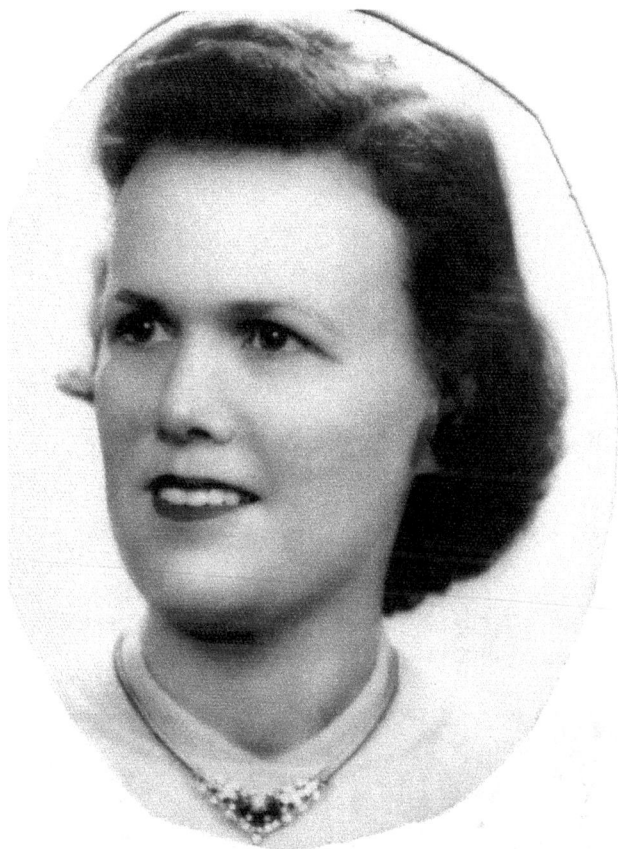

Portrait of Margarette ("Peg") Kummer. Jay's mother was a coal miner's daughter and the sixth of eleven children of Scottish immigrant Thomas Wilson Gibb and Lavona McLain, an Alabama native. As a parent, she appeared to be the total opposite of her husband. Peg was a good listener and encourager and wanted her children to have their own ideas and be individualists. *Courtesy of Jay Sebring Collections/The DiMaria Family.*

Tom was like most post-World War II boys of his era, who gallivanted through the neighborhood in his own world as solider in the woods or as his as cowboy hero, emulating the likes of Roy Rogers, Gene Autry, and Hopalong Cassidy (William Boyd). *Courtesy of Jay Sebring Collections/The DiMaria Family.*

The Kummer family in front of their Highland Park, Michigan home on Ferris Street, where they resided for approximately a decade. Bernard has his arm around Tom's sister, Geraldine ("Gerry") while Margarette has her hand on Tom's back, who appears to be around eight in this picture. The look of consternation on Bernard's and Tom's faces exemplifies the relationship dynamic of the two. *Courtesy of Jay Sebring Collections/The DiMaria Family.*

Dressed to the nines and donning a chic hat, Tom was developing a sense of style even as an adolescent. *Courtesy of Jay Sebring Collections/The DiMaria Family.*

Tom made this banner from his St. Benedict days. The photo of his classmates includes his lifelong friend, Jim Graham. St. Benedict's was a parochial grade and middle school down the street from the Kummer's Highland Park home. Tom was well-liked by fellow students, some of whom described him as likeable, creative, and the leader of the pack. *Courtesy of Jay Sebring Collections/The DiMaria Family.*

A trio of Tom's sketches as a teen reveals his passion for cars, women, and ships—all things that were vital to him as an adult. The ship demonstrates his pioneering spirit and his desire to reach beyond. *Courtesy of Jay Sebring Collections/The DiMaria Family.*

CLASS	I HIGH		II HIGH		III HIGH		IV HIGH		CLASS	I HIGH		II HIGH		III HIGH		IV HIGH	
	1947-48		1949-50		1950-51		1951-52		TOTAL CREDITS AT BOTTOM OF CARD	1948-48		1949-50		1950-51		1951-52	
ALGEBRA I	50	55							GREEK I								
ALGEBRA II									GREEK II								
CHEMISTRY									HISTORY ANC. & MED.	F	64 54						
ENGLISH I	F	68 54							HISTORY AMER.								
ENGLISH II									AMER. GOVT.								
ENGLISH III									LATIN I	F	61 54						
ENGLISH IV									LATIN II								
ETHICS	82	77							LATIN III								
FRENCH I									LATIN IV								
FRENCH II									LAW COMMERCIAL								
GEOMETRY PLANE									PHYSICS								
GEOMETRY SOLID									RELIGION								
ECONOMICS									SOCIOLOGY								
INTRO. TO BUSINESS									SPANISH I								
GENERAL SCIENCE									SPANISH II								
									TRIGONOMETRY								

TOTAL CREDITS

ADDRESS — BROTHERS OLDER / YOUNGER — SISTERS OLDER / YOUNGER

LAST NAME	FIRST NAME	MIDDLE NAME	PHONE NO.
Kummer	Tom	John	To. 5-7516

Tom's eighth year grades at St. Benedict show his focus was on anything but academics. He received four F's in Algebra, English, History, and Latin. His only saving grace was a B in Ethics. One teacher told his mother that "he doesn't contribute to class. All he does is stare out the window and smile." *Courtesy of Jay Sebring Collections/The DiMaria Family.*

Tom with his arm around an unidentified friend. His teen years
were marked by rebellion: smoking cigarettes, taking joy rides
from a local car dealership, and sneaking out at night. *Courtesy of
Jay Sebring Collections/The DiMaria Family.*

Naval enlistment papers for Thomas John Kummer, dated October 9, 1950. Because he was 17 at the time, Tom had to receive special consent from his father, Bernard. *Courtesy of Jay Sebring Collections/The DiMaria Family.*

Graduation class for Company 372, 2nd platoon, U.S. Naval
Training Center in Great Lakes, Illinois. Tom is on the bottom row,
second from the right. He is clearly the youngest looking male in
the platoon. *Courtesy of Jay Sebring Collections/The DiMaria
Family.*

Tom in the barracks, hanging out with a handful of
buddies during a break in basic training in Great
Lakes, Illinois. His bunkmates included George
"Buzzy" Piperato and Tom's Detroit childhood
friend, Terry Lanfear, who followed him into the
Navy. *Courtesy of Jay Sebring Collections/The
DiMaria Family.*

Tom in full dress blues, with rifle in hand, at Great Lakes with snow on the ground. *Courtesy of Jay Sebring Collections/The DiMaria Family.*

A stylish Tom in a Navy peacoat, slacks, and shiny shoes with a cigarette in hand, visiting family while on AWOL. *Courtesy of Jay Sebring Collections/The DiMaria Family.*

Tom taking a smoke break on the island of Guam, where he discovered his life's calling for styling hair. In this photo he demonstrates one of his early cuts, which is much different than his fellow sailors. *Courtesy of Jay Sebring Collections/The DiMaria Family.*

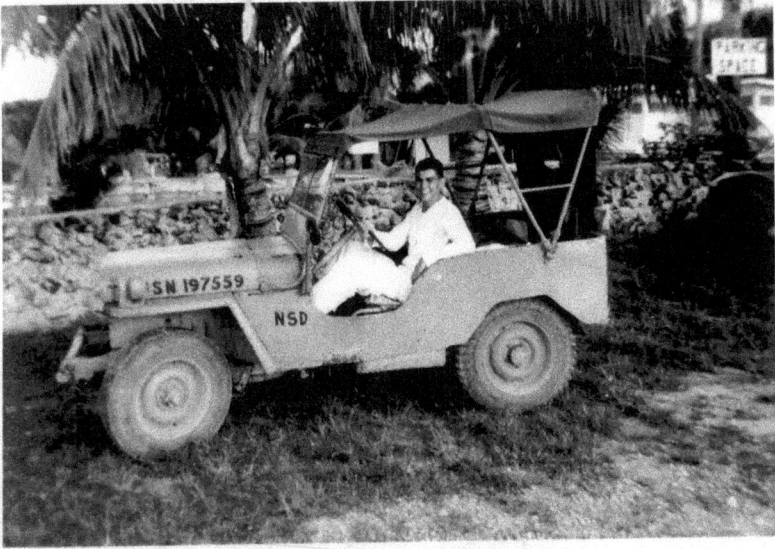

Behind the wheel of a jeep in Guam, Tom smiling for the camera.
Courtesy of Jay Sebring Collections/The DiMaria Family.

Tom with his arm around Larry Longlott. The two raised plenty of
hell in Guam and became lifelong buddies. Longlott reflected,
"We went everywhere together on Guam. We would find a way to
get out of working and sneak out. I was his first customer,
actually." *Courtesy of Jay Sebring Collections/The DiMaria Family.*

JUMBO PRINT AUG. 55

(Top) Tom standing next to Bernard at their Michigan residence, August 1955. The two grew closer after Tom's stint in the Navy. (Bottom) Tom is dressed up in a suit and tie with his admiring mother Peg next to him. *Courtesy of Jay Sebring Collections/The DiMaria Family.*

A grownup Tom with his three younger siblings, Frederick "Fred" (upper left), Margaret "Peggy" (upper right), and Geraldine "Gerry" (with glasses). *Courtesy of Jay Sebring Collections/The DiMaria Family.*

A resplendent Tom inside Grinnell Brothers Music House, a downtown mega emporium on Woodard Avenue. His job as a record store clerk was simply a waystation until he figured out how to get to California and realize his dream. *Courtesy of Jay Sebring Collections/The DiMaria Family.*

CHAPTER 5
REINVENTION AND REVOLUTION

Thomas "TJ" Kummer was a young man embarking on his passion and chasing his dream in the land of milk and honey. He was not a stranger in this strange land where anyone can run from their past, hit the reset button, and become whoever they want to be. He was at home here and, just as with many of his contemporaries, he was about to take advantage of the possibilities afforded to him in Hollywood.

Hollywood wasn't just a paradise everyone dreamed about. Whether it was as simple as a name change, a makeover from unnoticed brunette to blond bombshell like Marilyn Monroe, an image overhaul from star athlete to cinema cowboy as John Wayne did when he ditched his football cleats, if your dream was to be someone else, someone new, there was someone in L.A. who could make it happen.

For the young man from Michigan, reinvention meant breaking free from the limitations of his simple Midwest life and opening up a world where elegance mattered and fresh ideas about style were embraced. This is the place where Thomas Kummer would step down and Jay Sebring would eventually emerge. The reinvention and evolution of Thomas Kummer wasn't just in a name, but the entire game; it was in a whole new treatment and eventual industry for men that required society's embrace—a revolution well before Broadway's *Hair* celebrated "shining, gleaming, streaming, flaxen, waxen" locks in song.

The 1950s were a transformative time in American pop culture. With the creation of rock 'n' roll, the growing popularity of jazz music, the Golden Age of Television, and a paradigm shift in films, men's hairstyles of the decade were influenced by the likes of Elvis Presley, James Dean, Marlon Brando, and Tony Curtis.

In that era, men's hair was about short back and sides, clippers, petroleum jelly, and Brylcreem in stodgy, smoke-filled, and anti-quated barbershops. Film and television actor Robert Wagner said the scene for men's hair in the mid-1950s was simple, unsophisti-cated, and did not cater to individuals, especially actors who needed to stand out or have a certain look that matched the part.

> You walked into a barbershop. You had a guy who cut your hair. And you sat down when he cut your hair. There wasn't anything about, "What are you doing? What kind of part are you playing? What kind of guy is this?" There were only a couple of looks you could have.

There was no concept such as "hair styling" for men. Men walked into a barbershop, selected a standard look from a limited number of pictures on the wall, and the barber went to work. None of these stock cuts—from the Flat Top to the Executive—made men look their best or expressed their individuality. They were plas-ticized and rigid, completely devoid of any room for custom design. The seminal question a barber would ask of a client was, "Do you want the part on the left or right?"

TJ Kummer was intent on changing all of that.

Actor Dennis Hopper wasn't a fan of the barbershop scene that was, in those days, heavily connected to the AFL-CIO, which was a firmament of Eisenhower-esque male masculinity and had about as much charm as a straight razor.

"They weren't exactly putting a bowl over people's heads and shaving them, but the regular barbers in the United States were pretty gross at that time," said Hopper, who was a client of Tom Kummer's (though he only knew him as Jay Sebring) and, later, a friend.

It was clear that, at least in Hollywood, men were looking for an offramp from mediocrity and uniformity. The days of fixed ideals for cookie-cutter suburbanites were coming to an end in the socio-political and cultural arenas. TJ could see the writing on the wall and knew the environment was primed for him to make his mark. But the only mark he made leaving Detroit was rubber on asphalt. Somewhere between Michigan and California, TJ, and his friend Don Buday, who also had Hollywood aspirations, accompanied him on the trip. They ended up wrecking the vehicle. Peggy DiMaria remembers the incident more than six decades later:

> Don Buday was driving the car and my brother thought he could get a little sleep because they were going to drive straight through. You don't have to get a room and all that stuff. Cutting corners. And Don ended up falling asleep at the wheel and they had a car accident. My brother was okay, but Don broke his back and ended up in the hospital.[1]

TJ Kummer eventually arrived in the Golden State in the fall of 1955 on a Greyhound bus with two sweatshirts, one pair of Levi's, and a pair of desert boots. He held onto the boots and had them bronzed a few years later when he became successful beyond his

---

1. Don Buday not only made his way to California but ended up in the entertainment industry. He wrote several screenplays, including 1978's *Kiss Meets the Phantom*.

wildest dreams. In fact, the bronzed boots were a fixture in his house to serve as a reminder of where he came from and how far he'd come.

TJ quickly settled in East Hollywood. The location wasn't anyone's idea of heaven, but it was strategic. It was affordable, centrally located, and a twenty-minute bus ride to the place where he would learn his trade.

His first residence was an apartment at 4320 Lockwood Avenue. The twelve-unit complex was built in 1926 and located a few blocks south off Santa Monica Boulevard, not far from Los Angeles City College. Those who saw it said calling it an apartment may have been a stretch.

"He was living in the basement where all the cleaning supplies were kept, and it was pretty bad," said Gloria Vizer, who was one of TJ's first friends in his new hometown. "It was not good."

But TJ had no plans to stay there very long. He had ambition, vision, and a solid work ethic that would propel him to great heights. TJ had what only a rarified few grasp—he knew early in life what he was created to do and wasted no time starting down that path. He set about pursuing his passion at an age when most people hadn't even begun to develop a sense of self. That clarity of purpose drove TJ to make a way where there seemed to be none.

One of the many reasons he ended up in Los Angeles—besides its billing as the "Glamour Center of the World"—was that he couldn't find any schools in the Midwest to learn men's grooming techniques. TJ ruled out barber school right away, remembered Peggy.

He felt that cosmetology school would be a better avenue for him as far as cutting hair. He knew the things that he knew from cutting his own hair and cutting his friends in the Navy. Learning women's hair cutting, it's a little more artistic. Barbering, you didn't learn that.

He felt the trade, techniques, and approach to men's hair were outdated and lazy. Their paint-by-the-numbers look for all men didn't work for him. It bothered him that men's style hadn't evolved, and men were conscripted to an uninspired, formulaic appearance that, while sleek and dapper, offered little to express individual personality. This young visionary wanted to take men's hair where it had never gone before. The man's face, bone structure, and hair growth pattern would be the canvas on which he would create.

And he cultivated that foundation at Comer & Doran, a cosmetology school at the corner of Hollywood Boulevard and Ivar Avenue, a stone's throw from Grauman's Chinese Theatre, a world-famous movie palace[2] at the center of Tinseltown. The cultural landmark is known today for its ornate design and celebrity hand-prints, footprints, and autographs in the concrete of the theatre's forecourt. Even Jay Sebring might have had a star on the adjacent sidewalk of Hollywood's Walk of Fame had fate not intervened.

Founded by Comer Syprett and Grace Doran, Comer & Doran Beauty School was a chain of West Coast-based cosmetology schools with franchises in Hollywood, California; Reno, Nevada; Seattle, Washington; and Tucson, Arizona.

Syprett was a hairstylist, consultant, instructor, and appeared as a guest artist on television and radio shows and served as a hair consultant in motion pictures. Doran was an award-winning hair-stylist and member of numerous high-profile cosmetology groups. Gloria Vizer, a seventeen-year-old spitfire who started training students in 1954, said TJ could not have picked a better place to learn his craft.

---

2. Grauman's Chinese Theatre (now TCL Chinese Theatre) was the site of Quentin Tarantino's 2019 U.S. film premiere for *Once Upon a Time in Hollywood* in which Jay Sebring was a celluloid character fifty years after his death. The film was awarded two Oscars and considered an instant classic.

Comer & Doran was *the* school to go to if you wanted to learn hairstyling. They had a big reputation. It was a wonderful school. Good people. Many great stylists have graduated from their schools and have gone on to open their own salons. It was a great time in my life. I got to travel, meet interesting people, and do what I loved.

Gloria earned TJ's instant admiration when she drove him home one night to his apartment in her new '57 Ford Thunderbird.

"He [TJ] loved my car. I mean, really loved it," said Gloria, noting his fine taste in automobiles. "He said, 'I'm going to get myself a great car one day. You watch and see.'"

Being trained as a Comer & Doran beautician in the 1950s and early 1960s carried cache in the industry. Newspaper articles, announcements, and advertisements around the country boasted of Comer & Doran scholarships or returning beauticians with their new training and enhanced skills. The school was the Ivy League of cosmetology, and completing their program provided credentials that would ensure professional opportunities like no other school could.

TJ was a beneficiary of the GI Bill enacted by Congress in 1944, which sent more than eight million veterans to college and vocational schools between 1945 and 1956. The bill provided for tuition, books, supplies, counseling services, and a living allowance. It paid for most of his training at Comer & Doran.

The school required 1,600 hours of on-the-floor training and covered a lot of ground. Subjects included treatments and styling for skin, hair, and nails as well as sanitation practices and diseases. TJ even had to learn about anatomy and physiology in his courses, and he kept meticulous notes in his Comer & Doran manual. His notes show that he even took notice of a client's bone structure, down to the arms, elbows, wrist, hands, and fingers.

"Hair is the frame for the face," was a mantra Jay Sebring would constantly repeat when he became a household name a few years later.

According to Gloria, there were three types of students who attended cosmetology school in the Los Angeles chapter—those working in the entertainment industry who needed a steady job, those who wanted to make a career in cosmetology, and those who just wanted to score with the opposite sex.

> We had a lot of men who attended our school, a lot more than women. How weird, right? Some were gay, but mostly they were straight men. They'd asked me, "Where can we meet all the chicks?" Beauty school was a great start. When they discovered that, then they wanted to open their own business because they knew women would come to them.

TJ didn't lack in that area, either. With his slight and muscular build, good looks, impeccable style, and unique élan, he was catnip to women. Early in his training at Comer & Doran, he met seventeen-year-old Elle Elliot (Fiero), a petite and vivacious young woman who was half Italian and half Spanish. Later, his classmate became an Emmy-nominated stylist and had a long and distinguished career in the movie industry. She recalls, "TJ—as I knew him—was not a normal person. He was creative and quirky and unusual. Very eccentric. He cut my hair like a boy. It was before Mia Farrow had cut hers like that. Then he bleached it up and made it gun metal grey."

A rugged individualist with four years of military service, TJ Kummer was a glaring anomaly to the typical beauty school student. Even his tools stood out. The standard length of scissors provided in the Comer & Duran beauty kit was 4 ½ to 5 inches. TJ preferred his own 10-inch shears, said Gloria, which she noted: "I remember the shears he would use—they were those Filipino shears —the big ones. They looked like machete shears, and he just loved to cut hair with those machete shears." The massive implements certainly raised eyebrows and rattled nerves as Tom's beauty school subject and girlfriend experienced firsthand.

"They used to make me nervous," admitted Elle Elliot. That sense of danger and excitement attracted her to the Midwesterner as they dated, listened to jazz, and smoked weed. Elle cited a Halloween date where they got dressed up and competed for a door prize at an L.A. nightclub. Elle recalled that night for posterity:

> I took the bus to TJ's apartment, and then I kept waiting and waiting and waiting as he was filling in his goatee with an eyebrow pencil. And I kept saying, "God, how long you gonna be?" He said, "Well, you can always do the dishes in the kitchen. There's a whole sink if you're bored." So, I did that.
>
> When he was finished, he was wearing a red and black velvet cape and looking the spitting image of Count Dracula. We got on the bus, and he told me we were headed to a jazz nightclub. I really wasn't that much into jazz, but I was just going out with TJ and having fun. He said, "Now when we get to the club, we're going to win the door prize." And sure enough, we did.

At another party TJ hosted, Elle said she tried pot for the first time. It was not a rousing success, according to her.

> They put it in a coconut that was hollowed out and it was halfway filled with water. They put a joint in [one] end and I was told to suck really hard. And so, I sucked really hard. The joint went through the thing, and I swallowed it accidentally. TJ said, "I'll have to show you how to do it right." And I said, "To tell you the truth, I'm not that interested. I'd rather have a glass of wine."

Elle remembered another memorable party the two attended near Beverly Boulevard. It was hosted by a fellow cosmetology student named Vito.[3]

> Vito was a gypsy sculptor and was fabulous at it. He thought he was a Hugh Hefner type and had all the young girls. He was really into shock value and on Friday nights he would serve wine and show porno films. But not just regular porno films—porno films from the 1920s, so they were silent. But they were funny. You know what I mean, where everybody would laugh? Keystone Cops and porno. TJ loved it.

TJ enjoyed life and having fun. But when it came to schooling, he was all business. Gloria said TJ didn't just learn or take his craft, he attacked it with a fervor like she had never seen before or since.

> Your progress depended on the teacher who was instructing the class, who decided whether to move you to the next level or keep you back. The next level after instruction was putting you on the floor with clients, which is where TJ wanted to be. He was never afraid of anything. He not only wanted to move right to the floor, but right out the door so he could start his own salon. He was the most ambitious student I'd ever taught. He really wanted out of there.

Gloria said TJ Kummer had good reason to go out into the world. Like all big visionaries, he saw a void in the marketplace and wanted to be the one to fill it. He knew the mark he wanted to

---

3. Elle Elliott was most likely referring to Vito Paulekas, a well-known bohemian, artist, dancer, civil rights activist, and a leader of the Southern California counterculture scene of the 1960s and 1970s.

make on the world and didn't want anything to delay launching his dream. Even though he was ahead of his time, he knew he couldn't be the only person on the planet who saw the need for a style revolution and couldn't take the chance of someone beating him to the punch. She recalled him as a young man who thought with great clarity and vision.

> He told me his plans, his vision of what he wanted to do in this business. He was so enthusiastic. He wanted more of a unisex salon where there would be male and female clients. He didn't want to have the stigma of just a barbershop. And he wanted the style of hair to look more natural. He knew where he wanted to go and what he wanted to do. I have met rare artists who were just meant to be in the business, and TJ was one of them. What he did for men's hair was revolutionary.

It would take a few more years and a seismic shift in pop culture for TJ to realize his grand vision for men's hair. But when that shift happened, the world suddenly opened to a newly christened Jay Sebring, bringing with it wealth, women, a celebrity clientele that resembled an arm of the William Morris Agency, and the respect of his industry peers. He was catapulted onto a scene that most people only dream of observing, let alone defining. The beautiful and the talented embraced him and shared their world with him. However, unlike so many of his famous and wealthy patrons, TJ never forgot his roots or those who made it possible for him to succeed. He remained humble, grateful, and generous, using his clout to give others opportunities as well.

Gloria remembered a visit from TJ sometime in the early sixties, a few years after he graduated from Comer & Doran. But he was now Jay Sebring, a well-established stylist who was sought after by the Hollywood elite and the entertainment world. One day he pulled up in a large convertible Cadillac and whisked her away for a glamourous drive down their city's glistening streets. He was proud of his accomplishments, but he recognized the role Gloria played in his getting there, and he wanted to let her know in his own way he was thankful for her and the contributions she made to his career.

He drove me around Hollywood Boulevard that day and I could tell that he was so proud he had made it. He told me often, "You wait.... one day I'm going to have a car nicer than yours." And I'd always reply, "I hope so." I'm glad he did so well. He was so excited about his life and where it was going. I was so happy for him.

That special moment was also bittersweet for Gloria because all the hope she felt for TJ's trajectory would eventually be stolen in a night of madness and cruelty. She shared, "It was the last time I ever saw him."

CHAPTER 6
THE BALL HAS STARTED ITS ROLL

I t's less than ten miles from Crenshaw to West Hollywood, but the two sections of Los Angeles are virtually worlds apart. Yet, TJ Kummer found the predominantly black neighborhood of Crenshaw to be the launchpad for a storied career that would put in him in proximity to the greatest film and television studios in the world.

From the early 1900s, Crenshaw was a primarily White middle-class community. With the U.S. Supreme Court decision that struck down racially restrictive housing covenants in 1948, the makeup of the residents shifted dramatically, and the area evolved to become one of the most multicultural sections of the city. And, by the late 1960s, the communities around Crenshaw Boulevard—View Park, Lafayette Square, Baldwin Hills, and working-class Inglewood—had become associated with Black Angelenos.

"Crenshaw Boulevard is the main street of Black L.A. Has been, still is, and hopefully always will be," said Nina Revoyr, activist, college professor, and author of the acclaimed 2003 bestselling novel *Southland*.

The life of this neighborhood wasn't just about the promise of opportunity for minorities or an incubator for something bigger.

The struggles were real and pervasive as evidenced by the epidemic of violence that surged in the late '80s and early '90s as gangs and drugs, compounded by social, educational, and economic inequities, took their toll on this hamlet for urban artistic expression.

Revoyr describes it this way: "It is a boulevard of both aspiration and disappointments." And TJ Kummer found both there in his professional life.

Though TJ was young, resilient, and filled with hope for his future, getting where he wanted to be was going to be an uphill battle. In a letter penned to his family in Michigan during the early hours of Saturday morning, May 25, 1957, he chronicled his ups and downs in the City of Angels and the challenges he faced in feeling spread thin with too many demands on his time and attention.

> *Dear Family:*
>
> *I agree that it is a shame that I haven't got time to write to my family which you may think is impossible, but I know different. You see things haven't been going to well for me here, not that it makes much difference to me, because I feel as though I am doing just what I should be, and I am NOT complaining.*
>
> *The VA got my records mixed up and I haven't received a check from them since the early part of February. Therefore, I am working (by the way, I still haven't received any checks). I got a job at Al Lapin's Center of Color. (It is a beauty shop, and I am working at the desk, and at the same time bettering myself at my work). I'm up at 6:30 a.m. then I take my two-mile hike to school. I stay at school until time for work, which is at 4:45 p.m. I work from then until around 12 or 1 a.m., then I take a bus back to Hollywood, then comes the two-mile hike again only this time UP hill. This goes on for six days a*

week. For the seventh, Sunday, with the little time there is left after mass I clean my apartment and try and get enough sleep to hold me over for another week and try and cut or set a few friends hair in order to have enough money to carry me through the week and a few other things I won't take time to mention.

So now if you can find some time in there somewhere for me to write a letter let me know. I will be more than glad to do it. HA-HA. And as far as the people that ask about me, tell them that I'm doing just great, and that I am very happy with myself, which makes for pleasant living. I am of sound body and mind which I feel is all that I need in order to get whatever I want, and I am sure that all of the people that are interested will see for themselves the fruits of my efforts.

Another point which I would like to bring up that you may not agree with—I have quit trying to prove myself to anyone but myself. In other words, I don't care what other people think of me, and in order to properly lead my life, I can't. As long as I know that I am doing the right thing that is all that counts to me, and I know that anyone that thinks otherwise is wrong. I feel that if a person plants a wrong seed—they will find out as it grows, discard it and replant a new seed. Anyway, I have placed my own standards of living on myself, and I find that they are as good as any and better than most.

I hope with all of the wrong spelling, poor phrasing and so on, that I put across my point.

I received the $20,[1] and it came in more handy than you could imagine. Thanks, a lot. I've got to go to sleep now so that I'll be able to wake up in time. Thanks, a lot for your letters, and I really am sorry that I don't have time to write more

---

1. According to Sebring family archives and bank records, Bernard Kummer sent his son twenty-one checks over a three-year period from 1956 to 1959. The amounts ranged from $5 to $260.70 and were meant to support his education, bills, living expenses, and help launch his first salon.

often, but it seems there is always something in the way. I wish that you would understand.

With All My Love Always

Tom

The aforementioned Al Lapin was a top colorist in the hair industry and owned several beauty shops and schools in and around the Los Angeles area. He took TJ under his wing as his apprentice and later partnered with him when TJ became a rock star stylist. The location where he worked was at 6838 Sunset Boulevard,[2] an industrial-sized complex where a variety of cutting-edge hair and coloring products were produced. The product line's colors spanned the rainbow, from platinum-blonde to jet back, lime green and fire-engine red—hair colors that might not play so well in the Midwest at the time but were permissible in California. This opportunity with Lapin added an important extra layer in TJ's apprenticeship. Anthony DiMaria, Jay Sebring's nephew and director of the *JAY SEBRING....CUTTING to the TRUTH* documentary, said this was a crucial layer in his uncle's hair education.

> This is probably the first hands-on, direct exposure to the machination and chemistry of hair color products and processing that helped him understand hair care much better. Being in Lapin's color labs on a grassroots level served as a precursor to the origination of his own complete, organic, Ph-balanced product line.

After completing his 1,600 hours of study at Comer & Doran, TJ's hard work finally paid off. The California State Board of

---

2. The location has been used since 1973 as an outpatient treatment facility providing medical services, substance abuse, mental health, drug-free transitional living, housing for women with HIV, and prevention services run by Los Angeles County.

Cosmetology certified his first license in the fall of 1956, mailed to him at his new residence, 6206 Temple Hill Drive, Apartment 3, Hollywood. License No. H-3047 enabled TJ to operate as a "hairdresser and cosmetologist" for a full year, expiring on September 10, 1957. His first full-time job in his chosen vocation was at Shelley Hair Style in South Central Los Angeles.

The proprietor announced in grand style the hiring of his new stylist, renamed as "Jay Kummer," in a small but boastful advertisement in the *Angeles-Mesa* and *Inglewood-Morningside News Advertiser*. The ad, which was placed on October 10, 1957, coincidentally fell on Jay's 24th birthday. Accompanied by a thumbnail-sized black and white headshot, the ad read:

One of Hollywood's foremost stylists now practicing his hair dressing and beauty cultural abilities in this area:
COLORING
SHAPING
STYLING
Mr. Jay Kummer
Hollywood
"The haircut that styles."

Linking Jay to Hollywood was a strategic master stroke in terms of drawing clientele to the modest shop at 4427 Crenshaw Boulevard.[3] From the beginning, Hollywood had been an idol maker and trendsetter for all of America and the entire world. Style trends and hot topics rippled out from this entertainment epicenter like shockwaves of fashion. Suburbs like Crenshaw on the periphery of Hollywood were just as susceptible to the influence of the awe-inspiring big city lights and star-studded streets.

Jay was familiar with this neighborhood as well as others in its

---

3. The storefront still stands today and is currently a fashion boutique.

proximity. He had traversed these streets a few years before during his jazz club days with a couple of adventurous navy buddies while docked in Long Beach and his girlfriend Joanna from their Earl Bostic days. Among the many requisite sites to see were the jazz, R & B, and blues clubs on Central Avenue, as Jay did from his nights when hobnobbing with the likes of Lionel Hampton, Earl Bostic, Max Roach, James Moody, and Woody Herman.

"I didn't know where Sunset Boulevard was when I moved to L.A., but I sure knew Central Avenue," legendary music producer Quincy Jones recalled years later.

Those were glory days for Jay when he was in the navy and now working in near the same locales as some of these dizzying establishments must have provided him with some sense of familiar providence and sentimentality. Jay felt that, even on its worst day, South Central Los Angeles was a hundred times more exciting than the Michigan suburbs. A transformation of sorts was taking shape. What was once the proverbial playground for navy sailor Thomas Kummer would now be the very first business launchpad for the newly christened Jay Kummer.

Shelley Hair Styles featured seven stylists, a manicurist, and was marketed exclusively to women. The shop also sold and rented a wide variety of wigs, wiglets, falls, and cascades, a touch that most likely galled Jay, who still pined to open his salon exclusively for men.

However, Jay was like a sponge, and he let nothing go to waste in his quest to prove his concepts from a knowledge-enterprise point of view. He undoubtedly picked up a few publicity pointers from his employer, known only to the media as "Mr. Shelley," who was described as "one of the quietest gentlemen I have ever met in my life," wrote Eve Adams, a reporter with the L.A.-based *Star-News/Vanguard*.

"Due to the knowledge and artistry of Mr. Shelley, his studio is certainly getting to be the No. 1 hairstyling salon in the Los Angeles area," Adams wrote in a 1960s puff piece that read more like a paid advertisement. "Incidentally, I cannot give you a full name for Mr. Shelley, as, for professional reasons, he prefers and simply is known as 'Mr. Shelley.'"

Whether or not Jay was on a first-name basis or knew the real identity of Mr. Shelley is a matter of speculation. What can be construed as fact is that after a few months of wigs, women, and warts, Jay was fed up with women's hair, according to Peggy DiMaria.

> One of my uncles had passed away in Michigan and my mom and Jay spent some time together there, and he was saying how he wasn't enjoying doing women's hair. It just didn't suit him. He wasn't satisfied with it. He was sitting on the edge of the bed and my mom was on the other side. He was meticulously dabbing his fingers with wart remover because he had several on his hands. He tapped the warts and said, "This is not for me. I caught these warts from one of these women who came into the salon." He didn't like doing women's hair because he felt it was very artificial. He didn't like doing roller sets because everything was out of proportion. But when he got those warts, it was as if he was at the end of his rope.

The bottom line was that Jay would never be happy working for someone else. His vision and ideas about hair design were carefully thought out and curated over several years. They needed to be implemented by him and him alone because until now, no one comprehended what Jay did. Something that is revolutionary is often met with resistance or scorn since there is no reference point nor understanding of that which does not exist. His salon would become a lab where creatives could apply their craft with a wide cross section of customers: actors, music and record executives, professional athletes, doctors, lawyers, politicians, and even construction workers.

"I've had ample opportunity to observe every variety of men's hair," Jay later told *Playboy*. "My conclusions: the condition of most American men's hair is deplorable."

Jay felt that most men's hair was "burdened" with grease and oil, favoring unnatural hairstyles that were too short and bristly, which often made them look like "the village idiot."

Rather than a barber cliché slapped on the customer's head, Jay would design hairstyles for the configuration of a person's face. For an oval shaped face, he recommended hair at medium length with sideburns aligned with the cheekbone and that the hair part should start at the maximum recession. Hair should be full on the side of a square-shaped face to offset the fullness. Sideburns should be full and extend below the cheekbone. With this cut, a part is not necessary. With a round face, Jay wanted to de-emphasize the rotund jawline, and hair should be full on top and on the sides. A part is optional. And with the long face, the hair should lie fairly flat on top, but not short. Sides should be full, and the length of the sideburns depended on the length of the face. In this instance, a part was desirable. While these were basic guidelines for Jay, it was the nuance of a unique canvas that provided the finishing touch in which he created a custom cut for each individual.

Jay also had strong ideas on daily shampooing and conditioning, examining the hair after a shampoo free of adhesives, hot oil treatments for eliminating dandruff, and how to treat receding hair ("a young guy who has started to recede will automatically feel older"). And if faced with inevitable baldness, he recommended taking a bold stance and shaving the entire head like actor Yul Brynner ("this can be quite attractive if the head is a good shape, for it gives the head a better balance and clean-looking line").

These ideas for men's hair were far ahead of their time in the late 1950s, but an artist needs a clean designer's slate and a space to execute these ideas. For someone as ahead of his time as Jay, breaking new ground on someone else's turf just wasn't going to work, and it seems he may have explored a few options for realizing this dream before eventually opening his own salon.

Sebring's nephew, Anthony DiMaria, discovered an architect's rendering in the early-to-mid-2000s amongst family documents, linking Jay to actor Michael Pataki, a prolific film and television star (*Get Christi Love!*). On the rendering, Pataki was listed as potential partner in a space located at 5678 Sunset Boulevard,[4] a few blocks east of the Hollywood 101 Freeway. The blueprint suggests the two men commissioned an architect to draw a rendering for a "Proposed Men's Hair Styling" salon at this space. The plans included a reception area, a work room with several stations, two sinks, a tint room, and a restroom for men and women. Pataki died in 2010 and never revealed any insight into what came of the possible joint venture. "Whatever plans the two had for this men's only hair salon or why it didn't work out went to the grave with both men," said Anthony.

> The family doesn't know what happened with this location or what Jay or Michael Pataki had in mind. We don't know if he couldn't raise the money or if the idea turned into fog, or if the idea evolved or progressed into something else.

Pataki went on to have a decades-long career on the big and small screen while Jay went back to the drawing board, honing his ideas for the first men's-only hair salon in the country. As it turned out, waiting a bit longer for the idea to ferment turned out to be serendipitous. His next location would be far more modest and affordable. More important, it sat in L.A.'s sweet spot, straddling

---

4. The original building was razed to the ground, and the site is currently a Home Depot.

tony Beverly Hills, hip West Hollywood, the trendy Melrose district, and the iconic Sunset Strip, a glamorous thoroughfare and playground for Hollywood stars and rockers. More important, the salon was in proximity to CBS and Paramount Studios where a cadre of stars, entertainers, and network and film executives could stop in for one of Jay's life-altering cuts. But that was a few years later when the rest of the world finally caught up.

Throughout the latter part of 1958 and early 1959, Jay focused all his energies on opening a place he could call his own where he would call his own shots and carry out his specific vision of the invention he would usher into the world. Thanks to a final loan from Bernard Kummer in the amount of $260.70, Jay placed a $500[5] down payment to secure a small space[6] at 725 N. Fairfax in West Hollywood, which he found through Britton Realty, a Los Angeles-based realty firm. It was far more modest than the proposed Sunset location, but it was enough to get started. The rent on the narrow and rectangular-sized room was $85 a month. But it was all Jay needed, said Anthony DiMaria.

> You don't need much to open a salon. All you really need is a license, a chair, cabinet, a mirror, implements, a shampoo bowl, and you could be in business. But real estate is a completely different matter.

The same day Jay signed the lease—March 3, 1959—he penned a letter to his father back in Michigan, expressing his gratitude to Bernard for his belief, encouragement, and financing to help secure his dream.

"Thanks to a few fine people and yourself, the lease was signed

---

5. This amount is equivalent to approximately $5,000 in 2025 dollars.
6. The space was originally part of a deluxe six-unit complex that had plumbing to handle domestic and small retail use.

today," Jay wrote. *"I am in business for myself (no partners), and I am a very happy young man for the first time in a long while."*

Jay was unreserved in his optimism for his future. He believed in the diligence and hard work he had put in to honing his craft. He was confident that not only was the world ready for something new, but that he was the one who would deliver just what they needed. All the right things were in motion and his success was inevitable. As he wrote his father, "The ball has started its roll...."

What Jay didn't write or could possibly know was that there'd be lots of curveballs, too.

CHAPTER 7
PIECE BY PIECE

Jay Sebring's story is not one of overnight success. He wasn't one of the breakout stars that are the stuff of Hollywood legend—the dream that draws thousands to its beacon each year to this day.

His struggle was more akin to the likes of most seekers who pay their dues without "connections" or immediate results, but he wasn't waiting for the phone to ring. Jay was determined his hard work would pay off even if others weren't so sure.

Jay wasn't yet a blip on the Hollywood radar, his friends and family were questioning his life choices, and the public wasn't buying in to what he was selling.... yet. Jay was convinced it was just a matter of time for all of that to change.

He had a vision, a space, and a concept that would revolutionize—perhaps even create—an industry. All the pieces of the puzzle were there, but how it would come together was still in question. As it turned out, he did assemble his dream, piece by piece, with his own bare hands.

Jay had no discernible carpentry skills or even a rudimentary understanding of how to build things. But, for his salon, he learned how. He had to. Jay was on a do-it-yourself budget and outfitted his salon with his own two hands. He even carried lumber on his shoulder from a nearby hardware store because he didn't have a car. Jay relied on wit and grit and did things he didn't know he could do. To him, nothing was impossible.

A group of friends had promised to help him out, but they didn't bother showing at the appointed time. Jay quickly realized that Los Angeles could be a place where friendship was slippery, elusive, and transactional. Hollywood was filled with networkers, socialites, opportunists, manipulators, performers, and phonies, and Jay took note of who did and did not come through for him. The ones who did were rewarded with loyalty. The others were dropped quickly.

Bill Abbott, Jay's first hire, did pitch in to help him build a sink cabinet, desk, two partitions, a couple of signs, and a few other necessary things. Jay added the final creative touches in sketching out his storefront banner. When the salon opened on Tuesday, March 24, 1959, the space was no frills, but certainly functional for what he wanted to do. It was bright, classy, and simple. Jay brought his best foot forward with limited funds but in a substantial way. In time, the space would bud and fuse, ultimately becoming iconic.

"People seem to think that it looks better than if we had it made to order," he wrote in a letter to his parents dated April 5, 1959, a week after he opened the salon. *"And as I sit back and look at it, it does.... I have never believed in or worked so hard on anything in my life, and I think that it shows."*

Jay worked furiously day and night for three weeks to open the salon, acquiring more than a few blisters and callouses along the way. He only stopped to eat and sleep, bedding down in his shop with just a sleeping bag and pillow. No bed or couch. This saved him a substantial amount in rent money when "even 50 cents makes a big difference." Struggles were not foreign to Jay. After his mother's poverty-ridden Alabama roots, his service in war-time Korea, and his living in a utility room during his cosmetology days,

Jay must have considered retiring in a sleeping bag in the back of a shop on a major thoroughfare luxurious. Like all go-for-broke artists, disruptors, and visionaries, Jay was willing to do whatever it took to achieve success.

"The only thing wrong is that in working so hard on the shop we haven't had any time for the promotion of the business and no money left to advertise, so considering, we did well this week, and we are doing as much promotion as finances will permit," Jay informed his parents.

One of the earliest advertisements Jay took out was a small—some might say pitiful—ad in *Variety*. It certainly targeted the right audience, but it sat at the bottom of page fourteen. The ones who read it must have either been curious or wondered why it was there in the first place. It later paid off in spades.

All this hard work did not preclude Jay from needing or having a social life. In that three-week period when he was preparing his salon for opening day, Jay attended a weekend party hosted by Bob Beaumont. It was there where he met BarBara Luna, a Filipino-Italian stunner from Manhattan. The Broadway singer/actress had arrived in Los Angeles in 1958 and was trying her hand in Hollywood. BarBara had no problem finding work, and her career was rolling from the get-go, guest starring on several television shows, including *Perry Mason*, *Zorro*, and *Mike Hammer*.

Beaumont, who knew Jay, was BarBara's hairdresser. She said Jay caught her eye at the party, and there was an instant connection. Both were young, good looking, and had much in common. They talked about Hollywood, the hardships of the business, and what he was doing with his life. BarBara said of their early days together:

He was the cutest guy with this little twinkle in his eyes. He was so inspiring because he had this vision. He started to talk about his ideas about men's hair, and that he had just rented this little space on Fairfax. And he was down to his last buck, but he wanted to do this. His ideas were starting to get to me, they were so infectious. You could see that this something was so possible. I thought, *I gotta help this guy somehow.*

The two exchanged phone numbers and began dating almost immediately. BarBara knew Jay didn't have a dime to his name, but that didn't matter to her. According to BarBara, "Jay was a decent guy" who was "sweet, friendly, and calming." She can't ever recall him cursing or saying a negative word about anyone.

He was not an outgoing person, but he wasn't introverted. He was serious but had a great sense of humor. He was funny but wasn't really a joke teller. But you couldn't make fun of a serious matter. He would defend it up and down, which is one of the things I loved about him. He was just as serious about things as he was about his own business.

BarBara was dedicated to helping Jay achieve his dream, even sweeping floors at the salon and preparing the shop for its opening. They'd break for dinner and grab a bite at a nearby eatery on Melrose and Sierra Bonita called Joe's Steak Pick. BarBara grew sentimental when speaking of the eatery:

It was a little steakhouse with four tables and a guy named Joe was the bartender, the cook, the waiter, and he just loved Jay. I think he was Jay's first client. So, we'd go there, eat, then head back to the salon, sweep and put the shop together. He had a barber chair, a cape, and he was ready to give cuts.

It was at one of these late-night sessions the couple broached the idea of changing his last name. BarBara was all for it. To her, Kummer sounded hard, unnatural, and lacked a certain sophistication. She encouraged him to think of something that rolled off the tongue with ease but would also draw people into his establishment.

> Jay wanted to change his name, and, in the Sixties, there was a Hollywood agent by the name of Henry Willson who was responsible for changing a lot of actor's names.[1] He came up with such wonderful names. Jay was so glamorous and somehow Jay Kummer just didn't quite fit. The more we talked about it, the more he thought it was a good idea.

Not long after that conversation with BarBara, Jay had flipped open a men's magazine and came across a series of sketches of the Sebring racetrack in Florida. It drew his attention. He followed auto racing which, at the time, was a niche sport in the States. Being a Detroit native, he naturally loved cars. Jay told his mother in private conversation that he had been to the famed racetrack and had "experienced a streak of good luck" there. So did his friend and future client Steve McQueen, who later raced there in March 1962 as part of the World Champion circuit.

Jay liked the ring of "Sebring" as a business and professional last name. Shortly before opening his salon, and after a long debate, he made the change. When he shared the news with his parents over the phone, they were not fully supportive of the idea. Bernard was baffled that anyone would ever change their name. Peg, on the other hand, was amused and teased her son, "The name might have a ring to it. Kind of like 'Sebring a ling a ling a ling.'"

One of the final touches was the storefront awning bearing,

---

1. Willson was a talent agent known for cultivating unexperienced, handsome young men and turning them into stars who fit the "beefcake" physique popular in that era. He changed the names for Rock Hudson, Guy Madison, Tab Hunter, Robert Wagner, Troy Donahue, and Rory Calhoun, transforming them into matinee idols.

"Sebring Men's Hair Design," and a neon sign with Jay's signature featured in the window. He spent every cent he had on getting the shop up and running, so there wasn't much left for anything else.

It would be quite a while before Jay could afford much beyond subsistence. He worked himself to the bone, sometimes standing and cutting hair for twelve-to-thirteen hours a day on his feet without a break, still finding it hard to make ends meet. Some days there would only be one or two customers all day. At other times, none.

A salon requires repeat business and building up a clientele, which Jay didn't have. He was fighting an uphill battle on many fronts: adult males didn't understand the concept or didn't want to deviate from what they already knew. Getting a haircut wasn't an impulsive act and required a degree of deliberation. And his salon didn't get much pedestrian traffic. There was also the fact that Jay's cuts were $5—double what barbers were getting at the time. To enlist clients, there had to be awareness about Jay and what made him special, and that required marketing dollars he did not have. He cut friends' hair in hopes people would ask so they'd offer a referral. And there were times Jay was so desperate he would coax complete strangers in off the street, offering a cut for free, hoping that the next time they needed a quality cut they'd remember him. This move came off as desperate and it certainly didn't pay the bills, which were mounting after a few months of revenue stagnation.

The ones who did hear about the shop tried their best to squash Jay's salon. A group of teens from Fairfax High School gathered daily outside of the shop to give patrons entering and exiting a raft of shit about their new cuts, no doubt calling into question their masculinity. While this was nothing more than sport to them, they didn't realize the damage they were doing to Jay's livelihood.

"I just kept plugging away and refused to listen to what THEY were telling me," Sebring told Ele and Walt Dulaney in a 1963 interview for their entertainment column *Dateline*. "In this world you've got to decide whether or not you're going to live your life or let OTHERS run it for you."

Five months after he opened the Fairfax shop, Jay was on his last gasp of air, financially speaking. Checks were bouncing, the telephone and utilities were about to get shut off, and on top of that, he had a cold and developed strep throat. Jay was about as low as a man could get, and he felt terrible having to hit his old man up for help. It wasn't a matter of needing a check mailed to him; he required a wire transfer to keep the wolves away. This bleak situation was the catastrophe Bernard Kummer had hoped his son would avoid. He encouraged Jay to adjust his life plans to stem further reckless hemorrhaging. On August 18, 1959, he had to swallow whatever pride he had left to write Bernard a desperate missive about his circumstances, which were dire. It read:

Dear Dad:

I have been sitting here writing for about three hours, this is my eighth letter. The others are in little balls, in the waste basket.

I find it very hard to express myself. Partly because of my limited vocabulary and poor spelling, but most of all I want to put it in a way that you will be able to understand my point.

I feel that I know you pretty well being as that I only know you as a mature man set in his ways (based on high intelligence and his life of the past) so I will try. What I am trying to do is help you to understand me as the man I am developing into based on that knowledge from you plus what I have absorbed on my own and planting it in my field as you did in yours.

I feel that I am in the field best chosen for me as you do yours to you. Because this is the artist field doesn't mean that I am of a lesser caliber of a man than you were at my age, or that I have less intelligence in my field than you did in yours.

This being true, then where would you be now, if your

father was of the same caliber of a man in his field you are in yours and every Kummer thereafter you and got in back of you 100%. Where would you be now? (Looking at it from a business standpoint because that seems to be the topic now.)

Unfortunately, your father was of a much lesser caliber than you and you were forced to make it alone and you did very well as I think that I could without you.[2]

In other words, I want that break which you never had and so far, I feel I do, but a father doesn't stop being a father when his son is twenty-one he just loses his jurisdiction. At this point I am obligation free, seeking to you at this time of life, and I feel that although you don't have a lot of money to throw around, you do have a better mind than most of the people that I have met that do. I tribute this to your misfortune.

Just because I am in another city and in a different field doesn't mean that I am not part of the family.

I think that if we worked a little more together, we develop this into something that will be a credit to the family and a tremendous business success. I feel that I can handle the creative and artist end, but I could use your help on the business and financial end.

My bookkeeper helped me to get everything in order to send. These are my records from the 1st quarter that is the best I can do for now. I didn't know if I should send you just the breakdown sheets or the whole works, so I am sending everything....

If it weren't to this low point and I didn't have so much money in it already and I wasn't so sure that it will succeed, I wouldn't be asking you to stick your neck out.

It would take another letter three times this long to tell you what I need money for. I figure I need at least a thousand to

---

2. Bernard Kummer's father abandoned his family when he was three.

put me and the business well on its feet once and for all. It will
secure the business in other words and we together with the
money the business takes in will be able to grow and expand as
the money coming in will permit. If you can't see this from
what I have already written, you will either have to forget
about it as something not worth looking into or come out here
and see what is going on and give me a hand. In other words,
you have either got to trust my word or come out which I
would prefer but if you can't, please for the sake of both of us do
something.

> *With All My Love*
> *Always*
> *Tom*

P.S. I know that this letter probably sounds like a bunch of
nonsense and judging by the clipping I received today from you,
I guess you had the right picture right along, but I would just
like to keep it in the family if possible. And it's to the point that
something must be done. Wow I think this fever must have me.
Another letter will follow this tomorrow. Of my needs.

Bernard read the desperate letter with serious but loving concern. Jay's parents debated back and forth whether to send the money to their son. While they wanted to support and bolster Jay in his quest, the salon was slowly becoming a money pit for them.

"My dad didn't really understand what Jay was trying to do," said Peggy DiMaria. "At this point, he was wondering if this wasn't just a pipedream."

The legend and legacy of Jay Sebring hung precariously in the balance during this volatile period. Jay could always go back to Michigan and style hair for someone else, but he wouldn't get to lead the hair revolution that he had sensed was coming in the city that he loved so dearly. And that would crush him. Ultimately, Bernard and Marguerite decided to help their son and get him back on his feet. After years of support, Jay was fully aware of the strain this put on his parents' middle-class income. The end of the rope and his enterprise was in sight.

"When you think about it a little bit, it [the loan] made all the sense in the world," said Fred Kummer, Jay's older brother. "It was a good decision."

Another lifeline came from Jay's girlfriend, BarBara Luna, who connected Jay with his first celebrity client: entertainer Vic Damone. The postwar crooner and actor was at the height of his career, entertaining bobbysoxers, presidents, and royalty alike. Known for hits such as "You're Breaking My Heart," "On the Street Where You Live," and "I Have But One Heart," he had never been happy with his mane. He had dealt with curly, unruly hair his whole life and could never find anyone that made him look better. After BarBara sang Jay's praises, Damone gave him a shot.

"Jay cut my hair like I've never had before," said Damone a few years before his 2018 death. "It took an hour and a half. It was so small and in pieces. Never took a chunk out—he just carved it. It was like a work of art."

More than that, Damone's hair finally had *balance*—something Damone considered a major achievement.

"He cut it in such a way that it was all even, and I've never had that before," Damone marveled decades later. "After Jay's cut, I could run my hands and fingers through my hair, and it would just fall into place. Amazing."

Damone also knew of Jay's financial issues and gave him a $100 bill for the cut (equivalent to almost $1,130 in 2025).

"Jay was a gentleman and a very wonderful and centered young man," Damone said. "He was just very honest, sincere, and humble. I tried to bring him some business."

Damone, who appreciated Jay's artistry, brought Jay clients whenever he could. Damone said his friends loved what Jay did for them. However, it was barely enough to keep the shop open. Jay even discussed with him shuttering the business and moving back to Detroit, but Damone wasn't going to let that happen.

"Jay deserved success; he had such talent," Damone said. "Someone had to open the door for him. Someone had to introduce him. And that was me."

The vital introduction Damone made was to Jack Entratter, director of entertainment at the Sands Hotel in Las Vegas. Known as "Mr. Entertainment" to the showbiz industry, he was a host at the world-famous Stork Club and managed the Copacabana nightclub in the 1940s and early 1950s, using that currency (as well as financing from mobsters Frank Costello and Meyer Lansky) to gain entrée into Sin City in 1952. Today he is credited with elevating the quality of shows produced on the Vegas Strip and helping the city to become the "entertainment capital of the world."

He designed and built the Sands' famed Copa Room specifically to lure Frank Sinatra away from the Desert Inn, where he'd performed for a couple of years since that casino opened. He also signed Dean Martin and Sammy Davis, Jr., the core of what eventually became the Rat Pack.

Entratter was a meticulous dresser, had all his suits tailored (he had to at 6'4" and 240 pounds), flew in Learjets, and dated showgirls. He lived in a 5,000-square-foot apartment that included a guesthouse, a teahouse, a koi pond, and a pool. He had three chefs on duty to make whatever dish he desired. He also didn't carry cash but could buy anything he wanted, according to his widow, Corrine Entratter Sidney. She said in a 2007 oral history for the University of Las Vegas:

I had the power of the pencil. I could sign for anything I wanted. I had credit wherever I went. If I went to Caesars Palace with my niece to buy her outfits, I'd just sign for it, and they'd send the bill in care of The Sands.... it was an incredible way to live.

Entratter also had space at the Sands for a dentist and a barber and created a world where everybody came to him. When he took notice of Damone's transformative cut, an introduction was made, and the Vegas mogul flew Jay to see him. Jay worked his magic and made the already dapper executive look even better. Jay gave him the classic Sebring cut: timeless, classy, and masculine, making Entratter's profile even more attractive. It was the first time Entratter received a shampoo and custom cut with hands, scissors, and comb. Jay didn't employ any machinery or clippers except an edger, which he used to remove excess hair around the ears and neckline. This show of delicate finesse was a seminal event, even for Entratter, who was used to the best of the best.

Jay was in.

From 1960 to 1967,[3] Entratter regularly flew Jay to Las Vegas to cut his hair. Others began asking for "the flying barber's" services, including Frank Sinatra, Dean Martin, Sammy Davis, and Joey Bishop.

Canadian singer Paul Anka, who hung out and competed with the Rat Pack in Vegas for customers, said word began to spread quickly about Jay's incredible hair designs and what he could do with a pair of shears.

> Back in the 1950s, for all of us singers, besides your songs and working, your hair was the next important thing. So, we always wanted the guys who were the best. And Jay was the best. He would stylistically vibe into who you were.

Jay began 1959 as a new business owner who had spent his last dime getting operational. By the end of the year, he was about to

---

3. Entratter served as president of the Sands until Howard Hughes bought the hotel and casino for $15 million in July 1967. Entratter was a 15 percent stake owner, retired, and lived comfortably until his 1971 death of a cerebral hemorrhage at age 57.

take the hair and entertainment industry by storm. Though others had to be convinced, Jay knew the strife and struggles were worth it. This was the seminal period of vindication when Jay's ethereal ideas and dreams manifested in solvent form, unlocking a magical world where he would be granted entrée to stars, beautiful women, fame, wealth, sporty cars, and a chalet-style home in Beverly Hills —a life most wouldn't have the audacity to imagine.

More than anyone else, Jay Sebring was on the precipice of becoming the architect of ultimate masculine style of the 1960s, shaping the look of some of the coolest iconic figures of the ages. But soon—and equally important—he would create an industry for men's hair care and concepts that didn't exist before, which is approximately a $100 billion a year worldwide industry today.

"That was the start of the monster," BarBara Luna said.

CHAPTER 8
A JACK IN VEGAS

L as Vegas has always been known as a Mecca of Strange, but in the 1950s it was beyond surreal. With exploding nukes as a tourist attraction, Miss Atomic Blast beauty contests, and the electric cowboy "Vegas Vic" sign hoisted in 1951 that said "Howdy, pardner" every fifteen minutes around the clock, Vegas was a caricature of itself. And with a county sheriff busted for owning a brothel and a governor who made corruption and cronyism an art form, it was gaining a reputation as a place where anything goes.

But the storied history of the Vegas Valley didn't start there. Prior to flipping on the bright lights and outrageous antics, it was mostly a desert wasteland where predatory creatures of the human and animal variety roamed. Coyotes, black widows, scorpions, and rattlesnakes chased after unsuspecting prey, and desperados sought refuge from life on the run. The only humans that inhabited the land were a small group of Native Americans—the Southern Paiute peoples, also known as the Nuwu. As incentive, gambling was introduced to lure laborers and miners in the Southern tip of the mineral rich "Silver State" during California's gold rush. Then came the construction and completion of the Hoover Dam. The Valley had been a desolate stretch for which the U.S. railroad had transported its passengers on their way to other places and a land that failed to sustain the farmers who tried to tend it. Then the town hummed to life in the 1940s, powered by the jolt of the dam and the legalization of gambling. One powered the town, the other empowered the town.

With gaming as the state's fastest growing industry, mobsters of all flavors financed hotels and installed their own frontmen. The American postwar boom led a lot of people who were flush with cash (and had just survived World War II) to seek a good time and fortune.

After the December 1946 opening of the Flamingo (built by Del E. Webb and bankrolled by Benjamin "Bugsy" Siegel and members of the mob) the following decade saw the rise of resort-style hotels such as the Thunderbird, the Desert Inn, the Sahara, the Riviera, the Dunes, the Tropicana, the Silver Slipper, and the Sands. A formerly dusty hole in the wall had become the glitzy destination for the rich and well-appointed. Even in the oppressive desert heat, women donned fur coats and men wore tailored suits and slicked their hair. These glamorous venues drew the top entertainment acts in the country and offered an endless supply of extravagant buffets of rich foods and stylish cocktails.

In early 1960, Frank Sinatra was in Las Vegas to shoot *Ocean's Eleven* with a star-studded cast. This testosterone-filled ring-a-ding-ding crew of night crawlers took full advantage of all Sin City had to offer. However, the punishing schedule of filming, horseplay, drinking, and women were taking a toll on Sinatra. After a few weeks, he called a "summit" with Jack Entratter to discuss scaling back on his two shows a night commitment. Jack could not do anything to change that as he was under a contractual obligation to The Sands. But Sinatra insisted something had to change.

He proposed having Dean or Sammy come up and help him with a show.

"You want them to come, they'll come," Entratter said. This was the genesis of the suave and swanky crew known as "The Rat Pack" —Frank Sinatra, Dean Martin, Sammy Davis Jr., Joey Bishop, and Peter Lawford—who would run over the town like a pack of wolves for years to come. They had found (and founded) the entertainer's paradise, where top-tier performers could write their own tickets and had an eager entourage waiting in the wings to cater to their every desire. But for Jay Sebring Vegas was a business opportunity, not a playground.

Jay was thrust into this new world of entertainers and mobsters, working and befriending people who lived on a level he could barely imagine, and he had a new learning curve ahead of him. For most people, finding themselves within such a storied world of opulence, it would be easy to get swept up and lose their bearings. But Jay instinctively knew that 90 percent of surviving and eventually thriving in this environment was simply providing the best cuts and keeping his mouth shut about what he saw, heard, and experienced. Those Midwestern values served him well in this regard.

A January 19, 1960, letter (written on Sands letterhead) to his parents and siblings was surely a sanitized and wholesome version of what went on behind the scenes. It read:

> *Hi Family:*
>
> *This is the first chance that I've had to write. My health is good, and the shop is coming along better and better. The guy who owns this hotel flew me up to cut his hair. I am now often referred to as the "flying barber." Soon I hope to buy my own plane.*
>
> *I am planning on opening another shop within a couple of months. I am going to talk with people about it tomorrow. Will let you know what happens. I am sure that the talents God gave me will win out over all else, as they are now.*
>
> *I will fly back as soon as time will permit, until then take*

the best care of yourselves and pray for me as I pray for you, that someday we may be together again and that our individual desires be filled and link as one. In some way I feel sure this can be done. Faith has done more many times before.

Well, more and more of the star actors are calling me every day and I am quickly becoming known as the best in my field and that is only right because I am. But I know that you will be happy to know that every time you see movies or watch TV, you see some of my work. I would mention names but there are too many and by the time I do there will be more. But when I see you, which will be soon I hope, I will tell you all. Now to the next step has got to be money, right? Keep your fingers crossed. Soon we will be rich.

With All My Love
Always
—Hope you can read this soft pencil

Almost overnight Jay went from borderline poverty, sleeping in his one-chair shop, to the lap of luxury, flying on private jets, and embraced as "one of us" amongst Sinatra and the Rat Pack. He was suddenly thrust into a catered world where everything was his for the asking—as long as he brought those extra-long shears and magical hair designs.

What Sebring knew instinctively was that penetrating that insulated world didn't happen by showing up on their doorstep uninvited. You got invited by bringing something unique and special to the table, and Jay had that in spades. With Sinatra's effusive approval, word spread like wildfire, igniting diverse flocks of individuals seeking Jay's services and employment.

Jay hit the scene in Vegas at a serendipitous time when stars and planets were aligning to create a cultural movement that would ripple out through the world. Not only were entertainment icons being launched into the stratosphere, but the mores and conventions of society were being tested. Vegas had earned a reputation as the "Mississippi of the West," a desert city that practiced Jim Crow laws and could be outright hostile to Blacks.

They were allowed to work at the casinos, but only as cooks, maids, porters, and other "back of the house" jobs. Under no circumstances could they walk through the front doors of any casino. Entertainers didn't fare much better when it came to the respect afforded them. They were forced to enter the stage through back doors or the kitchen and, after they received their nightly applause, they exited the same way they came in.

It was during these times of racial strife that Jay's staff, clientele, and friends were completely integrated. There were Jews, Blacks, Italians, Hispanics, Asians, women, homosexuals, all working together side by side. Jay did not judge gender, color, or orientation. He gravitated towards high quality and the individual. At a time when racism in America was understood only as a Black and White issue, Jay supported his friend Sammy Davis, Jr. as he commuted to the performer's home to cut his friend's and wife's hair after the couple received death threats upon the announcement of Davis' marriage to May Britt.

African American Wardell "Del" Jackson was a peer and designer at Jay's Fairfax salon, now one of the most exclusive establishments in the world in 1961. Some of Jay's clients and friends included Sam Cooke, Quincy Jones, Sammy Davis, Jr., Bill Cosby, and Bahamian British actor Calvin Lockhart.

The taboos and judgments of polite society had no place at Jay's salon or his space in Vegas, and people were allowed to explore their desires in a place where indulgence was on the menu.

That said, even in the city where you could find whatever suited your fancy, no matter how unconventional it might be, there was a dark underbelly hidden from the view of tourists and players. Vegas was notorious for being "mobbed up," and was perpetually on the radar of the FBI. It might even be true to say that the legendary tales didn't go far enough in capturing what really happened there.

Jay was now an insider in this world of show and shade. But discretion was paramount for keeping that all-access card. That was easy to do in a town that mostly slept during the day and came alive at night. And no place was livelier in Vegas than the Sands at that time, according to Nancy Sinatra.

The Sands was built at the same time as my dad's house in Palm Springs, and we would fly back and forth between Las Vegas and the desert. My dad wanted to keep an eye on what was going on at the Sands 'cause that was his baby. Jack Entratter had two daughters, so I had pals. I remember when the Sands had a pool, finally, and we all sat around outside.

Nancy said that on one of those days in the sun, she was sandwiched between her father, singer and entertainer Dinah Shore, and David Sarnoff, an American businessman and pioneer of radio, music recording, and television. Sarnoff ruled over an ever-growing telecommunications empire that included RCA and NBC. Among his many accomplishments was a recording contract he extended to Elvis Presley in 1955, luring him away from Sun Records. She described a conversation between Shore and Sarnoff as even being interesting to a kid, who later became a recording and movie star in her own right.

Dinah was actually reading an encyclopedic explanation of what television was, and here I am this kid, you know, taking this all in. The Sands grew one building at a time, and each little building housed several hotel rooms. It was a wonderful place.

Nancy Sinatra said it was a place where wonderful things happened, and it was wonderfully run.

> The guys who owned the nightclubs in the east were what I would call "wise guys," had just moved out to Vegas and took over the running of these hotels. They were very generous with chips, "Here, go play. Have a good time." They gave you free drinks. Very heady, exciting time. Everything was more fun back then. That's where I met JFK. He was at the Sands when he was running for president, and my dad introduced me. He was in the audience when my dad performed there.

It was a time when $14 got you a round-trip ticket from Los Angeles to Vegas and where $100 could easily sustain you for the weekend. That included a room at the Sands and all the food and drink you cared to consume. A lot of business was conducted in the hotel's steam room, where the partiers could nurse themselves back to health after a night of revelry and where mafia dons could hold private conversations. It was even the site of a public prank on comedian Don Rickles by the Rat Pack that made the "Merchant of Venom" blush, laughed Nancy Sinatra.

> There was one night when Don Rickles, who was in the steam room with a towel wrapped around his waist, got pushed out the door. Now, picture this: the door to the steam room was right by the public pool. As they pushed him out the door, they grabbed his towel away. And he's standing there naked as they slammed the door and wouldn't let him back in. Some great times, great stories from that steam room. I'm so glad Jay got to be part of that.

In addition to Sinatra, the Rat Pack, Rickles, Peter Lawford, and Joey Bishop, singer Paul Anka was a part of the action. He fondly remembered his time running with the pack and getting to know Jay.

> You come into that environment late at night, two or three in the morning, and you got Sinatra, Dean Martin, Sammy Davis, Jr., and a bunch of women and you're in the steam room. And the haircut will be in four hours. Meanwhile there was fun and frolic. Back then it was Disneyland. It was the place where there were definite parameters, how to exist, how to dress, what to do. And part of that whole luster was not only the Rat Pack, but it was also getting a cut from Jay.

Jay's imprint on these legendary players and performers didn't just offer his business some long-awaited stability; it established his reputation. Jay's haircuts became a status symbol for high rollers, like private jets, luxury cars, beautiful women, and backstage passes. A cut from Jay became part of the package of what made a man. Jay was now a long way away from the struggling upstart in a tiny shop in Hollywood. He was building an empire.

To Jay's credit, he didn't just take it all in and keep it to himself. He began sharing the experience with others. Now with a little success under his belt, Jay was able to hire new cutters at the salon. Among them was Joe Torrenueva, a Filipino/Puerto Rican transplant from Brooklyn, New York, who settled into East L.A. in 1950. Known as "Little Joe" to his illustrious clients, Torrenueva is also a musician, recording artist, and actor. Along with Jay Sebring, Torrenueva is also one of the most talented hair designers to emerge from the twentieth century.[1]

---

1. Some of Torrenueva's famous cinematic cuts include Dustin Hoffman in *The Graduate*, Richard Gere in *Breathless*, and Michael Douglas in *Wall Street*.

As soon as eighteen-year-old Torrenueva graduated from beauty school, Jay immediately put him to work. He proved not only to be an excellent student of Sebring's method, but he also had a special way with people. He was humble, gentle, non-intrusive, empathetic, and instinctively knew how to keep a confidence. Jay recognized these qualities, and soon Jay asked his future protégé to accompany him to Las Vegas.... and the steam room at the Sands. The first time he entered that sacred spot, Sammy Davis, Jr. was holding court, telling stories, cracking jokes, and busting balls. He remembered:

> I'm standing there with this towel wrapped around me and Jay's standing there, and Neil, the guy who ran the steam room, is standing on the other side of me. Sammy spotted us and said, "Look at those guys—they look like cuff links!" Then Sammy said, "How do you like the steam room?" I said, "It's too hot." They all laughed.

Torrenueva found Jack Entratter equally hospitable and eager to please and could grant him almost any wish if he so desired.

> He said, "Kid, what do you want? You want some broads? You want to gamble?" I said, "Jack, I'm really tired, you know." I had just flown into town, and wanted to relax, maybe watch some television. The reason why I said that was I [was] embarrassed. I was nineteen years old, and I didn't want to get anybody in trouble.... and that was my introduction to the finer things.

Although the allure of these finer things was tempting, Jay knew he would be limited if he stayed in Vegas. As grateful as he was for the powerful leg up he was offered in this city of lights, he was equally aware that he was meant for more.

Jay knew a thing or two about the fashion world and perhaps sensed the time for a fashion-forward Vegas was going to have its run and a new frontier would be just around the corner. Jay instinctively knew that Hollywood was still the epicenter of where things happened and was a world he needed to conquer.

Ironically, that would come, not through his Vegas connections but after an epic film that had been delayed for over a year's span finally saw the light of day. His styling prowess for the lead actor put him on the map in the town where he had been longing to make his mark.

Hollywood was a little late in calling, and perhaps Jay needed his time in Vegas to prepare him for what was to come, but once the stars of the silver screen caught wind of his epic talent, his life would never be the same.

CHAPTER 9
A SLAVE TO FASHION

No one has been able to piece together exactly how Jay Sebring was introduced to movie star Kirk Douglas or why he was picked to design the actor/producer's hair for *Spartacus*, the most iconic film of his career about the historic slave revolt that took place around 71 BCE. Jay never told anyone on the record and Douglas does not give an account in his 1988 memoir, *The Ragman's Son*.

At the time he was approached, Jay was still struggling in his small Hollywood studio. He had yet to become the in-demand stylist to the stars, so his name wasn't on the lips of anyone with influence.

The best possible guess is that Douglas sought him out. As a fervent reader of industry and trade magazines, the most likely scenario is that Douglas came across Sebring's small but strategic ad in *Variety*, which started running in 1959—the same year *Spartacus* commenced its long and troubled production. Douglas did, however, confirm in his memoir that the "Spartacut" was an original design Jay created in his Fairfax salon after gathering intel from Douglas about the film and his role. He wrote in *The Ragman's Son*:

I wanted everything about *Spartacus* to be special and authentic. I went to see Jay Sebring, a genius with hair. Jay came up with the distinctive look for the slaves—hair cut butch on top, long in the back with a tiny ponytail. I don't know if that haircut set any trends in the early sixties, but everybody is walking around with a Spartacut in the eighties.

A press photo from April 1959 showed a profile of Douglas sporting his daring new cut and ponytail. The photo was nothing more than a curiosity and the studio's way to build momentum for the picture. Later that summer, British-born nationally syndicated gossip columnist Sheilah Graham boldly predicted in her June 23, 1959 "Hollywood Today" column: "When *Spartacus* is released, the teenagers will have a new hairdo to copy—the Spartacut—a top knot effect worn by Kirk Douglas and other gladiators in the $6 million epic."

Had Graham or Douglas mentioned Jay's name in any of this press, he might not have spent as much time as he did in Las Vegas and his career might have had a different trajectory. But that wasn't the way things unfolded. In those days, gossip columnists got their fodder directly from stars seeking to promote projects or keep their name in the headlines. These days, publicists do the legwork in this regard. Graham's column ran for thirty-five years and, at its peak, was seen in 168 papers. But gossip columns do not mention those in the periphery—it's all about the stars because their names grab attention—so Jay got no credit for his role in the soon-to-be-trending look. This was typical during Hollywood's "Golden Era." Who would write about, or even care to read about, a hair designer in the film crew with no credits or guild membership?

Jay would soon change all of that. After a year of desperate struggles and coming a hair's breadth away from a one-way ticket back to Michigan, Jay was aware of how fragile his vision and methods were when sustaining a business operation within common industry parameters. At the time, the mere mention of men's hairstyling (Sebring was always quick to emphasize "designing" versus "styling.") was embarrassingly stigmatized as useless, silly, superficial and most of all.... feminine! Jay realized he would need a publicist not only to get his concepts out there, but to educate the public about the worth and manliness of his unheard-of concepts and treatments. Eventually he did get as much attention as many of the stars he styled. In fact, though his name wasn't mentioned, the results of his work got better press than the star or the film.

Up to that point, Graham's small news item was about the only positive mention of the motion picture, which had a final price tag of $12 million when it completed principal photography.[1] The 197-minute epic seemed as if it had been snake bitten from its inception and is considered one of the most hexed films ever attempted to this day. Plagued by illness, injury, ineptitude, ego, and an unfinished script by a blacklisted screenwriter, *Spartacus* had the highest price tag of any film made in Hollywood up to that point.

Originally announced in January 1958, Douglas' epic woes began almost as soon as the project was revealed. Academy Award-winning actor Yul Brynner simultaneously announced he was making the same film at United Artists based on the historical novel by American writer Howard Fast.[2] After a lengthy battle with Brynner, Douglas beat him to the draw by luring big stars to his project.

"For the first time, I managed to get everyone I thought was perfect for their roles—Laurence Olivier, Charles Laughton, Peter Ustinov, and Tony Curtis," Douglas told UPI reporter Vernon Scott.

---

1. In 2025 dollars, that would be equivalent of about a $130 million production.
2. Brynner paid Fast $100 for his first option on the book, which sold approximately three million copies and was translated into 45 different languages.

But his troubles were just beginning to fester. Once filming got underway, director Anthony Mann appeared to be in over his head, consumed by the enormity and magnitude of the picture. The first week went well, but then he let Peter Ustinov run roughshod over him by allowing the British actor to direct, including adding lines and over-the-top actions that weren't in the script. Mann was soon replaced[3] by thirty-year-old Stanley Kubrick, who came with his own set of baggage—chiefly that he shot slowly and deliberately, which added to the film's bloating budget. His cast didn't respect him for a variety of reasons, the least of which was that he was not relational with people, was arrogant, and wasn't fond of bathing. Stuntman Loren Janes, who was Douglas' stunt double throughout the seven-month shoot, said the famed director was unkempt and the cast and crew tired of the "boy genius" act.

> He wore the same black suit and tie and white shirt every day. Jean Simmons complained to Kirk Douglas about his body odor. Kirk had to pull Kubrick aside one day after filming and tell him to take a shower and change his clothes. Well, Kubrick took a shower, and he changed his clothes—but the next time he showed up on the set—he was wearing the same suit, tie, and white shirt. He just had them dry cleaned.

One of Kubrick's first acts was to sack then-leading lady Sabine Bethmann, who was to play Varnia, the slave girl who falls in love with Spartacus. After a long search by the studio, Bethmann had been announced proudly by Universal as the studio's "new discovery." Universal even set up a *LIFE* magazine photo shoot for the

---

3. Mann was paid his full $75,000 fee after 11 days of shooting. He quickly found another directing job when he landed *Cimarron,* an unremarkable Western starring Glenn Ford and Anne Baxter.

German-born beauty, which signaled to the Hollywood press corps a future star was being minted. After two days of filming, Kubrick determined she had no depth or range. He coldly gave Bethmann the boot and she broke down in tears.

Midway through the picture, Jean Simmons was sidelined for six weeks with female issues that required major surgery and serious bedrest.

Co-star Tony Curtis was not immune to the curse on this production either. He split his Achilles tendon while playing tennis with Douglas. He required a cast for his lower leg and needed five weeks to recuperate.

Even Douglas fell victim to the film's plight. For the first time ever in his career, he was sidelined by a flu brought on by exhaustion, according to his doctor. Douglas did not step foot on the set for ten days, another expensive delay for Universal.

Spartacus' follies became almost daily fodder for entertainment journalists who gleefully wrote about every misstep and mishap along the way. It even drew the attention of columnist Walter Winchell and the *Hollywood Reporter* who revealed that the Oscar-winning but blacklisted Dalton Trumbo was the real writer on the epic film. Throughout the picture, he had gone by "Sam Jackson."

In October 1947, Trumbo and other members of the film industry who were suspected of being communists were called to appear before the House of Un-American Activities Committee, led by Wisconsin Senator Joseph McCarthy. Trumbo and his cohorts (labeled the "Unfriendly Ten") were blacklisted by Hollywood, and they retreated to Mexico City to lick their wounds until the blacklist was lifted. For several years, Trumbo wrote scripts—including the Academy Award-winning *Roman Holiday*—under various pseudonyms. Hollywood still wanted him but not the stink of the political scandal.

The very idea that Trumbo was writing *Spartacus* riled gossip writer Hedda Hopper and the American Legion, who were galled at the very idea a Communist sympathizer was gaining a foothold to re-enter the business. The American Legion, the world's largest veteran's organization, threatened to picket the film unless Trumbo was fired. These hit-piece articles and threats didn't halt or slow down the production, but they added to the intense pressure they were under. Like Trumbo, Sebring was an outsider. But unlike Trumbo, Jay had no proven track record or credits to his name—yet another example of how Douglas bucked the system with his risky production decisions.

What the public didn't know was that there was an equally controversial collaboration between the director and a "hair design-er." No doubt Jay relied on his artistic sketching abilities, as he did in his youth and throughout his career, to settle on the final look for the Spartacus character. He created a style that would embody the transformation of a helpless slave into the dynamic leader of a historic uprising like a warrior phoenix from the ashes.

Actor Robert Wagner recalled a similar experience with Jay a few years later, which worked out well for his screen character.

> When I did Alexander Mundy in *It Takes a Thief,* he styled the look for that. Jay asked, "What kind of part are you playing? What kind of guy is he?" He read the character and liked the character. This guy was a thief and a very kind of suave guy. Jay would draw some sketches and take a look at where we wanted to go and how he wanted to have it, and how it looked on you. But to do a stylization of your hair, shape your face and do it for a character. It was great.

Somehow, *Spartacus'* production continued to soldier on and weather the storm. The motion picture was originally slated at $6 million with a three-month filming schedule. In August 1959, *Spartacus* finally reached the finish line four months late, spending three times the budget. It was quite an investment for Universal, who estimated that the picture had to make $20 million just to break even.

On October 6, 1960, *Spartacus* made its film debut at the DeMille Theatre in New York City's Times Square. The 2,300-seat theater was jam-packed with film critics and fans, fully expecting a spectacle. They got it too: ushers and usherettes were decked out in togas and Roman jewelry while the press received souvenir kits filled with 8 x 10 glossy headshots and still photos, detailed notes on the production, and quotes from the star-studded cast, not to mention Douglas, a Hollywood star in the truest sense at the peak of his fame, in attendance with his smiling and adoring wife, Anne, on his arm.

On October 19, 1960, they repeated the exercise at Los Angeles' Pantages Theater. The Hollywood showplace, famous for being the former home of the Academy Awards, received a $125,000 facelift for the L.A. premiere of *Spartacus*, which was a benefit hosted by the Women's Guild of Cedars Lebanon.[4] The new theater décor kept with the theme of the early Roman period of the film while special projectors were installed to accommodate the Super Technorama-70 process in which *Spartacus* was filmed.

Spartacus went on to receive rave reviews from film critics around the world and shattered many previous box office records. It pulled in an astounding $30 million domestically and $60 million worldwide,[5] thanks in part to a half-dozen roadshow productions that ran concurrently in New York, Los Angeles, Boston, Detroit, Philadelphia, and Chicago. *Spartacus* was even big in Russia where viewers saw the slave uprising as *their* revolution—which greatly pleased Douglas, the son of extremely poor Russian Jewish immigrants. Closer to home, at UPI, a small story ran that President

---

4. The Women's Guild of Cedars Lebanon raised $100,000 for the premiere, the equivalent of about a million dollars in 2023.
5. Equivalent to almost $650 million in 2025.

John F. Kennedy sneaked out of the White House in early February 1961, during the middle of a snowstorm, to watch the three-hour epic at the Stanley-Warner Theater, the grandest movie house in the nation's capital. This notion gave the film the kind of press you just can't buy, which it needed desperately in the wake of such fraught beginnings.

It may sound excessive to say that a haircut saved a film, but in some ways that's not too far from the truth. For a project like this that found difficulty at every turn, any ray of hope could have a profound impact. Jay's design of the Spartacut was one of the few bright spots on the rocky road to success. Some might even say his creation gave Douglas inertia at a time when he must have doubted himself and his picture. It certainly boosted his confidence. It also solidified his vision for the character not unlike Charlie Chaplin's selection of a Derby and cane for his role as the Little Tramp or when Richard D. Zanuck ordered a screen test for *Planet of the Apes* so he could see what the mask would look like on screen. The reality is one simple prop, a piece of wardrobe, or a look can drastically transform an actor and help them truly step into the role that comes alive on the screen.

Douglas and Sebring shared a common bond when it came to risk taking and unwavering vision. Notably, for Jay to have swayed Douglas to accept a look for the film's lead character, which bore no known resemblance to any ancient Greek or Roman history, required an immense amount of *chutzpah*. Even Ralphie in HBO's *The Sopranos* (brilliantly played by Joe Pantoliano), nearly five decades later, took note of this in a 2001 episode titled "University."

"Look at Kirk Douglas' fuckin' hair!" he screamed at the TV

screen while watching the epic. "They didn't have flattops in Ancient Rome!.... nor did they have English[6] accents."

The saga of the *Spartacus* production reflected an important takeaway that modeled Jay's own journey. Though there were long, challenging days, lots of hard work, and more than their fair share of bad luck—the tenacity of those committed to seeing it through paid off in the long run. The success of *Spartacus* was a huge relief to everyone who invested in it, and the spillover didn't just enrich the actors and producers. Jay eventually saw a payoff as well, and it didn't just trickle in; it was like a flood, according to SEBRING cutter, Joe Torrenueva.

> One day I walked into the shop and people were lined up to get their hair cut. We're talking people like Paul Newman, Steve McQueen, Henry Fonda, Marlon Brando, Kirk Douglas, Richard Burton, Milton Berle, and George Peppard, with starstruck teenaged girls standing outside to get a glimpse. Chuck Connors came in specifically to get his hair cut like Kirk Douglas in *Spartacus*. Anyone who was anyone wanted to be inside that shop. It was an exciting place to work, and this was just the beginning.

From this point on, Jay's star was rising. His salon instantly doubled in size due to the overwhelming demand. He went from a one-man operation to employing eight stylists working day and night shifts, a receptionist, and a shampoo girl. He was able to buy the building where he had been leasing space and resided in the upstairs apartment. And he had a waiting room full of celebrity clients and top businessmen willing to pay his rapidly expanding rates.

---

6. This comment refers to the trio of British actors Laurence Olivier, Peter Ustinov, and Charles Laughton.

Jay was on his way to becoming as big in Hollywood as any film or music star he styled.

CHAPTER 10
DEMAND AND SUPPLY

t took close to a full decade for Jay to take his career from conception to a sustainable business. He followed the success of *Spartacus* with Marlon Brando's *One-Eyed Jacks*, and soon Sebring was developing a sterling reputation in Hollywood. Once lightning struck, it lit up every bit of potential Jay had and electrified it for exponential growth.

Jay knew the future was at hand. He was forging a career in a field that was not open to interpretation but needed to be reformed. He inspired innovation, and he wasn't just passionate about changing men's style, he was its architect. He sought to elevate the beauty industry by creating space for men within it. Before Jay came along, men had limited options and strict boundaries where hair was concerned. Jay was out to cut down those barriers and encourage men to express their attractiveness and individuality.

A groundbreaker in every sense of the word, Jay transformed musicians into rock stars and sex symbols, vaulted movie stars to the stratosphere, and added years to the careers of some established actors by improving their style. Gossip columnist Hedda Hopper once asked Milton Berle if he'd had a facelift, and he explained he'd just had a haircut from Jay Sebring. And Jane Fonda told a reporter that her dad's career was revitalized for another ten years thanks to Jay's styling and hair care.

Jay created timeless and iconic looks with his shears. In fact, there would be no men's hairstyling without Jay Sebring. Prior to the '60s, men had a handful of variations on the same theme—short and slicked back—but when Jay came on the scene, men's hair was given new life, freed from restriction and confinement to be free and natural.

According to *Los Angeles Times* film critic Charles Champlin, getting a barber cut was a miserable event.

"Before Jay came along, a barbershop was five chairs in a row and five guys all cutting hair badly. In my early days you got a bowl around your head, and it was awful fast," Champlin said.

It had always bothered Jay that the only luxury the common man permitted himself, in terms of personal appearance, was an occasional visit to the barbershop. He once quipped to a reporter, "French poodles get better clippings than men do."

Jay personalized the male haircut and, more than any cutter in Hollywood, gave his customers a style that was reflective of their personalities. As his reputation reached beyond his shop, he acquired a stable of stars who lent their heads to be his canvas, trusting him to create a look that was equal to their position in the zeitgeist. Frank Sinatra, Marlon Brando, Henry Fonda, Michael Douglas, and eventually the younger breed Paul Newman, Steve McQueen, George Peppard, Dennis Hopper, and Warren Beatty. They were all icons of the silver screen, and Jay was in part responsible for the looks we remember when we picture them.

With the flurry of big names and public figures, Jay offered privacy and exclusivity as a perk to a one-of-a-kind cut. There was a VIP door at the back of the building so his celebrity clients could slip in quietly to his private chair with no waiting. And their egos just ate it up.

Jay not only had the skill for delivering the optimal personal styling, but he also had an artistic instinct for crafting an indelible image. He took his role as peripheral servicer of clients to the level of being a coveted member of the team that made a star shine. He embodied the crucial ingredient that makes the best of the best in a dog-eat-dog town and industry where image is everything—a quality that was in high demand and short supply. Though journalists and others often referred to him as "hairstylist to the stars," Jay's unique vision and talents positioned him as a star among stars. Writer Dominick Dunne said Jay not only created imaginative cuts but also made it great theater.

> Jay had a private room because he had so many big stars. He made it like an event. Paul [Newman] was leaving when you came in. He got the TOWN. It was special. You felt special. It was expensive. It was worth it. And if you got into Jay's private room to have your hair cut, you'd made it.

It is not overstating things to say trendsetting is Hollywood's raison d'être, and with Jay's inimitable influence, his roster went beyond movie stars to business moguls, titans of industry, entertainment executives, and political power players who queued in line for hours or flew Jay to movie locales to experience his magic.

Increased demand necessitated Jay expand—the first of several additions that would take place over the years at the Fairfax shop.

The first expansion, though small, was substantial for Jay, allowing him to increase his capacity from one cutting station to five, then eight. He also employed a handful of full-time cutters, all carefully selected by him. They included Bernie Roberts, Jim O' Rourke, Buddy Markel, Felice Ingrassia, Darryl Wilde, and Art Schlick (who also went by Art Windsor).

Jay gave each one a key to the shop and told them, "You don't work for me; we work together." They also looked like one another. Sort of.

He outfitted every operator with lightweight French chambray shirts, a variety of colored pullovers with raglan sleeves and a zipper side, slacks, and indigo hip-hugger jeans. The look was hatched by Jay (inspired in part from his navy days) in collaboration with clothes designer Fred Segal, another relatively unknown upstart in West Hollywood at the time. Segal, whose name is seen blazoned on the sides of buildings to this day, said he and Jay were introduced by Sunset Strip club owner Elmer Valentine and made their foray into the Los Angeles zeitgeist around the same time. Segal said:

> We were both in sort of an embryonic stage. I think we helped each other very much. When people went into Jay's shop and saw the outfit, they'd say, "Where'd you get that?" They'd say, "Over at Fred Segal, right around the corner on Santa Monica and Crescent Heights." Then people would come in and say, "Oh, your hair looks great, where'd you get it done?" I'd say, "Sebring, Jay Sebring, right around the corner on Fairfax." So, I sort of became friendly with his customers and he was friendly with my customers.

The constant parade of clients now warranted two shifts to keep up with demand: 8 a.m. to 4 p.m. and 4 p.m. to 10 p.m. Some of Jay's employees opted to pull double shifts and were on their feet almost all fourteen hours. And, regardless of who you were in the societal pecking order, there was always a wait. Ken Mansfield, who was the West Coast district promotion manager for Capitol Records at the time, said he waited almost three months to get an appointment.

> It was really a tough and arduous process to get an appointment with Jay—we're talking months. But when I finally got my hair cut by him, the results were stunning. For the

next three nights, my head never hit the pillow because my hair looked so good. Finally, sleep got the better of me. But I never looked as good in my life as I did for those three days.

Sometimes even the biggest stars—icons who were not used to waiting for anyone—had to wait for Jay, according to Joe Torrenueva.

Jay was not a morning person, and he'd usually roll into work after noon and one time Henry Fonda was waiting for him. I got him seated, shampooed his hair, combed it out, and told him that Jay was due any minute. I dragged the process out for as long as I could and when I finally heard the rumble of Jay's sports car pull up in the parking lot, I breathed a big sigh of relief.

The expansion also enabled Jay to employ new concepts, which were perceived by the industry as "freakish." Actor Robert Wagner contextualized it this way:

It was hard to explain at that time, a guy like this. You say, "You know, there's a guy that stylizes hair." And you say, "Huh. What? Women have their hair stylized. You mean a guy is gonna go and have his hair shampooed, cut, and blown dry?" C'mon. Is he gonna wear a dress in the shop?.... or is he gonna wear a dress out of the shop! You know?

In *Hair Power*,[1] an instructional film for prospective SEBRING certified stylists, Jay revealed the following: "When I first started the

---

1. *Hair Power* was filmed in the summer of 1969; the reels were released from the lab a few weeks after Sebring's death.

hair designing business a few years back, I was considered bizarre, some kind of freak. But as time went on, I made up my mind that I was going to do all that I could do to elevate the profession."

These innovations included shampooing the client's hair with a very specific shampoo brush before the haircut to eliminate all polymer and sebum build-up from the hair and scalp, installing heat lamps, and supplying each designer with a stool on wheels to bring them eye-level for a more precise perspective when cutting the neckline, sides, and around the ears. He was the first to bring Solis hand-held hair dryers to America from Europe (today you'd be hard-pressed to find a household without one). As a finishing touch, cutters used light hair spray instead of creams, pomade, or tonics to hold the hair in place, giving his clients a more natural and free-flowing look.

Dean McClure, who met Jay while he was in high school and later became one of his cutters, said Jay was a visionary like Walt Disney.

> Everything Walt Disney ever did had never been done before and people thought he was nuts for what he was doing. That's what visionaries do—they see things others do not see. When Jay started, men came in with grease on their hair or just crappy looking hair. They'd take a seat in Jay's hair [salon], and they'd come out with a flawless looking haircut. They'd look like a totally different person. He totally remade their image, and it was quite astounding that it had never been done before.

Sebring not only changed the way people looked but changed the way he charged clients. He always had an initial consultation (for $15) to observe the man's bone structure (face and skull), learn his occupation (if he was an actor, what his current role was; if he was an attorney, whether he was a prosecutor, defense, or corporate attorney, etc.), and whether the man led a business lifestyle or one more casual and laissez-faire. After that came the cut with a $100 price tag.

Jay emphasized to his cutters:

> The first time you see your customer, it's good to see him with his head wet after the shampoo. That way you won't be influenced by the way his hair was styled before. There are three things to watch for: 1) the shape of his face, 2) the structure of his hair, and 3) his position in life. That means you'll need to ask him a few questions—get friendly with the man—as you're looking at his hair. Then you can start to make some moves and know what you're doing.

Standard consultation for a cut was 10-15 minutes. Additional time might be required for color, hair restoration, and hair piece consultations. During the consultation Jay would run his hands through the client's hair to determine texture and growth pattern. He would also feel the skull for flatness or protrusions of the head, particularly at the occipital bone and crown areas. After analyzing the man's face and bone structure, he would provide balance and sculpt by diminishing or creating fullness where necessary to style the most attractive look for the man.

"Having a new hairstyle for a man was a gigantic expression," Fred Segal noted. "It was sort of a revolution. I like to call it trans-formation from restriction to expression.... it was the beginning of a fashion."

As Jay's enterprise was expanding, so was his focus on the health and integrity of men's hair. He began experimenting with mild shampoos and conditioners and soon would hire chemists to create the best organic, pH-balanced hair care product line. And he had no qualms about prescribing his haircare product for his customers, said Joe Torrenueva.

Jay was really good at telling powerful people what to do, but he did it in the classiest way possible. For example, after he cut a guy like Henry Fonda, he'd get on the intercom system and call the front desk. He'd say, "Please get Mr. Fonda a brush and a bottle of shampoo, conditioner and spray," and Mr. Fonda wouldn't even question it. He'd pay the bill because he could afford it and be on his way. Jay knew the big money was in the products.

The products Jay sold at his shop were made specifically for him in conjunction with Al Lapin, and had a significant markup. A few years later, Jay would develop his own line of shampoo and other related products, which was the next piece of the puzzle for building his empire. Once he started selling his own products and not relying on someone else's supplies, both the profit margin and his prominence in the industry soared.

Another unheard of "freaky" practice Jay recommended was daily shampooing at a time when the common practice for men was to wash it just once a week. There was a fear that any more would cause you to lose it.

"You bathe and brush your teeth every day," Jay noted, "why wouldn't you shampoo your hair every day?"

Jay employed massaging and electrodes to stimulate and increase blood flow to the client's scalp to feed the hair follicles. For more hygienically challenged cases, he would use mild acid peels to eliminate scalp build up, opening pores and hair follicles that otherwise caused premature hair loss due to neglect.

For clients with patches of permanent hair loss, Jay used rice paper cut to the dimensions of the bald area where he would sketch the directions of the individual's natural growth pattern. The diagram was designed, then sent to a toupee manufacturer, and after completion Jay would cut the hair piece to blend naturally and fluidly with the existing hair. Bobby Darin, Frank Sinatra, and

William Shatner could attest to this process, and paid about $400 for the accouterment.[2]

Gordon Mullinger said his boss wasn't just a stylist; he was a true miracle worker.

> Henry Fonda came in and had all of these treatments that Jay had set up for him. And I'm here to tell you—I swear this is true—that he did start growing hair on his head.

As Jay's business exploded, the SEBRING enterprise needed a facelift. One was the shop's exterior. Gone was the black and white façade, awning, and neon light. Now, the storefront was adorned with textured driftwood with sleek, embossed silver signage: SEBRING....

There were three front doors inset with the center door parallel to Fairfax Avenue and each side door set at a forty-five-degree angle to the center stair entrance. The doors were stained dark brown, and each had a single circular red stained-glass window with an ankh in the center. The ankh became Jay's signature emblem and a great identifier of his brand. He gravitated to it in business and his personal life because the ancient Egyptian symbol represented virility and everlasting life.

Larry Geller happened to be walking past the shop when all these new and exciting changes were taking place and had a chance encounter with Jay, which ended up changing his life.

> I had just got out of cosmetology school and was awaiting my results from the state board. I was going to be a hair-dresser for women. One afternoon I went for a walk on Fairfax Avenue, and I see this—I wasn't sure if it was a salon or barbershop because it had a stained-glass window. I

---

2. In 2025 dollars, that's the equivalent of approximately $4,200.

walked in there and there's this young guy on a little ladder, hanging a small plant. He said his name was Jay Sebring.

Geller introduced himself to Jay, told him his story, and how he had plans to cut women's hair. Jay submitted to Geller that his shop was the first of its kind and that if Geller was open to being taught his method, together the two of them would be "pioneers" in their field. Geller took Jay up on his offer and never looked back, eventually becoming Elvis Presley's personal stylist. Geller said:

> Jay Sebring was so innovative and so important to our culture, which has never been fully recognized. Not only did he start men's hair in America, but he created the look for the men of the Sixties. Those were phenomenal years. Very exciting. That little shop on Fairfax changed our culture.

It also changed Jay's checkbook as well as that of his colleagues. At a time when barbers were receiving 75 cents to $1.50 per client, Jay obliterated the rigid pay ceiling, allowing him and his designers to charge what their talents and services were worth. Joe Torrenueva explained how Jay's system worked:

> All of Jay's cutters were on a three-year contract, and the first year he took 50% of every cut, but we got to keep the tips. The second year it was 55% and the third year it was 60%. The first year I cut I'd get $3, and he'd get $3. The next year I charged $7.50, and his cut would increase. Some people might have had a problem with this arrangement, but we were getting double what we'd get if we were barbers. Besides, this gave us an incentive to work harder because our rates continually went up as we got more experience.

According to a 1961 news article, Jay was clearing approximately $50,000 a year, equivalent to more than half a million in 2025 dollars. Steve McQueen, a kindred spirit who became one of Jay's biggest celebrity boosters, wasn't pulling in that kind of cash. At the time, McQueen was still contractually bound to his TV show, CBS' *Wanted: Dead or Alive*, and earned $750 a week, or $39,000 annually.

Once Jay had his professional life on track and began moving toward the success he'd dreamed of (but no one else thought was possible), he decided it was time to begin looking inward. He realized that building his career had required laser focus and consumed his life. For years this dyed-in-the-wool bachelor was driven to get where he wanted to be, and now that his business was stable and growing, he had finally arrived.

Jay had worked so hard and for so long that there was simply no work-life balance. His work at the shop took up all his time and energy. Sure, Jay had no shortage of women to date, but he had not found a person to share his life with, to enjoy the fruits of his labor and success.

While he enjoyed the playboy lifestyle to a degree, he felt the longing for more meaningful companionship tugging at him and he determined that it was time to consider settling down. He was approaching thirty years old, and the idea of a family appealed to him.

CHAPTER 11

TO HAVE AND TO HOLD
FOR ONE HELL OF
A RIDE

For Jay, breakups were not hard to navigate; he was kind, level-headed, and mature, and he managed to maintain friendships with his former lovers. It was being in long-term relationships that were casualties of Jay's many interests, female distractions, and an expansive libido.

Jay found it particularly difficult to sustain his relationship with actress BarBara Luna as his career flourished and his popularity rose. She played no small part in his success, introducing him to Vic Damone when his fledgling shop was struggling to take hold, but their paths began to diverge in the spring of 1960. She explained:

> My career was taking off and I had less time to help Jay. When I made a guest appearance on *Overland Trail* and met the star of the show, Doug McClure,[1] we became an item and then eventually married. I kept in touch with Jay, sending him clients, and we saw each other here and there, however, by then he was doing really well!

---

1. Doug McClure was also a loyal SEBRING client throughout Jay's career.

With his career success established, Jay was ready to shift focus to his personal life, and that is when he met Bonnie Lee Marple. Of course, Bonnie's stunning beauty was a gamechanger for the immensely independent Jay. A chance encounter led to a quick wedding and, just as with everything in Jay's life, he was launched into a new and exciting adventure in the blink of an eye. Bonnie (who later came to be known by her stage name, Cami Sebring) entered Jay's shop one day in late September of 1960 with her boyfriend, actor Mike McKee, who was seeking a cut from the "master." At the time, she was an exquisite seventeen-year-old model and an aspiring actress being groomed by 20ᵗʰ Century Fox.

"Cami and I went to Hollywood High, and she was a beauty," said Larry Geller, who worked for Jay until 1965. "Beautiful person. Very sweet."

Cami describes the moments after her initial meeting with Jay as almost magical, ethereal and sweeping.

> I was sort of twirling around in a [barber] chair and all of a sudden, I saw two wedding bells chiming over Jay's head. I had never experienced anything like that in my life. Every-thing was kind of mystical at this point. We had gone up to his apartment one night, which was over his shop. And we were sitting there and he said something, and I said, "I didn't quite hear what you said." And he said, "I didn't say anything." But I thought, *Will you marry me?* Two weeks later, we were married.

It sounds like a storybook whirlwind romance, but technically being a minor, she had some legal hoops to jump through, and getting her mother on board was very tricky.

With Jack Entratter in charge, shifting the venue to Las Vegas greased the wheels of the legal system, making it possible for Jay and his young bride to be wed. Entratter hosted the wedding reception at the Sands as he had done for many celebrities, including Dick Haymes and Rita Hayworth, Betty White and Allen Ludden, and Frank Sinatra and Mia Farrow.

"I flew to Las Vegas separately because there was a Mann Act,[2] being 17 years old," Cami said. "The Rat Pack were there, and it was a big celebration."

Because of this restriction, Jay and Cami had to play it by the book until they were officially pronounced man and wife, but the celebration was well worth the wait.

It was a small wedding—literally and figuratively. On Monday evening, October 10, 1960, the couple exchanged vows in the Little Church of the West, located on what later would become the Las Vegas Strip. The late Gothic revival structure was built in 1943 out of redwood and intended to serve as a replica of a typical pioneer town church. It was charming and picturesque, which didn't go unnoticed by Hollywood scouts. The church was used in a 1959 episode of *Perry Mason*, the ABC series *Vega$* also used it for a pair of episodes, and it was the setting for the classic 1964 film *Viva Las Vegas*, where Elvis Presley and Ann-Margret exchange their vows. And, of course, a slew of celebrity couples[3] actually got married there as well.

Vic Damone served as Jay's best man[4] while Janet March[5] stood in as Cami's witness for their nuptials. Jay was as handsome as ever, wearing a traditional black suit, white dress shirt, and skinny tie

---

2. The Mann Act, also known as The White-Slave Traffic Act, was a federal law passed in 1910. It criminalizes transportation of any woman or girl for the purpose of prostitution or debauchery, or for any other immoral purpose.

3. They include Betty Grable and Harry James, Judy Garland and Mark Herron, David Cassidy and Kay Lenz, Richard Gere and Cindy Crawford, and Noel Gallagher and Meg Matthews.

4. Damone is listed as Vito Farinola (his birth name) on Jay and Cami Sebring's marriage certificate.

5. The authors could not positively identify March but assume she was employed by the venue as a needed stand-in witness.

while Cami sported a stylish, tailored jacket and skirt, which were popular at the time. Justice of the Peace George O. Treem presided over the ceremony that lasted about ten minutes. A photo of the two snapped immediately after they were pronounced man and wife shows a deliriously happy Jay and his new bride, staring at him, equally giddy.

The Copa Room at the Sands was transformed for a lavish reception where the wedding party, invited guests, and showgirls were jammed into a VIP suite adjoining the showroom. Guests included Jack Entratter, Frank Sinatra, Dean Martin, Sammy Davis, Jr., and Sands Hotel host Charlie Baron. The suite was filled with wedding gifts, cards, flowers, decorations, and lots of champagne, courtesy of The Sands. Davis, who was especially fond of Jay, doled out gifts to the ladies in attendance, noted Cami Sebring.

> Sammy came in and started handing out little stuffed animals to all of the women but didn't give me anything. Then he went in the back area and brought a big box and started handing out every last toy. I look at Jay like, "Sammy didn't give me anything." I felt really strange and awkward. Then he presented me with this beautiful life-sized ram. It was beautiful beige with black feet and a black face. He said, "What are you gonna call him?" I said, "Sam the Ram." That's his name, and I have him to this day. It's fabulous.

Another photo from that day captured Jay fraternizing with client and friend Charles "Babe" Baron, an organized crime figure from Chicago and official greeter of the Sands Hotel. The 53-year-old Baron had ties to Al Capone, John Roselli, and Meyer Lansky, and he was twice acquitted of murder in the late 1920s and early '30s. He started out as a handbook operator for the Chicago Outfit, which ran a large illegal gambling ring. He later served as the general manager of the Havana Riviera under the Batista regime until Castro and his band of revolutionists overthrew the government in 1959, and Baron and many organized crime figures like him were forced to flee Cuba. He landed safely on his feet in Las Vegas, where he was employed as the host at the Sands. A year after his arrival, Baron had a 1% stake in the hotel. Charlie was a big fan of Jay's, and one evening had the newlyweds join him for dinner in his private booth.

Whatever illicit acts or deeds Baron committed in his younger days, he cleaned up his image in Sin City. Barron developed a reputation as kind and helpful; he made alliances with everyone from Nevada Governor Paul Laxalt to show business and sports celebrities such as Dean Martin, Paul Hornung, and Rocky Marciano, extending to casino dealers, pit bosses, and the shoeshine guy in the men's room. He even held rank as Brigadier General in the Illinois National Guard.

Cami had no clue Jay knew such people. She only knew Baron as a kindly, older gentleman. But, even after learning more about him and a few other powerful associates, she didn't fear them. Cami felt safe and at home with Jay. In fact, the only person she really feared was her mother, Kay Marple, who was caring and doting, but intimidating.[6]

Shortly before the wedding, the soon-to-be newlyweds enlisted Jay's friend Buddy Markel and his girlfriend to discreetly move her clothes and possessions out of the house while her mother was at work. Cami said her mother was not pleased initially.

> After the wedding I called my mother, and she was shocked and angry because she had come home, and all my belongings were gone. When she found out who I married, she

---

6. Cami's mother Kay "Cassie" Marple was a significant Hollywood figure herself as a Formosa Café hostess for decades.

screamed, "You married a HAIRDRESSER?!" My mother wasn't aware of who he was. Of course, when she met him, she loved him. Absolutely loved and adored him, which makes sense because he was an incredible human being.

The newlyweds remained in Vegas for their honeymoon, spending their days at the pool and their nights in showrooms, VIP suites, and celebrating with Jay's powerful and iconic Vegas inner circle, culminating in a post nuptial bash in a large private screening room atop the Sands. A few days later, they headed to Los Angeles, and Cami lived with Jay in his apartment above the shop. In their downtime, the couple listened to jazz, specifically the "Johnny Magnus Show" on KMPC.

"Everybody listened to Johnny Magnus at that time," said Joe Torrenueva. "He had this theme song that was a Count Basie song called 'Cute.' Johnny gave us all his albums we played in the shop. Great looking guy, handsome.... great hair."

Jay didn't just listen. He played the xylophone upstairs, Cami recalled.

"He loved that xylophone and scrambled egg sandwiches on wheat bread with ketchup and mayonnaise," she recalled. "Jay rolled the perfect joint, and he taught me too. I rolled a great joint then too."

A few weeks after tying the knot in Vegas, Jay and Cami Sebring were formally married in Saint Ambrose Church. Located at 1281 N. Fairfax Avenue in West Hollywood, the Roman Catholic church was approximately a block north of the SEBRING salon. Cami even converted to Catholicism, which she said was important to Jay.

Cami's mother hosted a reception after the ceremony on Sunday November 6, 1960. Then the whirlwind continued as the couple traveled to Detroit before the holidays to celebrate with Jay's family. His parents, Margarette and Bernard, his siblings Geraldine,

Fred, and Peggy, and several aunts and uncles gathered to fête the happy couple.

When the honeymooners returned to Los Angeles, they frolicked on Malibu beach, dined in exclusive restaurants, including The Cock 'n' Bull and The Steak Pit, and sped from nightclub to nightclub and out to Palm Springs in Jay's convertible Jaguar XKE. Jay and Cami also trekked to Joshua Tree, which was one of Jay's favorite retreats since his early days in California and throughout his time there.

In the desert they smoked grass beneath the stars, pondering the future and imagining the great beyond. The sky appeared to have no limits, but there a few things off limits to Jay where it concerned his new bride, Cami Sebring said.

> We were at PJ's, which was one of the real big nightclubs on Santa Monica and Crescent Heights, and Hugh Hefner was there all the time. Everybody went there. I was there with Jay one night and Hefner approached Jay, and he said he wanted to do a special layout with me as a focal point. He offered a lot of money and Jay said, "Nope. Ain't gonna happen."

Since its December 1953 inception, the allure of nabbing a *Playboy* spread was tantalizing to many a young aspiring starlet, but Jay understood that the sudden money and attention was chewed up and spit out in the Tinseltown gristmill and rarely led to a real career launch. At the time, the magazine was still perceived as controversial by many throughout the country and a full spread was a double-edged sword that carried a tawdry stigma for an ambitious but unknown actress.

"Jay told me at the table, 'Hef wanted you to do a layout'[7] and I

_____

7. According to Cami Sebring, the going rate for a *Playboy* centerfold layout at the

told him no,'" Cami recollected. "And I said, 'That's okay with me.'"

Cami also experienced Jay's life up close and personally in Los Angeles, witnessing his impact on the fashion world, the Hollywood crowd, and Southern California's elite. Cami noticed that Jay, without much effort, stood out in a town where everyone was a peacock.

> He (Jay) had that quiet magnetism; that's why everyone was drawn to him. He was a star in his own right. Everybody emulated him. He was a trendsetter. Everything he did people copied. When he got his black Porsche, Steve McQueen, who was his good friend and pal, went out and got an all-black Porsche because he thought it was great.

Jay's sense of style was undeniable, and he was developing a reputation for it. It wasn't just hairstyling that was putting him on the map. His taste in clothing was impeccable as well, and he made bold fashion choices, according to Cami Sebring.

> Jay was the first person I knew to wear leather pants. Then all the jet set did—they all started wearing leather. He was also the first person I know of to wear tailored jeans, though they were ironed and pressed. Denim shirts fit him to a T. Everything he wore was fitted. He had a grey pinstriped suit with red lining and a matching cape. I don't know how that sounds, but he looked magnificent and could carry and pull it off.

Of course, with Jay's slender build—he stood at 5'6" and

---

time was $1,500. Hefner persisted with offers of $3,000, then $5,000 after Jay continued to decline.

weighed approximately 130 pounds—everything looked elegant, sophisticated, and graceful on him. His physique was sleek and proportioned. He carried himself much like a European, with confidence, finesse, and refinement. He was everything most American men had not been able to capture in his day. In a word, he embodied taste.

In terms of Jay's temperament, Cami took note that he was even keeled and mild-mannered. He also had a deeply contemplative side, which captivated her.

> Jay was never the type of person to raise his voice. He was laid back, and should I say, "The King of Cool?" Nothing ever got him angry or upset. Never saw him enraged. He would think deeply about something and take the right steps that were appropriate for whatever the situation was.... he was a silent kind of guy. He observed and he looked. There was nothing insecure about him at all. He knew exactly what he wanted....he had big balls.

> And a brass butt.

Cami Sebring remembers the night Jay was cruising on a powerful Harley Davidson and was just learning how to ride it.

> We were driving around on Mulholland and going around the curves. And Charles Champlin and I were following behind him. And he spun out. Charles was just horrified, and I started laughing. I don't know why I started laughing because Jay just spun out and jumped up and picked it up and took off. When he's into doing something, he's into doing it. He wasn't gonna let anything get the best of him.

Jay and his Harley also left an indelible impression on his friend, American writer and author Dominick Dunne.

You didn't usually get people on motorcycles at your house in Beverly Hills. When he came in, he was in all leather. Even a hat. He had sort of a leather hat. There's nothing to describe except that he was an excitement.

The excitement was contagious, especially among women. Cami wasn't blind to Jay's past where it concerned the opposite sex.

Jay was quite a player before me. He used to carry a gun because sometimes the lovers would come home. And because he wasn't a big, burly guy—he was lean. So, he used to carry a gun with him all the time. Just bringing out the gun is enough to stop anyone.

After a year in the apartment, Jay and Cami bought a place that commeasured his success and taste. They found a quaint, rustic chalet nestled in L.A.'s Benedict Canyon. South of Sherman Oaks and west of Beverly Hills, homes there ranged from smaller one-story family residences to large estates. The two-bedroom, three-level Bavarian-style home was a perfect fit for Jay's sensibilities and expression—unique, rare, and exquisite. It was a glamorous and eerie house packed with history.

On July 7, 1932, MGM producer Paul Bern married Jean Harlow, one of Hollywood's biggest box-office draws in the 1930s. As a gift to Harlow, he built a home on a secluded Benedict Canyon perch at 9810 Easton Drive. It included stables and separate house quarters surrounded by a maze of slate stone steps navigating throughout the expansive hillside property. A few months later, on September 5, while Harlow was away filming *Red Dust* opposite Clark Gable, Bern was found dead in the master bathroom from a gunshot wound to the head.

Though the cause of death was officially ruled a suicide, questions about this remain to this day. Bern's former common law wife,

Dorothy Millette, who had a history of mental and emotional struggles, reportedly travelled to Los Angeles and visited Bern at the Easton residence the day he was killed. Two days later she jumped from the Delta King steamboat and her body was found in the Sacramento River.

Decades had passed since this mysterious scandal, and it seemed so far away—certainly nothing that would deter Jay and Cami from acquiring this perfect love nest. Cami Sebring said the house was enchanting and just right for them.

> The house we lived in on Easton was fabulous. We fell in love with it. It was designed by art directors of MGM at the request of Paul Bern as a gift for his wife. A product of the Prohibition, the residence had a maze of secret passageways from the master bedroom to the secluded steeple tower, a hidden wine cellar and a secret bar hidden by a library book cased wall.

Cami particularly loved the peg and groove floors, high wooden ceiling beams, fireplace, and the carved heads of John Barrymore and Norma Shearer overlooking the pool. Their dog, Tosh—a beautiful white German Shepherd Alsatian—completed the home.

"He used to swim in the pool all the time," Cami mused. "Actually, the pool was always so cold that we wouldn't go in it. But Tosh went in it all the time."

The Sebring residence was open to friends famous and eccentric alike. Gypsy Boots, Cami recalled, was "kind of this crazy guy and he always wore hardly anything.... just shorts and his hair always wild. He knew everything about health and nutrition, which was great because then I incorporated that for Jay. He'd come up a lot and bring us casseroles he and his wife made."

Cami said entertainer Bobby Darin was an extended guest

when the crooner was going through a rough patch with wife Sandra Dee. She recollected:

> Bobby was crazy about Sandra, madly in love with her. But he had a falling out with Sandra and needed a place to stay. Jay said, "Come hang out at the house." So, he did. One morning I was sitting down by the fireplace and Bobby comes walking down the stairs after a shower. And.... he has no hair. I didn't know that he didn't have hair. This is terrible, but I started giggling because Jay was very private about those things. He never discussed those kinds of things about his clients. But it was a kick. I loved Bobby, an absolutely fantastic, great person.

Another frequent guest was actor Stuart Whitman, who was a neighbor of Jay and Cami's. He lived at 9827 Easton Drive with his wife Patricia and their four children in a two-bedroom home, originally built as a hunting lodge in 1927. The Oscar-nominated actor said his first encounter with was Jay quite memorable.

> I almost got run over by the Cobra that Jay was driving going down Easton. He was hogging the road coming down and I was comin' up. It's a very narrow street and the neighbors would come out and say, "Who is that guy?!" Jay had the house just below me. He was my closest neighbor.

In time, the men would become close friends and would often visit each other at their residences. Whitman remembers Jay as "a cool cat" who later served as a best man in Whitman's second marriage to French-born Caroline Boubis in November 1966.

As Jay and Cami settled into their home and married life, their lives were borderline idyllic. She was a successful model and budding actress while Jay was disrupting his industry and shaping the look of his generation with his revolutionary concepts. They were young, beautiful, and lived in one of the most affluent zip codes in the country. There was nothing missing from their American Dream. Their inner circles were among the most influential personalities of the times and their lives were fulfilling and enviable. They were living out every person's greatest fantasy, perhaps tenfold.

Soon, the idea of kids crept into their conversations. It was important to Jay not only to create a family with the love of his life, he wanted to have children to carry on his legacy. As much as he worked to build his business and reputation to achieve his own goals, Jay dreamed of passing his vision on to the next generation. Cami specifically recalls one discussion that has stayed with her after all these years.

"He talked about the day he'd be driving down Sunset Boulevard in the convertible with his son beside him," Cami said, then took a long and thoughtful pause. "That was part of the dream that didn't come true."

CHAPTER 12
THE COST OF SUCCESS

By the early 1960s, Jay Sebring was not only famous within his industry, but he was also the gold standard for hair design and Hollywood cool. In a few short years, he transformed the look of the American male and took men's hairstyling where it never dared to go before. He implemented standards and practices that remain in place across the industry six decades after he opened his iconic shop on Fairfax. He was lauded by fashionistas, movie studios, esteemed actors, and the Hollywood elite. But Jay was also a disruptor, earning him a few well-placed enemies.

Word of Jay's magic was spreading nationally after features in *TIME* magazine ("The Sebring establishment is a 10-chair swinging bedlam."), *Cosmopolitan* ("A leading champion of the male right to compete in the battle of the sexes is Jay Sebring."), and *Motion Picture* ("All stars agree that his is the kindest cut of all! Out of this world!").

To accommodate the onslaught of demand, Jay purchased 723 N. Fairfax Avenue immediately south of the existing shop next to the center staircase leading above the entire building. Putting his touch on anything involving his salon, Jay equipped each stained wood door with $50 brass knobs and adorned the circular, red stained-glass window with a black ankh. The floor throughout the shop was black and white square tile except for Jay's private room located on the south side of the expanded location, which had red and black squares. Each stylist's station was equipped with an intercom and handheld hairdryers mounted in a stand, resembling a white oversized space-age pistol.

SEBRING.... as it was commonly known, was the hot spot offering the best cut in town and a social playground for Hollywood's elite to carouse and unwind. Journalist John Locksher provided an apt day-in-the-life glimpse into the shop in his article, "How the Hollywood Stars Get Clipped!" for *Motion Picture* magazine in July 1963.

Locksher observed a typical day in the life on the comings and goings of the SEBRING shop.

> There is an easy casual atmosphere about the most "in" barbershop in Hollywood and, because Jay Sebring takes as much time as he feels necessary, his customers often stage impromptu shows while they wait for their turn on "the throne." Bobby Darin clowns it up by using the whole shop as a set and the equipment for his impromptu act. Milton Berle brought in Mickey Rooney for his first cut. [During their wait], the two comics settled down to a face-slapping contest, which went on for almost ten minutes. There was almost a riot. Doug McClure and Vic Damone organize chess games. Now and again, George Raft will grab a broom and sweep up the trimmings. May Britt, Keely Smith and BarBara Luna have at one time, or another subbed at the reception desk.

Intense demand for Jay spread from the Fairfax salon to major movie studios, on location, in planes, and overseas. On any given

day, Jay might do a cut for Gig Young, Robert Culp, Chuck
Conners, Don Adams, James Garner, George Peppard, The Everly
Brothers, Dominick Dunne, and Stan Kamen, power agent with
William Morris, before heading to NBC Studios in Burbank to give
Andy Williams a trim, then return to the shop to take care of
Dennis Hopper, Paul Lynde, Tony Franciosa, George Chakiris, and
Stuart Whitman. With a full day already behind him, he'd still hop
in his sports car and head to the residences of Marlon Brando, Steve
McQueen, and Robert Wagner for house calls. But Jay worked on
his own schedule, star or not, according to a slightly amused
Wagner.

> You were constantly waiting for Jay. He was never on time.
> You just figured he was at Paul's [Newman] house doing
> Paul, and he'll be over here when he can. And he'd never
> say, "Hey I'm sorry.... I had to...." He had a great personal-
> ity. His humor was very interior. You'd ask him, "Jay, can
> you take this stuff [hair] out?" He'd reply, "No, I only bring
> it in [the hair clippings]."

In addition to servicing his clients at the shop or studios, there
was the commute to cut the guys in Vegas or snip Texas mogul Sol
West III on his private jet.

Jay had more than doubled his staff—from five to ten cutters
during the day and another ten for the night shift, including Sal
Orifice, Bud Kipp, Darrell Wilde, Bruce Hein, Jimmy Silvani,
Wardell "Dell" Jackson, Warren Peace, Joe "Little Joe" Torrenueva,
David Chavez, Harold (Dean) McClure, Paul Yamashiro, and
Anton "Woody" Green—but even that wasn't enough to lighten his
load.

"There was no other place that was getting the revenue that
SEBRING's was," noted Gordon Mullinger, Jay's personal assistant.

"There was no other place that was getting the publicity that SEBRING's was."

In *Rocketing Rhythms*—a nationally syndicated radio show that partnered with *Meet the Press* through the Armed Forces Radio and Television Service Collection—the show's host asked Jay a variety of questions, including which client had the most interesting occupation. It was a no brainer: Jamie Bravo.

"He's a matador. They wear their wife's pigtails in the back so I have to leave it a little longer where they can clip it on," Jay responded. He also broached the subject of his three female clients: Keely Smith, May Britt, and his wife, Cami Sebring.

Elaborating on his better half, Jay said, "She's a very young actress just starting into the field. She did a small part in *Love in a Goldfish Bowl* with Tommy Sands and Fabian."

At that time, Bobby Darin was signed to star in *If a Man Answers* with his wife, Sandra Dee. Bobby and Jay discussed Cami playing a supporting part as an alluring model. Cami was thrilled about what would be her first big break. But all was dashed when Sandra Dee, who was known to be prickly and challenging, threatened to quit the film if Cami was hired. It was Cami's first lesson in the big breaks and bad breaks of Hollywood.

By 1962, men of all ages were walking into barbershops across the nation and asking for the "Sebring Cut" to the bewilderment, and eventual ire, of thousands of barbers. This seismic trend was not only frustrating for the sedate old-school cutters, but also a challenging embarrassment.

"People would often ask the barbers, 'Why don't you do what that guy in Hollywood does?' 'Oh, I, we don't do that.' It was almost embarrassing to a barber," Joe Torrenueva remembers.

It was a flashpoint. The barber industry, like American society, was experiencing a cultural shift from antiquated and stale conventional norms to fresh progressive concepts of individual expression and lifestyle choices, which would explode in the latter part of the sixties.

Barbers had no idea what a "Sebring Cut" was, even though potential customers were willing to pay several times their going rate. This was hitting the entire barber industry in the wallet—and hard. To the typical barber, Jay Sebring was a beauty school fraud who was stealing their rightful share of the pie. The Barber's Union, which had been controlled by the mob for decades, flexed its muscle on Jay's shop. First, they harassed him, initiating repeated visits from the Barber's Board for various code infractions.

Gordon Mullinger attested to the fact that Jay was unfairly being targeted and put through the wringer.

> The board kept giving us the world's worst time because they wanted to close the place down. So, they were constantly coming in, and if the shampoo bowl was an eighth of an inch away (from barber's regulations) we couldn't use it. They were driving us crazy. Crazy!

When board inspections failed to close the Fairfax shop, The Barber's Union resorted to more direct, mob-like tactics, including verbal and physical threats.

"Jay was the odd man out in the barber's trade," noted *Los Angeles Times* journalist Charles Champlin. "He had to be careful at night.... [to watch for] someone creeping up on him because he really was an outlaw, wasn't he?"

Jay fought fire with fire, calling on a few friends of his own. He enlisted Jack Entratter and Charlie Baron in Las Vegas, as well as some underworld types from Detroit. Sebring protégé Joe Torrenueva confirmed their presence in the shop.

> Jay first told me about The Purple Gang when I was in Las Vegas. The Purple Gang came up again when we were

having hassles with the barbers. They were in the shop, standing in front of the shop, in the back of the shop. I mean these were big imposing guys. And Jack Entratter was also connected to the Purple Gang.

Michigan historian and Purple Gang author Paul R. Kavieff described the Detroit mob organization as "predominantly Jewish gambling operators, in Southeastern Michigan, who were some of the founding fathers of Vegas. The Purples were a high-profile violent organized crime group. Very violent."

Between 1927 and '32, the Purples controlled everything that went on in Detroit's underworld. An estimated 500 unsolved murders in that period have been attributed to the Purple Gang, including Michigan senator Warren Hooper in 1945. He was about to testify against powerful Republican party boss Frank McKay, who had significant ties to the crime organization.

Though gambling was illegal in Michigan for years, it was rampant in southeastern Michigan, and the Purple Gang expanded their operations into this territory, generating massive profits. They were very experienced and knowledgeable in gambling and casino operations and formed an alliance with Detroit Mafia leaders Joseph Zerilli, Pete Licavoli, "Papa" John Priziola, and "Black" Bill Tocco. In the '40s, the Ferguson Grand Jury was created to rid the region of all illegal gaming, and many Purple operators fled to Florida or Las Vegas.

A few Hollywood friends also lent their protection to the shop and its employees. Joe Torrenueva describes the additional presence on the scene.

The barbers wanted to put us out of business. We had bodyguards because there was a lot going on. A lot of tension in the shop for a while. Bob Phillips would walk me to my car. He was a huge guy, a Marine and an actor. He had the biggest arms I had ever seen. You didn't want to mess with this guy.

Robert "Bob" Phillips, a SEBRING client and friend, had served in World War II and was a military self-defense instructor. He also played professional football for the Chicago Bears and Washington Redskins before launching his acting career (*Hell is for Heroes, The Killers, The Dirty Dozen,* and *Killing of a Chinese Bookie*). He was a former bodyguard for Illinois Governor Adlai Stevenson as well.

It seems laughable that a beauty school graduate would have to stand up to and be successful in defying a labor union with mob influence, but the slight outlier from Michigan did.... with a little help from his friends. Eventually, the verbal and physical threats dwindled once the support and firepower for the SEBRING enterprise proved to be more than enough to avert their sinister actions.

Switching tactics, The Barber's Union launched an onslaught of legal attacks against the SEBRING salon, asserting only barbers were licensed to cut men's hair and cosmetologists were only licensed to do women's hair. Jay's defiant response was simple, "Hair knows no gender."

These battles would continue to play out intermittently throughout Jay's life. Shortly before his death, Jay (along with assistance from Joe Torrenueva and Sebring attorney Alvin Greenwald) finally introduced and passed new legislation that permanently established the right of cosmetologists to perform services on men and, conversely, the right of barbers to cut women's hair.[1]

If that weren't enough, Sebring's many visits to movie studios, sets, and filming locations were ruffling feathers with the Hair and

---

1. Jay Sebring and his new breed of men's hair designers, which was expanding in droves, faced many political obstacles throughout the course of their legal wranglings.

Makeup Union. Jay was granted studio passes daily to clip his clients' hair during filming. Resentment boiled over when Jay arrived on the 20th Century-Fox lot to cut actor Gardner McKay's hair, temporarily shutting down filming on the set of James A. Michener's *Adventures in Paradise*. Production resumed only after an awkward compromise that allowed Jay to supervise the film's hair-stylist's work on the actor, per McKay's demand.

Robert Wagner was a firsthand witness to this war of the shears and explained it this way:

> There was a big resistance to Jay as far as the studios were concerned. They didn't like him coming on the lot and coming into my trailer and cutting my hair. The makeup people did that. He had a lot to fight. The Makeup Union was very resistant.

Sebring's presence on studio lots became a top-secret affair. Frank Sinatra had a semi-cryptic pass issued to J. Sebring for access to the Warner Bros. lot while he was filming *4 for Texas*. The pass, dated October 30, 1963, listed the purpose for the visit as "Business Interview." Because the pass was issued by Sinatra, no one questioned its authenticity or legality, but Jay was walking a tightrope for business in and out of his salon.

The conflict reached an all-time high when Jay was escorted off studio lots and banned from future entry. Not to be dissuaded, entertainers simply began going to Jay's house or vice versa before filming. This resulted in production delays, but Hollywood's most powerful knew how to get what they wanted.

"You know what it costs to shut down a movie for an hour?" asked Larry Geller, one of Jay's first hires. "That's why the studios go crazy if a star pulls some crap."

For Jay, these union confrontations were becoming an obsession and an all-out fight to win that would last several years. Between business expansion, union turmoil, and constant demand, the young hair designer was spread thin, and all of this took a toll on his home life.

In an April 1963 article, "He Keeps the Stars in Trim," Jay confessed to the fact he had a beautiful wife he rarely saw and a beautiful car he never drove. He said, "The business keeps me hopping with the 12-hour day and the traveling bit. I keep flying to places like Las Vegas and New York to cut peoples' [*sic*] hair."

Peggy DiMaria explained that Jay's quest to reach the top of his field led to a busy and all-consuming time in her brother's life.

Cami would call my mom sometimes when my brother would still be at work. He would work sometimes 'til 10, 11, or 12 at night. And my mother expressed to my brother she [Cami] felt lonely. She was in the house all by herself. And one of the things I know of what my mom did say when she would talk to my brother on different occasions, and he would say "I'm busy doing this and that and I'm at work till 12 at night."

Cami Sebring confirmed this as well.

"I didn't get to see him that much because he was always at the shop cutting hair or he was going here or there to someone's home or to the studios," she said.

There was light at the end of the tunnel when The Barber's Union and Jay finally struck a deal at the end of 1961. The entire north side of the Fairfax location would be solely staffed by barbers, but only after being trained and certified in the SEBRING method of cutting, which would be applied to all barber customers. The south side of the shop was populated exclusively by hair cosmetologists and hair designers. The agreement was a win-win for the embattled renegade—doubling his establishment's revenue, succeeding in his mission to elevate the profession, and eliminating any further distracting hassles to close his Fairfax business.

With barbers in his shop, there was one compromise Jay wasn't willing to make, according to SEBRING stylist Dean McClure:

> He [Jay] was very annoyed The Barber's Union insisted he place a barber pole outside the shop, and he wasn't going to do it. Period. Jay was insistent his establishment was not a barber shop. He eventually did make a compromise—he allowed a tiny sign that read "Barber Shop" above one door. I was privy to a conversation he had one day with a barber on the other side of the room. I worked next to Jay and there was a partition between us. The barber admitted to Jay, "We should be trying to help you, not stop you." It was very troubling at the time, but Jay stood his ground.

With that battle in the rearview mirror, Jay was able to focus a considerable amount of his attention on what would become another first: a complete hair care product line carrying Sebring's name. After several years of exploring and mixing shampoo and tonic concoctions, Jay realized he would have to create his own to meet his standards and match the demands for healthy hair. He started by hiring chemists to provide the precise results he sought. He knew products were the future of his industry and would prove to be a goldmine for years to come. This was the beginning of what would be another brainchild for Jay—the SEBRING Product Division.

Eager to share the good news with his wife, Jay raced up Laurel Canyon to Mulholland Drive, only to find Cami and any trace of her gone from their Easton residence. For some time, the two had been living separate lives. The strain of Jay's battles and endless work demands were taking a toll on Cami, who lamented decades later regarding their parting.

That was a difficult thing. It would have been better if we were together more, I let a good thing go. I was young, and when you're young sometimes you don't have your head on straight. You can say a lot of "ifs"—*if* we were together that would have never happened. But you never know what's going to happen in life. But I did leave him. I left that part of my life.

In the wake of their split, Jay remained friendly with Cami. She recalled one night that, after a date with Hollywood publicist and agent Joe Sutton, he drove her back to her apartment after dinner. The two lingered after they parked in front of her place and Jay even came out to greet them. While the three talked, Jay's friend Art Schlick suddenly emerged, yelling at Sutton, "You're going out with my best friend's wife!"

As Schlick reached in the car, Sutton rolled up his window on his arm and stepped on the gas. Schlick ended up breaking his arm because of his loyalty to Jay. Joe Torrenueva said Jay returned Schlick's loyalty tenfold.

Jay comes in one day and he says, "You gotta do me a favor. Do you remember Art Schlick?" I said, "Yeah he's the guy that first cut my hair at the shop." Jay said, "Well, he was in an accident, and he broke his arm. He has these clients that he can't do, but he needs money. So, if you work for him— you charge $7.50 here, you'll charge $10 at his place. You keep 60% and you give him forty percent. He's in really bad shape. So, you would really help me out by helping him out. And he's a great guy." So, I said, "Okay."

Charles Champlin said it saddened him that Jay and Cami couldn't make their marriage work.

I had the feeling that it had the potential of being a really wonderful marriage. A wonderful relationship. And for as long as it lasted, I hope it was. Marriages are hard things to figure out. Why they work and why they don't work. And why they don't work better than they do. There's no answers to it.

Unfortunately for Jay and Cami Sebring, they had no answer how to save their marriage. They split in 1963, and their divorce was finalized in 1965.

"Jay took it very hard," Peggy recalled. "I think it was one of the hardest things that he ever had to deal with. He was calling home a lot."

With his family more than 2,000 miles away, and as the confidante of so many in Southern California, Jay still yearned for true love in this strange dog-eat-dog town.

CHAPTER 13
FRIENDS TO THE END

"'m a hard guy to have as a friend," Steve McQueen once told a reporter. "You know, I used to hang out only with the guys I knew before I made it. I thought the new ones were after me just because I was a movie star. Then I found out both kinds screwed me around just as much."

Because of his hardscrabble Midwest upbringing, McQueen had significant trust issues well into adulthood, always assuming people were conspiring against or using him, and finding it hard to believe that anyone had his best interests at heart. His alcoholic parents—products of the Roaring Twenties—shuffled in and out of his life, frequently abandoning him and leaving him to be shuttled between relatives throughout his childhood and adolescence. This rocky foundation fueled a distrust and paranoia that grew exponentially along with his fame.

McQueen's inner circle included his wife, Neile, motorcycle racer and stuntman Bud Ekins, L.A. nightclub owner Elmer Valentine, and fellow actor Tom Gilson. The latter was surprising considering how McQueen viewed everyone in Hollywood—the land of gladhanders and backstabbers—as a potential competitor. McQueen was ruthless with classmates when studying under Lee

Strasberg at the Actors Studio in New York City and insensitive when he heard about the passing of James Dean.

"I'm glad Dean's dead," he told actor and writer John Gilmore. "Makes more room for me."

When McQueen got his first taste of stardom in the CBS TV series *Wanted: Dead or Alive* (1958 to 1961), he could finally let down some of his guard, though not much. He did so with Gilson, an actor under contract to Twentieth Century-Fox (*Rally Round the Flag, Boys!*), who guest starred on two episodes of the show.

The two men hit it off because their personalities were so similar. They both were rowdy drunks, but also charming and loveable rascals. They made this work for them in Hollywood, but there was a big difference. Steve found a way to control the rage that boiled just below the surface; Gilson, on the other hand, was not capable of taming his demons.

On the night of October 6, 1962, those demons got the better of Gilson and he lost the battle. At the time, Saundra Edwards, his common-law wife—a shapely and stunning brunette, part-time actress, and *Playboy* model—had custody of their nine-month-old son. The couple had broken up three months prior, and Edwards had moved into her sister's Van Nuys apartment with her three children (their infant, plus two children, ages 6 and 3, from a previous marriage).

The two met on the set of the 1960 film *The Crowded Sky* and embarked on a whirlwind romance. No doubt Edwards was attracted to Gilson's bad-boy image, but living with him was another story. He had a nasty streak that was fueled by booze, and he turned emotionally and physically abusive when his intoxication level got out of control. This was his state on October 6 at around 1:00 a.m. when he called Edwards at her sister's apartment and threatened her in what she described to police as a "strange" voice.

Gilson showed up at the apartment (her sister and brother-in-law were at a party) to make good on his threats—he banged on the doors, demanding to see their son, and then he forced his way through the kitchen door. Edwards herded her children into the living room away from the enraged intruder. As the hulking 6'4" man came at her, Edwards turned a 12-gauge shotgun on Gilson and warned she would use it on him if he took another step.

"Go ahead, I don't care," he replied. "If you don't, I'll kill you and the kids." Then Gilson advanced on her. Edwards took aim and blasted Gilson through the heart, sending him reeling backward. He was dead before he hit the floor. Edwards was charged with murder, but a week later, the coroner's inquest jury panel ruled the shotgun slaying a justifiable homicide.

Gilson's autopsy concluded he suffered from acute alcoholism.

McQueen served as a pallbearer at Gilson's funeral—the same role he later performed for both Jay Sebring and Bruce Lee.

Gilson's death left a void in McQueen's life, and Jay was just the person to fill it. He and McQueen met in late spring 1962, shortly before McQueen departed for Germany to shoot the epic World War II film *The Great Escape,* which would turn him into a major movie star. It was Jay who gave McQueen his iconic cut for his breakout role as Captain Virgil Hilts, along with styling the film's core stars James Coburn, James Garner, and Richard Attenborough. Jay created a look that was short, sharp, layered, and beautifully cut to the shape of McQueen's Roman-shaped head. It defined McQueen the way McQueen defined cool.

For the deeply competitive actor who constantly sought to be top dog, Sebring's touch to McQueen's hair was transformative. He designed a balanced frame that would best enhance McQueen's face and skull shape by directing attention to McQueen's most powerful feature: his eyes. Sebring's indelible brush strokes are the trademarks that would ultimately define Steve McQueen.

Nancy Sinatra noted Jay's contribution to the lasting influence of the characters Steve McQueen portrayed and brought to life on the silver screen.

These iconic images, a lot of that was because of Jay's work. Once he locked in on a style for the actor, that actor was set. I always think of Steve McQueen because to me that's the most obvious one. Steve in *The Thomas Crown Affair* was the epitome of the Jay Sebring man. It made him an icon. That movie did it for sure.

Cami Sebring pointed out that Jay's impact on his clients went far beyond a haircut, and that especially applied to McQueen.

I don't know that Steve McQueen would have had the impact that he did after he met Jay because Jay, okay I'll say it, was such a cool human being. His demeanor and just the way he was. He influenced so many people. And they wanted to be like him. Steve really appreciated Jay. *The Thomas Crown Affair*, that was Jay. That was totally Jay.

To Joe Torrenueva, it was Jay's dedication to quality in every aspect of his lifestyle that made Sebring a trendsetter in Hollywood's most elite circles.

He knew style. He knew what to put on—the Brioni suits. Jay had the Cobra which was very hip. He had two Cobras. The way he dressed. I saw other actors dress like him. McQueen was influenced a lot by Jay. He just had a lot of style. He knew how to do it.

Jay was one of the few people Steve McQueen not only needed but wanted in his life. McQueen, like all great movie stars, knew that his physique, appearance, and style were his most prized assets, and having Jay in his corner was essential. Jay knew just how to enhance his good looks to be progressive and classic yet timeless.

But their relationship wasn't simply professional. The time

McQueen spent in Jay's chair forged a true and lasting friendship. McQueen was known for being a taker, but he was loyal to the friends that mattered to him. In 1963 when *LIFE* magazine was developing a photo-essay on McQueen to document his ascension to the top of the Hollywood ladder, he invited photographer John Dominis into his world, who shot approximately forty rolls of film. The layout featured various high-quality photos of McQueen at work and play, including pictures of him with his wife, Neile, at their Hollywood and Palm Springs homes, racing motorcycles in the Mohave Desert, speeding along Sunset Boulevard in his rare sports car, etc. One of the outtake photos that Dominis snapped but didn't make the article was a picture of Jay giving McQueen a trademark cut in his private room.

In the photo Jay is meticulously trimming his client's hair while McQueen is quietly reading—most likely a motoring magazine. Not a word was spoken, but the silence was a demonstration of the comfort level between the two men.

McQueen also brought others to enjoy Jay's cuts, like Frank Hill, who worked intermittently for the movie star from the 1960s to the late 1970s.

> McQueen never liked it when my hair was longer than his and so one day, he calls me up and says, "Frank, drop what you're doing. I'm going to take you to get your hair cut." So, about a half hour later he picked me up in a sports car and brought me to Jay's salon on Fairfax. Jay was a great guy. He didn't strike me as a typical Hollywood hairdresser type but a real man's man. They talked about cars and real-life stuff while Jay cut my hair. I could tell he and Steve were tight. I walked out of the shop with the greatest haircut of my life, and then when we got in the car, McQueen told me how much it was going to cost me—and my jaw dropped. He [was] always pulling shit like that on me.

Jay and Steve were very much alike—self-made, military men who were renegades with a zeal for life that included beautiful women, fast cars, jazz, and transcendental enhancers. They were rugged individualists and iconoclasts who brought the same level of intensity to their professional and personal lives.

As their friendship deepened, they recognized they had quite a few things in common, said Larry Geller, who knew both men.

"Steve and Jay were very much alike and close, close friends," Geller said. "Jay, like Steve, was very straightforward and honest and wasn't shy about letting you know his true feelings."

Their passion for fine automobiles and racing brought them even closer. McQueen raced motorcycles and cars competitively, but Sebring could more than hold his own on the urban streets of L.A. to the ire of various police departments throughout Southern California. According to Sebring's personal and probate records, attorney Harry E. Weiss represented Jay in seventeen traffic cases from 1965 to 1969.

Laurel Canyon and Mulholland Drive were favorites for their sharp bends and steep climbs, offering hairpin turns that would terrify their driving companions. Former SEBRING assistant Gordon Mullinger recalled one such excursion.

Jay was driving like a bat out of hell, and I would purposefully take a steno pad. It was like a game, and I would focus down on the pad and Jay would be saying things and I'd go "Uh huh, uh huh." And Jay would keep looking at me because he was speeding like you couldn't believe. He just wanted to see if he could get a reaction from me. I was bound and determined that I wouldn't even flinch. So, I would sit there and go, "Uh huh, uh huh, uh huh," and meanwhile inside I'm going, *Oh my God, we're never gonna make it! We're not gonna make it! I know we're not!*

Jay's friend and employee Amos Russell also found Jay's driving over the mountainous canyons and windy terrain hair-raising and an exercise in fear.

Laurel Canyon was the road he liked to drive. He'd be coming around the mountain like, "What's he tryin' to prove here? Win an Oscar or somethin'?" He drove fast! I'm not kidding. Not exaggerating at all. There's a lot of stiff curves up there, you know, and a lot of people be drivin' too fast and thinkin' too slow. But my God, I said, "Where we goin'? You know? Slow down!" He used to let the rubber burn. Put the pedal to the metal. As a rule, I wouldn't complain much, but I tell him as we goin' up, I said, "You gonna drive fast, I catch a cab right now. I'm in no hurry. I'm in no hurry!" And he could drive that Jag. He loved to drive. And the Porsche, oh my God, that poor Porsche, he like wore that thing out. We used to come around the corner on two wheels. Look like he was on two wheels comin' around the corner. Took it to *another* level.

Quincy Jones, who was friends with both men, said McQueen trumped Jay in the fear department.

"Steve was worse. He always wanted to do his own stunts and stuff," Jones said. "He drove so fast that he scared the shit out of me."

Even former Formula One racing driver Jackie Stewart took note of Jay's love for machinery.

Jay was a motoring enthusiast, which is probably why he was keen to cut my hair. He was driving a Porsche at this time, and he knew all about the Grand Prix racing world. I had driven in India, New Zealand, South Africa and Riverside, California, and he was well into what I was doing and where I was driving in those days.

Perhaps this fast and loose approach to driving was a foreshadowing of the trajectory their lives would follow. Jay would soon extend his driving skills to the racetrack with close friend (and then racing neophyte) Paul Newman, who later became an accomplished racecar driver. The two practiced and competed extensively at Jim Russell[1] Racing Drivers School in Snetterton, England and Brands Hatch racetrack in Kent, England.

In addition to fine automobiles, women also revved them up, and both Sebring and McQueen revved up their share of women, noted Nancy Sinatra.

> Jay was like a magnet. Whether he was shaggy haired, which he was at times, or neat as a pin, short above the ears kinda hair, he was extremely attractive and sexy. And he would look at you over those shades of his and you would melt. One time we were all at the Daisy, and there was a crowd on the dance floor, and I didn't know what was going on. And I looked over there and right in the middle of it all was Jay.

The Daisy, Luau, The Candy Store, The Factory, The Playboy Club, the Galaxy, London Fog, the Unicorn, the Hullabaloo, Ash Grove, Sneaky Pete's, and Elmer Valentine's Whisky a Go Go were Hollywood's playground. The latter, where McQueen had a booth, is the site where he met screen siren Mamie Van Doren. Van Doren, a reigning sex symbol in the late '50s and early '60s, was pegged by

---

1. Russell was one of the leading players behind the action sequences of the John Frankenheimer's 1966 film *Grand Prix*. He was responsible for dressing up Formula Junior cars as F1 machines and coached the leading stars, including James Garner, to handle racing cars.

studio honchos as the next Marilyn Monroe. She recalled an LSD-laden tryst that started at the Whisky on Sunset Boulevard and ended up in bed at the Benedict Canyon home of Jay Sebring, who was hosting a mod-style party.

Mamie said when they arrived at Sebring's Tudor mansion, the party was in full swing with people splashing around the pool. Others wandered around the home, drinking and smoking pot. McQueen summoned Mamie into the bathroom to drop some Sandoz acid and have sex. Mamie said they were heady days and hallucinogenic times, and acid wasn't hard to find.

> You could get LSD over the counter then. Also, amyl nitrate. You could get that as well if you said you had a heart murmur or something. I had a carpenter who was always doing LSD. I asked him about it because I thought it sounded like Lucky Strikes. Cary Grant said his doctor was giving it to him for his problems. Everyone had a problem back then.

Quincy Jones said he experienced wild times as well with Jay and McQueen and fondly reflected on his days with the two men.

> Steve and Jay and I were inseparable. We'd drive to Steve's house on Oakmont and have dinners all the time and, uh, some stuff we probably shouldn't talk about. But most cats that end up hanging out with each other, it's about common interests—imbibement, girls, human interests. We had no limits.

Like all good friends, Jay and McQueen had their fair share of disputes and disagreements. Sometimes it led to taking a break from each other. Just as the two shared many similarities they were vastly different in other aspects of their lives.

Both were alpha males. Steve fought his way through an unstable youth with a constant need to prove himself. He was introverted, but a competitor to a fault. Conversely, Jay was raised in a very grounded, stable family environment and competed only with himself to prove his vision dreams and goals.

In this Hollywood context, Jay was certain of his role as the main attraction. For Steve, who made his living being the main attraction for many years, feeling second-fiddle to anyone on any level was difficult. Neither man was secondary to the other, but Steve met his match in Jay. This inevitably led to clashes that challenged and bruised both egos from time to time, according to Joe Torrenueva.

> I'd get these strange phone calls every once in a while, from Jay, telling me that Steve was going to give me a call any minute asking for me to cut his hair. They'd put me in the middle, but I found it funny and odd. I didn't make a big deal of it and said, "Okay." A few minutes later Steve would call and ask, "Joe, can you cut my hair? Jay and I aren't getting along so good right now." And because Jay gave me a heads up letting me know it was okay, I said, "Sure, Steve." Then a few weeks later I'd see Steve in the shop getting a trim from Jay, and everything was okay.[2]

Torrenueva said neither of the men ever disclosed what those disputes were about or how they started. He just chalked it up to the fact that both men were strong-willed and ego-driven, and those elements were bound to clash every now and again.

Fred Segal observed an idiosyncratic difference between Jay and Steve:

---

2. After Sebring's death, Torrenueva cut Steve McQueen's hair for three films— *Junior Bonner* (1971), *The Getaway* (1972), and *Tom Horn* (1980).

I asked Jay if there was anything I could give him or do for him because of him sending me customers, how much I appreciated it. I offered him an outfit, I think three. No way. He wouldn't take it. That is a very high-level, authentic character trait that I don't think he wanted anything for nothing. Before I personally met Steve through Elmer Valentine, years before that, through Jay I met Steve. He was so excited about the clothes Jay's crew was wearing, that he was going to the Olympics to represent the United States motorcycle team. And he made them all wear Fred Segal jeans to the Olympics. That was a big, big thing. He also wanted to fight me once behind my store 'cause I wouldn't let him return twenty-one pairs of pants he had for six months. I wouldn't fool with Steve. He had a pretty good temper.

The two men were a united front, however, when it came to McQueen's career. It was Jay who created McQueen's iconic looks for *The Great Escape, Love with the Proper Stranger, The Cincinnati Kid*, and *The Sand Pebbles*—the latter being a not so sentimental nod to his navy days when his GI cut was sheared high and tight, not to mention embarrassingly short. Jay singlehandedly turned McQueen into a sexy matinee idol by lightening his blond hair in *The Thomas Crown Affair* and created the superstar's best-known haircut in *Bullitt*, the defining movie of his illustrious film career. McQueen's first wife, Neile, credited Jay's gentle prodding for helping convince her husband he should take the part.

McQueen, a middle-aged hippie at heart, had serious misgivings about the role. He felt his carefully established rebel image would betray his younger audience. The thought of playing a police detective during the emergence of the counterculture frightened him. Days after he received the script, Neile subtly floated the idea past him.

"No way am I playin' a cop," he said, getting emotional. "Those kids call 'em pigs, man. What are you trying to do to me? Why, those kids would turn on me so fast it'd make your head spin!"

A few days later when Jay visited McQueen's house (dubbed "The Castle" by the superstar and his friends) to give Steve a trim, Neile felt as if she had an ally—albeit a loaded one. She wrote in her 1986 memoir, *My Husband, My Friend*:

> Both men were high as kites, and I took advantage of the situation by getting Jay to agree with my reasoning that playing a cop might actually enhance Steve's image with his young fans rather than compromise it. Everybody was of the opinion the script wasn't particularly good, but I felt very strongly about the salability of the title. I knew Steve could play *Bullitt* in his own oblique and unconventional way.

An early 1968 photo captured the two men on the set in San Francisco, deep in conversation. What was said between them remains a mystery, but the image says everything you need to know about their dynamic—Jay is doing the talking while McQueen listens intently.

Bullitt premiered on October 17, 1968, at Radio City Music Hall. The movie wasn't just a smash; it was a juggernaut. It not only started a trend but became the gold standard for all chase films. The film has also stood the test of time with its stylistic approach and dedication to cinema verité. In 2007, it was voted into the National Film Registry so these heart-pounding scenes could be preserved forever. The motion picture exceeded everyone's wildest dreams— and earned a whopping $50 million in the United States alone.[3]

The film gave McQueen all the power, money, respect, and

---

3. Equivalent to a $460 million in 2025 dollars.

glory he could ever have imagined. It was also his fifth hit film in a row and his biggest success to date. He had made the rare transition from movie star to producer to pop-culture icon. McQueen had already achieved amazing success, but *Bullitt* pushed him through the stratosphere. The legacy and presence of this role is indelible to this day, sealing Steve McQueen's status in the zeitgeist as "The King of Cool.... and Jay Sebring as the kingmaker."

Three weeks before McQueen's 1980 death, he lay in a Mexican cancer clinic recounting his life to a "spiritual advisor." He didn't feel sorry for himself, wasn't morose or asking, "Why me?" at the age of 50. He was lucid, reflective, and looking ahead to the future, thinking his best days were in front of him even if his cancer-ridden body said otherwise. And when Jay's name was brought up, he smiled and closed his eyes.

"Jay Sebring was my best friend," he said.

CHAPTER 14
ENTER THE DRAGON

Ever the renegade, Jay Sebring was a free-thinking individualist from the start. While that is the fire that fueled his drive to innovate and break new ground in an established industry, it also resulted in repeated conflict. Jay was not intentionally combative, but his confidence and crystal-clear direction led to the defiance of his father and superior officers in the navy. It got him into fistfights with good ol' boys and scorned boyfriends, feuds with The Barber Union and mob heavies, and even occasional clashes with high-profile clients.

Now, at the apex of his career, Jay found himself in an enviable situation: his clients needed him more than he needed them. That was evident when he stopped cutting Elvis Presley's hair. "The King," known for his impeccable Southern charm and manners, rubbed Jay the wrong way or vice versa. SEBRING alumnus and Elvis Presley stylist Larry Geller said their parting was real and irrevocable.

"Jay did Elvis' hair, and they didn't get along. They didn't like each other," Geller said.

"They clashed and they didn't want to see each other anymore. It's all chemistry."

On another occasion, Jay told his secretary, Gordon Mullinger, to fire his client, the Tony-winning Robert Goulet, because he was a "pain in the ass." When Jay felt charitable toward a client but didn't want to personally cut his hair any longer, he'd send them off to one of his protégés. But kicking them to the curb wasn't an issue, either, said Joe Torrenueva.

Jay was very strategic about which clients he kept and the ones he didn't. The ones he kept were not only the upper echelon in the entertainment industry but would sing Jay's praises to the media—guys like Sinatra, McQueen, Newman, and Vic Damone. Jay was very smart in that way.

Constantly pushing boundaries meant Jay sometimes pushed buttons. Jay was no stranger to adversity or physical confrontation, and being of slight stature, Jay had to ensure he had ways of protecting himself. He trained hard in martial arts and leaned on his military firearms training to protect himself in dicey situations, noted Larry Geller.

Jay had many sides to his personality. He had a propensity, something to do with violence and safety. He was very concerned about his safety. He hired someone to protect him by teaching him karate. He hired Ed Parker, one of the great American masters who brought karate to the West.

The martial arts movement in the United States began to take its foothold in the early sixties. It was the dawning of the karate and Kung Ku craze that would soon capture American culture in film, television, and even popular music ("Kung Fu Fighting" by Carl Douglas) in subsequent decades. In California, the pioneers were Kenpo grandmasters Ralph Castro in San Francisco and Ed Parker in Pasadena (both of Hawaiian descent). In Southern California,

Parker was the go-to karate expert for influential Los Angeles figures and Hollywood celebrities who attended his classes and booked him for private sessions. By 1963, Parker owned several dojos and made several television appearances (*The Art Linkletter Show* and *The Lucy Show*) and had written two books: *Kenpo Karate: Law of the Fist and Empty Hand* (1960) and *Secrets of Chinese Karate* (1963).

Parker also generated healthy revenue from his private Hollywood students Garry Cooper, Darren McGavin, Blake Edwards, Robert Wagner, Warren Beatty, George Hamilton, and Frank Sinatra, as well as some of the industry's top stuntmen. Parker would eventually become Elvis Presley's singular Kenpo mentor and instructor, and he later served as a bodyguard when the King began touring again in the 1970s.

Jay studied extensively with Parker in the backyard of his Easton residence, which was equipped with a body bag that hung from a poolside awning. Decades later, Darlene Tafua, Ed's daughter, recalled a particularly memorable workout session.

> My dad was very fond of Jay even though Jay's dog bit him one day when they were training in Jay's backyard. He always laughed telling the story because the dog thought my dad was attacking Jay.

Former SEBRING cutter and stylist Sal Orifice[1] witnessed Tosh's attack on the instructor and recalled it in his book, *Tripping with the King and Others*.

> Jay arranges for us to take private lessons at his house. Our instructor is Ed Parker, a big powerful Hawaiian. When Ed

---

1. Orifice was originally assigned by Sebring to cut and style Presley's hair, but they eventually parted ways. In April 1964, Larry Geller became known as Presley's personal stylist and was intermittently employed by him until his death on August 16, 1977.

arrived, Jay and I and Jay's gigantic dog are kicked back poolside. Ed waves to us as he comes down the stone steps leading to the pool. The monster canine eyes him.... [she] growls deep and throaty, then takes off running. [She] viciously pounces on Ed. Ed twists and turns avoiding the dog's huge jaws. Jay swiftly subdues the dog and chains her to a post. "Man, holy fuck! Sorry about that! You alright?" "That's okay," says Ed calmly. "I'm fine."

We head for the house—I spot a trickle of blood on Ed's arm and there's a tear in the seat of his pants. This guy could have snapped the dog's neck if he wanted to, yet he was absolutely composed while the dog was trying to bite a chunk out of his ass. He doesn't seem ruffled at all. I'm duly impressed. I believe I just had my first lesson in the martial arts.

Kung Fu masters Ming Lum and James "Jimmy" Lee had a significant influence on Parker. One day Jimmy called Parker to tell him about a kid named Bruce Lee who was living in Seattle, Washington. Parker eventually met him in Oakland while visiting Jimmy and said of Lee:

When this kid punched, he could pop air. He was a very cocky kid, very cocky. There were a lot of things he didn't know, but all you had to do was let him watch one time and that was it. He was such a natural athlete. He was very nice to me, but cocky. Having said that, he was able to produce.

In August 1964, Parker held the inaugural International Karate Championship Tournament at the Long Beach Municipal Auditorium. Also known as the International Karate Championships, Parker's tournament launched the careers of numerous martial arts superstars including Mike Stone, Chuck Norris, Bill "Superfoot"

Wallace, and Benny "The Jet" Urquidez. That 1964 tournament was one of the most pivotal events for martial arts throughout the United States and for Bruce Lee, a young, unknown martial artist from Oakland, California.

Linda Lee Cadwell, Lee's widow fondly spoke about her famous husband's electric charisma.

> Bruce and I were married August 17, 1964, in Seattle, and in the same month Ed Parker invited Bruce to make an appearance at the Long Beach International Karate Tourna-ment. Ed, who had known Bruce for years, invited Bruce to give a demonstration. Bruce was very charismatic in his demonstrations. He spoke to the audience a lot, joking, and was very entertaining along with his mastery of the martial arts. He would call people up from the audience and demonstrate his "one-inch punch" and high kicks.

Sal Orifice recalled in his 2010 book making the trek from Los Angeles to Long Beach in Jay's latest prized vehicle, a Shelby Cobra.

> We're chug-a-lugging down Benedict Canyon onto Sunset Boulevard, then on to the 405 freeway. Jay led foots the gas pedal, whooshing the Cobra to ninety-five miles an hour in about three seconds. Now we're weaving in, out, and around traffic like we owned the freeway. It's un-fucking-canny. Not a cop in sight. We arrive at the arena in record time. Jay, being a trophy presenter, scouts off to the "celebrity seating area." I'm twenty rows behind.
>
> When Bruce comes out, an expectant hush hangs over the arena. Bruce does the humble bowing bit, then bam! He springs at least six feet straight up, then rolls on the floor like a basketball, then spreads flat out like a crab, then jumps and twists like a panther, then, shit—man, he just

went on and on. Every move impeccable. The guy has major chops. Big time moves. I'm profoundly impressed. Two weeks later, Bruce Lee comes to Jay's house to give us private instruction.

Jay was honored when Parker asked him to present trophies to tournament champions along with Parker and his wife, Leilani, during the awards ceremony at the conclusion of the championships. Jay was not only impressed with the young martial artist from Oakland, but he also recognized a similar revolutionary and kindred spirit in the Jeet Kune Do creator, said David Tadman, a Bruce Lee historian.

It wasn't until the Ed Parker Internationals that Bruce was able to showboat on a large scale what he was, who he was, and what he can do. It just so happened Jay Sebring was in the audience and saw Bruce. When you see Bruce doing this demonstration at that time, no one ever saw this type of martial arts before. This was something far out, something different, something new. Jay was far out, doing new things. He was a revolutionist. There's that saying, "great minds think alike."

A few months later Jay was cutting the hair of television producer William Dozier in his Fairfax Avenue private room. The *Batman* executive informed Jay he was looking for an Asian actor who could fight, was good-looking, and had the charisma to play a lead role. Without hesitation, Jay informed his client he knew someone who perfectly fit the bill.

"Your man is Bruce Lee," Jay said coolly. Lee, a philosophy major dropout, was an almost impossibly hard sell as a neophyte actor. He didn't have a single Hollywood credit to his name, nor did he reside in Southern California. Jay explained that Bruce had acted in films during his youth in Hong Kong, but Dozier was unimpressed. Sebring persisted, insisting the producer at least view Lee's demonstration film from Ed Parker's Invitational.

On Thursday January 21, 1965, Jay set up a meeting with Peter Bren, son of film producer Milton Bren,[2] and William Dozier at his 20th Century-Fox office. Sebring's black book planner reads:

10 A.M.– Showing of Karate Film–William Dozier's Office–20th Century Fox–With Peter Bren.

The meeting was a success. Dozier finally saw Lee's extraordinary talents and made a call to the Lee residence in Oakland. Linda Lee Cadwell described the momentous occasion decades later.

> I took a phone call when Bruce was not home. And this was just totally out of the blue, "Hello, I'm William Dozier, I produce movies in Hollywood…." We had no idea there was going to be a phone call like this, or even any idea at all that Bruce would ever be interested in the motion picture business in Hollywood. Because when Bruce came to the United States, he never had the idea of going into acting or anything. He was strictly going to be teaching martial arts. That was his dream. So out of the blue comes this call from William Dozier "Well, would you ask Bruce to give me a call back?" Bruce came home and I said, "Bruce, this guy, this producer, wants you to call him." And Bruce is as puzzled as we are because we didn't know about Jay yet and how this whole thing worked out!

In a letter dated January 25, 1965, from William Dozier to

---

2. Peter Bren's father Milton Bren was a movie producer and married Academy-Award winning actress Claire Trevor in 1948. Peter Bren later became a successful real estate developer and died in 2019.

Bruce Lee, the producer finalized the logistics for the screen test. It read:

Dear Bruce,
*   Per our phone conversation, I shall expect you in my office at twelve o' clock noon on Friday, February fifth. At that time, I shall reimburse you for your PSA round trip ticket.*
*   Very truly yours,*
*   William Dozier*

The screen test originally was to consider Lee in the lead role for Dozier series on a Charlie Chan adaptation of *Number One Son* but ultimately served as a test for the part of Kato in Dozier's *The Green Hornet.* Jay personally drove Bruce to his life-changing screen test in his Cobra. Gordon Mullinger had recently left Jay's employ to work for 20th Century-Fox in the financing department and was on the lot the day of the screen test.

It just happened that I was walking out of the studio office right at that moment. Jay almost hit me. He had no idea who it was and then he looks, because he was gonna say, "I'm sorry are you okay?" He came out of the car, and he goes, "Oh my God, you've got to come back to work for me. I won't take no for an answer." And then he said, "I want you to meet somebody. This is Bruce Lee and I'm bringing him to the lot because I arranged for an appointment for him to try out for the role of Kato." And of course, Bruce Lee did get it. Which again shows you the influence Jay wielded.

It is impossible to overstate the roles Ed Parker and Jay Sebring played in altering the trajectory of Bruce Lee's life and career at this time. And Bruce, with his talents and vision, deftly rose to meet the opportunity of a lifetime or, more accurately, an opportunity that would result in such a historical and global reach. Soon Bruce and Linda Lee would relocate to Los Angeles with their newborn son Brandon. In a letter dated March 11, 1966, Bruce wrote to his newfound Hollywood advocate, mentor, and trusted friend:

Jay,

I've been back two days now and busy like hell packing. James Lee is working and as soon as I have the opportunity to borrow his car, I'll cash that check and send you a personal money order.

Belasco called and said that he has talked to both you and Dozier—I've told him to arrange acting lesson for the 21st of this month, which is Monday from this coming one. I hope to move into town in the middle of next week. I'm going to Bernie Walters and let him know the landlord of my coming so he can have everything ready. Walter's enthusiasm is decreasing when he found out he couldn't open a Kung Fu school with me. He wants to become an assistant instructor. In fact, I had Dan [Parker's assistant] drive me to the airport. He is one hell of a nice guy. I should write him and thank him.

After figuring out all of the expenses—like $200 for moving, monthly rent plus gas and light, car payment, everyday need—I need to have some private lessons going. The best would be through your introduction I can teach the better group and thus not have to teach too many people. My acting lessons are only three times a week, so I can have a lot of time on my own. When you have the opportunity, I hope you can work on it for me. I thank you.

In closing, let me express my sincere thanks for the many things you have done for me during my stay in L.A. You ARE a friend, Jay. Thanks again.

Bruce

P.S. I know Las Vegas will leave you exhausted, *but I do hope you will work on the lessons I've left near your phone. By the way, a pedestrian warned me that you have a '65 plate on your Cobra—check on it if you don't know—just wanted to let you know.*

This was the beginning of a friendship that would endure until Jay's untimely demise on that fateful Friday night on August 8, 1969, said Linda Lee Cadwell.

Jay and Bruce had a relationship that went on for years between the time they met late '64 till Jay's passing in '69. There was about five years where they had a very close relationship. They would trade professions. Jay, of course, was a famous hairstylist to the stars and Bruce was very fussy about the way he wanted his hair to be. So, Jay would cut Bruce's hair and Bruce would teach Jay Kung Fu lessons.

Bruce learned from Jay's example during these interactions that he could charge as much as he was worth. This was particularly true in Hollywood as he amassed a clientele of private students with endless resources through Jay's introduction to Hollywood's elite A-listers. Cadwell said Jay was the common denominator when it came to building her husband's star students.

Jay was cutting the hair of a lot of stars like Steve McQueen, James Garner, Vic Damone, James Coburn. There were many, many who were very interested in self-defense. And Jay was the one who hooked Bruce up with these people for Bruce to teach private lessons. Bruce knew what Jay could charge for haircutting, so he applied that to his Kung Fu lessons. So that if you make the price higher, people will think it's more valuable. Of course, the truth was, it was more valuable.

Damone said that, through Jay's introduction, he started working out with Lee whenever the opportunity arose. Though the lessons extended far beyond the martial arts, said Vic Damone.

Bruce didn't only show you moves; he would talk to you about the psychology of it—the inner peace, the balance of your body and how you don't ever tense up. It was like you had to be loose in order to make a move if you're gonna protect yourself. They [Jay and Bruce] would come to see my show at the Sands, and we would use the stage to work out in the afternoons.

This one particular time we just finished working out and we were going to get something to eat. If you know Vegas at all, you have to walk through the casino to get to a restaurant. So, we meet this guy "Big John" Hopkins, Sammy Davis' bodyguard. I mean this guy is really big and strong and he's saying "Hi" to Jay, and I and I introduced him to Bruce. Bruce is in the middle, standing right in front of John, who was smoking a cigarette. John raises his hand or arm to say hello to someone behind Bruce, and all of a sudden Bruce had Big John's arms up, and he kicked his foot over, so he was completely powerless, and Bruce was going into his throat with both hands, like the points of his fingers. I said, "Oh my God, whoa, whoa, whoa.... what are you doing Bruce?!" Bruce said, "He was gonna hit me!" and John says very gently, "No, I was waving at someone behind you." Bruce says, "Oh, I'm sorry."

Fred Segal described his experience with Lee tantamount to working with a top Zen master.

When he (Lee) came into the store.... he would kick up, standing up, he would kick his foot up, all powerful force and stop right at my chin. And I never flinched, and he loved it. But Bruce Lee, he sticks in my mind like Jay. Bruce is one of the transformations of the entire vocation that he did. He was like in the embryonic stage of that. So, Bruce, Jay, and me had a connection all in the same level.

Cadwell observed that Jay's influence on Bruce was ubiquitous.

Jay had an overall influence on Bruce, style-wise. Not just the hair, but clothing and cars. This was all part of Jay's style. And Bruce learned a lot from Jay. Bruce came to this country when he was eighteen years old. So, he had a lot to learn about American styles, expressions, everything. And then Hollywood, that's a whole different America, right? I credit Jay with being one of his initial teachers in that regard.

Sebring's impact on Bruce Lee's look and style was profoundly transformational, as is obvious when comparing him pre- and post-Sebring. The Sebring imprint on Lee's movie star image and persona is indelible—an influence he incorporated throughout his entire career.

Joe Torrenueva remembered when Bruce would come into the shop to have his hair cut and schmooze with the guys.

Bruce would come in [during] that whole craze of everybody wanting to take karate. I was taking karate and some of the other guys were also taking karate or judo. But Bruce came in with Wing Chun and his style, Jeet Kune Do. So, we would go in the back parking lot on Fairfax and compare styles. The Japanese use their hands as weapons like a hammer, a spear, a knife, whereas the Chinese use their bodies like animals—the praying mantis, the lion, the bear. It was like "Show me how you punch" or "How do you kick?" or "Hey Bruce, show Sal [Orifice] that one-inch punch thing!" It was great. A lot of good times in that parking lot.

The Lees and Torrenuevas would eventually become close friends, sharing meals together, visiting on Sunday afternoons, and celebrating birthdays.

While Dozier set up production for *The Green Hornet*, Bruce spent his time teaching private lessons and honing his acting skills in classes at the recommendation of talent agent William "Billy" Belasco, also a Sebring client. Belasco was handling actors Bobby Sherman and Sal Mineo at the time and would go on to produce *The Carey Treatment* with James Coburn, *They Only Kill Their Masters* with James Garner, and *The Last Hard Men* with Charlton Heston and James Coburn (1976).

On February 12, 1976, Belasco's dear friend, Sal Mineo, was stabbed in the heart by Lionel Williams, a criminal with a long rap sheet with charges ranging from bad checks to robberies. In a sad twist of fate, on the night of February 26, 1976, grief-stricken Belasco was offered a ride home after several cocktails during dinner at The Palm Restaurant in West Hollywood. A member of the restaurant staff drove Billy home in his car to provide safe passage. The two were involved in a car crash on Sunset Boulevard's "Dead Man's Curve." The driver survived but William Belasco was killed. He was forty-one years old.

The Green Hornet finally premiered on September 9, 1966, and ran for two years with twenty-six episodes in all. The series starred Van Williams as Britt Reid, Bruce Lee as Kato, and Wende Wagner as Lenore Case. The show followed Reid as he fought underworld crime with the assistance of his stunningly beautiful secretary and

Kato, a Kung Fu expert, traveling in Reid's sleek, fully armed vehicle known as the "Black Beauty." The series enjoyed worldwide success, short as it was. Lee's skills and talents stole the show so much so that in China the show was re-titled *The Kato Show*.

When Ed Parker was asked by a reporter if Bruce Lee was really that good, he had a ready and sensible answer.

"Well, at one time, Bruce was teaching Joe Lewis, Mike Stone, and Chuck Norris, so, you know, he was pretty good."

But Lee was not infallible.

When Lee was on the set of *The Green Hornet*, he had an altercation with a stuntman named Gene LeBell, a world-class martial artist, twice national Judo champion, and master grappler. Stories abound in Hollywood that LeBell picked Lee up, slung him over his back (a "fireman's carry"), and paraded him around the set after Lee roughed up one of the stuntmen, a tale whose lore has grown over the decades.[3]

"Stuntmen and wrestlers have their own brand of humor and at first Bruce didn't take my little joke too kindly," LeBell said in an interview at the end of his life. "Eventually he realized we were just welcoming him into our group and before long he fit right in with the rest of the rowdy stuntmen."

Van Williams star noted that Lee was long on athleticism but short on temper.

> He and our stunt guys didn't get along that well because Bruce wanted to do it his way. Low light and back lighting were also issues. Because Bruce was so fast and everything, it caused issues. Bruce was in a black uniform with a black mask, black cap, with black shoes, and if he wasn't lit just

---

3. This incident was never discussed by Gene LeBell, who granted several interviews over the years about Bruce Lee. The scene between LeBell and Lee was loosely interpreted by Quentin Tarantino in 2019's *Once Upon a Time in Hollywood*.

right, he'd bust open a door and all you'd hear was a bunch [of] yelling and screaming and people flying around, but you never got to see Bruce because he was moving too fast. So, we finally proved to him after showing him two or three times that he had to slow it down. We learned a lot of lessons on that show.

This was the first television program to expose authentic martial arts to America. The show was groundbreaking, historically speaking, because it was the very first time an Asian man played a lead role in a major American television production. At that time, most of Hollywood thought Asian actors to be incapable of playing any significant lead or supporting roles, and that included depicting actual Asian characters.

It wasn't until Bruce Lee was first introduced to the world on millions of television screens across the globe in *The Green Hornet* that Hollywood filmmakers stopped treating Asian actors as cartoonish servants and sidekicks. It had been routine to hire white men to play Asian parts. The casting of John Wayne as Genghis Khan in 1956's *The Conqueror* was arguably the worst casting choice in U.S. cinematic history. Mickey Rooney's outlandish portrayal of I.Y. Yunioshi in *Breakfast at Tiffany's* (1961) was personally disturbing and offensive to Bruce Lee.

But that would soon change.

Lee as Kato dazzled audiences and changed the perception of Asian actors in the Hollywood studio system. While there would be several challenging twists and setbacks for Lee in the years ahead, he went onto become one of the world's biggest box office attractions and movie icons with hits such as *The Big Boss, Fists of Fury, Way of the Dragon,* and *Enter the Dragon,* opening the door for Asian actors all over the world in the decades to come.

Lee historian David Tadman noted Jay's syncretic impact on the legend of Bruce Lee:

When you see all these Bruce Lee documentaries, read all the Bruce Lee books, you don't really hear about Jay Sebring at all. If it wasn't for Jay, Bruce would not have become a star. He would not have entered that Hollywood circle. Because of Jay, this all happened.

A chance meeting between two innovators in seemingly unrelated fields led to an enduring friendship. A casual conversation between a stylist and his client produced a profound and history-making shift in movie casting and production. But, for people like Jay and Bruce who were made to be great, to be outstanding, these moments were anything but accidental.

CHAPTER 15
THE GO-GO GENERATION

On November 22, 1963, President John F. Kennedy was assassinated in Dallas, Texas, by Lee Harvey Oswald. The entire country was in shock and practically stopped in its tracks while the nation mourned the loss of their leader.

Later that evening, an enterprising L.A. restaurateur made a miscalculation that would cost him a star performer. The events of that day were harbingers of a great cultural shift that would bid farewell to the staid era of the Eisenhower fifties faster than the shimmy of a go-go dancer's hips.

Bill Gazzarri owned an Italian restaurant on La Cienega near Beverly Boulevard that featured family recipes, a piano bar, and a small dance stage. Gazzarri was a self-styled tough guy who smoked cigars, dressed like a Chicago gangster, and worshipped Frank Sinatra. He was all about image but was also tight-fisted.

At the time, Johnny Rivers was the house entertainment, and he was building a loyal following with his mix of South Louisiana-style blues, rock 'n' roll, and blue-eyed soul. Rivers' burst of success happened quite by accident. A week into his residency at Gazzarri's, actress Natalie Wood and an entourage took to the dance floor while the paparazzi snapped away. The photos were circulated to many national and trade publications and, according to Rivers, Gazzarri's was practically minting money.

"The night after that, you couldn't get near our door. It was just jam-packed," Rivers said. "People were lined up and down the street, trying to get in there; you know how it goes in Hollywood."

But after the JFK assassination, Rivers was reeling. Naturally, he thought Gazzarri would follow suit out of respect for the fallen president and informed him that he wasn't coming in that night.

"Well, what do you mean?" asked Gazzarri. "We're open."

"Nobody's open tonight!" Rivers countered. Gazzarri didn't budge.

Rivers went home to Baton Rouge for Christmas and never returned to Gazzarri's. Years later, Rivers reflected: "Bill wanting me to work the night Kennedy got assassinated made my mind up to take the new deal, so basically I did and that's how it came about."

The new deal was an offer from Chicago native Elmer Valentine —rumored to be a bagman for Al Capone—who had relocated to the West Coast and joined a handful of partners to open PJ's on Santa Monica and Crescent Heights. The restaurant and nightclub were situated across the street from Fred Segal's up-and-coming clothing store.

Segal reflects, "All those guys that owned PJ's sent me people all the time when I was starting out. I wish Elmer was still alive. He was my customer. He supported me unbelievably and he was one of the great supporters of Jay."

Valentine named the place after his favorite New York City bar, PJ Clarke's, located in Manhattan's midtown eastside. This Los Angeles venue at 8151 Santa Monica Boulevard is where Trini Lopez recorded two live albums for Reprise Records, which included his 1963 cover of Pete Seger's "If I Had a Hammer." The single sold four million copies and launched the entertainer's career. It also put PJ's on the cultural map.

His timing was fortuitous. By the end of the 1950s, Hollywood's original Golden Age was circling the drain and plunging downward—or dropping like flies. Tinseltown's playgrounds, nightclubs, and watering holes that had offered the type of nightlife where Jay thrived had begun to change. A younger, hipper crowd was emerging, and those venues had set their sights on catering to teens and young adults with very different tastes. Glamourous watering holes, nightspots, and supper clubs like Ciro's, the Mocambo, Cocoanut Grove, and Cafe Trocadero had become passé almost overnight.

Somewhere in the early to mid-1960s, glamour was traded in for a grittier, mod aesthetic. Teens and young adults were getting wilder and less refined. Men's hair was getting longer, and women's skirts were getting shorter. Clothes were getting tighter. Marijuana replaced booze as the intoxicant of choice, and the sexual revolution —thanks to the over the counter offering of The Pill—meant marriage was no longer a rigid prerequisite for having sex. Nancy Sinatra observed:

> The sixties were an interesting time, I think primarily because of The Pill. The Pill came along and suddenly we were free. We could take a contraceptive pill orally and go out and have a great time and not worry about getting pregnant. So, it really freed up the women and I think probably the men as well.

The new Sunset Strip crowd ditched convention and anything they deemed inauthentic. They wanted something all their own.... something that had never existed. And Elmer Valentine—a recently divorced man on the precipice of middle age—knew exactly what to give them.

Valentine's cosmopolitan exposure from his tours in the military and rubbing elbows with Chicago's social elite (including knowledge of underworld dealings) made the entrepreneur an adroit mover and shaker in Los Angeles. He saw opportunity where others saw empty buildings. His next venue promised to give this new generation something fresh, something they'd never seen before.

The "guy who looked like all seven dwarfs" (according to actor Jack Nicholson) spent the summer of '63 in Europe and returned home ready to burst onto the scene with something new. On that majestic trip, he had ogled their women (and most likely bedded a few), feasted on rich food during lavish dinners, and scoped out Europe's emerging mod club scene. What he saw and experienced invigorated him.

Valentine had just sold his interest in PJ's and was looking for a new nightclub concept to bring back to Los Angeles. He found it when he stumbled on Paul Pacine's Le Whisky à Gogo, the hottest club in Paris. It was a simple concept, but the action was off the chain: the deejay spun records while mini-skirted young women danced the night away and men sprang for alcohol.... lots of it. The locals called it a "discothèque."

"So, I came back to Los Angeles, and I wanted to open a discotheque," Valentine said. "I wanted that badly. 'Cause I saw what was happening—the frenzy and the people and the lines."

When Valentine explained to Rivers[1] that he and his partners were ready to take over a dying establishment at 8901 Sunset Boulevard called The Party[2] and turn it into an American discotheque called The Whisky a Go Go,[3] Rivers said that was all well and good, but wondered what that had to do with him.

"I'd like to sign you for a year and have people play records in between your sets so people can keep dancing," Valentine explained.

---

1. Rivers was also a loyal client of Jay's whose hair was also cut by SEBRING stylist Art Windsor.
2. No small wonder it was dying. The Party was a former bank building.
3. The Whisky had to spell its name without the 'e' because Los Angeles city zoning laws prohibited clubs to be named after a spirit or anything or product that promoted alcohol.

In addition, he added his special touch to the place: a female deejay named Patty Brockhurst who played records in a booth that was suspended over the right side of the stage. The former cigarette girl spun her tunes between Rivers' sets and entertained patrons by dancing; thus the idea of the go-go dancer was born. Not long after, Valentine added a couple of large glass-walled cages affixed above the other side of the stage where go-go dancers wearing short, fringed skirts and knee-high white boots shimmied to The Frug, The Swim, the Mashed Potato, and the Watusi.

The Whisky opened on January 15, 1964, and hosted a gala event that rivaled any major Hollywood movie premiere, featuring a red carpet, klieg lights, and a bevy of Hollywood stars in attendance. Cary Grant, Gina Lollobrigida, Steve McQueen, and Jayne Mansfield were among the patrons who danced the night away. Joe Torrenueva said it was the place to be and to be seen.

> I had been to all the other clubs in Los Angeles but there was something completely different about the Whisky. It *exuded* sex appeal. A lot of times celebrities make these places and movie stars attract beautiful young women. That in turn attracted the paparazzi at the entrance to see who got out of their cars. That whole era on the Sunset Strip was electrifying.

Author and biographer Stephen Davis (*Hammer of the Gods: The Led Zeppelin Saga*) noted that Jay was Hollywood royalty perched amongst his famous friends and clients.

> Steve McQueen had his own booth. Jay Sebring had his own booth. Warren Beatty had a booth. One of the regulars, Jay Sebring, was regarded as much a celebrity as the movie stars he worked with. And he had a booth.

It became the most important rock club of the 1960s and early 1970s, hosting future Hall of Fame acts such as The Byrds, Buffalo Springfield, The Doors, Janis Joplin, Love, The Kinks, The Who, Frank Zappa and the Mothers of Invention, and Led Zeppelin.

The Whisky a Go Go became a cultural Mecca in the sixties, with an eclectic mix of celebrities, young women, pimps, drug dealers, criminals, strippers, and plenty of underground characters,[4] according to an FBI field officer investigating the club for racketeering. His May 15, 1964, report took note of Steve McQueen frequenting the place and wrote:

> This unique entertainment phenomenon continues to draw capacity crowds and features live and recorded Watutsi music and dancing.... it is probably the most popular spot on The Sunset Strip.

The club was emblematic of the new era ushered in with all the fanfare of glittering lights, fluttering fringe, and freestyling moves. And the days of refined and tailored looks, dinner clubs, and posh night spots for the rich and famous were over. This world became Jay's playground, and he was definitely one of the cool kids.

For many of the players running in those circles, the tide changed in an instant and they couldn't keep up. Their scene quickly faded once 1964 rolled around with The Beatles, long hair, go-go style, pot/psychedelics, and a new sense of freedom came sweeping in. Joe Torrenueva, who was also a musician on the Latin club circuit, said the times-were-a-changin'.

---

4. Valentine employed mob hitman Felix Anthony "Milwaukee Phil" Alderisio to help him whenever there was trouble in his club or business dealings. At one time, Alderisio was considered the most feared assassin in the underworld. Federal authorities estimate he was personally responsible for approximately ten gangland executions. He died in September 1971 of a heart attack while serving a stint in federal prison.

Everything was so much looser and freer at that time. LSD was starting to come on the scene because it was not illegal at the time. The guy who manufactured it, Owsley Stanley, I cut his hair at SEBRING. He had a ton of hash and pills, but mainly he manufactured and sold mass quantities of "Owsley Acid." He was a chemist and audio engineer, but Owsley was also the money behind the Grateful Dead. I remember one time he brought them in the shop so I could cut their hair. I'm telling you; it was a crazy time and we seemed to be at the center of it all.

While the sounds of The Beatles, The Stones, The Kinks, The Who, and the first wave of the British Invasion were making their way across the pond and through the radios of America's teens, word of Sebring's skills had reached in the other direction and piqued the interest of the Fab Four. Soon, Gordon Mullinger received a request from their famed manager.

Brian Epstein called the office and wanted to make arrangements for The Beatles to be cut at SEBRING's, and Jay was perfectly willing to do it. And then the legalities started to come in. They contacted the city, and the city wouldn't give them the permit, because the only way they would consent to do it is if Fairfax Avenue was blocked off, and they would not do it.

It might have been for the best. The Beatles (minus Paul McCartney who was most likely canoodling with actress Peggy Lipton) did manage to squeeze in a midnight trip to the Whisky where Jayne Mansfield joined them for a drink. It was a dream come true for John Lennon who had fancied the late '50s screen siren since her starring role in *The Girl Can't Help It*. Sporting a beehive hairdo and wearing a mauve cat suit on a hot August night,

Mansfield had aged considerably after cycling through the Holly-wood studio system. After a few drinks, she tugged at Lennon's hair and asked if it was real. He peered at her breasts through his Wayfarers and asked an equally fair question.

"Well, are those real?" he countered.

Mansfield, who had been out of vogue for a few years, brought with her a legion of paparazzi, who began snapping photos of the Beatles cavorting in a corner booth with the starlet. The Beatles found the scene too wild and intrusive, and left after ten minutes.[5] Despite this experience, The Whisky was quickly becoming Holly-wood's hotspot.

The 18-to-21 crowd was moving in, and anyone over thirty was washed out—everyone except the likes of Jay Sebring, Elmer Valen-tine, and Steve McQueen, who managed to navigate this transition with all the cool they brought to everything they did.

The same cultural shift was happening in Europe, according to women's hairstylist Vidal Sassoon, who was starting a women's revo-lution for hair in England at the same time.

It didn't just happen on Day One in 1960. It didn't happen that way at all. You must remember fiscally up until the Sixties; Britain was out of it. Depression of the Twenties and Thirties, the war '39 till '45. People had no houses because the bombing was so drastic. If you look at history, new ideas come out of hard times. Lethargy comes out of soft times. Energy comes out of hard times.

Jay was in a phase of his own hard times. He was still reeling

---

5. George Harrison was so enraged by the intrusion of the paparazzi that he tossed a drink at Robert Flora, a photographer with United Press International. Harrison later wrote to his parents that he had to fight his way to the table with the assistance of Mal Evans and a couple of Los Angeles County sheriffs. Then they had to fight their way back to their car.

from one of the most difficult personal chapters in his life: the ending of his marriage with Cami. But changing times and a recent invention would provide a slow but soothing balm for Jay during his recovery, even if just a distraction.

Gordon Mullinger shared a memory of this time in Jay's life.

We threw a big cocktail party that Jay came to which thrilled the living daylights out of me. He was out on our balcony. There were women across the way that were out on their balcony. And the next thing I knew, I looked over there and there was Jay with the other women on the other balcony.

Larry Geller said Jay was definitely a ladies' man and remembers a party at the Hollywood Hills home of Bernie Roberts, a SEBRING stylist.

Jay was a stud, man. Everyone knew that. Definitely a ladies' man. No question. Now, remember this is the Sixties. We were at a party in the Hollywood Hills. Jay and I wanted to smoke a joint, so we walked into the bathroom and there were a couple girls there. We took out the joint and started smoking it and one of the girls said, "You guys really want to party?" Jay said, "Party?" In just moments, Jay and his new friend began undressing.... yeah, he was a ladies' man. Absolutely. Not ashamed of it either.

Actor Max Baer, Jr. was a SEBRING client who knew Jay socially and would run into him at various L.A.-area nightclubs. Even though he didn't know Jay all that well on a personal level, he certainly knew of his reputation as a ladies' man.

He was jumping everything he could. But that was no different than anybody else our age. If you weren't married, or if you were married, I guess. You know, it goes to your head. Any kind of fame goes to your head. It doesn't matter what it is. Whether you're a singer or a dancer or an athlete, or a politician. Fame breeds strange but similar bedfellows. Anytime you achieve fame, it's easier to get laid. You haven't changed, but it's easier to get a yes on the phone for a date even if you don't know the girl. But they know who you are.

Jay was finding his social sea-legs again and, in the process, stumbled on a branch of his industry he never imagined would be in demand.

Longtime friend and SEBRING client Peter Knecht recalled when female "personal grooming" was yet to be a trend and Jay played a part in another kind of hair revolution.

There was a time when I was dating this gorgeous blonde and you know in those days, the girls weren't trimming their private areas like they do these days, right? So, I called up Jay and I said, "Jay, I need a favor." And he says, "What is it?" I said, "I'll come over, I don't want to talk about it over the phone." So, I came over and I introduced him to this beautiful blonde. And I said, "Jay, I need you to trim her beaver and make it look good.... like you do, like you know how." He looks at me and he says, "What are friends for? Right?" And that's how it was. We smoked a joint, trimmed the beaver, and we were on our way. Those were the sixties, man.

"The Player" era in Jay's life was a transition out of one love and into another great love of his life. Soon, things in Jay's life would change in ways no one could see coming.

CHAPTER 16
EXQUISITE BEAUTY

The allure of post-World War II Los Angeles was contagious, and the bright and shiny city attracted a massive influx of seekers. Initially, the aeronautical and military industrial complexes—boosted by the GI Bill—brought tens of thousands of families to Southern California for its spacious track homes in lush suburbs. Thanks to Detroit's automobile boom, the spider web of freeway arteries made the urban sprawl accessible.

In 1962, one such family, Lieutenant Colonel Paul "PJ" Tate, his wife Gwendolyn (later known as Doris to the public), and their three daughters—Sharon, Debra, and Patricia—moved to their newly built home in scenic seaside Rancho Palos Verdes.

Like so many dreamers who gravitate toward the promise of California, and more specifically the glistening hope of Hollywood, the Tate's eldest daughter had a grander scheme with stars in her eyes.

Sharon Tate was born on January 24, 1943, in Dallas, Texas, and at only six months of age she became a pageant contestant and was awarded "Miss Tiny Tot of Dallas." However, those awards and accolades did not insulate her from some of the built-in hardships that came with being a military brat. The family moved frequently, changing cities and schools, making it difficult for Sharon to maintain friendships and a grounded environment.

Colonel Tate's assignments required his family to shuffle throughout Texas, Washington, and ultimately to Vicenza, Italy, where Sharon graduated from Vicenza American High School in 1961. In addition to her extraordinary beauty, Sharon refined her gift for making great, lasting impressions on everyone she met. She exuded kindness, class, and humility, creating a presence that would serve her well as she pursued a career in entertainment.

Her first film experience was on *The Pat Boone Chevy Showroom* in 1959 in Venice, Italy. Boone recalled of that first encounter with the stunning young lady:

> We took my show to Italy, France, and to Austria to do half-hour musical shows. And so, we started in Venice and while we were filming for two weeks in Venice, there was a young girl who was standing on the sidewalk watching us in our gondola doing music, you know, on the sidewalks and wherever we were performing in San Marcos Square with all the pigeons flying everywhere and landing on us. And this girl was there watching, and my wife Shirley was talking with her for quite a while. This young girl, a beautiful, young seventeen-year-old kid from a military family had stars in her eyes. She and Shirley got very talkative and friendly. She hoped to be an actress.

Sharon's mother captured the sequence in San Marcos Square with the family's eight-millimeter camera. Boone continues, "I met her, and we even included her in a scene in one of my musical numbers in which I was out there, pigeons everywhere, and she was feeding the pigeons in the middle of the song. As we got friendly and when we weren't shooting, she told me about her ambition to come to Hollywood and become an actress."

The father of four young girls at the time, Boone was cautious in his advice to the ambitious teenager:

> I suggested there was a place—Chateau Marmont—where a lot of actors and actresses would hobnob, and if she got a good acting coach, she might get a break. But be on your guard and don't sell yourself for this dream which may never happen because no matter how talented you may be, it may never happen, and you'll ruin your life if this is what you're hooking it on. But I wasn't that final. I was telling her that career can be too fickle and just be careful.

Despite Boone's cautionary advice, the determined teenager became even more encouraged and driven after her "chance encounter" with the legendary crooner, which resulted in Sharon's very first credit captured on film.

A few years later, while still in Italy, Sharon had the opportunity to work as an extra in *Barabbas* (1961) starring Anthony Quinn and Jack Palance. And later, she was in *Hemingway's Adventures of a Young Man* (1962) starring Richard Beymer and Paul Newman. Beymer, who played the film's lead role, was so impressed with Sharon's attitude and beauty, he encouraged the worldly young woman to pursue a career in Hollywood and connected her with his talent agent Hal Gefsky. Beymer and Tate also dated briefly.

However, before that could happen, she had to make her way to Hollywood. She spent most of her waking hours devising ways to head to the States to capitalize on her first credit, including forgoing her college education.

"College isn't going to help me become a better actress," Sharon blithely told her parents. The comment didn't go over well with them. They went back and forth over this terrain until the military intervened. Not long after the worldwide release of these films, Paul Tate was assigned to Fort MacArthur in San Pedro, California, just south of Los Angeles. It was decided that Sharon would head to Los Angeles before the family got settled in the U.S., and immediately signed with Gefsky, who enrolled her in several acting and voice classes. To be in the center of the action, the aspiring actress moved to an apartment in West Hollywood, where she met actress Sheilah Wells who had roles in *Dr. Kildare*, *The Green Hornet* (and later *The Blues Brothers*). Wells said of their first meeting:

> I came to Los Angeles in the early '60s. I was an actress under contract with Universal. We were introduced by Hal Gefsky who was my agent and Sharon's agent. And what was funny is that she said, "Well, I'm getting ready to move. Where do you live?" And I said, "I'm at 1148 N. Clark." And she said, "Oh my gosh, I live right next door." So, we went back to my apartment, and she said, "Oh, this is so nice.... uh, maybe I can just move in here?" And that's how it started all in one day.

Wells found Sharon to be a darling spirit, a kind and good, dear friend.

"Everyone adored her, you never heard a bad word about her," Wells said. "There was a naïveté about her, and I don't think she ever realized her beauty."

Even though Gwen and her daughter Sharon were only separated for a few months, Gwen said in the 2012 book *Restless Souls: The Sharon Tate Family's Account of Stardom, the Manson Murders, and a Crusade for Justice* by Alisa Statman and Brie Tate that she felt "fragmented without her [Sharon]" and suffered from "a mountain of anxiety." She began seeing a psychologist and confessed that because Sharon was so far away, she was worried she might get hurt and wouldn't be able to get to her fast enough to help.

"Mrs. Tate, what do you think is going to happen to your daughter?" the therapist asked.

"I'm not sure," Gwen replied. "I just have a horrible feeling she will be attacked or maybe even murdered."

The psychologist smiled, politely dismissed the notion, and asked Gwen what she thought the chances were of her daughtered being murdered. Gwen said she had no clue.

"Try a million to one," he said. "Now, you give that statistic some thought, and I think you'll see how irrational your fears are."

Gwen was prescribed sleeping pills and was diagnosed with acute separation anxiety disorder. While the pills and the diagnosis were helpful, those nagging feelings that something might happen to Sharon never dissipated, even when the family reunited again in California.

After a year in Los Angeles, Sharon had not landed any speaking role credits until she finally got her first break. During a screen test for the CBS sitcom *Petticoat Junction*, Sharon caught the eye of Filmways producer Martin Ransohoff. Actor Max Baer Jr., who played Jethro on *The Beverly Hillbillies*, remembers meeting her at this time.

"I met Sharon over on the lot at General Service Studio where they were testing for *Petticoat Junction*," he said. "Sharon was always sweet."

Sharon was cast as Janet Trego, Miss Hathaway's assistant, on *The Beverly Hillbillies*. The network liked Sharon so much that she appeared in fourteen episodes, culminating in "The Clampetts vs. Automation" on May 12, 1965.

Like many upstarts in the industry, Sharon was getting an education on the set, learning the craft and valuable life lessons. She was also working off the set, meeting movers and shakers, and attending industry parties and awards shows.

Sharon met actor Philippe Forquet, the son of a wealthy French aristocrat. As a member of the celebrated Théâtre Mouffetard in Paris, France, Forquet was discovered by American director Robert Parrish in 1962 who gave him a key role in the film *In the French Style*, which co-starred Jean Seberg and Stanley Baker.

While filming *Take Her She's Mine*, Forquet met and fell in love with Sharon and her exquisite beauty. Their relationship turned serious quickly and their union made the rounds in the industry trades. By Christmas 1963, the two were engaged, but it unraveled after a few months. Behind the Tinseltown PR machine, the relationship was tumultuous, and rumors of cheating and abuse abounded. According to Sharon's mother, their relationship ended after one of Forquet's tirades put her in the hospital emergency room with two broken ribs. After Sharon's death, Forquet claimed she had been the aggressor in the relationship and cut him in the chest with a wine bottle. Regardless, the relationship ended abruptly when Paul Tate threatened him within an inch of his life —and with deportation—should he come near Sharon again. Their parting cleared the way for a seminal meeting between Sharon Tate and Jay Sebring. And their lives would irrevocably be changed.

Much has been written about Jay Sebring and Sharon Tate, but how they crossed paths remains an enigma. The details of their fated first encounter vary, but the result was a bond—romantic, platonic, or otherwise—that would remain unbreakable to the end.

Larry Geller recalled a night when he, stylist Gene Shacove, and Jay had dinner at the Luau in Beverly Hills after trading haircuts. "Gene says, 'Jay, a new starlet has come to town that is the most beautiful looking person I've ever seen in my life. Her name is Sharon Tate. You won't believe her.'"

Elmer Valentine opened The Whisky a Go Go at roughly the same time Sharon moved in with Sheila Wells at the apartment on Clark Street, a two-minute walk from what was rapidly becoming the hottest spot on the Sunset Strip.

"We lived right up the street from The Whisky. Oh, my goodness, we could hear the music on some evenings," Wells said. "We knew Elmer Valentine, so it was pretty easy for us to get in and everything."

The same was true for Jay who applied his finishing touches to Johnny Rivers' hair in the dressing room before Rivers took center stage, flanked by go-go dancers on raised platforms. There have been many reports that Jay and Sharon met at a party Elmer hosted at the Whisky one weekend in November 1964.

Hollywood publicist Joe Hyams wrote in his 1973 memoir, *Mislaid in Hollywood*, that he helped put the two together. He wrote:

> Jay Sebring looked questioningly at my reflection in the mirror as he stood behind me clipping my hair. "Do you know a girl named Sharon?" "What's her last name?" "I don't know. I saw her at a screening last night and she gave me a come-on.... I want to meet her. She's something special."

Hyams said he liked Jay and took note that he drove a black Lincoln Continental with a telephone just like his idol, Frank Sinatra.

> Although he charged $15 to $500, depending on the amount of traveling involved, he worked on me for free because I sometimes wrote about him and the goings-on at his shop. We were friends and frequently talked about girls while he worked on my hair. "What was the name of the film you saw?" I asked him. "Damned if I can remember. I saw her when I came into the screening, and I blanked for the rest of the evening. But we were at Paramount Studios, and I think she's under contract there." I picked up Jay's red telephone and called a publicist at Paramount. He told me

producer Martin Ransohoff had a girl named Sharon Tate under personal contract.

Hyams cupped his hand over the telephone and repeated the information to Jay. He nodded. "'Does he know anything about her?' I repeated the question. 'She lives with a French actor, I think,' the publicist said."

Jay nodded as Hyams relayed the information.

"'It figures that someone that beautiful would already be taken," Jay said. "But is there any way you can arrange for me to meet her? She doesn't know it yet, but she and I are going to have a common destiny.'"

Two days later, Hyams arranged a luncheon meeting with Sharon at Frascati, a Belgian restaurant on the Sunset Strip. Hyams recalled of that meal:

She was as beautiful as Jay described. "The studio told me I wasn't ready for publicity yet," she said after ordering a diet lunch of a hamburger patty with cottage cheese and peaches. "Who told you about me?"

Hyams told her his friend had seen her at a screening and described her as the most beautiful woman he had ever seen.

"And who is your flattering friend?" Sharon asked.

He told her it was Jay Sebring.

"Is he kind of small and slight and very sexy looking?" she asked with a smile.

Hyams confirmed that was Jay. An hour later, Jay appeared at the table—just as the two men had planned. After brief introductions, Hyams left the two alone. He assumed all went well. When he visited Jay a few weeks later at his Easton residence, he looked at the top of the stairs and spotted Sharon in a negligee, "looking radiant as sunshine."

She walked down the stairs and then gave Hyams a kiss on the cheek.

"Thank you, Cupid," she said in a sweet voice.

Sheilah Wells shared Sharon Tate's perspective on their meeting:

Sharon said, "Oh I've met someone I really, really like." "Oh really?" "Yes, his name is Jay. Jay Sebring." And I said, "Jay Sebring.... I know that name." [Sharon said,] "You know, he's the hairdresser, the hair guy." And I went, "Oh. Hmmm, that's interesting." At that time there weren't men hairdressers or stylists, or whatever they were called. So, it was unusual, and I was really looking forward to meeting him. You could tell they were in love and truly adored one another. That was very evident. They laughed a lot.

When Jay bonded with something or someone, it was deep and most often lifelong. Friend and SEBRING cutter Sal Orifice recalls learning of Jay's new love in a conversation with his former boss:

"It's been six months since Cami and I split up.... I met someone. She's something else. Beautiful," Jay revealed.

"You smitten, man?" Sal quizzed.

"Smitten? Maybe. But I still think of Cami."

"What's her name?"

"Who?"

"Your new love."

"Sharon Tate."

Even as the romance between Jay and Sharon was heating up, Jay and Cami were still very close and spiritually bonded. They remained so throughout his life despite their separation.

Stuart Whitman, Jay's friend and neighbor, remembers Jay and Sharon's early days as a blissful, happy, and inspiring couple.

A girlfriend of mine was living with me at the time, Wende Wagner. She brought up Sharon Tate and Jay happened to be there, which was quite often. And there was this budding romance that took place. It was like love at first sight. It was a wonderful thing to see right in front of my eyes these two people just getting along so well. And both were really handsome, both of them, yeah.... very playful, giggling all the time. It was quite special.

Soon Sharon would be spending most of her time with Jay at his Fairfax shop and at his Benedict Canyon home. Dominick Dunne recalled seeing Sharon at the shop while getting his hair cut.

Sharon and Jay were madly, madly in love with each other. There's no doubt about it. And often when I'd have my hair cut, she would just sit there on a chair with this beautiful, beautiful golden hair. She was like a Botticelli. I mean, she was that beautiful. So, we'd have good, fun talks during the haircut time.

Gordon Mullinger was also crazy about the new woman in Jay's life and was effusive in his praise of her.

I loved Sharon. Absolutely loved Sharon. Sharon was honest, forthright, pulled no punches. She would come into my office and sit and talk with me every day. She would confide in me. She was rigorously honest. To a point that some people, like columnists, would get upset with her when she would come out and be very forthright with an answer such as "Yes, Jay and I are living together. Why? What has that got to do with anything?" Things like that.

Sharon found herself at the epicenter of one of the most exclusive locations on the planet with a daily parade of Hollywood's most influential power players and nearly every film and recording artist seeking the talents of her new beau. Jay was a star among stars and had a following of his own.

Sheila Wells said, "I have a friend Betty who was raised in Los Angeles. She told me, 'Oh we used to go over and stand outside his shop.' She went to Fairfax High School. And I said, 'Oh, so you could see all the movie stars?' And she said, 'No, no. We were waiting for Jay.' So, he had his fan club. His own groupies."

Like so many who knew Jay, Sharon was taken with Jay's success, his inimitable style—the clothes he wore, the cars he drove, where he vacationed, and the home where he resided. Sheila Wells remembered:

> He always dressed so beautifully. Sharon liked that 'cause she could wear his clothes. And he was always beautifully dressed, that struck me. Sharon loved to drive and I remember her taking me to the airport in Jay's Cobra. We were going ninety miles an hour and I still missed the plane. I'll never forget that. Jay's house was sort of Tudor architecture with different nook and cranny rooms. It was fun, and of course the story that went with it—Paul Bern and Jean Harlow. You went in there going, "Oh my God, this history." It was a little bit creepy but very intriguing. Sharon loved that part. I mean this is part of Hollywood history and Jean Harlow was here.

Kurt Zacho, who grew up next to Jay on Easton Drive, remembers Sharon visiting the house and what she wore that day:

> She had on an overcoat. It was a rainy day. I guess she had thrown on the overcoat to go to an interview and was going to pick up her dress at the dry cleaners on the way, but the

dress wasn't cleaned yet. She was running late so she had to go to the audition with just the coat on. When she came back, they delivered a script here for her. My mother invited her in and told her to have a seat and gave her a drink and told her repeatedly to take her coat off and make herself comfortable. Sharon described the situation at the dry cleaners and that she wasn't wearing much underneath her coat, so she wasn't going to take it off. She was like a goddess. I just remember very beautiful big eyes and blond hair. She was pretty much the first person that got me excited, I guess as a male in my young age.

The Tate family gathered up at the Easton residence for special occasions. Sharon's mom, Gwen, was a frequent visitor with her sisters Patricia and Debra in tow, including times when the couple was away working.

Jay and Sharon were glued together as much as possible, spending time with her family in Palos Verdes, his family in Las Vegas, on film sets, traveling to Italy and Hawaii, and around Los Angeles. Friends and family regarded the couple as a perfect match. Sharon's sister Debra said Jay was heavily scrutinized by her parents, but he passed with flying colors.

He was very charming and dissuaded any anticipation of failure. Jay did that with such style and grace. They loved him. He won them over in about, oh, I would say the first eight minutes upon meeting them.

Peggy DiMaria recalled a time in the sixties when Jay and Sharon came to Las Vegas to visit with her and her new husband, Tony. The newlyweds had recently moved to Las Vegas from Detroit to work with Tony's brother at Salon Di Pompeii in Caesar's Palace but were 200 hours short of Nevada state requirements.

Struggling, Peggy worked as a telephone operator at the La Concha Hotel and Tony worked in room service at The Dunes Hotel. She shared:

> I was expecting at the time with Anthony and the next day Sharon brought me a box with a bow. It was a blue pullover with kind of green circles with a hood on it, but very light weight. It was like a poncho, but it was great for me while I was pregnant. She was a very sweet, kind person. She was into her career and everything, but she had taken the time to think about what she felt would be a little nicer for me to have since I was expecting.

Gwen and Paul Tate were impressed with Jay's character, military background, and success. Sharon's parents viewed him as a perfect match for their eldest daughter, acknowledged Debra Tate.

> Jay was an absolute invite into the family on all levels. Mom and Dad saw him as potential son-in-law material as well as a great individual, promising personality with an outrageous potential for extreme success. Not just casual success, extreme success. So, Jay was a very coveted, precious entity in our household.

In early 1965, Jay met privately with Paul Tate for his approval to ask for his daughter's hand in marriage. The couple soon became engaged and lived together like a married couple. On May 1, 1965, Jay co-signed for Sharon's new green 1965 Buick Riviera at Executive Car Leasing. Sharon's film and residual checks from the Screen Actors Guild were sent to Jay's home and business addresses as well as her bills from the car dealership, and from wig, makeup, and clothing stores, including Fred Segal. Segal recalled:

When Sharon would come in with Jay, I'd do with her like I did with many gals, especially the knockouts. So, I pulled the jeans down as far as I could get 'em. And then I'd have to push the hip in so they could zip 'em. It fit everybody so tight because the indigo denim fabric stretches when you wear it. It's gotta be fitted tight. So, I'd push in the hip and Jay would zip 'em up. Then I had a tailor on the premises that did the bottoms on the jeans.

Jay also played a role in shaping Sharon's acting career. He didn't agree with the strategy and overall vision of Sharon's agent, Hal Gefsky. For instance, he questioned why he would agree to Sharon being veiled under a dark cropped wig on a sitcom that concealed all she had to offer. Jay knew Sharon's success would not come from being a character actress, but in being herself. He understood Gefsky's and Ransohoff's approach—classes and incognito small TV parts—but he felt they had a formulaic mindset that was limiting to the unique beauty. Jay was sure Sharon would best be received by audiences cinematically where her presence could shine.

Jay also knew how crucial a top-notch agent is for effectively opening doors and packaging deals beyond co-starring roles in television sitcoms. On February 1, 1965, Jay set up a meeting with friend and client Stan Kamen, a powerhouse agent at the William Morris Agency. In order to not burn bridges while getting her out of the contract with Gefsky, they agreed to share commission with him on all future projects Kamen booked for her.

A few months later, Jay and Sharon flew to Hawaii to join the Valentine and McQueen families to celebrate Easter weekend. Elmer Valentine's daughter Kimberly recalled them renting a series of cottages. Judy Garland was also there with her lover, Mark Herron, and her daughter, Lorna Luft. Kimberly Valentine said that trip included spending some special time with Jay.

We were all on a boat and Jay was teaching me games like tic-tac-toe and other games the whole time on the boat. Sharon seemed irritated that Jay was spending his time on the boat teaching me games.

On the island, the kids had an early bedtime and slept in a separate room while the adults partied into the night, said Kimberly Valentine.

One night we saw a bunch of smoke coming from one of the cottages. We told our parents, and they ran over to try and put the fire out and at one point there was an explosion. And after the fire department came out and put the fire out, I remember Steve saying, "Fuck, fuck! Fuck me!" He described seeing numerous jugs of water in Garland's house and he threw one of them on the fire, but it exploded because it was actually 100-proof vodka. We were staying in a huge house, so Judy Garland and her family stayed with us overnight till their house was cleaned up.

The Honolulu Advertiser documented the fire on April 15, 1965, with an article titled "Judy Fights Fire with Tumbler." Despite the chaos, the festivities continued through the weekend.

In 1964, producer Martin Ransohoff acquired the rights to adapt Robin Estridge's book *Day of the Arrow* for film in conjunction with MGM. Shortly before filming began on September 13, 1965, the title was changed to *Eye of the Devil,* starring David Niven, Deborah Kerr, Donald Pleasance, and Sharon Tate. Production of the occult thriller was plagued early on by mishaps and postponements. The film's original lead actress, Kim Novak, had to be re-cast after she was thrown from a horse, injuring her back. Filming was halted again when director J. Lee Thompson (*The Guns of Navarone*) fell ill.

Jay visited Sharon in Europe, and the couple took advantage of the filming delays to travel around Sharon's old stomping grounds in Italy. For a novice film actress working on the epic set with a highly esteemed veteran cast, one would expect the task to feel daunting, but Sharon rose to the challenge and was embraced by the cast. Niven was particularly fond of Sharon, and the two became fast friends. The star gave Sharon a Yorkie named Guinness —the first of several Yorkies in her life. They would become her favorite breed.

Before Sharon's return to Los Angeles for the holidays, Jay had Sharon's Buick painted and had a stereo installed in the car. The couple spent Christmas and New Year's at their Easton home with the Tates and Sharon's new member of the family, Guinness. Photos captured that day show Jay and Sharon snuggling on the sofa, Jay hugging Guinness at his hidden bar, and Sharon and Gwen at the Christmas tree with canines in tow. The holidays were festive and a welcomed break, but perhaps briefer than the couple and her family would have liked.

Soon Sharon returned to England to resume filming *Eye of the Devil*. The film wrapped in early 1966 and was eventually released in the United States on December 6, 1967, to lukewarm reviews. It was a box-office failure. The film did little to boost Sharon's career as a *New York Times* critic characterized Sharon's performance as "chillingly beautiful, but expressionless."

The couple returned to their normal routine at Easton, with barbeques at the Tate residence and occasional excursions to Las Vegas for work and play. Jay's brother-in-law, Tony DiMaria, remembered a show they took in at the Sands featuring Sammy Davis, Jr. He remembered that night at the glamorous hotel and casino in vivid detail.

Jay had just come back to our table after doing Sammy's hair. George Peppard was there, and he came running over to Jay. Jay introduced us all. It was very exciting for us because we were just newly married, and he was one of the first celebrities we ever met.

Debra Tate said Sharon took several Vegas runs with Jay for pleasure and to hang out with his sister, Peggy and her husband Tony DiMaria, who were now living there.

Sharon went and met with the family and the comment was that they were lovely people and that she was welcomed into his family's household as Jay was into our household. Jay and Sharon were very well suited for each other. Jay was a little apprehensive [about marrying her] because of a divorce he had gone through. He wasn't quite ready to commit at that point in time and Sharon was.

Still, according to Stuart Whitman, their fate together "looked like it was written in stone. And then I kinda kicked myself that I ever gave Sharon Victor Lownes' telephone number." As fate would have it, this decision began a series of events that led to a truly unforeseeable outcome.

"T.J." (Jay) Kummer's personal cosmetology book from 1956, which contains his notes and philosophies on cutting men's hair. *Courtesy of Jay Sebring Collections/The DiMaria Family.*

An early ad touting "Jay" Kummer, announcing his arrival at Shelley Hair Styles in the Crenshaw section of Los Angeles. *Courtesy of Jay Sebring Collections/The DiMaria Family.*

DEC 60 •

Jay expanding his salon with the help of friend and fellow stylist
Art Windsor inside the Fairfax shop, December 1960. *Courtesy of
Jay Sebring Collections/The DiMaria Family.*

DEC 60 •

Jay sharing a meal with friends Art Windsor (sitting) and Buddy Markell (standing) and an unidentified female in Los Angeles, December 1960, right as his salon was starting to take off. *Courtesy of Jay Sebring Collections/The DiMaria Family.*

Exterior photo of SEBRING Men's Hair Design, Jay's iconic salon on Fairfax Avenue in Los Angeles. *Courtesy of Jay Sebring Collections/The DiMaria Family.*

Through the introduction of Vic Damone and Sands Hotel
President Jack Entratter to Frank Sinatra and the Rat Pack, Jay
first struck it big in Las Vegas before finding success Hollywood.
Jay cut every member's hair except for Dean Martin.

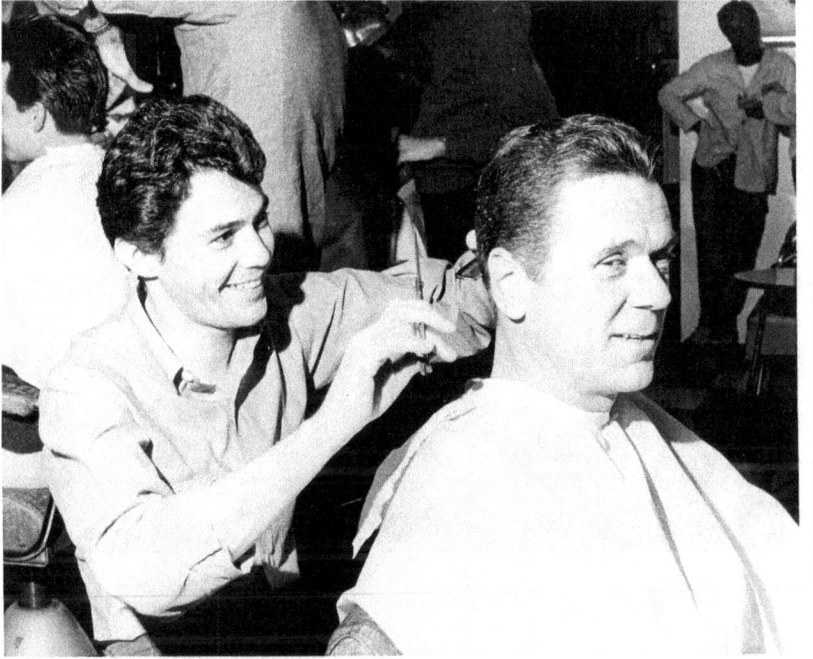

A smiling Jackie Cooper getting his hair cut and styled by Jay Sebring in his Fairfax shop, which was teaming with celebrities by 1961. *Courtesy of Jay Sebring Collections/The DiMaria Family.*

Singer/entertainer Bobby Darin was not only a client but a close friend of Jay's. Cami Sebring recalled that Darin was a salon fixture. "Every time he came to have Jay cut his hair, he would come and sit on the stairs. And I would come and sit with him," she said. "He said growing up he used to sit on the stairs and dream about his future, 'It reminds me of when I was a kid.' So this was his favorite place to sit when he would wait for Jay. And sometimes you had to wait for Jay a long time." *Courtesy of Jay Sebring Collections/The DiMaria Family.*

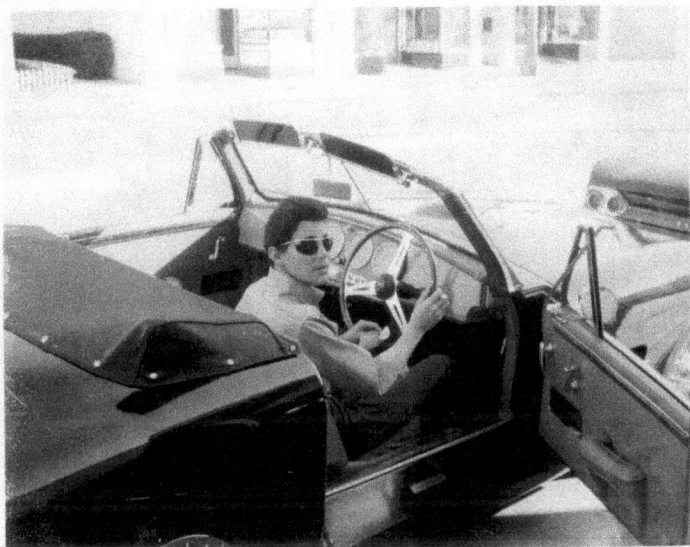

Jay's newfound success allowed him to indulge in his love of driving and owning high end sports cars. In this photo he's driving an Aston Martin DB2. *Courtesy of Jay Sebring Collections/The DiMaria Family.*

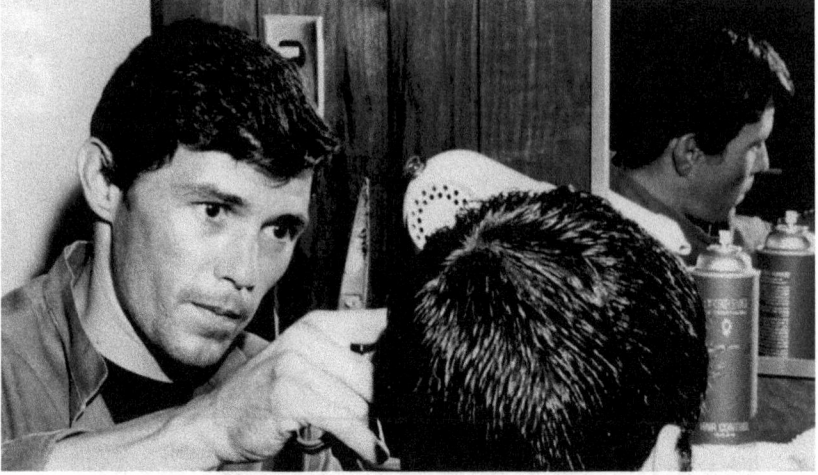

With his trademark Filipino shears, Jay goes to work on singer Johnny Rivers' hair. His clientele wasn't limited to Hollywood stars but included music entertainers, captains of industry, and high-end businessmen. *Courtesy of Jay Sebring Collections.*

A star among stars, Jay Sebring's influence transcended a haircut. Steve McQueen consults with Jay, his Hollywood style mentor, on the set of *Bullitt*. The actor valued Jay as his "best friend" according to a death bed interview. Sebring was responsible for giving "The King of Cool" his trademark look— short, sharp, layered, and beautifully cut to the shape of McQueen's Roman-shaped head.

Jay with his SEBRING staff at the Fairfax salon, circa 1962. Word of Jay's magic was spreading nationally after features in *TIME* magazine and other prestigious publications. His one-station salon quickly expanded to almost a dozen chairs. *Courtesy of Jay Sebring Collections/The DiMaria Family.*

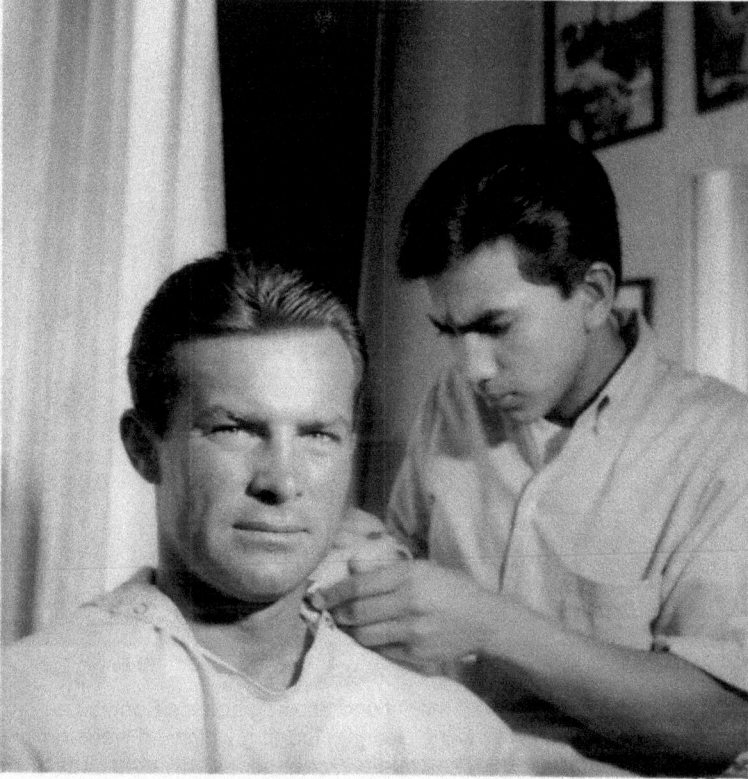

SEBRING protégé Joe Torrenueva cutting the hair of actor Robert Conrad in the mid-1960s. Sebring and Torrenueva were also responsible for legislation for California salons going unisex. It was another revolutionary feather in Jay's cap that would ultimately manifest itself in permanent global implications. *Courtesy of Jay Sebring Collections.*

A chance encounter with model and aspiring actress Bonnie Lee Marple (later known as Cami Sebring) led to a whirlwind wedding on October 10, 1960. The couple exchanged vows in the Little Church of the West in front of entertainer and best man, Vic Damone, and matron of honor Janet March. The couple split in 1963 and finally divorced in 1965. They remained close until Jay's untimely death. *Courtesy of Jay Sebring Collections/The DiMaria Family.*

Bernard Kummer looks proudly at the SEBRING....salon sign while Peg (arms crossed) and Cami stand in the background with mutual admiration to allow Bernard to have his moment. *Courtesy of Jay Sebring Collections/The DiMaria Family.*

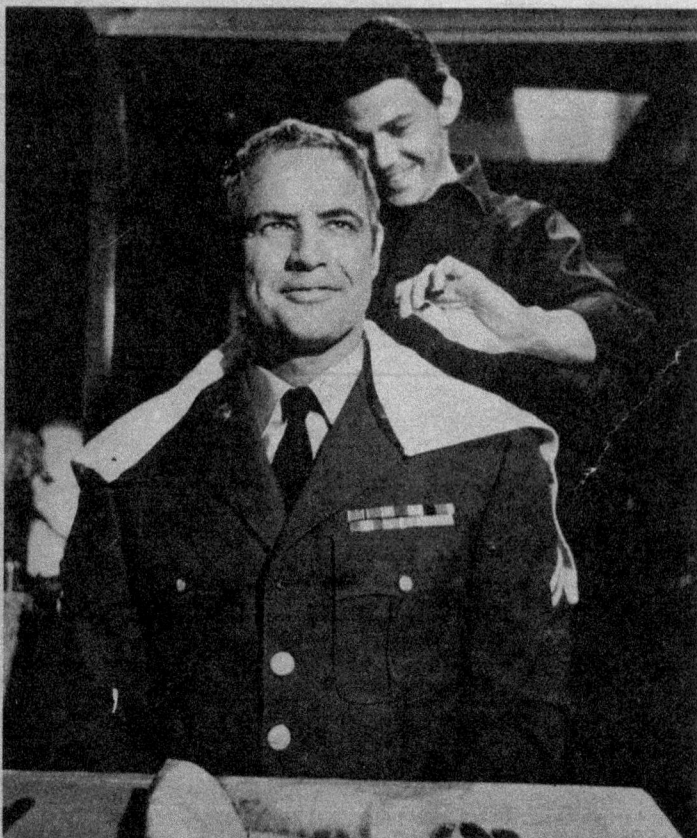

Marlon Brando got a modified G.I. cut from Sebring for a new military role.

By the early 1960s, Jay had conquered Hollywood as evidenced in this newspaper clipping of him giving Marlon Brando a trim on the set of the Universal Pictures comedy *Bedtime Story* (1964).

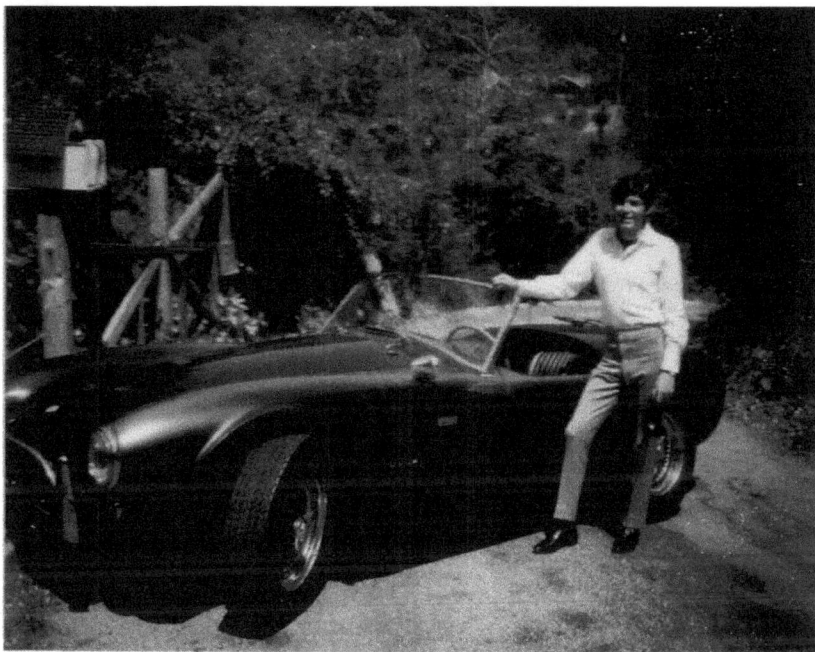

Jay posing next to his midnight blue 1963 Shelby 289 Cobra, which was his favorite sports car. Jay often raced pal Steve McQueen as well many others through the streets of Los Angeles and actor Paul Newman on racetracks in California and at Brands Hatch Raceway in England. *Courtesy of Jay Sebring Collections/The DiMaria Family.*

About a year after his marital split with Cami, Jay and actress
Sharon Tate began dating and eventually became engaged. They
shared their first Christmas together in December 1964. The
couple, inside Jay's Easton Drive home, appear ecstatic in this
photo. *Courtesy of Jay Sebring Collections/The DiMaria Family.*

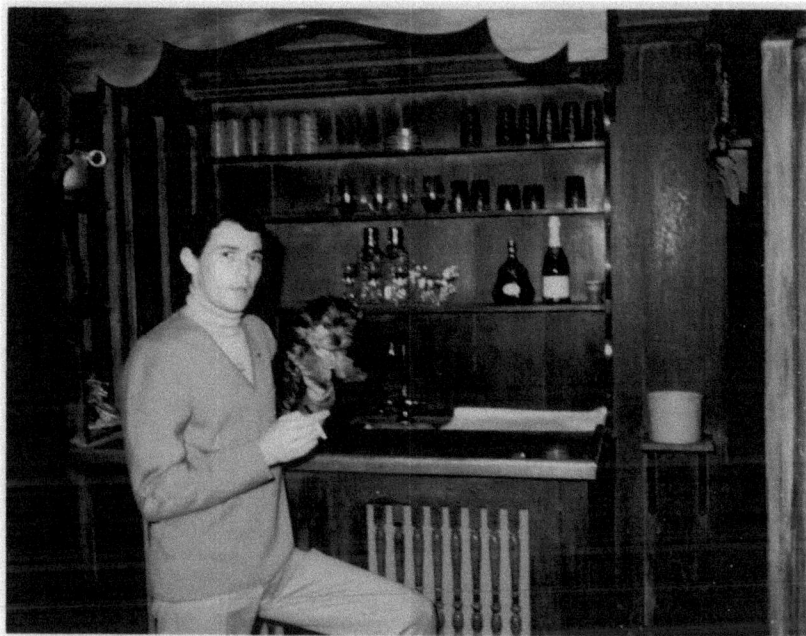

Jay standing in front of the bar inside his Bavarian-stye home at 9810 Easton Drive in Los Angeles' Benedict Canyon. The home was built in the 1920s and was the former residence of movie star Jean Harlow. *Courtesy of Jay Sebring Collections/The DiMaria Family.*

Jay and Sharon on vacation in Italy in 1965. *Courtesy of Jay Sebring Collections/The DiMaria Family.*

Jay and Sharon's love for each other extended to their respective families. Sharon and her mother Doris pose next to a Christmas tree in Jay's home.

Paul Tate with his arm around Patricia Tate, Sharon's younger sister. *Courtesy of Jay Sebring Collections/The DiMaria Family.*

Tuesday, February 9, 1965

40th day – 325 days follow

REGARDING TRAFFIC TICKET: GO TO DIVISION
NUMBER 63 ASK FOR JUDGE FREUND'S BAILIFF
- RON ROTHMAN - RON KNOWS ABOUT THE
SITUATION AND HE WILL TAKE CARE OF THE MATTER.
DIVISION NUMBER 63 LOCATED ON PURDUE STREET

1:30 P. M. - APPOINTMENT AT SEBRING'S WITH
            JAMES DE VOSS - PROSPECTIVE
            TEACHER FOR HAIR DESIGNING
            COURSE - 838-1803

CASH -
    BOB PHILLIPS   PROMO
    DENNIS JAMES $20.00
    MILO FRANK   20.00 $40.00

CHARGE -
    GEORGE CHIKARIS $20.00
    DOMINICK DUNNE   20.00 $40.00

With Jay's status in the entertainment industry came certain perks. In a daily reminder entry for February 9, 1965, Jay is given specific instructions how to dismiss a traffic ticket with a local judge. Other items in the daily reminder include a hair appointment with a prospective teacher and what he charges his famous clients actor George Chakiris and Dominick Dunne, then a television producer. Jay's $20 fee at the time is equivalent to about $200 in 2025. *Courtesy of Jay Sebring Collections.*

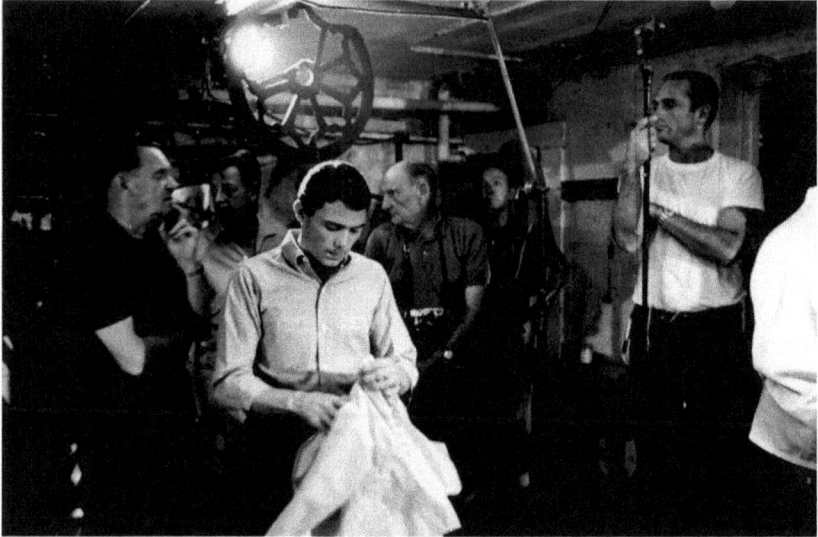

Jay was no longer an industry figure working behind the scenes. He began appearing in front of the camera on a variety of talk shows and television cameos. In 1965's *Synanon*, starring Chuck Connors, Stella Stevens, and Alex Cord, Jay appeared as a character in the film. In this on set photo, he's preparing a scene with actor Alex Cord. *Courtesy of Jay Sebring Collections.*

CHAPTER 17
EXPAND THE BRAND

Branding was barely a concept, much less a part of the common vernacular in the 1960s. It probably wasn't even a term Jay Sebring would have used, but he certainly employed the idea and intention in every facet of his business.

Jay—the world's busiest and most in-demand hair stylist—had a day planner booked from morning to night, every day of the week. Yet he still found time to think beyond the walls of his studio and even set his sights on expanding men's hair design throughout the world.

Jay had the qualities necessary for a visionary leader: emotional intelligence, creativity, good communication skills, resilience, boldness, a collaborative spirit, and most important, a growth mindset. Quiet and deliberate in his leadership, he might not be what you'd expect for a business tycoon, yet he embodied everything that ensures success. Visionary leaders see what others can't see, and that was one of Jay's greatest gifts, as Joe Torrenueva explained:

> Jay knew he could only cut so many heads in one day and charge so much per haircut. Getting into merchandising and franchising was a natural progression to him, but others

in the field simply never saw beyond the walls of their shops. Jay was different in that way.

And Jay understood that, in order to grow his empire, he would have to branch out into other services and opportunities. He was developing hair care products, a training school, SEBRING location expansions, and SEBRING certified shops where barbers and stylists from around the country would pay him a substantial fee to learn his method, which allowed the graduates to promote themselves and their shops as "SEBRING Certified."

Hair guru and stylist Hector Rodriguez regards the influence Jay had on the salon paradigm then, and now.

"His work was very comfortable," said Rodriguez, who owns Cush, a Beverly Hills salon, café, and gallery on La Cienega Boulevard. "You could have a drink, people loved to hang out there, and that's what I've tried to do here."

The brilliance of many of these ventures was the passive income they would generate. Jay could impact people around the country and change the way they looked without having to be there in person.

The moves Jay was making with his brand were as progressive as the ambitions of the Beatles company, Apple Corps, which was formed a couple of years later. But, where Apple failed spectacularly, Jay excelled because of this key difference: John, Paul, George, and Ringo sometimes had competing visions of how to run their entertainment corporation rather than one clear direction.

Jay's plan included several divisions, but all of them worked in concert to expand and enhance the Sebring brand. He knew haircare products were perhaps the most important and lucrative part of what he wanted to accomplish. He knew through experience that product was much more profitable than hair design and cutting. He worked diligently over a period of years with a group of experts and chemists on a high-end shampoo, conditioner, and hairspray, offering a product unlike anything else on the market. Joe Torrenueva recalled how hard Jay worked on this aspect of his business:

> I remember Jay spending many hours in meetings up in his second-floor office with people working with him on his product line. Jay was a perfectionist, and he wasn't going to put out something unless he was 100 percent satisfied. If it had the SEBRING name attached to it, it was going to have to live up to his standards.

Jay also directed a significant amount of his profits back into his business and toward his new product line because he felt that it was a good investment. His assistant Gordon Mullinger watched the company's bottom line and pushed Jay to save money.

> I would make Jay's paycheck out and I wouldn't give it to him. I would deposit it in his account and pay off bills with it. Now, the money that Jay earned was fantastic because if I really concentrated on that budget, I was able to knock out a lot of the accounts right off the bat. And Jay would live on his tips. There was never a time from my very first week that Jay ever came in and said, "Hey, what did you do with my paycheck?" The money he got from tips was unheard of. I mean, I could live on it today. It wasn't a case that he would ignore it. He was very knowledgeable on how much profit that he would make per bottle of hair spray. He could tell you down to the penny.

Post-World War II advertisers began placing a high priority on beauty, especially hair and makeup products. Several companies launched new shampoos and conditioners during this beauty-conscious era. But most of these lines were aimed at women. Men didn't really give much thought to what they put in their hair other than tonics, creams, or elixirs, which loaded down the scalp with more oil than it could naturally handle. Then they might wash that out with a bar of soap at the end of the week—a thought that repelled Jay.

"Their hair looks like a cat with water on its back," Jay said. "A man can have a good, full head of 350,000 hairs, but if it is very fine and he uses oil on it, the oil mats the hair down, and you can see it right through to the scalp."

Jay not only wanted men to think about how their hair was cut, but how they treated their follicles, and to restore them to good health. This was achieved by using an organic-based compound that stimulated the scalp while eliminating grease, polymers, and petroleum jElles from the hair and scalp pores. Jay claimed his protein-rich products gave the client's hair a chance to restore its natural growth and regain its luster and natural body. Larry Geller affirmed this decades later.

> We told people not to use harsh chemicals in their hair because a lot of people were losing their hair. We gave hot oil treatments. We had this solution that would actually peel the scalp. We did a lot of experiments.... he (Jay) always wanted to start a line of products, but he was so busy, and much was going on in his life. He never got around to it while I was with him.

Two years after Geller left the salon to work exclusively on Elvis Presley's hair, Jay's product line was ready. Jay focused on pH balance to establish the foundation of his product line. Jay understood that any alkaline product will cause a dry, itchy scalp and would be too harsh on the follicles, causing dry, frizzy, brittle hair resulting in breakage; acidic products are equally damaging, causing the hair to become dull, limp, and prone to breakage. To enhance and maintain the best health and integrity of the hair, Jay created formulas that matched human hair's pH balance, which is neutral non-acidic and non-alkaline. Since his early days at the Lapin Lab, and through years collaborating with chemists, Jay determined that his conditioner must also contain a protein additive to restore and maintain the luster and vigor of hair.

Each product (shampoo, conditioner, and hairspray[1]) came in a cylindrical cannister and featured silver lettering. The SEBRING name was placed prominently at the top, the ankh symbol was in the middle, and then "FOR MEN" was positioned below that, underscoring his intended target market. He wanted men to feel they could pamper and care for themselves while reinforcing their masculinity.

Not only did Jay spend an inordinate amount of time creating his product line, but he also gave much thought to how he would introduce it to the public. He booked time at some of Los Angeles' most exclusive department stores, sketching hair designs for prospective clients, offering demonstrations on his technique, and pitching his product line at the end of each session. He even gave away an innovative "shampoo brush" he developed so customers felt they received something of value—a strategy taken from the Fuller Brush Company playbook from a few decades before. But the brush wasn't just a gimmick. In Jay's case, it was important to the SEBRING process. The brush was effective in removing any remaining debris or buildup from the scalp and hair while shampooing, before applying conditioner.

The end game in these demonstrations was to get the word out, to get product in the public's hands, and to develop a relationship with exclusive department stores to act as a SEBRING outlet. Jay

---

1. Sebring had even developed a line of men's cologne, but it did not connect with the public. This extremely rare item usually fetches about $1,500 on Internet auction sites.

had been moving a lot of merchandise through his Fairfax store and added a lot of profit to his bottom line, but this next step would put him on a whole other level of distribution and income by providing the products at all SEBRING Certified shops and franchises.

The SEBRING International complete product line was introduced in 1966—years before similar product-lines such as Sebastian (1972), Sassoon (1973), and Paul Mitchell (1980) were created.[2]

The Sebring name carried clout in the American Southwest where men were quicker to accept his ideas about hair. On the East Coast, men were still clinging to staid, business-like cuts, while the warmer, milder climates and the creative demographics of the West were more conducive to Jay's personalized looks and free-flowing style.

Eventually the rest of the country would catch up. In the meantime, Jay opened two more spaces, adding Palm Springs, California, and Las Vegas, Nevada, to the growing franchise by 1965. These cities were selected because Palm Springs was a massive hub of refuge for many Hollywood film and television personalities, recording artists, and entertainment executives. Also, a growing majority of entertainers and business executives on the Las Vegas Strip were SEBRING clients, necessitating a location there. In a few more years, Albuquerque, New Mexico, and San Francisco, California, would proudly add SEBRING marquees to storefronts.

Jay was ten steps ahead of everyone else in his industry. In some instances, he was light years beyond. In addition to contemplating and later creating his own line of hair products—something most might consider to be better left to major corporations with deep pockets—he also came up with an idea for a men's finishing school in England. One of Jay's most outstanding characteristics was that he didn't just have great ideas and chase dreams to make himself a

---

2. Paula Kent and Jheri Redding started their shampoo line, Redken, in 1960.

valued commodity. He sought to give this gift to the world. He wanted everyone to have the opportunity to feel confident in who they were, how they looked, and bring out their best qualities. Cami Sebring reflected:

> He told me his dreams and one of those dreams was to have a castle in England. It would be a finishing school for men where they would learn everything about women, and how to treat women. About music, art, self-defense, dressing.... everything that would completely polish a man.

The finishing school would also involve many of Jay's famous friends and associates. He would enlist Bruce Lee and Ed Parker, both martial arts legends during their lifetime, to teach self-defense. Fred Segal would be on hand to personally fit clothes, and they would offer driving lessons courtesy of Formula One champion Jackie Stewart. Jay met Stewart through Roman Polanski who later directed a full-length feature documentary on the racer titled *Weekend of the Champion* (1971). Stewart recalled of Jay:

> In those days I had long hair like the Beatles. It was the Swinging Sixties in England. So, I had very long hair and Roman had recommended Jay Sebring to me. I went to Jay's place quite often when I was in Beverly Hills or sometimes, he would come to my hotel—usually the Beverly Hills Hotel or the Beverly Wilshire—to cut my hair. I used all his products. He supplied me with shampoo and conditioner, and all the other bits and pieces.
>
> He was a good-looking man, well connected, and friend to the stars. We had a lot of nice lunches and dinners. I brought my wife over a few times, and we danced a lot. These were nice times. Nice group of movie people. Jay, Sharon, Roman and I remember Mia Farrow.

We went to a nice dinner place where music played. I remember dancing with Mia to "Hey Jude" by The Beatles. We all slow danced in those days and made the most of it.

A letter from Stewart, who was in Switzerland at the time, demonstrated his fondness for Jay and his artistry. It was dated October 11, 1968.

Dear Jay,

Just a wee Scottish note to say thank you again for looking out for me so well when I came to the coast.

Your haircut has been remarked upon a considerable amount. Motor racing has really arrived when after winning the U.S. Grand Prix I was taken to be interviewed by TV and radio, and the press, perhaps 150 in all, and during this interview the question continually cropped up as to "who cut your hair?" and "where the hell did you get that haircut?" I think this is really new heights in motor racing and I am sure added a great deal of colour to their race reports!

In addition to all that I really did enjoy my visit and to meet you all. It really is a rather swinging group. I will of course be coming back around October 24th. I look forward to that very much.

As the present time I am staying in John Whitmore's flat as my wife has taken our children to see their grandparents, so I will try to get John to scribble a note at the bottom of this letter.

Thank you once again for your kindness in giving me the haircut and accessories to go with it. In the meantime, don't shunt into any of those racing cars, don't get too high while you drive and put your foot in it at the right time.

Cheers!

Jackie

Expanding the brand also meant sharing his hair-cutting technique with others. Jay developed a school. Barbers from across the country traveled to West Hollywood to study and learn the SEBRING method. Seeking his creative approach, shampooing, cutting, styling, products, business acumen, stylists came in droves to elevate their skills and grow their bank accounts. Gordon Mullinger helped organized the new enterprise. He remembers:

Jay and I put the school together. We had no problem getting people that wanted to come. It was older men and young barbers that definitely wanted to have a shot at their piece of the pie because certification from SEBRING was a status symbol.

Indeed, it was a very positive symbiosis. Jay appreciated his colleagues' desire to learn his methods, and the barbers valued the opportunity to improve their craft and elevate their rates and lifestyles. Jay was quite cognizant of the fact that a large segment of his students was already accomplished with decades of experience. Respectful of this, he encouraged them to implement the SEBRING technique with their existing craft.

Barbers, cutters, and stylists across the country could also pay a $1,000 fee to become "SEBRING Certified" by coming to Los Angeles and learning the methods and technique directly from Jay. They could also sell his exclusive product line in their stores once they passed the course. Albuquerque stylist Jim Markham, who charged about $5 a haircut at his shop, was one of the takers.

Markham said he read about Jay in the April 1965 article Jay wrote for *Playboy* magazine. In the 2,000-word piece, which came with a color photo of Jay at work, as well as illustrations of four facial structures, he presented a comprehensive guide to individualized haircuts and correct hair care. He explained in the article that over a six-year period he had seen a potpourri of clientele—actors, producers, directors, doctors, lawyers, politicians, construction workers, and teens—and how many of them needed his help. Jay wrote:

> With such a wide cross-section of customers, I've had ample opportunity to observe every variety of men's hair. My conclusions: The condition of most American men's hair is deplorable. Their heads are burdened with grease and oil. They favor totally unnatural hairstyles. Most men wear their hair too short and bristly. And more men than realize it wind up looking like the village idiot.

Markham was not only intrigued by Sebring's forthrightness, but his special technique for designing hair as well. He was also astounded that Jay could charge and collect such a large fee ($30 at the time) for one of his cuts. Markham was twenty-three, a divorced father of two children, and had a barbershop that fizzled in 1966. That same year Markham won the national men's hair-styling championship in Dallas, Texas.

After Markham finished reading the article, he picked up the phone and dialed SEBRING in Los Angeles, asking to speak to the owner. Somehow, he got through and issued an offer that he'd help Jay distribute his line of products in New Mexico. In return Jay would teach him the SEBRING technique, which eventually occurred at the Fairfax shop in late 1967. Jay thought Markham was perhaps a bit cocky but was intrigued. He told him that it would cost him $1,000 to watch him work. And if he was interested in opening a SEBRING franchised shop, he could apply the amount toward the $10,000 franchise fee.[3] Markham recalled for *American Salon* in 2019:

---

3. That amount is worth nearly $100,000 in 2025 dollars.

He said, "Why don't you come out to California, and we'll see?" So, I flew my plane to Los Angeles, where I met Jay. I cut one half of [his client] Van Johnson's hair, and he cut the other. It was obvious straight away that his shear technique was better—Jay's technique cut and shaped hair to the frame of the face, which was critical and still is revolutionary today.

After that meeting, Jim Markham soon opened the first SEBRING franchise in Albuquerque, New Mexico.

The SEBRING brand had now expanded beyond the reaches of the Golden State. Over time, Jay would develop national, then global aspirations.

CHAPTER 18
THE TASTEMAKER

With a great new love, a thriving enterprise, powerful influence over emerging trends, and the world as his oyster, Jay found new opportunities outside of hair opening to him in unexpected ways.

These were the halcyon years. At any given point in time, you could find Jay popping up on your favorite TV show, penning an article in the hottest magazines, making a cameo in a feature film or even making guest appearances on late night talk shows. For a guy who had his sights set on a specific path that was more behind the scenes than front and center, Jay was on a trajectory to high-profile stardom far beyond his chair.

In the span of a decade, Jay went from struggling to pay rent and asking his parents for help in financing his dream to becoming the rock star's rock star. He created the iconic look of Jim Morrison, made Steve McQueen a matinee idol for the Beatles' generation, and was the personal stylist for the entire Rat Pack. In the anatomy of Hollywood, Jay was the nucleus, and the stars were drawn to him like electrons, seeking foresight that would propel them to the highest strata.

Jay wasn't leaving hair behind, but his own celebrity was

becoming an industry unto itself. It afforded him opportunities in areas such as film roles and production, as well as providing a voice for influencing gentlemen's lifestyles.

Tom Kummer's rising star in Hollywood as "Jay Sebring" was a massive source of pride for his family in Detroit, Michigan. His sister Peggy DiMaria was particularly delighted with Jay's massive success.

I remember going to grade school with one of the movie magazines under my arm. I happened to have it opened on my desk with my brother's picture. Of course, when my friends would ask me, I would say, "This is my brother." And they were in awe of it. My parents saved every clipping they ever saw of my brother.

And while most who knew Tom Kummer in his early years expected he would break away from an ordinary life, he exceeded those expectations by leaps and bounds. He had been in their living rooms as a neighbor and friend, but now he was there on their TV screens, in movies, on the pages of their magazines, and with a different name.

On November 15, 1961, a local Michigan Legion Hall had *The Steve Allen Show* on the television while Detroiter and St. Benedict's alum Martin "Marty" Halloran was drinking a Stroh's beer with half a dozen of his buddies when the host announced he was about to have his hair washed and cut live on air.

"Ladies and Gentlemen, Jay Sebring!" Allen said enthusiastically.

Halloran was astounded. "I says, 'That's Tom Kummer!'"

He couldn't believe it. It had only been five years since Tom had called Halloran on the phone and asked him to come over to the house in Six Mile to give his old Cadillac a push start toward Los Angeles.

Since his childhood in Highland Park, Michigan, Tom Kummer had existed in his own world. He was a vivid dreamer, and the fantasy world of his fertile imagination demanded tactile substance and full commitment. In his Highland Park childhood fantasies, he dressed in full gear as a doughboy fighting the Germans and as the Lone Ranger or Zorro in the wilds of Ferris Avenue, tangling with bad guys. When Tom was not in the war-torn trenches of Alsace or on his faithful horse, the boy sketched numerous drawings of curvaceous pinups, Western settings, and Hollywood actors like W.C. Fields, William Powell, and James Cagney.

For childhood friend Jerry Millen, the transformation of Tom Kummer of Highland Park, Michigan, into Jay Sebring of Hollywood, California, made total sense.

One of the things I really remember more than anything else is Tom used to put on little skits in his garage at 55 Ferris Street. And his mother was there all the time. She backed him in everything he did. It was a little bit of singing and acting, but Tom was behind the whole thing directing. So, it wasn't surprising to us that he went out to Hollywood and the whole thing.

Jay was featured in the "Hollywood, USA" episode of NBC'S *Hollywood and the Stars* that aired on January 2, 1964. Oscar-winning producer and long-time Sebring client David Wolper (*Roots*) profiled him in a surprising addition to the program's slate of celebrities. Actor Joseph Cotton's inimitable narration sets the scene for the piece:

This is the SEBRING house of hairstyling. The customer's hair is cut while wet here then shaped to the head and to the personality. This unusual expression of male vanity is costly, and analysis and haircut can cost from $7 to $25.

One of Hollywood's indestructibles, Henry Fonda, is in once a week while making a picture. He has to appear unchanged on the screen while the production takes weeks to finish. Jay Sebring's job is to snip away about a quarter of an inch a week, which by the inch makes for a pretty expensive haircut.

The demand for Jay as a personality, not just as a hairstylist, was increasing. On January 28, 1963, he made his first and only national gameshow appearance on one of America's most popular and enduring programs, *To Tell the Truth.*

"Only one of these men is the real Jay Sebring," the announcer proclaimed. "The other two are imposters and will try to fool this panel—Tom Poston, Peggy Cass, Barry Nelson, and Kitty Carlisle —on *To Tell the Truth* with your host Bud Collier."

In typical fashion, the panel asks each guest, known as #1, #2, #3, questions to determine the person of interest. While the individual in question was usually culturally relevant or fascinating, the panel was always comprised of well-known personalities and celebrities.

Unlike typical gameshow guests or contestants, Jay had no interest in notoriety, the limelight, or jumpstarting an acting career. For him, this appearance was a huge chance to spread the word of his innovations on a national level, well beyond his elite Hollywood converts. It was the second time Jay spoke directly to a national television audience. It started off as he had hoped it would when the show's host Bud Collier read:

I, Jay Sebring, own and operate the most exclusive men's hairstyling establishment in the world. I charge $25 the first cut and $15 thereafter.... I am personally responsible for the hairstyling of Steve Allen, Elvis Presley, Henry Fonda, Peter Sellers, Milton Berle, Sammy Davis Jr., Eddie Fisher, and

Marlon Brando. Flying east to appear on *To Tell the Truth*, I made two stops: one in Las Vegas to cut Vic Damone's hair, and another in Palm Springs to perform the same service for my old customer, Frank Sinatra. Signed, Jay Sebring.

The three prospects then took their seats, and the panel soon commenced their comments and questions. It wasn't long before a few of the panelists began poking fun at the seemingly outrageous cost for a SEBRING cut.

"How long before the poor guy has to shell out the next fifteen dollars?" Peggy Cass asked to much laughter. Veteran actor Barry Nelson pressed further: "What would I tip after a $25 job?"

"Nothing!" Peggy Cass barked. The audience exploded with laughter, immediately agreeing with outrage.

What was anticipated as a breakthrough for nationwide enlightenment quickly twisted into mockery of Jay and the hair care industry for men. This would be another baptism by fire for the upstart. While his innovations and brainchild were introduced to America in primetime on millions of TV screens, his concepts were simultaneously mocked nationwide as superficial, supercilious, and outrageously expensive.

This was a seminal moment for the ambitious Hollywood outlier because the desired outcome held with it a double-edged sword. In one of his first massive publicity breaks, Jay learned a valuable lesson: media can be a useful marketing tool and an engine of commerce in which humiliation and mockery are an entrenched commodity. In future appearances, Jay would keep an eye out to prevent perceptions that Sebring concepts—unusual as they might have been—were not to be mocked but understood.

With a slew of television appearances under his belt, the next logical step for Jay was gracing the silver screen with his presence, though not through personal efforts, but culminating from Jay's producer clients. In September 1964, Jay arrived on a film set, this time with no fear of studio union lockout or grief from set security. This also marked the first time he'd set foot on a film location as a member the Screen Actors Guild (SAG) rather than as the guy cutting a star's hair. Jay Sebring was a Taft-Hartley player[1] who portrayed a barber in the black and white feature film *Synanon*. The Columbia Pictures film starred Chuck Conners, Alex Cord, Stella Stevens, Eartha Kitt, Richard Conte, and Jay's former girlfriend, BarBara Luna.

The film follows Cord, a struggling junkie, in his journey to clean up at the Synanon rehabilitation center[2] oceanside on the Pacific Coast Highway in Malibu. Jay's scene, and most of the location's scenes, were filmed at the actual facility.

It was a first for Jay as he would not be behaving and speaking naturally, sharing his concepts and techniques. He was tasked with bringing someone else's vision—playing a character rather than being himself. Ever the perfectionist, Jay was experiencing some anxiety to deliver a noteworthy performance, and he did show signs of butterflies on set. In one scene, when Connors and the gang escort Cord to his sacramental hair initiation at Jay's Synanon basement station, Jay rises from where he is seated, reading the newspaper, and reaches for the hair cape. He knocks an implement to the floor, stops, retrieves the item, and places it back on the counter before draping his reluctant client. For a man whose hands moved so deftly when he was in his element, this fumble was an indication that he wasn't quite at ease. But once Connors, Cord and the actors hit their marks, Jay uttered his lines in his usual understated cool.

"Rare, medium or well done?" he asked as he draped the junkie

---

1. The Taft-Hartley Act of 1947 was a provision that allowed non-union members to enter a union (in this scenario the Screen Actors Guild) when a producer pays his/her dues to join.
2. Synanon later morphed into a group cult in the 1970s. It was disbanded in 1991 after several of its members were found guilty of a variety of crimes, including attempted murder.

with a styling cape, then cut the lead character back to his first steps to recovery.

Months later, Jay would add another title to his budding repertoire: magazine writer. In April 1965, *Playboy* published a six-page article by Jay Sebring titled "Topping Off the Well-Groomed Man." The tone and content of the article was consistent, which was to extol the worth of men's hair design and to educate the masses on the importance of hair care and hygiene. His persistent message began to chisel away at long held myths and wives' tales plaguing men for decades, even centuries. Dennis Hopper recalled:

> It's funny. People can drop a line on you, and you think about it every day. When I'm brushing my hair, I think about this almost every morning. And because I was losing my hair Jay said, "You know the reason men lose their hair and women don't?" I said "No." He said, "Because women brush their hair!" It's just one of those lines when I'm brushing my hair and I think, *Well I should be brushing my [hair] more.* It's one of those lines I think about almost every day. So, every day I think of Jay.

Word about Jay was finally spreading well beyond Los Angeles and demand for him as a guest or subject was growing exponentially. Gordon Mullinger remembered a slightly unorthodox appearance request in June 1965.

> Gypsy Rose Lee had a TV program in San Francisco and called me up. She said, "Do you think that Jay would consent to come up and be on my program and let me interview him?" So, I went in and explained to Jay who Gypsy was (a burlesque entertainer turned television host) and came back to the phone and said, "Yeah, absolutely. He'd love to."

Mullinger watched the segment live on television and almost cringed at Jay's unfiltered honesty.

> Now, she has him on the program and that morning Jay and I had had one of our budget discussions (before his trip to San Francisco). She asked, "Jay, is your business really as big as they say?" And he turned around and said, "Well, my secretary just told me I'm three thousand dollars in debt on one of my bills. So, I guess it is."

Not all of Jay's television appearances were business related. In what most likely was a cheeky roust amongst friends, long-time client and TV producer William Dozier cast Sebring to play "Mr. Oceanbring" on his campy but wildly popular show, *Batman*. The episode, "The Bat's Kow Tow," aired on December 15, 1966. It featured Julie Newmar as Catwoman along with her minions Eenie, Meanie, Miney & Moe, conspiring at Mr. Oceanbring's salon when the dynamic duo crashes the party. A fight erupts between Batman and Robin and Catwoman's four hoodlums.

Bedlam ensues as Mr. Oceanbring runs from vase to vase to protect the expensive masterpieces from destruction during the mayhem.

"BING!!!"

As the crime fighters battle the gangsters, Catwoman makes her sleek escape. *"KAPOW!!!"*

The Dynamic Duo finally emerges victorious. And as the dust settled, after successfully preserving every prized possession, Mr. Oceanbring relaxes and rests against a nearby sculpture, causing it to tumble to the ground and shatter.

"DRATS!!!"

Shifting back to the printed page, Jay agreed to pen an article for *Esquire* magazine in 1967. The composition included sketches drafted by Jay to illustrate his points. While the piece contained

standard Sebring insights on hair, Jay provided additional insights
and suggestions for presidential candidates Ronald Reagan, Lyndon
Baines Johnson, Richard Nixon, and Robert F. Kennedy, along with
very detailed drawings of each candidate sketched by Jay to demonstrate his ideas. He went to great lengths as an author and artist for
the magazine's article; however, when the piece was published, Jay
was apoplectic. Though the article contained his writing, none of
his sketches were included by the magazine. Paul Greenwald said
the omission left a bad taste in Jay's mouth.

> Jay was upset because it wasn't his artwork. It was very
> disappointing to him because he had done the graphics and
> a makeover of the candidates. When the magazine was
> published, they weren't his drawings. They weren't his
> concepts at all, and he was very upset. And what I learned
> from my father [Alvin Greenwald, Jay Sebring's attorney] is
> that he would not accept the check for payment. In fact, he
> sent the check back.

On April 12, 1967, Jay would again appear on televisions
nationwide, this time on the American western series *The Virginian*.
In the series' fifth season episode, "The Strange Quest of Claire
Bingham," Jay seemed increasingly at ease with his thespian chops
as the collected, charming barber of Shiloh where he tends to James
Drury's follicles.

After the cut, the two characters exchange friendly jabs:

Jay: There, how do you like that?

The Virginian: Jay, you're an artist. Unfortunately, what I
wanted was a barber.

Jay: Next time you better count your ears before you leave.

Jay was sure to adorn his character with an attachable
SEBRING moustache, which could be purchased at his Fairfax

shop as an accoutrement. Jay's mischievous side certainly delighted in this.

Jay's world was expanding in directions he never expected or intended, but his life was an adventure to him, and he was open and eager to see where it would go. Other areas of his world were about to intersect, and he would face a whole new set of challenges.

CHAPTER 19
LONDON CALLING

I n June 1965 the sky provided no limit for Jay—he'd met his perfect match in love with Sharon Tate, the SEBRING product line launch was on the horizon, and demand for his talents and unique take on style had extended beyond America's shores. Jay, ever the intrepid entrepreneur, had set his sights on going global. First stop: a hop across the pond.

The seismic shift of London from the impoverished, gloomy, war-decimated capital of England to the world's well-spring of art and style emerged out of brutal times, propelled by youth, money, and sexual carpe diem. England's post-war baby boom resulted in the largest population explosion since Roman times. In 1965, nearly half the population of England's urban cities were aged twenty-five or younger. Artists, designers, writers, and publishers flocked to the "Great Wen." The disposable income of Londoners was at a historic high with most households grossing more than 150% of living costs monthly.

Londoner Vidal Sassoon described the economic boon this way:

Fiscally, up until the sixties, Britain was out of it—Depression of the twenties, thirties. The war started in '39 and lasted until '45. People had no houses because the bombing was so drastic. About 700,000 people were killed during the Luftwaffe raids over Britain. [After the war] there was an enormous amount to be done. The fifties was hard times. There was still clothes and food rationing. If you look at history, new ideas and energy come out of hard times. So, in the sixties suddenly there was the young fiscally were earning damn good money. They could spend; they could create.

Fashion and music exploded with zeal and expression. Mary Quant's boutique BAZAAR on King's Road was flooded with women seeking her most recent iconic design—the miniskirt—named after her favorite vehicle: The Mini. Fashionistas Peggy Moffitt and Twiggy popularized mod-style with their Sassoon bob and asymmetrical haircuts, distinctive makeup, and false eyelashes.

Similar movements and trends were brewing in Los Angeles, but the strife and horrors of WWII directly impacted the United Kingdom, which exponentially accelerated the creative revolution in London.

Jay arrived in "Swinging London" on June 16, 1965, to scope out potential new digs. Jay would commute to Europe seven times before the year's end, both for business and to accompany his stunning bride-to-be. England held exciting opportunities for both Jay and Sharon.

He flew to France on August 21 to help Sharon settle in for filming her first starring role in a feature film. *Eye of the Devil*, directed by J. Lee Thompson, was a British supernatural horror film with witchcraft and occultic themes. It also starred David Niven, Deborah Kerr, Donald Pleasance, and David Hemmings. British Wiccan and occultist Alex Saunders was brought on as a technical adviser for the film's ritual scenes.

In the weeks leading up to principal photography, Jay and

Sharon jetted between Paris and London—setting up bases at Hotel Des Saints, a flat at Belgravia Mews, and at Eaton Square (paid for by Filmways) in London. While preparation for Sharon was the focus, the couple's time together during these months played out like a honeymoon with a limousine at Sharon's disposal (also covered by Filmways), shopping at Harrod's, Harold Leighton, Dior Boutique, and Mary Quant's BAZAAR boutique. As idyllic as this time was, demands in the States required Jay's return to Los Angeles.

Friction was brewing at the Fairfax shop between barber Felice Ingrassia and several others on the barber side of SEBRING's. It's unclear the source of Ingrassia's resentment toward Jay, but with Jay's frequent absences, it had room to fester. Jay was spending significant periods of time giving demonstrations throughout Southern California and in San Francisco in particular, styling on film locations and at movie studios, in Europe, and being featured on television shows.

To accommodate for demand, Jay had transformed the upstairs Fairfax apartment into an additional private room so other stylists could use his station. This meant that Jay was spending less time in the shop downstairs and more time upstairs in his private room. SEBRING designer Dean McClure felt the absence of his mentor at the shop, which wasn't good for anyone.

"I think we kind of lost touch with Jay when he moved upstairs," McClure said. "We just lost that connection."

Interest in Jay and his reputation was reaching epic heights. Actor George Peppard insisted that Jay be flown to Dublin, Ireland, to cut his hair in defining his role as WWI German ace Lieutenant Bruno Stachel in *The Blue Max*, an expense 20th Century-Fox covered within the film's $5 million budget. The transcontinental cut was highly publicized, one publication noting, "Sebring, by plane, car, and helicopter, arrived, performed the 'custom clip.'"

It certainly grabbed the attention of Hedda Hopper, whose

August 28, 1965, column headline blared: "He'll Get a $2,500 Haircut." Hopper wrote: "George was always a frugal guy, and this story is hard to believe, but I'm told it's true. He's flying Jay Sebring to Dublin to give him a haircut at a cost of $2,500."[1]

This milestone established Jay's *Blue Max* cut as one of, if not, the most expensive haircuts in history. American film director Quentin Tarantino shared that during research for his film *Once Upon a Time in Hollywood,* he learned the following:

> Jay had a policy and that was "Okay, I'll fly out; I'll do the haircut, all right. I get paid $1,000 a day. I do not cut on the day that I arrive. And I don't cut on the day I leave. $3,000, that's the deal. And you put me up." So, if Steve McQueen is in New Orleans doing *Cincinnati Kid* and needs his hair cut, he wants Jay to cut it. Is a haircut worth $3,000? It was to Steve McQueen.

Jay had been riding high on the waves of success that were breaking on the shores of Hollywood and the many other places clamoring for a piece of him. The 1960s were proving to be a time of rapid and radical change, not just for Jay, but for the whole world.

But in the U.S., the country had been shaken by the Civil Rights Movement, which was finding its legs. And Jay's life was beginning to see the ripples of unrest as well. Upon returning to Los Angeles from Ireland, Jay learned several of his cutters had walked out in the middle of the night. The departure, led by Felice Ingrassia, included barbers Art Fields, Bernie Roberts, Jimmy Silvani, and Jim O'Rourke. Jay's protégé Joe Torrenueva felt for his mentor and stated for the record:

---

1. This amount would be nearly $25,000 in 2025 dollars.

There was a big exodus in 1965, and a whole bunch of guys left, maybe five or six people. And that hurt Jay. All of a sudden, we were minus about six guys. Maybe they felt "We should do this" and "We should do that." But Jay knew where he was going. So, they left.

This act took a massive financial and emotional toll on Jay. Each cutter had become quite talented in their own way and developed large clienteles, which they took with them, no doubt impacting Jay's bottom line. Jay had shared his concepts and trained each cutter extensively over the years. A loyal person by nature, Jay took their walkout particularly hard. Not so much the investment into his staff, but the abandonment by those he considered friends. The men shared their space, their time, and even their clients throughout the years, except for Ingrassia.

Gordon Mullinger described the strain that existed between cosmetologists and the barbers at SEBRING during this time:

There was tension between Felice and Jay. However, I don't know that it was Felice so much as somebody else who was involved with Felice and was dead set on getting him to go out on his own. Which he did.

Ingrassia went on to open Dynasty on Highland and Sunset Boulevards, which existed for many years, competing head-to-head with Jay for business. Within a year of the walkout, O'Rourke, Roberts, Silvani, and Fields all moved on from Dynasty and either opened shops of their own or partnered with each other.

In the latter part of 1965, Jay continued to navigate his business and personal obligations. In addition to maintaining his business expenses and overhead, Jay paid for Sharon's car and her SAG dues while she was filming in Europe.

While she was away, Sharon stayed on the radar in the States through a feature article in *ELLE* magazine that drew a lot of attention. In the piece she described a frightening dreamlike encounter with Paul Bern's ghost at Jay's Easton residence one evening when Jay was away. She said she spotted a "creepy little man" one night while in her bedroom whom she believed to be Paul Bern. Tate said the apparition entered her bedroom but ignored her and seemed to be looking for something that was important to him. She said when she ran from the room, she encountered a spirit, its throat slashed and tied to the staircase with a white cord.

Reporter Dick Kleiner claimed Sharon told him the story at some point in 1966,[2] and he regurgitated it in August 1969, days after her murder, trying to find some meaning in the re-telling.

"It was just a creepy story, when Sharon Tate told it to me in early 1966," Kleiner wrote in a piece titled, "Did Sharon Have a Premonition?" "But now, three years and five murders later, it has acquired something more than creepiness."

This particular story became a component of the lurid *Helter Skelter* mythology, being repeated time and again after her death. There is nothing to suggest any truth in it, yet it got traction in what was already a grisly and tragic event that didn't need any embellishment to capture the world's attention.

Jay returned from England on December 11, 1965, giving him enough time to prepare for the holidays. Ten days later, Jay received a Western telegram from his fiancé at 12:26 p.m. on December 21:

MR SEBRING
9810 EASTON DR. BEVERLY HILLS (CALIF.)
SWEETHEART ARRIVE FRIDAY PANAM
FLIGHT 212
I LOVE YOU

---

2. Kleiner is referring to a November 18, 1965, issue of *ELLE* magazine in which Tate made the claim about seeing the ghost of Paul Bern.

SHARON

Jay picked up Sharon at Los Angeles International Airport on Friday, December 23, with Guinness, her Yorkshire Terrier puppy, and the couple spent the holidays at Jay's Benedict Canyon home. Sharon's mother joined them, and the three celebrated the holiday season together.

Even though these were happy times, there were undercurrents of tension between the two. Peggy DiMaria observed the couple up close and their thoughts on marriage:

> Sharon was wanting to get married, and my brother didn't feel that was the time for them to get married. He seemed comfortable in that Sharon was going to pursue her career and he was pursuing his career.

In early January 1966, Sharon returned to her Belgravia Mews flat in London to resume filming *Eye of the Devil* while Jay was preparing the launch of his complete hair care product line. Publicity around Sharon began ramping up as she was featured in an article titled "School is Over, So Sharon Sails Out" on January 31, 1966. In the piece, Sharon revealed:

> I was up for a TV series in Hollywood, and Mr. Ransohoff took one look at me and said: "It's films for you, baby, and no one sees you from now on." So, I went to school. I did nothing but study for two and a half years. Now it's all happening. I'm just finishing my first film with David Niven and Deborah Kerr—*Eye of the Devil.*

She went on to proudly state, "I used to be naïve and bashful. Not anymore. I'm full of electricity, vibrations. I'm even allowed to have a boyfriend now. I'm engaged to Jay Sebring." Almost a month later, she gave the first in-depth interview of her career for *Weekend Magazine* at London's Dorchester Hotel.

As filming wrapped, Martin Ransohoff and Filmways were in pre-production for the company's next project, *Fearless Vampire Killers,* to be directed by a young and brilliant, if not mercurial director, Roman Polanski. The Polish émigré was a hot new name in London's film society and had delivered two critically acclaimed films—*Repulsion* (1965) starring Catherine Deneuve and the award-winning *Cul-de-sac*[3] starring Donald Pleasance and featuring Jacqueline Bisset. Ransohoff was determined Sharon Tate was a perfect fit for the lead role of Sarah Shagal in his new horror-comedy.

Exactly how and when Sharon Tate met Roman Polanski is wildly speculated, but the nexus is certainly London and Tate's second feature film.

Jay's neighbor, close friend, and client Stuart Whitman recalled what was ultimately the beginning of the end of their relationship:

> Sharon got a job in England, and she was gonna be there for a month or two. And I said, "You have to look up this friend of mine, Victor Lownes. He's building Playboy in London and he's giving parties from time to time, and you'll meet some interesting people." I had no idea that she would then also fall in love with Roman Polanski. So....

Lownes recounted over the years to several writers that he met Polanski through film producer Gene Gutowski, who was at his house in England when the actress and director met. It wasn't exactly love at first sight, but they exchanged phone numbers at the end of the night. Polanski's house was around the corner from where Sharon was staying. A few days later they had dinner and

---

3. *Cul-de-sac* won the 1966 Golden Bear Award at the Berlin Film Festival.

headed back to Polanski's place. But, according to his 1984 autobiography, *Roman by Polanski,* they first stopped at a friend's house to pick up a cube of acid. They tripped and then made love at dawn, according to the director:

> What had impressed me the most about her, quite apart from her exceptional beauty was the sort of radiance that springs from a kind and gentle nature; she had obvious hang-ups yet seemed completely liberated. I had never met anyone like her before.

Even though Sharon and Jay were still involved, it was not a big deal to Polanski who looked at monogamy as nothing more than a Western convention. And with Jay reticent to tie the knot, perhaps Sharon gravitated toward an alternate course with enticing future possibilities.

Their relationship kicked into high gear soon after filming got underway, and Sharon eventually moved in with Polanski. Jay, unfortunately, was more than 5,000 miles and an ocean away.

Breaking up with Jay was incredibly difficult for Sharon, who deeply cared about him. Her close friend and actress, Sheilah Wells, recalled Sharon writing her a letter from Europe.

"She told me she had met someone named Roman," Wells said. "She felt really sad about Jay, but she hoped they would always be friends."

And they were in time. But it took a while to get there.

Often, Gwen and Paul Tate would send audio cassette recordings to each other in lieu of letters when the intelligence officer was away in Vietnam or Asia. One such recording captured a conversation between Gwen and actor Stuart Whitman at Sebring's Easton home about Jay and Sharon's split while Jay was going to pick up Sharon from the airport.

"Jay needs to find a woman," Gwen said.

"I think Sharon took a powder on Jay," Whitman responded.

"I think so," Sharon's mother answered.

Debra Tate said that, despite the love they had for one another, the shift between Jay and Sharon was surprisingly amicable.

"Sharon called Jay over to Europe to give Roman the 'once over,'" Tate said. "To give the seal of approval or the 'boot' so to speak. And they all became very good friends."

On February 12, 1966, Jay arrived in London. Roman described his first encounter with Jay at a restaurant in a polygraph test with Los Angeles police in August 1969:

> I felt very, you know, uneasy. Then Jay came and sat at the table and shook my hand and kissed Sharon's hand. He said, "I just wanted to meet you." It was not traumatic.... it was a very relaxed type of thing, "I wonder how you are," and "I think I like you," and asked if we were happy. That was the first meal with Jay. Afterwards there was several occasions I wanted to avoid him. It was sort of, I felt guilty sort of. But when I came to Los Angeles and started living here maybe two years, I saw him more and more often. He used to come to our parties, etcetera, and then I started liking the guy very, very much.

It didn't take long for the press to catch wind. On March 16, 1966, Hollywood columnist Earl Wilson headlined his article on their coupling, "Hot Romance in in Europe: Sharon Tate and Roman Polanski of *Vampire Killers*," adding salt to Jay's wounds. As the breakup started to sink in, it would be some time before Jay would get his bearings back. It was baffling for many, including friend and designer Fred Segal.

"I don't know what, know why she ended up with Roman Polanski," Segal said. "It was like a shock to me. I know Jay was in shock for a year."

Writer Dominick Dunne also attested to this.

"He was so devastated," Dunne said. "And it was like he went through a period of mourning."

Andee Nathanson became friendly with Sharon Tate while working at Jax, a celebrated Beverly Hills women's boutique owned by Jack and Sally Hanson.[4] They specialized in tight pants, sweaters, and thigh-high mini-skirts. Tate was a customer and grew friendly with Nathanson, a nineteen-year-old Philadelphia transplant who later became a photographer, author, and artist. She said Sharon tried to set her up with Jay after their breakup, but he was not emotionally ready.

> Sharon was very nice to everyone, and we became friends. She wanted to fix me up with Jay and I spoke to him on the phone one night. But it was very clear to me that he was still very much in love with Sharon. We never went out.

Jay, who was very sexually expressive, found it hard to become intimate with others for a while during this phase. Jozy Pollock, an English-born entertainer and performer, was in the process of getting a divorce from her husband, professional magician Channing Pollock, when she met Jay at Sneaky Pete's bistro on the Sunset Strip.

"Jay was with Steve McQueen, and they both hit on me," Jozy said. "I knew Steve was married, so I never entertained the thought of going out with him and kept talking to Jay."

The talk led to a few dates, but she said they never consummated the relationship.

"I never slept with him. We just hung out," Jozy said. "We

---

4. Jax was such a success that it enabled the Hansons to open The Daisy in 1962, a trendy nightclub/discothèque on Rodeo Drive. In 1971, Jack Hanson turned it into a lunchtime restaurant.

weren't exclusive. I'm sure he dated other women. I dated other guys. He was a lovely person. Very cute. Always well dressed and manicured. He was a ladies' man, but we just hung out."

While Jay was getting his sea legs back, Sharon and Roman were quick to plan their nuptials. They were married at Chelsea Registry Office on January 20, 1968, a blustery winter day. Barbara Parkins, Tate's *Valley of the Dolls* co-star, served as maid-of-honor.

The reception was a swinging sixties mod-style affair held at The Playboy Club in Mayfair where champagne was served by buxom bunnies, and they frugged the night away. In attendance were Joan Collins, Anthony Newley, Victor Lownes, Candice Bergen, and Michael Caine. Collins remembered a special moment she shared with the bride that night:

> Sharon was one of the most beautiful brides I had ever seen at her wedding to Roman in 1968. Sharon looked ravishing —her long blond hair was done in intricate coils and laced with baby's breath. I too had a complicated hairdo of the times, and we had a sweet picture in which we laughingly compared our "do's." Roman in his Beatles jacket looked like the cat that found the cream. It was a fabulous wedding, and everyone had a fabulous time.

As much as Jay cared for Sharon, he was not present for their wedding. It's not known if he was invited or not—most likely not. But no doubt he saw a widely distributed photo by the Associated Press of the couple gaily skipping down the stairs at the Chelsea Registry office. It had to smart. Through it all, he kept a stiff upper lip.

Peter Knecht shed insight on Jay and his relationships with past loves:

There are some guys that can't handle that, and they become enemies, and they lose all those beautiful years together and all that time together rather than be smart and continue a relationship on a different level and become lifelong friends.

Vidal Sassoon noted whatever pain Jay might have experienced, he got over it eventually. "In London, Jay came to my flat with Sharon Tate," Sassoon said. "I think Sharon was already married to Roman Polanski. But they remained close.... they were great friends."

Jay's brother-in-law, Tony DiMaria, was surprised by the turn of events and the shift in Jay and Sharon's relationship from lovers to friends, explaining:

It kind of amazed me that after the breakup they were such good friends. As I remember, there didn't seem to be any hanging on at all. Even after the breakup he continued to date and see women. Jay was always able to pick up and start relationships with really beautiful women.

Sometimes we go through losses that seem big enough to break us. Jay's girl and half of his crew had walked out on him, and a lesser man might not come back from something like that. Jay found himself at a crossroads. It wasn't the first time and wouldn't be the last.

CHAPTER 20
THE BEAUTIFUL PEOPLE

By the mid-to-late sixties, Jay had established himself as a leading voice in men's hair and as a wildly successful, well-known entrepreneur. His clients were the top tier of society, he drove expensive sports cars, and he had his pick when it came to women after he and Sharon were no longer an item. He was living a beautiful life as one of the beautiful people of Hollywood and was managing to straddle two generations. In an era when the ethos was that no one over thirty could be trusted, Jay was one of the few still dialed in and hip enough that both youth and adults in one of the world's hottest towns bought what he was selling.

The post-World War II years of Eisenhower, Kennedy, the Rat Pack, and *Bonanza* were now considered old hat and corny. Even though it was only a few years in the rearview mirror, the suit-and-tie crowd of the late fifties and early sixties belonged to another era. The new youth wanted something different, something they could call their own.

The counterculture was emerging, protesting the war, pushing the boundaries of fashion, radicalizing popular music, experimenting with drugs, and freeing themselves from the constraints of traditional views on sex.

The year 1967 was the tipping point for one of the most radical shifts in societal structures on a global scale, and San Francisco, Berkeley, and Los Angeles were the hubs for the most pivotal activity. Actor/director Dennis Hopper, who identified as a beatnik, a hippie, and a Bohemian, said L.A. was his home but the Golden Gate City was where he drew his inspiration.

> I would go on the weekends almost every weekend to Haight-Ashbury to watch the Jefferson Airplane, Lovin' Spoonful, The Byrds, and the Grateful Dead. It was a very powerful time. Everything was changing. The music was changing. Fashion was changing. And movies were about to change.

Movie audiences were getting hipper, feasting on rich offerings such as *Bonnie and Clyde*, *The Graduate*, *Cool Hand Luke*, *In Cold Blood*, and *The Trip*. Hopper made his biggest contribution to the cultural revolution with *Easy Rider*. It was written in 1967 and then filmed and edited in 1968 with a modest $400,000 budget. When it was released the following year and grossed approximately $60 million, it turned Hollywood on its head and helped kickstart the New Hollywood era of the 1960s and 1970s.

"We'd gone through the Summer of Love, and nobody made a movie about the hippie movement until *Easy Rider*," Hopper said. "At that time there had never been a movie made that had its own soundtrack."

Hippies were pushing the conventional parameters of the time, bringing to it their long hair, Bohemian styles, progressive political ideologies, and outspoken opinions. They expressed themselves through a variety of mediums and places. Even courtrooms.

Peter Knecht, who represented Jay and a plethora of celebrity clients, explained the shift taking place in the sixties:

> I was the district attorney for Beverly Hills, which incorporated the Sunset Strip. Kids would come into my courtroom wrapped in flags. And I would relate to them. We hated the war. Everybody was in revolution.

Some of Jay's contemporaries identified as hippies and adopted that lifestyle. David Milch, an Emmy-winning writer, producer, and creator of *NYPD Blue* and *Deadwood*, describes the movement this way:

> So now people my age could say, "Oh, I'm not an asshole. I'm a hippie. I'm a fuckin' hippie!" Suddenly being confused had been translated into a philosophical position. "I'm not confused, excuse me. I'm not confused. I'm searching for a new truth."

It was also a very confusing time, said Gordon Mullinger.

> You would hear about picket lines and protests. And they would go up and ask these young people, "What are you doing here?" "Well, I'm protesting." "Well, what is it you're protesting?" "Well, I don't know." And you went, "This is real craziness."

American music journalist and historian Stephen Davis aptly described the young person's perspective during the heyday of the Age of Aquarius:

> We didn't want the old stuff; we didn't want our parents'

culture, and it spawned the 1960s. We wanted a counterculture; we wanted something that belonged exclusively to us.

The Human Be-In at Golden Gate Park in San Francisco and June's Monterey International Pop Festival kicked off the peace and love movement, known as the "Summer of Love." This social phenomenon saw nearly 100,000 people—mostly teens and young adults—flood twenty-five blocks of San Francisco's Haight-Ashbury neighborhood. They went there in search of glamour, ecstasy, free love, and communal utopia. They hung out at Golden Gate Park, smoked weed in coffee shops, and danced in trippy ballrooms to psychedelic music pioneered by bands such as The Grateful Dead, Jefferson Airplane, Quicksilver Messenger Service, and Big Brother & the Holding Company.

One of the ruffians that made a name for himself in the hippie underworld was a thirty-two-year-old ex-con named Charles Manson who had had been paroled in March 1967 from Terminal Island—an unusual, low-security prison in the heart of the San Pedro Port in Southern California. He thumbed his way north to San Francisco where he found a two-story Victorian crash pad in the heart of the Haight where he lived from April to November 1967. It was here where he resided with the initial cohorts of what would later be known as the Family. Amassed through wayward layovers and chance encounters, they included his then-girlfriend Mary Brunner, a librarian in nearby Berkeley; Patricia Krenwinkel, a college dropout who followed Manson from L.A. to San Francisco; Lynnette "Squeaky" Fromme, who famously went on to attempt an assassination of President Gerald Ford; and Susan Atkins, a mousy but voluptuous North Beach stripper who became an additional Manson hanger-on. The house at 636 Cole Street was conveniently located near a free clinic where these ladies were frequently treated for vaginal infections.

Once he got settled in, Manson quickly adjusted to the mores of Haight-Ashbury: he panhandled, hustled pot and LSD for small-time dealers, committed petty crimes, dropped acid at Grateful Dead shows, bedded teenaged runaways, and played guitar for spare change, desperately trying to launch a musical career. He was fed through a variety of soup kitchens and well-meaning ministries that catered to the "lost souls" of the hippie crowd. The Living Room, a Christian mission located in the heart of Haight-Ashbury, was a place where hot gospel and food were served daily. Lonnie Frisbee, a hippie preacher who later became a central figure in the Jesus Movement recalled Manson occasionally dropping by the mission for meals. He said Manson told everyone he was Jesus and the devil while taking advantage of their services.

"He would put us down for what we were doing in the community," Frisbee said. "Of course, this was while he was enjoying our delicious soup!"

But the Summer of Love was just that—a season. The Edenic idealism these seekers hoped for quickly disintegrated into a dystopian nightmare. There was plenty of violence, sexual assault, manipulation, deceit, STDs, and drug addiction.

"San Francisco was the first big experiment," said television writer, producer, and Yale English professor David Milch, "but people got a little tired of the body lice pretty quick."

Hair icon Vidal Sassoon rejected this social trend and distanced himself from any such assertion.

"We were nothing of the hippie movement; we were workers," Sassoon said. "We worked fourteen hours a day. We grafted; we created. We weren't hippies."

While Jay certainly didn't adopt the hippie lifestyle—as Sassoon described, he was much too ambitious and industrious—he incorporated some of the more hedonistic aspects of their ethos into his life. His hair grew longer, his clothes more casual, and his attitude toward sex certainly more *laissez faire*. Jay was always expressive with women before the height of the sixties with BarBara Luna, Jill

Howarth, Cami Sebring and, of course, Sharon Tate. Despite his recent breakup with Sharon, Jay remained consistent in his desire for smart and beautiful women. They included actresses Bebe Louie (*Once a Thief*), Kathy Kersh (*The Americanization of Emily*), and Las Vegas Showgirl-turned-Oscar-nominated actress Valerie Perrine (*Slaughterhouse-Five*).

Jay's passion for women rivaled his passions for his innovations. Patricia Bosworth describes in her 2011 biography, *Jane Fonda: The Private Life of a Public Woman*, a tryst between Jay and Jane that took place one evening at a party at the Polanskis' Hollywood residence:

> One night Vadim watched Jane disappear into a bathroom with Jay Sebring.... He had been Sharon Tate's lover and remained her close friend since her marriage to Polanski. Sebring and Jane didn't reappear for at least a half-hour.... For some reason the Polanski housekeeper got upset at the locked bathroom and began banging on the door. "What's going on in there?" she screamed. That woman had taken it upon herself to look after the morals of the Polanskis. She had her work cut out for her. Finally, Jane opened the door and marched out followed by Sebring. Her clothes were in disarray. Their flirtation had been interrupted, Vadim noted, but Jane seemed indifferent. "I hate it when something is half-finished" was all she would say, and she drifted past Vadim and into the living room.

Alcohol consumption gave way to smoking more pot, dropping LSD and, later, cocaine use. Neile McQueen-Toffel recalled in her book, *My Husband, My Friend*, a Friday night when she first dropped acid with her movie star husband Steve McQueen with Jay and Sharon present:

LSD was then the drug of the moment. Everyone seemed to be doing it, and Steve was anxious for me to share this experience with him. I was very apprehensive, disapproving, and very uptight about the whole idea. Drugs were not my cup of tea. Steve, however, was insistent, claiming that there was nothing to worry about. The four of us would be together and it would be a wonderful time.

It was anything but a wonderful time. It turned out to be a bad trip for her, who ended up seeing an "army of snails" crawling through the garden and up the walls of her beautiful Brentwood mansion.

"That experience was enough to validate my belief that drugs were no good," McQueen-Toffel wrote.

That certainly didn't stop her husband or Jay who both used it on occasional weekend getaways to Joshua Tree National Park in the Mohave Desert, about 140 miles east of Los Angeles. Dennis Hopper recalled several trips in the early 1960s, both to the desert and on acid, with Steve McQueen, Ted Markland, Tom Gilson, and Owen Ore, and laughed at the memory of their antics:

> We'd go on weekends and Steve would take his trailer out there, and we'd all drop acid. Ted Markland had a chair he called his "Father's Chair" on top of this little mound or hill on Joshua Tree and we'd all sit in the chair at one time. We'd spend the night looking at the stars. And we took everybody from The Rolling Stones to The Beatles. I mean, we took everybody.

But Jay's jaunts to the Yucca Valley weren't excuses to trip or bliss out. Joshua Tree and its grand boulders, spectacular rock formations, yucca trees, and 250 different species of birds embodied the mystical elements of Jay's innate sensibilities. It was a gateway to an untouched timeless patch of earth beneath the infinite cosmic possibilities that exist beyond earthly comprehension. Jay thrived on the outer limits and was drawn to Joshua Tree for all those components. Cami Sebring, who started visiting the desert in 1960, said Jay was drawn there for several reasons.

> He actually had his own experiences with extra-terrestrials, and it wasn't pie-in-the-sky. He knew there were other beings, other solar systems and galaxies. How could there not be other life out there?

The Sebrings usually headquartered with resident friends or The Joshua Tree Inn.[1] The Spanish Colonial style 10-bedroom inn was established in the thirties and was laid out in a square horseshoe. It was there where Jay befriended owner-managers R.O. and Ruth Murphy who were Catholics in their late sixties and hailed from Wisconsin. No doubt he was drawn to these elderly, salt-of-the-earth, kindly, hospitable Midwesterners who probably reminded Jay of his own parents.

After Cami and Jay broke up, he introduced the wonder of Joshua Tree to Sharon, and she enjoyed the desert as much as Jay. Sebring photo archives show a July 1968 trip to Joshua Tree with Sharon and Roman Polanski, and Mia Farrow and Peter Sellers, who were dating at the time. Writer James Poe (*Around the World in 80 Days*) was also there with his wife, English film actress Barbara Steele. Jay was accompanied by an unknown female companion, completing the circle of matched-up couples, some of them garbed in beads, headbands, and leather vests with fringe.

It might have seemed strange to outsiders that Jay and Sharon

---

1. The Joshua Tree Inn is where country rock pioneer Gram Parsons overdosed on a combination of morphine and alcohol on September 19, 1973. Parsons, McQueen, The Rolling Stones, and Jay shared the same pot and LSD source, an elderly bearded man named Sid Kaiser, who attended Jay's funeral.

were there together with other people and remained close even in the company of their significant others, but not to those who knew them.

Actress BarBara Luna recalled that Jay went to Europe to meet Roman because he wanted to be sure he was good for Sharon.

> He was protective of Sharon. He wanted to be sure that she was doing the right thing. Jay and Sharon remained close friends. And he was so cool. You know, "As long as you're happy." He was just so decent.

Debra Tate posits the following:

> Their relationship had switched gears completely and was more like brother and sister. I suppose at that point in time there was never an issue of distrust or anybody sneaking behind anybody else's back. Between you, me, and the four walls, I do believe down the road, had something happened to Sharon and Roman's relationship, which there was no indication of at the time. But I think Jay probably would have wanted to have been right there to move back in on the love that he denied himself at an earlier point in time.

Some friends, such as Fred Segal, thought the two were still in love and wanted to stay close. "I just felt they were together," Segal said. "But I may have also felt his love, maybe his love was greater, and it energized the both of them. I felt then what I feel now. And I felt them together."

Besides, they were there to unwind, have fun, and perhaps have a transcendental experience or two. Dozens of slides from Jay's personal collection chronicle the eventful weekend. The most iconic picture of that weekend was of Jay standing alongside his '68 Porsche on a Joshua Tree highway at dawn, apparently after an adventurous evening, in a white shirt open to his navel with a cigarette in hand. The sun is highlighting the distant mountain skyline. His hair is tousled, his clothing stylish, and he is the essence of cool.

Polanski told writer Ed Sikov that they went to Joshua Tree "because of its reputation for UFO sightings. It was very much in vogue."

According to Sikov, on one of those nights, the group was engaged in a deeply spiritual and mystical discussion about "eternity, stars, and alien life forms." The playful Polanski, who stood at a distance, tossed a stick at them from the darkness. Rather than spook them, it sparked their imaginations.

"Did you hear that?!" Sellers whispered.

"What *was* it?" Farrow asked.

"I don't know," Sellers replied, "but it was fantastic. *Fantastic!*"

The Murphys were always happy to see Jay, but they were especially appreciative that Sebring introduced his Hollywood inner circle of friends to their cosmic hideaway. After their stay, R.O. Murphy penned individual letters to them, thanking them for visiting their establishment.

On July 9, 1968, Murphy wrote to Jay on Joshua Tree Inn letterhead:

Dear Mr. Sebring:

We have written a note of appreciation to YOUR guests that spent a couple of days with us. We enclose copies of each, as we felt you might be interested. They should be a reminder of your hospitality.

Needless to say, we are very grateful to you for bringing them up here.

You will note that we did not write to Mr. Poe. We could not decipher the name of his street—and I could not find a similar name on the map I could dig up.

We have had many calls—phone—for you since you left. One from Mr. Manning (?) that seemed quite urgent. I suggested—and he concurred—that you were probably in Palm Springs with Steve (McQueen). But, as Steve would probably have an unlisted number, that was no help.

Please tell Mr. Poe that if he would write plainer—or if I could read better—I would have written him a "Thank You." You tell him and the lovely wife we meant well.

Thanks again.

JOSHUA TREE INN

R. O. Murphy

The life Jay was living at this time was out of this world, or at least a world away from where he grew up and even the way he lived when he first landed in Hollywood. It was an era like no other, and Jay was just beginning to explore all the possibilities that lay out there for him. It wouldn't be long before he would venture beyond Los Angeles, beyond styling hair, and into even greater adventures.

CHAPTER 21
TRIAL AND ERROR

The year 1968 went down as one of the most volatile years in 20th century America. Great leaders of our country—Martin Luther King Jr. and Robert Kennedy—were assassinated. The Democratic National Convention in Chicago erupted in chaos as the National Guard sprayed bullets and tear gas into crowds of young protesters. On the other side of the country, the Black Panthers prowled Oakland, California with shotguns in hand, searching for their own form of justice. College students openly and defiantly protested the Vietnam war, burning their draft cards and American flags. Revolution was in the air, and significant youth movements of the day threatened to topple the government.

Anarchy and confusion abounded everywhere you looked, and the world was struggling. But Jay Sebring found hope and opportunity around every corner. Stepping outside his comfort zone, Jay began exploring new passions within the body politic and the silver screen, giving him yet another dimension to his already impressive scope of influence. Jay also cast his gaze beyond L.A. to expand his business and extend his enterprise even further.

Starting in 1966, Jay began a dialogue with California Congressman Thomas M. Rees, a well-respected Democrat who represented the 26th Congressional District, which covered a large portion of Los Angeles. Their correspondence was initiated through an introduction by Jesse "Big Daddy" Unruh, whose tenure as the 54th Speaker of the California State Assembly ran from September 19, 1961, through January 6, 1969. The lifelong California Democrat and the state's 26th treasurer had been a SEBRING client since 1962.

Rees soundly beat his Republican opponent in a December 14, 1965, special election to fill the seat of former Representative James Roosevelt who had accepted an appointment to the U.S. delegation of the United Nations. A staunch Democrat, Reese looked to address issues involving mass transit, air pollution, recreation, and Medicare during his term in Congress. A few months into his term, Jay reached out on behalf of Sharon's father, Paul Tate.

Tate was an Army intelligence officer whose work was classified, often involving cloak and dagger scenarios in places such as Vietnam and Korea. His nickname conferred by his base peers was "Ice Cube" for his ability to stay cool under pressure. After the family moved back to the States in February 1962, Tate was assigned to Fort MacArthur, a U.S. Army installation[1] in San Pedro, California. He worked there as the assistant operations officer to the 47th Artillery Air Defense Brigade, which oversaw the training of Army Antiaircraft Artillery Command for troops in Vietnam. That meant he still had to travel back and forth to Vietnam for months at a time. Jay took it upon himself to intervene for Paul Tate who once said, "He [Jay] was like a son to me."

A letter in the Sebring family archive from Rees' aide Lloyd Winburn to Jan Faulstich, an Army representative, demonstrated Rees' hand in getting the Tate family stateside again.

---

1. For a period of about a year, Paul Tate's neighbor down the peninsula was inmate Charles Manson, who was housed on nearby Terminal Island prison from 1966-67.

To: Jan Faulstich

From Lloyd Winburn

Date: March 24, 1966

While we were unable to modify Major Tate's orders in order to keep him in the country, we should now press to have him reassigned to the States.

Through a copy of this memorandum to Jay Sebring, I am recommending that Major Tate apply for transfer back to the States, and I would appreciate if you could explore with the Department of Defense the best procedure for handling this request.

We have thoroughly investigated this case, and Congressman Rees believes it is absolutely a must that the Major be assigned where he can be with his wife.

Rees' efforts on behalf of the Tate family led to a personal and professional relationship between him and Sebring, which turned out to be mutually beneficial in the ensuing years. Jay believed he could use a powerful political ally, and Rees saw Jay as a gatekeeper to celebrities and high-profile clients, which was especially useful during an election year.

Unruh was considered by many to be the most powerful Democrat in the state and took over the running of Robert F. Kennedy's presidential campaign when he officially threw his hat in the ring on March 16, 1968.

Kennedy's election campaign got a big boost two weeks later when President Lyndon B. Johnson stunned the nation in a televised speech on March 31, announcing that he would not be seeking a second term in office.

California was crucial to the "first brother," as Kennedy faced heavy opposition within his own party, which included Vice President Hubert Humphrey and Eugene McCarthy, a U.S. Senator from Minnesota and prominent critic of Johnson's handling of the

Vietnam War. Kennedy was late in entering the race and went on to campaign in the Democratic primaries in Indiana, Washington, DC, Nebraska, Oregon, and South Dakota. He then wended his way to the City of Angels in April for a $250-per-plate fundraiser held at the Sportsmen's Lodge, an iconic Los Angeles gathering spot on Ventura Boulevard. On March 21, 1968, Jay received the following invitation from Congressman Rees:

Dear Jay:

You are cordially invited to a reception honoring Senator and Mrs. Robert F. Kennedy, Sunday, March 24, 7:30-9 p.m., in the Empire Ballroom, Sportsmen's Lodge, 12825 Ventura Boulevard, North Hollywood.

I hope you can attend, as this is Senator Kennedy's first visit to California since his entrance into the race for his Presidential nomination.

Sincerely,

Thomas M. Rees

Member of Congress

Jay not only attended the fundraiser, which drew about 300 people, but also had several of his influential friends in tow. Among them were Roman and Sharon, Paul Newman and Joanne Woodward, Warren Beatty, and Sammy Davis, Jr. Along with other Hollywood glitterati,[2] they met and mingled with RFK and his wife, Ethel. Jay had gotten a lot of publicity mileage a few years before when discussing the 1962 presidential candidates' hair. He was complimentary of John F. Kennedy ("President Kennedy takes good care of his hair. The way he combs it suits his personality")

---

2. Other celebrities and Hollywood personalities who endorsed Robert F. Kennedy's 1968 presidential bid were Robert Vaughn, Arthur Miller, Rosemary Clooney, Andy Williams, Candice Bergen, Rosey Grier, and John Frankenheimer, who directed and produced ads for Kennedy.

and had advice for Richard M. Nixon ("Vice President Nixon's hair was styled wrong, accentuating a receding hairline.")

Robert Kennedy was complimentary of Jay in a signed letter dated April 10, 1968, addressed to him at the Fairfax salon:

> *Dear Mr. Sebring:*
>
> *I'd like to take this opportunity to thank you for supporting the reception at the Sportsmen's Lodge.*
>
> *I was greatly impressed by the warmth and enthusiasm of the people of Los Angeles, and your generosity and efforts meant a great deal to me personally.*
>
> *I am looking forward to seeing you the next time I am in Southern California.*
>
> *Best wishes.*
>
> *Sincerely,*
>
> *Robert F. Kennedy*

Unruh also sent a letter of thanks to Jay, closing with a tragically ironic projection: "We have a good campaign going and I'm sure we will win."

Kennedy returned to the Golden State, placing a lot of hope in the California primary. He had recently experienced victories in Indiana and Nebraska, but a six-point loss in Oregon. A loss in California, insiders said, might make the New York Senator reassess the race. He had campaigned furiously for eighty days, traveled more than 50,000 miles by plane, car, and bus, gave hundreds of speeches in airport stops, courthouses, supermarkets, and even on the roof of a car when his motorcade was swarmed to a stop. It all boiled to down to the June 4th California primary. His team was headquartered in Los Angeles' Ambassador Hotel, where he arrived shortly before midnight.

Then the unthinkable occurred. Kennedy was assassinated by a twenty-four-year-old Pasadena resident named Sirhan Sirhan. Jay was most likely not there that night at the Ambassador Hotel—he never spoke of it if he was—but he most likely saw RFK's death the same way journalist Ed Cray did.

"I think the dream—I'm being very emotional here—I think the dream died in June of 1968," Cray said. "Sirhan Sirhan took away, in my opinion, the last great hope for a generation."

In the wake of Kennedy's assassination, Jay grieved the loss of this national leader and relived these events as a nightmarish déjà vu. Gordon Mullinger remembered how this unfolding event impacted Jay.

> If something happened that Jay was very touched by, [he] wouldn't necessarily want you to know how vulnerable he was feeling. But the day President Kennedy was assassinated, I went into his private upstairs office. He was very, very, very emotionally distraught about it. But the minute that somebody else came in, he immediately, you know "All right Gordon.... well now...."

But, as profound as this loss was, it didn't distract Jay from moving forward. He would soon have his attentions redirected by an opportunity from a familiar playground in the form of an offer for a mysterious film role opposite Jane Fonda.

Academy Award-winning screenwriter James Poe had known Jay since the early 1960s. He was a prolific writer of film, television, and radio. His work on *Around the World in 80 Days* (for which he won an Academy Award in 1957 for Best Adapted Screenplay) led to other big studio films, including *Cat on a Hot Tin Roof*, *Lilies of the Field*, and *Toys in the Attic*. In 1965, he signed a contract with Columbia to direct films; however, by the end of the decade he still had not gotten his shot. He was convinced he would after his screen adaptation (co-written with Robert E. Thompson) of *They Shoot Horses, Don't They?* a 1935 novel penned by Horace McCoy.

Set in the 1930s, the novel was a riveting parable about the
bitter times of the Great Depression in America, using a competitive dance marathon in a shabby ballroom as a clever allegory for
one of the country's bleakest periods of the 20th century. It was
filled with colorful dance contestants representing all walks of life,
desperate to win the $1,500 prize. Poe said he had written a menac-
ing, scene-stealing pimp character for Jay in his final draft to play
opposite Jane Fonda.

"I have the pimp show up halfway through. First time you only
see him as a silhouette in the crowd," Poe told journalist Michael
Dempsey for *The Hollywood Screenwriters: A Film Comment Book*. "I
did a screen test with him. He was fantastic."

Poe elaborated on why he wanted his friend for the part:

> Jay was small, intense black eyes, black hair, a glittering,
> brooding manner, and irresistible to women. He was, he
> was a friend. I found him amusing and right for the part. I
> wrote it with practically no dialogue. I just wanted to get
> the feeling of him. He was very much like an early John
> Garfield, incidentally, which was what the picture needed.

Even Jane Fonda felt Jay was right for the movie. Poe wrote in a
postcard to Jay dated July 18, 1968, from Paris, France:

> *Jay,*
>
> *Jane Fonda is absolutely delighted about the idea of playing
> opposite you! She says there are only two things worth visiting
> in Los Angeles—the Farmer's Market and Jay Sebring. Barbara
> and I are in Paris and miss you mightily. Thank God you don't
> know what's here. You'd padlock the shop.*
>
> *Love,*
> *Jim*

Soon after Poe and Thompson turned in their script, Palomar Pictures president Edgar Scherick purchased the property in early 1968. He offered the project—with Poe's blessing—to the producing team of Bob Chartoff and Irwin Winkler. They loved the idea, but felt the script needed a rewrite[3] and the $900,000 budget needed to be reconsidered. They were also vocal in their concerns about Poe's ability to direct, feeling he was arrogant and possessive of the material. Scherick brought in ABC Pictures to help finance the film, which boosted the budget to $4 million. Suddenly, this became "an important film," Poe said.

The movie was offered to Mia Farrow first, but her fee of $500,000 would have eaten up a majority of the budget. It was then offered to Jane Fonda who charged and received $650,000. She also received director approval; however, over time, she was unimpressed with the script and became less enamored with Poe. He was bounced from the project by ABC Pictures' new president, Marty Baum, a former talent agent with the Ashley-Famous Agency. Poe's removal also neutered Jay's role in the picture. In perpetuation of their thwarted tryst from the year before, Sebring and Fonda would, yet again, fail to consummate their silver screen relationship.

Poe had spent three years and made a massive financial and creative investment in optioning this novel for $25,000 (with an additional 25K owed), only to have it yanked away from him. While back door betrayal and dog-eat-dog tactics are the norm and not the exception in the entertainment industry, these were detestable traits to Jay. He believed Freddie Fields, his friend and Hollywood powerhouse agent, would be the perfect ally to right the course for his devastated friend. A letter discovered among Sebring's

---

3. Poe claimed about 90 percent of the movie was his script. He said, "In the rewrite, dialogue was changed. The relationships were not changed. No new characters were added, but a very important character was deleted. That's the character of the pimp."

personal collection from Poe to Freddie Fields details the saga and seeks guidance on what recourse he might have.

Unfortunately for Poe, director Sydney Pollack had taken over, much of Poe's blood, sweat, and tears were swept away, and there was nothing that could be done to reverse the trajectory of this project.

Despite profound tragedies and twists in Jay's life and inner circles, opportunity continued to knock for him; but where politics and entertainment were fair-weather friends, opening another shop was an unquestionably smart move.

Jay always had his eye on the ball where franchising was concerned. His relationship with the Pacific Northwest began with his days in the navy, but now that he had some money in the bank, he could experience the Golden Gate City in style. San Francisco was a totally different vibe and aesthetic from Los Angeles.

"San Francisco wasn't a big city at the time, but it had a lot of cachet," said Sandie Wernick, president and founder of a Bay Area boutique marketing group. "It was filled with a lot of socialites and powerful people and was a lot of fun. It was a swinging place."

In addition to lots of colorful people, the city was the commercial, financial, and cultural center of Northern California. It featured amazing architecture, world class museums, and hipster hangouts. It oozed charm, elegance, and personality. It also had a lot more wealth than Los Angeles, something that didn't go unnoticed by Jay.

After becoming the base for the gold rush of 1849, San Francisco became the largest and most important population, commercial, naval, and financial center in the American West. It continued to develop as a major business hub throughout the first half of the 20th century, and it was home to the highest concentration of millionaires, philanthropists, and social elites. They included the Hearsts (Hearst Newspapers), the Hewletts (Hewlett-Packard), the Driscolls (Weyerhaeuser Company), the Crockers (Crocker First

National Bank), the Spreckels (Spreckels Sugar Company), the Strausses (Levi-Strauss & Co.), and the Folgers (Folgers Coffee). Jay developed a personal relationship with heiress Abigail Folger through his friendship with Roman and Sharon.

Commercial Street was a discreet alley in the heart of the Financial District and seemingly the perfect place for an elegant parlor devoted exclusively to men's hair. It was named MacBlum's (advertised as "San Francisco's first gentleman's grooming establishment") after its owners Ray MacWade (a hair designer) and Art Blum (a successful publicist and agency head).

The shop at 629 Commercial Street opened in September 1965 and sat directly across from San Francisco's U.S. Mint. It was built prior to the 1900s and featured massive oak doors, brick work, big windows, luxurious furnishings, and state-of-the-art fixtures. Its owners, like Jay, felt successful men needed posh pampering and a place to call their own. While it might have sounded like a classy establishment, one of its owners had a questionable reputation.

Blum, who died in 2003, ran a very successful public relations agency. However, some have alluded that it was mostly on the back of Herb Caen, the iconic humorist whose column ran in the *San Francisco Chronicle* for six decades. Wernick, who briefly worked for Blum before starting her own public relations agency, said his success was due in large part to his relationship with Caen. She explains, "Art was close friends with Herb Caen and anything he said ended up in the paper. That relationship with Herb was the magic formula to his success. Art used it to get clients and to get women."

Blum, an old-school salesman, showman, and shrewd judge of business clients, lived in a man's world and conducted his business the same way. He was proud of the fact that his business was housed in a place that once was a brothel, Wernick recalled.

"Art was a pig and didn't hide it," Wernick said. "A lot of women who worked for him resigned. I did, too."

And yet, the place struck a chord and met a need for a growing clientele.

MacBlum's offered green and black marble booths for full-service "hair designs," scalp and hair conditioning, manicures, shoeshines, and a library-lounge reception area.

It certainly sounded like a place "inspired" by Jay, but the business struggled and lacked key ingredients for longevity: Sebring's vision and name. By 1968, MacBlum's also introduced weekly art exhibits and a noon-hour lingerie show. These were advertised as "cultural diversions."

These events were highly successful according to Patricia Fripp, who was hired as a hairstylist in February 1969. She recalled how she was brought on:

> My friend Wendy worked there for a few months. This place sounded fun, and I asked, "Are there any openings?" Wendy told me, "In two weeks, Ray MacWade and three other stylists were leaving to open their own salon." I got there two weeks ahead of their exit. They needed a manicurist and receptionist. I said to Art, "If you can get a good manicurist, hire her. I am a great women's stylist, and I will be a men's stylist. If I take the job, you must promise me I can get trained for a stylist."

Blum made good on his promise, and in time, Fripp became a star stylist in her own right.

According to Fripp, MacWade no longer wanted to be in business with Blum and set up shop elsewhere in the Golden Gate City and, later, in Los Angeles. Blum saw a grand opportunity to elevate the shop when he read an article about Jay.

Demand for Jay's services were at an all-time high, and San Francisco was a logical, expansive leap. He was looking for a location when he received a call from Blum who had read in an article that Jay was considering opening a shop in San Francisco. Fripp said Blum picked up the phone and called Jay to make an offer he couldn't refuse.

> Art contacted Jay and said, "You don't want to open your own salon. You want to be my partner." One Saturday after- noon after work, my best friend Frankie and I, stayed late to polish and clean. We made that salon, that was magnificent anyway, into a diamond, to set a good impression for Jay Sebring. The following day, Jay came in with his business manager John Madden, and they came to an agreement with Art.

It was the right city, right building, right setup, and a set of right circumstances for Jay who had to make few changes to set up his next salon location. Certainly, Jay put his touches on the new place, affixing his name and logo above the front door and adding a photo of himself and a few iconic SEBRING clients on the walls, but inside not much else was required. It was an easy transition in a year when Jay was experiencing searing frustration and staggering accomplishment.

Jay had big expectations for the San Francisco salon and high hopes that the rest of the year would be smooth sailing. But when he crossed paths with a gang of midnight marauders a few months later, those ambitions would become nothing but another thwarted destiny.

CHAPTER 22
YOU'VE COME A LONG WAY, BABY

From the time Jay Sebring made himself known in Hollywood to the day he premiered his satellite salon in San Francisco—the span of a mere decade—he went from barely having two nickels to rub together to amassing his own little empire that put him close to being a millionaire. His going rate when he started was $5 per cut, but the new shop would command a $55 price tag for his styling and an additional "hair design fee" for the first session.

The star-studded gala for the SEBRING salon opening in San Francisco stood in stark contrast to the lackluster launch of his shop on Fairfax. In his early days, he gave away free haircuts to gin up business; now eager patrons were flying in from all over the country and internationally to directly experience Jay's talents and/or support his latest enterprise.

When he was getting started, Jay lived in spartan quarters in the back of the business space; in this new era of success, Jay was expanding his real estate portfolio and had luxury accommodations wherever he chose to lay his head at night. Among them was a houseboat in Sausalito he rented from Ron Reynolds, owner of a discothèque in North Beach (San Francisco's entertainment district).

For Jay, the new salon wasn't a necessity; it was an indulgence. He explained to Albert Morch of the *San Francisco Examiner* that he opened the new location "mainly because I love San Francisco, and it will give me an excuse to come up regularly."

One of the keys to his success, in addition to being the best and knowing how to convey his concepts to the right people, was the acquired financial attribute: don't spend your own money. Jay's many high-profile clients provided a wellspring of investors who made his expansion possible without going to a bank or dipping into his own reserve. His benefactors included Warren Beatty, Paul Newman, Joanne Woodward, Lou Adler, Steve McQueen, Michael Pollard, and Herb Alpert. Additionally, coffee heiress Abigail Folger invested $5,000.

Jay sent invitations for his May 24, 1969, champagne opening to an exclusive group of influential people and the Bay Area's press. At the bottom of the invitation: *"On hand will be Joanne Woodward & Paul Newman."*

Newman was a champion of Jay's talent and an enthusiastic investor in his business. It was announced that the opening would include many of his Hollywood clients, including Steve and Neile McQueen, Herb Alpert, Michael J. Pollard, and Lou Adler.[1]

One of Jay's close friends, Bruce Lee, also received an invitation but responded he was out of town. In a letter postmarked May 26, 1969, Lee wrote back to his friend. Its tone was kind, playful, and familial:

Jay,

Thank you for your invitation. I just got back from New

---

1. As it turned out, Newman and Woodard, Beatty and Christie, and Lou Adler actually showed up.

York a few days ago. While there, I was trying to locate you,
but, alas, SEBRING is moving to San Francisco! What's this?
Faster than Bruce Lee! You've been moving around.

    I didn't learn of your staying in Northern Calif. until Steve
[McQueen] called the other day. A houseboat and all—what a
life! Rocking all the women to death....

    I won't be able to able to make the trip this time but will
definitely drop by to see you next time when I come up. I too
have some important and interesting projects coming up. When
I see you, I will talk to you in detail.

    In the meantime, take good care and have fun.
    Your friend,
    Bruce

Weeks before the opening, Art Blum's publicity prowess was in full throttle, announcing SEBRING's arrival to the Bay. He arranged for various types of exposure in the *San Francisco Examiner* in the run up to the opening. One such piece was an article written by Mildred Hamilton, accompanied by two large photos in which Jay gave a demonstration and dispensed hair care advice mixed with personal anecdotes. He used the head of Dennis Powers, an artistic director with the American Conservatory Theater, to demonstrate a cut while he talked.

"Anyone who has hair gets the same treatment. The main thing is to make it easy to care for so it will fall into place and make the man more attractive," said Sebring, turning his attention to Powers. "You have your part on the wrong side. Milton Berle wore his part wrong for forty years. So did Henry Fonda. And his gray hair looks so great now because we use a conditioner to drab the yellow out of the gray."

Of course, Jay discussed his triumphs in Hollywood, which every scribe was eager to print because of what he could command for a cut.

"My most expensive haircut cost $2,500," Sebring said. "I was flown to Ireland to cut George Peppard's hair in *The Blue Max*." He said he had recently flown to New York to cut and style the hair of Dustin Hoffman and Mia Farrow for their *TIME* magazine cover portraits.[2]

Hamilton noted that, at thirty-five, Sebring was an accomplished man who indulged in auto racing, photography, martial arts, and had a line of men's grooming products plus another shop in Albuquerque. Sebring recalled his salad days for the reporter, telling Hamilton he arrived in Los Angeles on a Greyhound bus with two sweatshirts, a pair of Levi's, and a pair of desert boots.

"I kept the desert boots and had them bronzed recently," Jay said. "They are on my coffee table, a reminder in case I ever get to the point where I don't appreciate what I have."

As fate would have it, those bronzed shoes not only served as a humble reminder at Sebring's Easton residence but have remained a cherished keepsake in Jay's family throughout the decades.

The SEBRING San Francisco shop opened as planned, housing a sitting area, six stations with mirrors, a section for hair dryers, and a large office in the back for Jay. On the morning of May 24, 1969, Sebring International at 629 Commercial received a flood of well wishes and congratulations. Among them, a Western Union Telegram from the Kummers in Detroit, Michigan, saying:

DEAR TOM:
WE EXTEND CONGRATULATIONS ON THIS
OPENING OF YOUR LATEST SALON. BEST WISHES
TO YOU, YOUR STAFF, AND ASSOCIATES. THE

---

2. The photo shoot coincided with the release of the 1969 film *John and Mary*, produced by SEBRING client Ben Kadish. SEBRING shampoo and conditioner containers were strategically placed on the bathroom counter in one of the scenes.

FAMILY SENDS ITS LOVE TO THEIR BROTHER,
AND OUR SON.
MOM AND DAD.

Jay's parents were unable to attend the opening as Bernard was battling health issues after the removal of a kidney.

Meanwhile, at Jay's Sausalito houseboat, the celebration began early in the day with a revolving door of Sebring friends marking the occasion, including Warren Beatty, Julie Christie, Lou Adler, John Phillips, and actor/screenwriter Gary Conway. Jay even made time to give Paul Newman a private haircut on deck, which was captured by a photographer. In the photo Jay is cutting the nape of Newman's neckline while his subject is looking ahead, as the two coolly sipped on a couple of ice cold Schlitz beers.

After the trim, Jay freshened up and changed from his white turtleneck and leather jacket to a Brioni suit and tie. Lt. Col. Paul Tate and his daughter Patricia dropped by before the formal opening.

Patricia Fripp describes the Commercial Street gala opening that commenced later that day:

> Our opening was spectacular. I was the hostess. I stood at the front desk and greeted our guests. In walked Paul Newman and Joanne Woodward. Paul Newman is the first example I ever met of a truly charismatic personality. He was plainly but elegantly dressed; he walked in with a can of beer. He glowed. It was just like in a movie where the background is blurred. Later that day, Warren Beatty and Julie Christie turned up.

A British native, Fripp would become the first female men's hair designer at the San Francisco salon. Today Fripp is a successful speaker, executive speech coach, and was elected the first woman president of the National Speakers Association. She said Jay had a typical male mindset regarding women and she had to work hard to earn his respect.

> Jay inherited me, and naturally I had to prove myself to him. When he first came to the salon, he said, "Women in the L.A. salon can make a lot of money as a manicurist." I said, "That's great, but I'm not a manicurist, I'm a stylist." Afterwards, Jay's business manager, John Madden, apologized to me for Jay being so tough on me. He had earned a great reputation and naturally his standards were understandably high. At the time, my experience was that many men were rather chauvinistic.

Yvonne DePatis-Kupka[3]—a SEBRING-trained (via Gene Shacove) employee at the West Hollywood salon—does not recall any strange or chauvinistic interactions with Jay. She reflects fondly on her time with Jay.

> He was generous and kind and handsome and just charming as all get out—one of the most amiable people. And it was always on the up and up. There was never any kind of weirdness, it was always straight up. "This is what we're gonna do."

And, by 1969, several women were cutting men's hair at the Fairfax location. Fripp accompanied Jay to demonstrations at local department stores. She said she not only learned the art of cutting, but also how to sell SEBRING products.

---

3. Depatis-Kupka has been nominated for three Emmy Awards for her work in television. She was also a stylist on Quentin Tarantino's *Once Upon a Time in Hollywood*.

Jay was a showman and wonderfully dressed. But the secret behind SEBRING was to make people feel better when they left than when they came in. I also learned from Jay when you meet really interesting and affluent people, learn as much [as] you can about them. Working in the Financial District, I could learn about business from my successful clients. I took advantage of the opportunity and received great advice from very successful people.

Fripp said haircare was also an important part of the SEBRING experience, and that people should not only walk out with a great haircut, but quality products to treat their hair afterward.

"No one ever walked out of SEBRING without our black packaged products in their hand," Fripp said.

After the shop finally officially opened for business, Fripp saw Jay almost every day for three months.

"He'd stay in San Francisco from Monday to Friday on his houseboat in Sausalito then fly back to Los Angeles on the weekends," Fripp said.

The last time Fripp saw Jay, he gave her a kind word and thoughtful gesture she said she'll carry with her always.

Every Friday evening, all the stylists stood at the end of our booths and shook hands with Jay as he left. That last night as he shook my hand, he kissed me on the cheek and said, "You're doing terrific haircuts." To me, that was like being acknowledged by God. Decades later, I have never forgotten.

Jay's reputation and influence created a symbiotic relationship with powerful people from all facets of society. He enjoyed the perks of those relationships in elevating his own lifestyle, but he also parlayed his cache into changing the industry for his colleagues. He formed a guild along with protégé Joe Torrenueva that allowed hair-dressers and barbers to work together in one space, enabling all shops to provide unisex services. This concept of integrating barbers and beauticians in the same establishment was unheard of—not only in Los Angeles or the United States—but the entire world.

The International Hair Designers Guild set its roots in late 1967 with Sebring as President and Joe Torrenueva as Vice President. Torrenueva had opened his salon, Little Joe's Artistic Tonsorial Parlor, on the third floor of 9000 Sunset Boulevard in 1966 with his mentor's blessing. Torrenueva said his parting with Jay was on good terms because he did it the right way.

> The walkout from a few years before really hurt Jay, and I wanted to make sure that when the time came for me to leave, I would tell Jay face-to-face. Jay really respected that, so we started as friends and parted as friends. It was important to me to always maintain a friendship with Jay because the man had done so much for me. He had done so much for men's hair.

The Barber's Union war with Jay and other hairstylists never really went away. There were periods of peace, but also times of plotting and power plays. The Union had the money and capacity to court lobbyists and formulate special interest groups to successfully pass legislation designed not only to protect their interests but to block what Jay felt was the natural progression of the profession. By 1967, the feud erupted when a new law prohibiting cosmetologists from cutting men's hair was challenged by hairstylist Sherman Bone, owner of shops in Glendale and in Hollywood on Melrose Avenue. He challenged the law by suing both the State Board of Cosmetology and the State Board of Barbers Examiners, asserting it was unconstitutional on the grounds that it was arbitrary, discriminatory, and unreasonable.

When Torrenueva brought this to Jay's attention, Jay felt that forming a guild and getting other hairstylists, designers, and even barbers to join would help protect all their common interests. Jay was listed as president, Torrenueva as vice president, and Bruce Hein as guild secretary. Jay's personal counsel, Alvin G. Greenwald, served as their attorney and advisor.

"The male segment of the general public," Greenwald said in a press release issued by Jay, "has a constitutional right to select the grooming services it desires."

While this statement was true, men's hairstyling was still in its infancy and was lacking muscle compared to their counterparts. At the time, California had about 27,000 licensed barbers in the state with approximately 65% of them belonging to the union. Since 1941, a state law permitted fifty-eight counties within California to establish a minimum price for a cut through majority vote. That didn't leave much room for the more ambitious ones to charge more for what they felt was a better cut. So they wanted to diversify and include women to boost their income. But they couldn't because prices were fixed through legislation, and it would be a violation of anti-trust laws. Torrenueva explained:

> Many up-and-coming barbers wanted to start cutting women's hair and the union wasn't having it. It was unfair because they had studied hard for their tests, spent money on tuition learning their craft, only to be told no.

Barbering was changing, and so were hairstyles. Long hair was in, which meant a sharp decline in barber shop business. From 1966 to 1967, there was a 15% drop,[4] according to Quinton (Red) Carter, a Barber's Union official for Local 1000 in Los Angeles County, who was quoted by the *Los Angeles Times*.

---

4. By 1969, there was a 30% drop in business.

"A barber who did 86 haircuts a week, which was average, found himself doing about 73," Carter said. "There's been little improvement."

Employment within the industry also saw an 8% drop within that year, and apprentices, who had to spend 1,248 hours[5] in a barber college and had to pass two state exams, were quitting left and right. In June 1968, less than 50% of apprentices were working at the trade. Barbers were getting $3 a cut, and Jay's cutters were getting significantly more. Again, the old guard was looking to find a way to put him out of business. However, the upstarts felt differently and wanted to venture into women's hair. With SEBRING's success, cosmetologists were also open to cutting men's hair. Jay and Joe thought there was no reason each party couldn't do both, but when Sherman Bone went to court, he was denied.

On November 14, 1967, Los Angeles Superior Court Judge Ralph H. Nutter upheld the state attorney general's contention that the law was a valid exercise of the legislative power to "define the scope of the licensed occupations."

Torrenueva was talking to one of his clients, Milton G. Gordon, while giving him a cut, and apprised him of the situation. At the time, Gordon was the commissioner of real estate, then became the California State Treasurer under Governor Pat Brown in the late '60s. He told Torrenueva it sounded wrong and asked what he could do for him.

Gordon called Kenneth Cory, a businessman and Democratic Assemblyman from the 69th district in Orange County who served in the California State Senate from 1967 to 1974. Cory agreed to sponsor a bill that, in essence, would allow barbers to cut women's hair and for cosmetologists to cut men's hair and work in the same

---

5. At the time, cosmetology schools require 1,600 hours of training, mostly in cutting, setting, dyeing women's hair, permanent waving, and hair straightening.

space as well. Torrenueva said the bill was a game changer for men's hair.

> The bill basically said if you're a hairdresser or cosmetologist and you've been cutting hair for a number of years, you're allow to take the barber's test. You didn't have to go to barber school, but you had to take the test and pass.

The test was divided into three parts: oral, practical, and written. It was not easy and required a serious period of study. The bill came with a fifteen-month window, and after that, it was closed to hairdressers. Torrenueva remembered a lot of people took the test.

> A lot of them passed and a lot of them didn't because they didn't study. Hairdressers didn't shave men, so that's one segment where we had to really study. Jay and I had studied hard for this test as we were going to be the president and vice president of this guild, so it was imperative that we passed.

Assembly Bill 244 was passed by both houses and signed by Governor Ronald Reagan. The first date to take the test was Monday, August 11, 1969. Tragically, Jay Sebring, Torrenueva's friend and mentor, was murdered on August 9, two days before. It took all the strength he could muster to get through it, but Torrenueva passed. He recalled his emotions that day:

> I was seriously grieving for Jay, but I had to do this for him because we worked so hard to get this through. I had to do it; I just had to. This laid the groundwork for everyone to work together now. Before, they couldn't. I now have both licenses, but I only went to school for one.

Jay Sebring and Joe Torrenueva were responsible for California salons going unisex and introducing legislation that granted the right of cosmetologists to cut and style men's hair and barbers to cut women's hair. Jay's defiant declaration years earlier, "Hair knows no gender" was now backed by law.

It was another revolutionary feather in Jay's cap that would ultimately manifest in permanent global implications.

CHAPTER 23
THE FAMILY

By the time Charles Manson and his acolytes migrated from San Francisco to Los Angeles, L.A. had shapeshifted from a relatively conservative stronghold into the New Age and cult capital of the world. The end of the '60s would see it become home to hundreds of false prophets, gurus, eccentrics, and cult leaders. All these metaphysical shysters promised enlightenment and higher consciousness through wide and varied paths but delivered questionable results.

Perhaps it's the moderate climate, permissive attitudes, the allure of the West, or some other mystical pull, but many of the most famous cults and fringe religions in American history have deep ties to the Golden State dating back to the 1800s. Groups such as the Moonies, Peoples Temple, Synanon, Children of God, Heaven's Gate, and the Source Family set up shop and drew thousands to their "sacred" spaces. The lure of pied pipers drawing naïve seekers to their West Coast lairs has even extended into the modern era with the likes of NXIVM and reincarnations of some older cults that were forced to "rebrand."

Many cults evolve out of an often-innocuous unifying purpose and become distorted as the lust for power consumes and corrupts susceptible individuals, and vulnerable devotees surrender to them.

Synanon was originally established as a drug rehabilitation center in Santa Monica but transformed into a violent nonprofit cult in the 1970s with approximately 1,300 members and $30 million in its coffers. But they eventually filed for bankruptcy in 1991.

NXIVM started off as a self-help and women's empowerment group that offered hope to desperate women. Behind the veil it was operating as a sex pyramid scheme. Keith Raniere was a schlubby puppet master who forced his followers into manual labor and a 500-calorie a day diet to maintain what he felt was an ideal weight for the opposite sex. The enslaved women were also branded with his initials and those of his protégé, *Smallville* actress Allison Mack, who groomed sex slaves for Raniere.

Jim Baker (not to be confused with Jim Bakker the televangelist for the PTL Club and convicted felon) was a wealthy middle-aged businessman and former U.S. marine who served in World War II before moving to Hollywood to become a stuntman. In 1969, he opened The Source, which was considered the first health restaurant[1] in the country. The Sunset Strip establishment brought in close to $10,000 a day and attracted luminaries such as Steve McQueen,[2] Goldie Hawn, Joni Mitchell, John Lennon, Warren Beatty, and Julie Christie, as well as a bevy of scantily clad Aquarius-era demoiselles. The Source[3] was featured in the 1970 film *Alex in Wonderland* and in Woody Allen's classic *Annie Hall*.

---

1. Baker's first L.A.-based restaurant, the Aware Inn, was located at 8288 Sunset Boulevard. Years later, the building was transformed into the Viper Room, outside of which actor River Phoenix died of an overdose.
2. McQueen and Baker were, in fact, good friends and fellow marines. McQueen frequented both The Aware Inn and the Source restaurants when visiting the Sunset Strip.
3. The cult was also the subject of an excellent 2012 documentary, *The Source Family*, directed by Jodi Wille and Maria Demopoulos.

Baker soon became enchanted with esoteric spiritualism and ditched his suits and ties in favor of flowing white robes, turbans, and leather sandals. He also grew a long, white Moses-style beard and shoulder length hair, and dubbed himself "Father Yod." He lorded over a commune of 150 young people—a majority of whom were young, impressionable, and nubile women—thirteen of whom became Yod's "spiritual" wives. They all lived and slept together, walked around in the nude, and recorded trippy psychedelic music in a mansion known as "The Mother House" in the Los Feliz neighborhood of Los Angeles. They also worked at the restaurant during the day. Joe Torrenueva recalled:

> Every morning I'd drive to work to my office at 9000 Sunset Boulevard; I'd see Father Yod and his young disciples walking up and down the Sunset Strip. They were a true sight to behold in their beautiful white robes and sandals. They always held up traffic.

The Manson Family also started off as something else, too, though theirs wasn't any kind of "higher calling" or seeking a deeper consciousness. It initially was started by a habitual criminal who wanted to get laid and desperately sought affirmation in a society in which he was an undeniable failure and self-perceived outcast. What began as an unemployed ragtag group of three eventually expanded into a crime gang, expanding upwards to 40 to 70 people[4] that operated on car theft, prostitution, pimping, drug dealing, credit card/check fraud, and petty crimes and burglaries. They would morph into a strange bunch of criminals, dropouts, and runaways who frequently performed "creepy crawls" where they broke into homes as the owners slept. They stole valuables and

---

4. The higher figure considers the dozens of transient figures who came and went as they pleased.

rearranged household items like furniture just for the sake of making mischief. As the gang expanded, so too did its expanse of violent crimes. It would only be after the summer of '69 that the so-called "Family" would be ubiquitously crowned "a Hippie cult" in headlines throughout America, their notoriety enduring for over a half-century and beyond. Thus, another notch was added to the long list of California cults. But the extensive criminal history of the Family spanning from late 1967-1974 define the clan as a crime organization.

The commune certainly embodied all the hippie optics: long, unkempt hair, shabby clothes, a Herculean disregard for personal hygiene, and lifestyles true to all the earmark Aquarius mantras: "free love," "free drugs," and Timothy Leary's timeless "Turn on, tune in, drop out." The title of "hippie" and "cult" conveniently served as an interchangeable cautionary tale at a pivotal time in America when establishment culture was being challenged by sixties' youth movements. Hippies embodied and embraced the counterculture movement throughout America, and California was Ground Zero.

The leader of this so-called "Family" was a thirty-something ex-con named Charles Manson. Whereas Jay had spent his life trying to make something of himself and enhance the lives of others, Manson was a dark force. He had spent much of his life in various correctional facilities for a range of crimes, including petty theft, robbery, armed robbery, auto theft, molestation, pimping, and violations of the Mann Act (aka The White Slave Traffic Act). While Manson was known to be involved in four separate acts of molestations while in these facilities, he was also molested and beaten during his numerous incarcerations.

No match for larger, tougher inmates, the diminutive prisoner was forced to develop unorthodox tactics of self-defense. This consisted of conning and acting repulsively insane to navigate through threatening confrontations and attacks.[5]

Manson also developed deft veteran jailhouse jargon and philosophical gobbledygook to stymie or win over menacing, dimmer inmates. Throughout his days behind bars, Manson voraciously consumed philosophical literature and developed an interest in Dale Carnegie's *How to Win Friends and Influence People* and Scientology, which cultivated in his wizard-like performative diatribe. This skill would prove most valuable to Charles Manson in how he would perform years later to promulgate his counterculture status.

Once released, "Charlie," as he was commonly known among friends, embarked on a meandering coastal trek hitchhiking along the Pacific Coast Highway back and forth from the Pacific Northwest to Southern California. Eventually Manson would acquire a second-hand van to facilitate his commute. While he aspired to be a famous rock star with his trusty acoustic guitar always in reach, the odd, tiny man, who was rejected by his mother early in his childhood, held deep-seated disdain for the conventional family structure, civil society, and anything considered to be establishment.

Manson noted large factions of California youth in the late 1960s now seemed to distrust authority, government, even their own parents. They hungered for an alternative, an escape, from antiquated or perceived corrupt rigors and establishment society. And he was poised to take advantage of this shift in the zeitgeist.

After only a few weeks as a free man, Manson spotted a target some eight years his junior for a possible interlude. He caught the eye of Mary Brunner, a homely and quiet twenty-four-year-old library assistant at the University of California, Berkeley. Brunner

---

5. Manson coined this latter tactic the "Insane Game." It mostly worked, though a few inmates saw through this act and literally penetrated his veneer. When Manson was on death row in 1971 at San Quentin, he was "punked" by a dangerous and aggressive Aryan brotherhood inmate who forced the once-dominant Family leader into the submissive role of prison bitch/sex slave.

allowed the former convict to crash at her apartment. The two soon became lovers, and Manson convinced her to quit her steady job and travel with him along the California Coast. Before long, the couple found themselves in Venice Beach where Manson encountered a visibly distraught nineteen-year-old named Lynette Fromme sitting on a curb. Sensing an impressionable, kindred mind, Charlie mused, "Your parents threw you out, didn't they?" He was right. She had recently been kicked out of her parents' home and was quickly convinced he was a magical psychic. She was captivated. Manson and Brunner now had a new companion in their aimless journeys.

In Los Angeles, Patricia Krenwinkel was living with her older sister who was battling heroin addiction and had recently attempted suicide by slashing her wrists. Krenwinkel was working a mundane job at the Insurance Company of North America when her sister's neighbor, Billy Greene, dropped by with a man he knew from prison. His name was Charles Manson. She said in a 2016 parole hearing:

> My sister had a friend who lived down the beach from us and he had done time at Terminal Island. When I met him [Manson], he was playing music, and my sister invited him back to stay with us, and he stayed with us for about three days.
>
> He started saying things to me that I thought *This is the first person ever that seemed to see what was going on.* He was 33, I was 19. He was so self-assured and what he would say seemed true to me. He said, "You're unhappy. Why don't you just leave with me? You're beautiful to me. I love you." It's everything that I ever wanted to hear someone say. Maybe he's the one I can eventually marry?

Manson shared his plans with his new lovestruck mate in the

days ahead. He said he intended to look for his mother, visit his parole officer in Washington state, and become a music recording artist. Krenwinkel was prepared to go with him but consulted with her friend before taking the big plunge. She recounted in 2016:

> Prior to leaving with Manson, I talked to Billy Greene, and he said, "Manson and I used to plan on getting on a bus and just traveling the United States with some gals and have a good time." I said, "Should I do this? He said, 'Yes.'"

Life on the road with Charlie appeared to be idyllic. It included music, marijuana, and lovemaking with the Pacific Ocean as a backdrop as they drove north to Washington. One day into Krenwinkel's relationship with Manson, Charlie had tossed a curveball their way when he picked up Fromme in L.A. It quickly dawned on Fromme that Charlie and the other two females were intimate. In fact, Brunner would become pregnant with Manson's child that summer. But Charlie was quick to reassure Krenwinkel she was number one, and the others really didn't matter.

"He would tell me, 'You're the only one. I love you the most,'" Krenwinkel said.

As the months waned, so did their pooled resources. Manson resorted to his old ways, gradually pimping out his three ladies on the road.

Sporadic stops throughout rural Washington and Oregon yielded limited opportunity and cash flow for the mobile brothel, so the four sought a denser community that embraced their "free sex, free drugs" lifestyle while providing greener pastures to sustain their un-livelihoods. The Haight-Ashbury district in San Francisco was utopian catnip for the illicit and unkempt nomads. They would stay in an apartment on Lyon Street, a crash pad on Cole Street, or a flat on Haight, exchanging chemicals and bodily fluids with as many as 20-30 people in a night. Krenwinkel recalled those days:

We traveled up to Haight-Ashbury; it was a different time and place. It was all these people and things were very communal. It was all these groups of people—men, women —and all these ideas of free love, free drugs. It was this kind of explosion of these different ideas. And they started naming people "hippies."

David Milch provided some philosophical context of this counter-culture epicenter.

A New Generation has come of age that is asking questions, which is a kind of high falutin' [*sic*] way of saying, "Nobody knows what the fuck is going on." And suddenly being confused had been translated into a position, into a philo- sophical position—FREE LOVE.... which is just a way of being confused with more pussies involved. Or whatever the orifice of choice is. What did the sailors tell us.... "Any port in the storm"?

Haight-Ashbury would serve its purpose for a time, adding interested friends and subsequent additional cash flow. Among their new colleagues were Ella Jo Bailey and dark-haired, dark-eyed Susan Atkins who recalled meeting Charles Manson when he was playing his guitar at a party where she was staying on Lyon Street.

"The song that caught my attention the most was 'The Shadow of Your Smile' and he sounded like an angel," Atkins said. When he finished the song, Atkins approached Manson and kissed his feet.

Before long, Atkins was standing nude before a full-length mirror, hand in hand with this virtual stranger, fourteen years her senior, when he asked, "Have you ever made love with your father?" Atkins said she had not. Manson asked if she had ever *thought* of making love with her father. She replied yes.

"All right, when you are making love.... picture in your mind that I am your father," Manson said. The troubled topless dancer was hooked.

It was just a matter of time before complete abandon and indulgence in the Haight would cast a dark shadow over the district with bad trips, STDs, body lice, and overdoses. David Milch explained that a huge cultural shift was taking place.

> San Francisco was the first big experiment and Los Angeles was responding to and trying to figure out how to market these new "truths." The film and recording industries were experiencing expanding energy and capitalizing on the changing times.

Manson realized that, if he was going to be discovered, he would have to place himself in the center of the pop culture universe. Thus, in a converted school bus, Charlie, Patty, Squeaky, Mary, Susan, Ella Jo, and a few guys drove south on the Pacific Coast Highway, conning, prostituting, and peddling their way to Tinseltown.

The budding "Family" arrived to find Southern California both hospitable and inhabitable. They hitchhiked and hopped from one crash pad to the next, from Topanga Canyon to Laurel Canyon, from Malibu Beach to East Hollywood or the Pacific Palisades.

Through a mutual friend, Manson met Harold True, an intense medieval history major at California State University at Los Angeles, who rented a home with a few other students on Waverly Drive in Los Feliz. Always up for an interesting time, True assured Charlie that he and the girls were welcome to stay any time, which the gang often did. It is crucial to note that Harold True's party crash pad for the Mansonites was right next door to eventual victims and

Gateway Markets grocery owners Leno LaBianca and his wife Rosemary.[6]

In the summer of '68, filming commenced at Spahn's Ranch for *The Ramrodder*, a low-budget sexploitation film that included Catherine "Gypsy" Share and Robert "Bobby" Beausoleil in the cast. Beausoleil, a musician frustrated with the scene in San Francisco, had recently moved to L.A. and was crashing at the Topanga Canyon home of his friend and fellow musician, Gary Hinman.

Beausoleil recalled to *Oui* magazine in its November 1981 issue:

> He [Hinman] gave me the loan of his basement, and he was very rarely home. Gary Hinman was not somebody you could be close with.... He was just somebody that I knew among a crowd of people in Topanga Canyon. His ideologies were very different from mine. He was into communism and all that sort of thing. I couldn't relate to that at all. He was a political science major with a piano on the side for some kind of an income.

Beausoleil and Share bonded during the late 1968 production of *The Ramrodder* and began living together. Soon after, the pair encountered Charles Manson during a party at "The Spiral Staircase

---

6. Leno LaBianca's first wife, Alice, wrote a book called *No More Tomorrows*. In it, she quotes many of Leno's letters sent to her and his children. On pages 409–410, she quotes an April 8, 1969, letter from Leno. It partially reads: ".... no new burglaries, thank goodness! No new clues, either. There has been a plain clothes detective hanging around here occasionally, but I'm beginning to doubt as to whether the 'culprits' will ever be caught.... LA is getting to be a pretty scary place. There are a group of hippies that have taken over Griffith Park and two 'pot parties' have been broken up by the police just next door. That's a little too close for comfort." The letter was sent four months before the murders, and according to Linda Kasabian, the Family attended these parties at that time. Kasabian also testified that she arrived in L.A. around the July 4th holiday, which would place her at True's house even closer to the murders.

House" in Topanga. Bobby and Charlie began jamming, appreciating each other's musical abilities.

"I joined a band, The Milky Way, that Charlie was in," Beausoleil said in the same issue of *Oui*. "That's how I met him. He was a very talented songwriter, good musician, lyrically, just excellent. He was somebody with an incredibly intense, vivid, expanded imagination because of all the time he's done."

In the spring of 1968, Beach Boy drummer Dennis Wilson picked up Patricia Krenwinkel and Ella Joe Bailley hitchhiking on Sunset Boulevard. He invited them back to his house. Krenwinkel immediately phoned Manson to inform her man that she was partying in the rock star's mansion. In a flash, Manson showed up with additional women to satiate Wilson's every desire. Manson was certain that this was his big break, and that Wilson was his ticket to a record deal.

Wilson allowed the clan to "hang" at his Pacific Palisades mansion for a few months, and the gang ate his food, drove his cars, sold his gold records, charged up his credit cards, and amassed an astronomical doctor's bill to treat the rampant venereal disease from their wild sexcapades. He once confided his tab for this social experiment was approximately $100,000 in 1969 dollars.[7]

In an ironic twist of fate, Wilson was hitchhiking on Sunset Boulevard when he was picked up by a tall, athletic young man named Charles Watson. In appreciation, Wilson invited Watson into his home to join the festivities. In 2016, Watson recalled this life-changing moment at a parole board hearing:

> I was living on Pacific Coast Highway between Sunset and Topanga. And I was driving home one day, and I picked up Dennis Wilson of The Beach Boys. I was all starry-eyed and everything. And I went into his home and that's where I

---

7. That's equivalent to about $877,000 in 2025.

met Charles Manson and the girls. So, it was like things were just falling into place to meet Dennis. And while he was off on tour, I would take care of his house for him.

Around the same time, Beausoleil and Share encountered Leslie Van Houten, a cute recent high school graduate, at a party in San Francisco. Van Houten expressed finding a higher purpose in life, and the "worldly" duo convinced the former small town homecoming queen she could find that purpose with them back in Los Angeles.

Manson supplied Wilson with all the girls and party favors he could want, but his generosity came with expectations. He pressed Wilson to introduce him to friend and music producer Terry Melcher (The Byrds, Paul Revere & the Raiders, and The Mamas & The Papas). Melcher was also the son of Hollywood screen legend Doris Day and was living with actress Candice Bergen in a well-known exclusive ranch-style home at 10050 Cielo Drive in Benedict Canyon. Eventually, after a lot of prodding and courting, Wilson introduced Charlie to Terry Melcher. The two got along fine, even became somewhat friendly. Manson and Watson visited Melcher at the Cielo residence, and he visited Manson at the dilapidated Spahn's Movie Ranch in the San Fernando Valley, their latest residence. Manson was ingratiating himself to all the right people, including Neil Young, who thought Charlie had something.

"I can see these things in other people. You can see it and feel it," Young told a reporter from England's *New Musical Express* in 1985. "Manson would sing a song and just make it up as he went along, for three or four minutes, and he never would repeat one word, and it all made perfect sense, and it shook you up to listen to it."

Manson felt the right producer could launch him to superstardom. Melcher was interested in recording Manson and wanted to make a documentary about him and hippie commune life. Unfortunately, Manson gave a terrible audition at Spahn Ranch, and Melcher backed out after he witnessed Charlie viciously fighting with a drunken stuntman. In 1979, Melcher reflected that his rejection, which was nothing personal, led to something else.

"You meet people and audition them, and it can be Paul McCartney.... or Charles Manson," Melcher told *Sounds* reporter Sandy Robertson. "Jealousies, and in some cases incredible ambition, and if they don't get the right kind of reaction their ambition turns to hatred, anger...."

But it wasn't a bad audition that made Melcher a target of Manson's hatred, according to one insider. He said the producer not only made certain promises, but helped himself to a few of Charlie's women, according to journalist Ivor Davis, who covered the trial and knew all the players, including Melcher. He said of the famous producer:

> He [Melcher] did partake of the girls, as did his pals, including Dennis Wilson. They formed an exclusive little club whose drug-fueled members aimed to bed as many groupies as possible. They called themselves the "Golden Penetrators."

Adding insult to injury, Dennis Wilson eventually cut off Charlie and his harem of hairy hippies. After footing a six-figure bill for their antics, the Beach Boy drummer wanted to avoid a conflict with Manson and simply walked away from his home and disappeared for a while. Wilson had leased the 8,000-square-foot home, and when the contract expired, the owner kicked out the remaining squatters.

Banished from paradise by the rich and famous, Charlie and his crew were forced to seek refuge large enough to accommodate fifty-plus holdouts. A Manson acolyte connected to a fifty-five-acre ranch out in Chatsworth cut a deal with eighty-year-old George

Spahn, who was legally blind and unable to maintain the property. It was agreed that Charlie and the now commonly referred to "Family" could reside at the ranch in exchange for labor, upkeep of the grounds, and maintenance of Spahn's horse rental business.

After Manson's bitter rejection from Melcher, an end to their gravy train, and the financial strain of an expanding commune, the atmosphere among the Family started turning dark and sinister. Manson began hearing hidden messages in The Beatles' *White Album* and took it upon himself to interpret that for his minions— chiefly, that a race war was about to commence and the Family had to be ready. He called it "Helter Skelter."

Despite having a free roof over their heads courtesy of George Spahn, the finances required to support a commune of nearly 50-60 adults, not to mention the children and continual flow of friends and visitors, were weighing heavily. Drastic measures were employed, including dumpster diving for food at nearby restaurants and shopping centers. Some of the more resourceful members of Charlie's Angels would offer sex and other acts to grocery store clerks who set aside food for them on their routine runs.

Prostitution, drug trafficking, and credit card fraud alone no longer covered the costs required to exist in California. In the months leading to July 1969, the Family turned to a wider range of felonious acts to sustain themselves—grand theft auto, check fraud, burglary, dune buggy theft, conspiracy, assault, extortion, torture, attempted murder, and murder.... and this was just the beginning.

Watson was floating back and forth between the ranch and the Hollywood apartment of Rosina "Luella" Kroner, his girlfriend. Upon learning that Kroner had become successful at selling drugs in significant quantities, Manson told Watson he wanted a piece of the pie. Watson described what happened next—a decision that most likely ignited the powder keg that unleashed one of the most notorious murder rampages in U.S. history. Watson recalled for a parole board at a 2021 meeting:

Manson asked Rosina for money, but she refused. Manson said, "That's not good enough, you have to get some money from her." So, I came up with an idea that I could possibly get some kilos of drugs. TJ Walleman was also in the Family and knew a dealer he had purchased kilos from before.

The drug dealer Watson referred to was African-American Bernard "Lotsapoppa" Crowe. Watson said a drug deal worth $2,750 went down on July 1, 1969. between him, Rosina, and a couple of people he believed were involved in the Black Panthers. Watson portrayed himself as the "mule" who would take the money from Rosa's source and return with kilos of marijuana. He revealed at the parole meeting that they "scammed $2,750 from these drug dealers and brought it back to Manson that night."

Then all hell broke loose.

Crowe called the ranch asking for "Charlie," intending to threaten Charles Watson, who had just burned the dealer on a massive amount of goods. But Manson picked up the phone to hear Crowe demanding his money and threatening to come out to Spahn with his crew and kill everyone. Manson believed Crowe would make good on his threat and devised a plot to meet him at his apartment in Hollywood to repay the cash. Manson enlisted Walleman to calm Crowe down under the guise of returning the money or promised goods, and then he would distract Crowe while TJ shot him. Manson reasoned to Walleman, "You got us in this mess, you've got to clean it up." When the pair arrived at Crowe's apartment that evening, Walleman froze, forcing Manson to shoot "Lotsapoppa" in the abdomen. When he collapsed and lay motionless on the floor, Manson assumed he was dead. Before fleeing, Manson absconded with an oversized leather jacket with fringe— the very same jacket Manson wore for his booking photo by LAPD.

The next day, fear and paranoia spread like wildfire at Spahn, anticipating certain Black Panther retaliation. The Family had heard a radio report that a Black Panther's body had been dumped at a medical facility on the UCLA campus, and naturally everyone thought it was Crowe's corpse.

Manson and the Family's game might have won over teenagers, hippies, and amorous Hollywood types, but Watson, T. J. Walleman, and Manson soon realized they likely fucked with the wrong people. With the nation literally going up in flames in racial strife, Black leaders were being assassinated, and now they had just murdered a Black Panther, Manson and his clan believed Helter Skelter was coming home to roost. And "coming down fast."

Desperate for protection, Charlie enlisted The Straight Satans, a Venice-based motorcycle gang, as a deterrent.... of course, in exchange for sex and drugs. Money was drying up in the sweltering summer heat and The Family's safety was in imminent peril. The Family was in desperate need of funds and a plan out of a deadly situation.

In the days leading up to July 24, 1969, Manson, Beausoleil, Atkins, Brunner, and Bruce Davis hatched a plan to extort a large sum of cash from Gary Hinman, a friend of Beausoleil's who had peripheral social involvement with the Family. Manson was under the impression Hinman was a trust fund kid. Since he participated in several Family festivities, Manson determined Hinman "owed" an amount upward of $20,000. It was also rumored that Hinman had been involved in "cooking up" a bad batch of mescaline in a drug transaction with the Straight Satans through the Manson Family,[8] even though Gary Hinman had no previous experience or history of drug dealing.

On July 24, 1969, Susan Atkins, Mary Brunner, and Bobby

---

8. Hinman's "occupation" as a drug dealer was refuted by Robert Beausoleil at a January 28, 2022, parole hearing. He stated for the record, "He [Hinman] was not a drug dealer, in my opinion. Though he did sell marijuana to mostly friends. He cooked up a batch of mescaline from peyote buttons he had come into.... it was something he was experimenting with."

Beausoleil arrived at Gary Hinman's Topanga Canyon residence under the pretense of a casual social visit. Almost immediately, Beausoleil informed Hinman, "We want the money." The UCLA Philosophy graduate was confused, and declared he didn't have any cash. Beausoleil phoned Manson with the bad news but Manson insisted, "Don't leave without the money." Beausoleil decided to search the premises for cash or valuables after handing the gun to Atkins to keep watch over Hinman in the kitchen. Atkins eventually let her guard down and Hinman was able to seize the weapon from her as she yelled out to Beausoleil. As he rushed into the kitchen and eventually wrestled the gun away from Hinman, the three struggled for the weapon. But first, a round was errantly discharged into a kitchen cabinet because of the commotion, causing Mary Brunner to phone Manson and inform him of the ensuing chaos at Hinman's shakedown.

A few hours later Davis and Manson, with machete in hand, showed up and confronted Hinman, who remained completely boggled. Manson told Beausoleil, "This is how you do it," and slashed the entire left side of Hinman's face from cheek to ear, severing his victim's ear in half. As he left, Manson instructed Beausoleil, "Don't leave till you get the money."

Hinman was bleeding profusely. Atkins and Brunner located dental floss in the medicine cabinet and the cohorts attempted to "stitch" Hinman's ear back together. Desperate to stay alive, Hinman agreed to sign over the titles of both his vehicles to Manson but remained insistent that he had no money or pile of cash.

The next day Manson told Beausoleil over the phone, "You know what you have to do." After hanging up, Beausoleil walked up to the man who kindly let him live rent free at his Topanga Canyon residence and plunged a Bowie knife into Gary Hinman's chest multiple times. Somehow, Hinman remained alive, gurgling and struggling loudly for breath for an agonizing length of time. Brunner, Atkins, and Beausoleil each took turns suffocating Hinman with a pillow. The killers hastily made their escape, but not before leaving messages in Hinman's blood on the walls of the crime scene: "POLITICAL PIGGIE," along with paw prints creeping upward. They also left desperate and cowardly clues intending to frame the Black Panthers and lead law enforcement to put the heat on them.

But that plan was derailed when Beausoleil was noticed by a Los Angeles Sheriff's Officer who was conducting a routine patrol on August 6, 1969. After being questioned, Beausoleil was arrested for suspicion of auto theft and the murder of Gary Hinman, who was sleeping in his murder victim's vehicle. Police also recovered Beausoleil's knife during a search of the car.

Now Manson and the Family faced several ominous likely fates —frightening bodily harm from the Black Panthers (for retribution of the drug burn and "murder" of Bernard Crowe) and/or jail time for the murders of Bernard Crowe[9] and Gary Hinman should Beausoleil slip up while in police custody. Desperate to stave off payback and incarceration, Manson concocted a scheme to pit their enemies against one another and spring one of their own from jail through copycat crimes.

They would accomplish this by convincing law enforcement that the Panthers had killed high-profile types in Beverly Hills exactly as they had at the Hinman Topanga Canyon murder scene. The motive was to eliminate the Black Panther threat by framing them for mass murder and to exonerate Beausoleil and The Family of their crimes while also sending a message to Terry Melcher.

In Manson's desperate, twisted mind, all roads and intersections for escape and delusional vindication would lead to the "Hollywood people" at Cielo Drive.

---

9. Manson and his cronies' incorrectly believed Crowe was killed after Manson shot him in the abdomen. Crowe not only survived but testified on behalf of the prosecution in court.

CHAPTER 24
EXPOSED

J ay Sebring's vision for his business was limitless, but the more successful he became, the more he felt the strain of significant time constraints.

Promoting his salon expansion and product line, giving demonstrations at department stores, servicing his clients, traveling to and from movie sets, and frequent visits to San Francisco, Las Vegas, and New York took up every minute of his day. Jay had to figure out a way to tackle his daunting workload so he could still have a personal life. This led to an older and wiser Jay Sebring working smarter.

The first step in making it possible to be in multiple places at once and meeting all the demands on his time and abilities was to produce a training film called *Hair Power*. The 106-minute film was shot by Barry Feinstein, a talented artist, photographer, and filmmaker who worked with presidents, rock musicians, and movie stars.

The stark but powerful image of Bob Dylan on the balcony of his New York apartment that graced the cover of the singer's third album, *The Times They Are A-Changin'*, is an example of Feinstein's work. After that iconic album was released in 1964, Feinstein shot hundreds of album covers for other top artists, including The Rolling Stones, The Byrds, George Harrison, Janis Joplin, Eric Clapton, and Ike & Tina Turner. Most likely Feinstein met Jay on the set of *Bullitt* in San Francisco when he was commissioned by Steve McQueen[1] to shoot the movie stills.

Jay opened *Hair Power* expressing his intentions:

Hi, my name is Jay Sebring and I'm thirty-five years old. Before I entered the hair business fourteen years ago, I made up my mind that I was going to do all that I could to elevate the profession. But strangely enough, my biggest stumbling blocks have come from the profession itself and the laws of the profession.

Hair Power covered many of Sebring's tips, techniques, and implementations, and featured his product line. He also performed different distinctive SEBRING haircuts on actor Peter Lawford as his subject. While Jay used several models in the film, the former Rat Packer was the only head on which Jay demonstrated two separate techniques: the Fox Cut and the Free Form Cut. That segment begins as Jay walks into frame to find Lawford seated in the barber chair smoking a cigarette.

Jay: Peter, what are you doing here?

Peter: There's rumor in town that there's a guy on Fairfax doing free haircuts.

It was a clever and funny quip, but Jay wanted *Hair Power* to be taken as seriously as he treated the profession and the way he revolutionized it. Peggy DiMaria, also a hairstylist, said:

---

1. Feinstein's *Unseen McQueen* chronicles his friendship with "The King of Cool." The 2013 coffee table book captures candid images of McQueen in fast cars, racing pits, working on engines, and during the production of the action feature classic *Bullitt*.

Jay got into a very specific way of men's hair cutting and really perfecting men's hair cutting. He wanted other people to have that same chance. But he took it a step further rather than how you would learn in school to duplicate certain procedures. He wanted people to be taught and shown how to be able to do a haircut and have the guidelines that they could perfect a haircut after they learned all the procedures. Then, they could create on top of that.

Though filming included Jay driving to the shop in his Porsche, leaving his house with a beautiful blonde on his arm, and coolly sauntering into the Fairfax shop, it wasn't just a demonstration film or a vanity project for Jay to show off, according to his nephew, Anthony DiMaria, who included some of the footage for the 2020 feature documentary, *JAY SEBRING....CUTTING to the TRUTH*.

Jay wasn't promoting his success as much as he was sharing his lifestyle. He's expressing his personal style and concepts—how he dresses, what kind of car he drives as well as his personal and professional philosophies on hair technique, each hinged on high quality and personal expression. To Jay, it was all one and the same. This was an intrinsic component of the SEBRING concept which Jay was aiming to inspire in the viewer: Be the best you can be and express yourself. This, in addition to his concepts.

The film also included some of Jay's most powerful and introspective quotes, such as:

- "So far, my greatest contribution to humanity has been my hair care and grooming concept. This seminar will be my contribution to the profession. I hope that you will accept it with the same integrity in which it is being presented."

- "The purpose of the film you are about to see is to pass on to you the findings and the knowledge that I have acquired over the years. As time goes on, styles will change as they have in the past. But the basic concept will remain the same. And that is what we are endeavoring to present to you here in its simplest form."

- "You will best benefit yourself by keeping an open mind and forgetting most of what you have learned in the past. Because after all, the usefulness of a bowl is in its emptiness. And now we will begin with some basic fundamentals...."

SADLY, JAY NEVER VIEWED *HAIR POWER*. PROBATE RECORDS FOR the Superior Court in Los Angeles show a creditor's claim from General Film Laboratories dated August 6, 1969, indicate charges in the amount of $736.85 for two separate films—a 16-millimeter reel of Kodak film approximately 3,835 feet in length, and a duplicate for $65.

According to Anthony DiMaria, only two or three copies of the original film existed. Jay's father Bernard Kummer owned one copy, and a few years later had it transferred to Betamax by Jay's brother-in-law, Tony DiMaria, as a family keepsake. The other set of reels were kept at the Fairfax Salon until an individual absconded with them when SEBRING International changed hands following Jay's death. Segments of *Hair Power* have shown up in various forms over the years, including websites like YouTube.com, but never the full-length version.

"We don't know how those clips got into the public domain, but it certainly wasn't from our family," Anthony DiMaria said.

Another strip of film not intended for public circulation surfaced later with photos that offered a peek inside the way Jay's world was shaping up. He and Sharon had been spending more time together again—four times in the last week of their lives—as both of their lives were seeing big changes, particularly the imminent arrival of Sharon's unborn child.

Three days before Jay submitted his footage to the film lab for *Hair Power*, film rolls from two separate cameras (one was Jay's Nikon) were taken. They reveal Jay and Sharon sharing a lazy day by the pool along with Roman and Sharon's housemate Wojciech Frykowski at 10050 Cielo Drive, a beautiful home in Benedict Canyon, less than two miles from Jay's home.

The picturesque three-bedroom country cottage-inspired farmhouse was perched high on a plateau at the end of a long, winding private drive and sat behind a gated driveway. After record producer Terry Melcher and his girlfriend, actress Candice Bergen, abruptly moved out, it was rented to Roman Polanski and Sharon Tate on February 12, 1969, for $1,200 a month. Owner Rudi Altobelli—a music and film talent manager to stars such as Henry Fonda, Katharine Hepburn, Buffy Sainte-Marie, and Valerie Harper—bought the property in 1963 for $86,000.

"It was magical. You'll never find another view like it," Altobelli recalled to television journalist Martin Bashir. He used the guesthouse as his private quarters while he rented out the main house to others.

In August 1969, Jay and Sharon, along with Cielo Drive houseguest Wojciech Frykowski, were enjoying the space while Roman Polanski was in London preparing his next film, a science-fiction thriller titled *The Day of the Dolphin*.[2] Sharon's belly was growing

---

2. After the murders, Polanski abandoned *The Day of the Dolphin*. Eventually producer Joseph Levine purchased the rights from United Artists. He installed Mike Nichols as the new director under the banner of Avco Embassy Pictures. The film was released in 1973, starring George C. Scott, Trish Van Devere, and Paul Sorvino.

with her first child on the way, and Jay was by her side keeping close tabs on the mother-to-be.

The images taken with Jay's Nikon (confiscated and developed by the Los Angeles Police Department after the murders) reveal an intimacy between them that proves their bond remained close. The photos showed them lounging by the pool on a lazy day; Jay in a skimpy bathing suit, fresh out of the pool, holding a beer in one hand and an arm around Sharon; also, Wojciech hugging Sharon's pregnant belly; a shirtless Jay blow-drying Sharon's hair in the bathroom at the Cielo residence. It seems clear from the photographic evidence that the bond between Jay and Sharon transcended their breakup. While many in Hollywood considered the Polanski marriage ironclad, some in Jay's inner circle believe the former couple never stopped loving each other. Others have said Sharon's relationship with Roman was waning and she was considering ending it.

Roman had earned a reputation among Sharon's closest friends as being demanding, controlling, hypercritical, and abrasive in his critiques. Actress Joanna Pettet, a good friend of Sharon's, told writer Ed Sanders that Roman had a high level of control over his wife.

"He told her how to dress; he told her what makeup he liked, what he didn't like," Pettet said. "He preferred her with nothing, no makeup."

Others, such as Sharon's father, Paul Tate, also viewed Polanski with a degree of skepticism. Many times, Paul overheard the two bicker and quarrel when he'd drop by for visits, according to various friends and intimates. Polanski's constant rebuttals and belittlements didn't endear him to his father-in-law (who used Jay as a yardstick for comparison). And then there were Polanski's indiscretions, which were frequent and sometimes flagrant. Even Paul knew about them, which made his disdain even greater.

Alisa Statman, co-author of *Restless Souls*, said that, according to her research, Sharon's parents did not trust nor respect Polanski.

Based on the audio letters between PJ and Gwen at the time, they did not like Polanski. They knew he was constantly fooling around on Sharon and that did not sit well with either of them. After listening to Polanski's polygraph, PJ was definitely suspicious of Polanski's culpability. Gwen went to visit him [Polanski] in the late 1980s while she was lecturing in Switzerland. I think she was still looking for some type of closure on the rape charges[3] but never received it. Being a victims' rights advocate, this did not sit well with her at all. PJ absolutely despised Polanski after the rape charges.

They spoke twice a year while Gwen was alive because she instigated the calls in August on the remembrance of Jay and Sharon's death and at Christmas. I moved into the house in 1993 after Gwen's passing and the only phone call I remember from Polanski was when he asked for the Tate family to write a letter of support to the DA for the charges to be dropped and for him to return to the US. Both Patti and PJ declined that request.

It seems domesticity wasn't a part of Polanski's DNA—at least,

---

3. In 1977, Roman Polanski was arrested for having unlawful sexual intercourse with 13-year-old Samantha Geimer. After some legal wrangling, he accepted a plea bargain and served just 42 days in prison. However, he fled the United States a year later while still under probation when word got back to him that he was going to face imprisonment on additional charges by a judge looking to make an example of him. In 2024, attorney Gloria Allred filed a civil suit on behalf of a Jane Doe claim that Polanski plied her with alcohol and raped her in 1973. She too was a teenager at the time. The Jane Doe case that would have brought Polanski back to Los Angeles in August 2025 has been settled out of court to the satisfaction of both parties. The settlement led to the case being formally dismissed.

not at that time—and his past probably played a role in how he conducted himself in relationships. Polanski was heavily influenced by the scars of the Holocaust that seeped into his everyday decision-making, including his beliefs on monogamy: "Live for this moment and let tomorrow take care of itself."

As a Holocaust survivor, his pregnant mother was taken to Auschwitz where she was sent to the gas chamber and died shortly after her arrival. His father told him to "Get lost" when the Nazi's invaded their Krakow Ghetto, and he roamed the Polish country-side to avoid the German troops. He survived but didn't fully escape. Later he revealed that German soldiers had taken aim and used him for target practice. After the war he was reunited with his father in Krakow. Then, in the early 1960s, he moved to France to pursue his film career.

Sharon was warned about Polanski by many close friends, family, and business associates, including producer Marty Ranso-hoff, who was responsible for setting up her career in Hollywood. He had seen the director up close and in action when it came to the opposite sex. When Sharon announced her intention to marry Polanski, Ransohoff crudely cautioned her that she was making a big mistake, both career-wise and personally.

"Married? Sharon, he's fucking everyone in town that has a pair of tits!" he told her. But it fell on deaf ears. She reasoned that Euro-peans had a more *laissez faire* attitude when it came to sex and that it was simply more out in the open and less inhibited. She wanted Ransohoff to see that she was happy in love. Ransohoff knew her blasé attitude might change over time and that she was going to wreck her career over him. He countered that Polanski was all about himself and didn't give a shit about anyone else.

"It doesn't matter who he's been with, he still comes home to me," Sharon said defiantly to Ransohoff. "He makes me feel whole and alive. He's helping me find out who I am; no one, including you, has given me that freedom before."

That discussion was their last. Sharon decided to sever their relationship, though it came at a severe cost. She'd still have to pay Ransohoff 25% of her earnings until the option on their contract expired. Sharon was willing to (and did) pay to avoid hearing any more negative feedback about Polanski.

Paramount studio head Robert Evans, who hired Polanski twice —for *Rosemary's Baby* (1968) and *Chinatown* (1974)—noted that Sharon "was under her husband's spell." He also noted, "It was where she wanted to be."

Sharon once shared with Evans how they made their Hollywood marriage work.

"We have a good arrangement," she said. "Roman lies to me and I pretend to believe him."

Her decision to love Polanski unconditionally meant looking the other way often and, ultimately, losing herself. According to friends Gene and Judy Gutowski, Sharon had a work assignment while she and Roman were living together at 1038 Palisades Beach in Santa Monica, so Roman decided to take a vacation 300 miles away in Big Sur. They witnessed Roman invite a Balinese model to spend the night with him at the vacation home they shared. The next day, the model departed for the airport and, a few hours later, Roman greeted his wife with a loving kiss as she disembarked the plane. Judy told Sharon about her husband's brief indiscretion when they got back to Los Angeles, but Sharon didn't do, much less say, anything about it to her husband. It seemed to be part and parcel of their marriage.

If the revelation hurt Sharon, she rarely showed it to family and friends. She was still deeply in love with Polanski and told a reporter at Cannes in May 1968:

He's very sympathetic, very sensitive, very intelligent and a combination of explosives. You don't notice any one part of Roman—he comes at you in one dynamic blast! Roman is such a beautiful, mad human being. Sometimes things are difficult, sometimes good, but it makes life twice as interesting. He's wise, wonderful, and brilliant and he knows everything. Roman has helped me to grow tremendously, it's about time wouldn't you say? Because of him and his acting business, I'm starting to see things for what they're worth. Because I used to take everything at face value. Because when I say something, I mean it... so I used to feel that everybody else meant what they said, but of course that wasn't true, and life isn't that sweet and simple. I guess I kind of lived in a fairytale... looking at everything through rose-colored glasses, I probably always will.

Others in their inner circle said Sharon was animated and bloomed like a flower whenever Jay was around, but in Roman's presence, Sharon's personality underwent a dramatic shift. Polanski sucked all the oxygen out of the room. Sharon was subdued and low-key, if not somewhat controlled.

Publicly, Sharon was standing by her man. However, others who knew her couldn't help but notice Jay's ever-growing presence in her life once she became pregnant. The more Roman wasn't around, Jay was, it seemed, and it didn't go unnoticed.

"Jay went with Sharon Tate before Roman Polanski did," Kirk Douglas wrote in his autobiography, *Ragman's Son*. "There was talk that their romance still continued, even that the baby might have been Jay's."

While the Polanskis were navigating married life, Jay was actively enjoying single life again, dating Valerie Perrine, Connie Kreski, Suzanne Peterson, Sharmagne Leland St. John, and a bevy of attractive women in Los Angeles, Las Vegas, San Francisco, and New Mexico. Another beauty who appeared on his arm on occasion was Barbara Leigh, a model-turned-actress looking for a break in the business.

In the summer of 1969, Leigh went looking for transportation at a used car lot on Wilshire Boulevard and Cox. She was eyeing a 1963 champagne brown Chevy Malibu but didn't have the credit to purchase the vehicle. The salesman said he might be able to help her land a co-signer and introduced her to Jay. She recalled what he was like in a 2025 interview:

> Jay was my knight in shining armor. I remember the first time I saw him. I thought he was handsome and kind, but he reminded me of my brother Jimmy. Both were short, dark-haired, and possessed a quiet and calm demeanor. Yet, he had a powerful presence. He co-signed on the loan; I got the car, and we started hanging out a little. He showed me his unique home, which he thought had a ghost living there. He told me he saw an apparition on his stairs.
>
> He took me to a dinner on Sunset Boulevard and a couple of parties. For whatever reason, he had to help me, show me things, and by doing so, enriched my life. I think he saw something in me that he liked, maybe an innocent young girl who needed a break. Maybe I reminded him of someone? Jay showed me kindness and was one of the first people in this town who helped me without asking for a thing in return. He was always a gentleman with me.

Despite a very successful, active bachelor life, the interactive bond between Jay and Sharon was unshakable. Dominick Dunne, an astute chronicler of the entertainment business and Jay's client, also was of the belief that Jay still carried a torch for Sharon and that his affection was returned.

> Roman and Sharon sort of adopted Jay as a family friend, which always surprised me because playing the passive friend never seemed like Jay to me. He loved her. Never got

over her. Theirs was a great love story. You know that marriage [Polanski and Tate's] wasn't gonna last. I mean, he was adultering around. Roman was always going to be that way.

Fred Segal said the connection between Sharon and Jay never waned, nor went away. Nor did it make any sense that she wasn't with Jay.

I don't know why she ended up with Roman Polanski. It was like a shock to me. I know Jay was in shock for a year. Maybe longer, so I don't even know what happened there. Jay once brought Roman Polanski in the store. I never had a connection or energized with him. I almost felt the loss that Jay felt at that time.

Love is difficult to explain but it comes from the heart. That's the difference between sex and romance—sex lasts an hour; romance can last a lifetime. I think Jay had that original heart connection with Sharon.... I just felt they were together. I didn't get the Roman Polanski thing at all. There wasn't that deep love that I felt from Jay with Sharon.

Jay's neighbor Kurt Zacho was about ten years old when he saw Jay and Sharon going for a walk shortly before their tragic murders took place. He recalled that 1969 meeting nearly five decades later:

I met them on the street as they were coming down the driveway. I remember he introduced me to her, and she gave me a hug. I just assumed they were married because when they walked down the road, as far as I remember they were holding hands. They were walking together, and they just looked like a couple to me.

But there were just as many people who felt Roman and Sharon were happily married and still in love. Andee Nathanson, who was friends with Sharon, said there was no question in her mind they were very much a couple.

> They were in love and there was no getting around it. You could tell just by being around them. It wasn't even a question in my mind. I don't care what anyone says, Sharon and Roman were happily in love.

Debra Tate was also insistent that her sister was deeply in love with Roman Polanski during their marriage, not with Jay.

> I do believe, down the road, had something happened to Sharon and Roman's relationship, which there was no indication of at that time.... I think Jay would have wanted to have been right there to move back in on the love that he had denied himself at an earlier point in time. I just can't see her with anybody else other than Roman. She was so devoted to that relationship.

During filming of *The Wrecking Crew* (1968), co-star Elke Sommer and her husband, Joe Hyams, invited Sharon over for dinner while Roman was out of the country. Hyams, a writer, noted something was off about the pair.

> Later we sat around the coffee table in the living room gossiping. The conversation turned to marriage. "I think it's a completely unnatural way for people to live," Sharon said. "People just can't remain sexually attracted to each other day in, day out. It's just not possible." "Your marriage seems to be going alright," I countered. "I'm glad it seems that way."

Sharon's voice intimated something other than what she said, but I let it pass.

A few weeks later, Roman returned to Hollywood and came with Sharon to our house for dinner. It was the first time I had seen them together and I noticed that whenever he was even in the same room with her, she was withdrawn and silent, whereas whenever I had seen her on her own or with Jay, she had been light-hearted and animated. Still, I found Roman to be one of the most interesting and charming men I had ever met.

Sharon's friends Joanna Pettet and Barbara Lewis had lunch with Sharon on August 8 at the house on Cielo Drive, along with Abigail Folger and Voytek Frykowski. Sharon had been in London with her husband and pleaded with him to have their baby there, but Polanski was adamant his wife give birth in the United States, so she had come back to Los Angeles in mid- to late July. She also told Pettet that she suspected Polanski of having an affair. She told Ed Sanders this anecdote for his 2015 biography of Sharon:

> She wasn't devastated—she had just said she had heard that he was fooling around, she wasn't surprised about it. You know, Roman and Sharon, they had, not an open relation- ship, but I know it was a very, uh, a 1960s marriage, where you could maybe fool around with somebody, and it wasn't going to be the end of the world. But she was not happy about the report she had heard. She didn't mention Michelle.

Michelle was Michelle Phillips, an original member of The Mamas & the Papas, who Sharon considered a friend. Phillips recalled a special moment they shared in 1968 to Debra Tate for her book, *Sharon Tate: Reflection.* "When we were in London, she told me she was pregnant, but that Roman didn't know yet, and with that sweet mischievous smile on her face said she wanted to smoke one last cigarette before telling him that night."

Later, Michelle Phillips finally admitted to her tryst with Polanski in a 2001 *Vanity Fair* article about the murders.

> The police were questioning everyone. Everyone was flushing drugs down the toilet. For some reason, they suspected my husband, John Phillips. "Would your husband have any reason to have any animosity toward anyone in that house?" they asked me. I told them I had a night in London with Roman. I felt bad about that because of Sharon.

While Sharon seemed willing to look past Polanski's string of one-night stands and flings, it was quite another thing to have an inner circle affair. Sleeping with strangers was easy to write off as a European eccentricity, but Roman being intimate with one of her friends would have brought it too close to home. The nature of his indiscretions or perhaps the mounting number of them must have begun to trouble Sharon enough to seek some legal options, which she did through Alvin G. Greenwald, one of Jay's attorneys.

The two men met through Greenwald's son, Paul, who was a longtime client and friend of Jay's. He recalled how they bonded and maintained their friendship:

> I see that Jay has this Magnavox stereo system, and I started in grammar school installing electronic systems. So, I said to Jay, "This isn't really set up right. There's a much better way to do it." And he said, "Oh, you can do that?" I went and did all the work to install the system, but I made a deal with him, that was a lifelong deal—"I'll do the work on your electronics, whatever you want. Can you pay me for the

parts, and cut my hair?" From that day on, I never paid for a haircut. And we became good friends and then I introduced Jay to [my] dad [Alvin] and Dad became his lawyer.

Greenwald, an extremely private attorney, told Anthony DiMaria for his 2020 documentary *JAY SEBRING....CUTTING to the TRUTH*, that Sharon met him in person shortly before August 8, 1969. He revealed: "I drew the papers for the divorce.... the divorce from the director Polanski. Sharon was going to tell Roman when he got back from London. And we drew the papers for that."[4]

In the early 2000s, Anthony DiMaria, along with his mother, met with writer Tom O'Neill. O'Neill had left a message for "Jay's sister" at her place of business, claiming to be working on a piece focusing more on the victims' perspective.[5] Peggy agreed to meet with him. After nearly two hours, O'Neill finally got to a question he was intent on asking and referenced a conversation between Sharon and her friend that hinted at Sharon's plans to leave Roman. O'Neill asked Peggy, "Do you know about any future plans Jay and Sharon may have had?" Both Jay's sister and nephew also observed what seemed to be the writer's keen interest in Sharon's baby.

Peggy responded in an even and measured tone:

I can tell you what I know. I know that my brother and Sharon were very close on several levels. And whatever plans they may, or may not, have had remains between them because they were struck down before the prime of their lives.... That's what I know.

---

4. Greenwald held on to this secret for nearly five decades.
5. O'Neill's book, *CHAOS: Charles Manson, the CIA and the Secret History of the Sixties*, was eventually published in 2019 on the 50th anniversary of the murders. No information shared with the author from Jay Sebring's family was included in the publication.

CHAPTER 25
HOT AUGUST NIGHT

The summer of 1969 was a historically hot season in Los Angeles, literally and figuratively. Temperatures soared into the high eighties—abnormally sweltering for the City of Angels—and the friction among Angelenos was peaking. Culture wars as well as political ones raged in a dark and fevered climate.

Los Angeles historian, essayist, and author Don "D.J." Waldie noted that Los Angeles changed a lot in the late 1960s, struggling to maintain its former way of life.

What had been promised to a lot of people as a place of leisure and life in the sunshine, and to a certain extent, easy living, began to get a little harsher, a little coarser. In part because of growing population, but also in part, more kinds of people were rubbing shoulders…. Los Angeles began to see rifts between its Black and Caucasian populations, between its Anglo and Latino populations. The [1965] riots in Watts were a powerful dividing time that separated what seemed like a simpler city to a much more complicated and hazardous city. Los Angeles began to acquire this apocalyptic kind of quality where it was either sunny all the time or on the verge of collapse and chaos.

Turbulent times extended beyond Los Angeles with the entire country gripped in a dangerous, pernicious Cold War between the United States and the Union of Soviet Socialist Republics. Nancy Sinatra said the late 1960s were a dark time in the United States.

Morally we started to sink in America. I think primarily because we were seeing such horrors with people being assassinated. I remember my first feeling of fear was when Khrushchev took off his shoe at the United Nations and started hammering it on the desk. I got scared. I thought, *Why is he doing that?!* Nations throughout the globe were bracing for World War III. It was only two-and-a-half decades since WWII.

However, 1969 did not hold only doom and gloom. On July 20, America would be bound by national pride and euphoria through the manifestation of a promise from President John K. Kennedy kept posthumously when Apollo 11 landed on the moon.

Journalist Ed Cray remembered this proud and historical moment for the country.

It was awe inspiring. It just had such an emotional impact that we had reached beyond, as they say, the surly bounds of Earth. We couldn't get a damn rocket off the ground at the beginning of the decade. Seven years later, we had men on the moon.

Better days were ahead, and the sky was the limit. Jay and Sharon experienced that iconic "step for mankind" together, and it was memorable, according to Debra Tate. She told Anthony DiMaria the following in one of their many conversations:

> The very last time I saw Jay was about the same time that I saw Sharon for the last time. It was the moon walk. My mother, father, my little sister, and I were piled [on the king-sized bed] in Sharon's bedroom. Because he was a little late, [Jay] actually came running into the room, did an aerial, sat up in a pose, and landed perfectly right smack in the middle of the bed. That was Sharon's house on Cielo Drive. We were all up there watching the moon walk.

Jay's endeavor to expand certified and franchised salons nationwide as well as landing the SEBRING product line's introduction for national consumption was on course to reap its rewards. And Sharon was reentering his sphere.

Outwardly, Jay's and Sharon's lives seemed to be on separate personal and career trajectories; yet, after her return to the States from Europe, Jay and Sharon spent more time together than not, even though Jay had business to tend to and Sharon was eagerly preparing for the arrival of her first child. Inner-circle candid discussions on the stability of her marriage aside, the pregnant Sharon Tate was focused on giving birth to her baby, whom they were to name Paul Richard Polanski.

Los Angeles Police discovered Jay and Sharon had seen each other at least four times in the week leading up to August 8, 1969 —the night of the murders—and many believe the two had rekindled their romance.

Fred Segal observed a unique chemistry between Jay and Sharon.

"I just felt they were together. But I felt then, what I feel now," Segal said. "And I felt them together. I didn't get the Roman Polanski thing at all."

Actress Barbara Leigh also noted how close they seemed to be. She recalled attending an informal get-together at the Cielo Drive house shortly before the murders.

> Sharon had a gathering at her home on Cielo Drive. It was more of a small gathering of friends rather than a big party. I remember she wore a maternity top and looked beautiful. You could tell she was pregnant, but she was a small lady. And very gracious—she was very sweet to me. I was so out of place. I had no clothes, no manicured nails or proper makeup, and my southern accent was still pretty strong.
>
> I was a wallflower, and I was welcomed but ignored once inside. I was a pretty girl to look at but had nothing to share or teach this sophisticated group of people. The only person who spoke to me that night was Ena Hartman, an actress that I would later co-star with in *Terminal Island*. Jay later told me the gossip was that I was a lesbian. I hardly knew what that word meant.
>
> Jay spent most of that night tending to Sharon, whom he worshipped. Most of the time when Jay and I talked on the phone, it was about Sharon. I just listened. He was definitely in love with her—to their dying day.

THERE ARE ONLY TWO PEOPLE ALIVE ON THE PLANET TODAY who know exactly what occurred at the 10050 Cielo Drive residence in Los Angeles where five souls were shot, stabbed, bludgeoned, and suffocated[1] to death. The two surviving witnesses—

---

1. Sharon Tate's unborn son, Paul Richard Polanski, slowly suffocated approximately 15-20 minutes after his mother expired.

Patricia Krenwinkel and Charles "Tex" Watson—were also the perpetrators.

What is known is this: Shortly before or just after midnight Friday, August 9, Linda Kasabian, and her accomplices—Watson, Krenwinkel, and Susan Atkins—armed with bolt cutters, a long rope, two hunting knives, a bayonet, and a long-barrel .22 Long-horn handgun, chugged up a Benedict Canyon hill in a beat up yellow 1959 Ford Galaxie and pulled up outside the secured gate of the residence.

Watson was very familiar with the layout due to his acquaintance with Terry Melcher, the property's previous tenant. He climbed the pronged telephone pole to cut the wires leading to the home, and then he, Atkins, Krenwinkel, and Kasabian scaled the wall and approached the residence. Eighteen-year-old Steven Parent had been visiting William Garretson in the guest house and was in his car at approximately 12:15 a.m., preparing to leave.

The three jackals hid in the bushes while Watson blocked the car as the recent high school graduate headed towards the electronic gate to push the button to open it. Steven rolled down his car window and stared, confused, as Watson emerged from the darkness, his gun trained on his hapless victim.

"Halt!" Watson yelled. Startled, Steven kept his foot on the brake but left the engine running.

As Watson approached the teenager with the gun in one hand and a bayonet in the other, there was a frantic, brief interaction between him and Steven. Most likely he told him to put the car in park.

"Please don't hurt me," the teen pleaded. "I won't tell anyone."

Sensing what was coming, Steven raised his hands while Watson slashed at the young man, lacerating his skin on the palm of his left hand between the little and ring fingers, and severing Steven's wristwatch. Watson then unloaded four bullets at point-blank range into

Steven's torso, making him the first victim at Cielo Drive. Watson then reached into the vehicle and turned off the engine's ignition.

Watson led the way to the entrance of their targeted crime scene, and he either slit or removed the screen of the window to the right of the front door and raised the window. He climbed through it into the home and opened the front door to provide free passage for his cohorts, except for Kasabian, who stayed outside and acted as a lookout. Watson and his counterparts sidestepped the two large blue steamer trunks that had arrived that afternoon with Sharon's belongings from Europe. They cautiously surveyed the living room and the loft perched directly above the brick fireplace. The three assailants observed a man asleep on the living room sofa.

Watson poked the slumbering Wojciech Frykowski with the Longhorn. The Polish immigrant was foggy and asked, "Who are you? What do you want?" His reaction enraged Watson, who kicked Wojciech in the head.

"I'm the devil, and I'm here to do the devil's business," Watson uttered, according to testimony.

Atkins then used a towel from the house to tie Wojciech's hands behind his back. Watson stood guard with an upraised gun. He motioned to Atkins and Krenwinkel to scope the residence. The culprits made their way down the hallway to discover Abigail Folger in the guest bedroom reading a book in bed and dressed in a nightgown. She kindly waved at Atkins, mistakenly perceiving the killer as a friendly visitor. Atkins smiled and waved back.

Atkins also observed Sharon, who was in her bra and panties, conversing with Jay on her bed in the master bedroom. Jay's back was to Atkins and didn't see her, and Sharon didn't take notice.

Krenwinkel and Atkins quietly returned and informed Watson that three additional people were in the back bedrooms. He nodded and the pair took their knives and tricked Abigail, Sharon, and Jay into the living room. There have been several references to Susan

Atkins' description of the victims walking into the living room as shocked or frightened.

There is some indication, however, that Jay might have initially thought these unknown guests to be some kind of hoax until he observed Watson with the gun. Brother-in-law Tony DiMaria opined about what he thought might have happened that night.

> There were practical jokes that went on at different times. And it's my thinking that Jay thought this was a practical joke at first. I don't think he was taking this seriously. He was going along with it until they got in the room when they were all together and he realized what was starting to happen. Then it was too late.

It was hard for them to fathom such a surreal scenario like this unfolding in such a safe and secluded home. Having a peaceful evening disrupted in such a bizarre way and being caught off guard made it difficult for them to respond appropriately to the danger they were facing.

As Abigail, Sharon, and Jay entered the living room, Jay asked "Who are you? What are you doing here?" to which Watson shouted, "Shut up. One more word from you and you're dead." Wojciech then warned, "He means it Jay."

When Sharon hesitated, Watson leapt forward, grabbing her arm and jerking her toward him as he flipped off the hall light with his elbow. Watson then ordered all of them to line up in front of the fireplace. Sharon must have sensed what was coming at that point and began to cry.

"Shut up!" Watson shouted.

Jay stared hard at Watson, not believing his insensitivity. "Can't you see she's pregnant?"

There are numerous accounts in testimony, published documents, and Vincent Bugliosi's bestselling *Helter Skelter* that vary and contradict one version after the other regarding what led to Watson firing the first (and only) fatal shot inside the residence. Regardless, that gunshot set off a chaotic chain reaction that altered what was intended to be an orderly execution of the occupants of the home, whoever they were. In some portrayals, Jay was pistol whipped after verbally defying Watson; other accounts claim Jay, Sharon, and Abigail were bound and tied before being brutalized. Atkins contradicted herself on the stand during trial regarding the rope. However, there are several irrefutable accounts in court testimony of Jay's last actions conspicuously absent from Bugliosi's book.

While there is no public definitive account of Jay's last actions, long-time friend and mutual devotee to self-defense Vic Damone was baffled by the reports he heard.

"The only thing I couldn't understand is when the Manson people went and did what they did, I wonder...." he said, "I wonder if there was anything that Jay could have done."

With his extensive training with firearms and self-defense, Jay knew there was no way to defend against a gun. Bruce Lee's wife, Linda Lee Cadwell, reiterates what her husband used to say:

Anybody with a gun can overcome somebody, no matter how much training they had. But Bruce would train for situations when people would have a weapon. In particular, it would be the element of surprise.

The element of surprise is exactly what Jay attempted in the moments leading up to enduring his very first fatal wound (as confirmed by testimony and autopsy findings). Once Jay realized the situation was not a prank or a robbery but was an attack with perilous intentions, he became actively defiant. After Watson physically manhandled Sharon, Jay charged the gunman while attempting to throw a blow with a clenched fist when he saw an opening to potentially thwart the inevitable. In a flash, Jay quickly advanced and lunged towards Watson when the gunman briefly turned his back to Sebring.

Debra Tate learned from her father's own investigation that, "once they realized the events were not some kind of hoax, Jay started fighting with everything he had."

In his original trial testimony from September 1971, Watson confirmed Jay seized a moment to physically attack him, but Atkins alerted him of Jay's aggression. In trial, Watson recounted the events:

Question: What happened when the group was in the room then?

Watson: A guy started toward me and—

Question: Was this the man that had been on the couch?

Watson: No, it was another person.

Question: What happened then?

Watson: And I was.... I remember I was kind of running or jumping back and forth behind the couch and making funny noises and Sadie [Susan Atkins] said, "Watch out!" or something and like that and I turned around and I emptied the gun on this man.

Question: You say you "emptied the gun on this man"?

Watson: Yes.

Question: How many times did you shoot him if you know?

Watson: I don't know, I just shot, you know. I don't know how many times I shot him.

Question: Did you do anything else?

Watson: Then I went around the couch and started stabbing him.

Question: This is the same man you shot?

Watson: Yes. Patricia was already over there stabbing him and I went over and did the same thing.

In Watson's 1971 psychiatric evaluation, he confirmed: "The girls were bringing everyone into the room. A guy (Jay) came *running* toward me. I know I shot the guy until the gun was empty and then I stabbed the man."[2]

One of the bullets fired pierced Jay's exposed left armpit and lung, traversing downward through the lower spine. The bullet exited Jay's body and rested between skin and shirt against Jay's belt. The Longhorn was, in fact, not empty but jammed, and Watson resorted to slashing Jay's outstretched left fist, making a perpendicular slash across the knuckles of Jay's left pinky and ring fingers.

During her trial testimony, Atkins corroborated that Jay was not compliant:

Atkins: Sharon said something to the extent that she is pregnant. Jay Sebring said, "Can't you see she's pregnant? Let her sit down."

Question: Before Sebring said that, had Tex ordered Abigail, Sharon, and Jay to do anything?

Atkins: Yes. Tex ordered them all to lie down on their stomachs in front of the fireplace.... Jay Sebring didn't follow Tex's orders and Tex shot him.

Forensic specialist Dr. Michael Baden established that the bullet itself caused a lot of internal bleeding but would not have incapacitated Jay immediately.

"It would have impaired him by internal bleeding, so he could have struggled for a bit," Baden said. "The stab wounds are very prominent on the back."

With Jay bleeding out on the floor, Sharon and Abigail became hysterical as Watson tried to regain "order" by saying they wanted money. Watson then looped one end of a rope around Jay's neck and threw the other end over a wood ceiling beam and wrapped it around Sharon's neck.

---

2. In Watson's October 15, 2021, parole hearing, he confirmed once again that Sebring caught him off guard. "I got scared and I shot him. And then he went to the ground, and he was still moving. I went over and stabbed him."

Suddenly, Jay began struggling to get to his feet, simultaneously gasping for breath as he was drowning in his own blood. Watson rushed Jay and repeatedly kicked him in the face with his steel-toe boot, causing massive facial contusions and breaking Jay's orbital socket. With Watson focused on Jay, Wojciech freed himself from the sofa and fought with Atkins as he scrambled toward the front door. Atkins clung to him and stabbed his legs.

At his trial, Watson was asked how long he attacked Jay Sebring in the second assault. Watson answered, "Until Sadie hollered at me, and she was fighting and stabbing a man going out the door."

Bugliosi's co-prosecutor, Stephen Kay, remembered the following decades after the murders:

> Frykowski ran and Susan Atkins stabbed him in the leg at least 3 or 4 times.... And he did get outside. Watson followed and pounced on him. Hit him over the head 13 times with the butt of his gun. Folger ran out the back of the house. Krenwinkel chased her with an upraised knife, chased her all the way out of the back of the house, all the way around to the front grass and then pounced on her.

"You got me! I give up," Abigail said. "I'm already dead."

As Abigail and Wojciech were being butchered by Watson and Krenwinkel on the front lawn, Sharon was being held at knifepoint by Atkins, strung together with Jay in a tandem noose. Stephen Kay recalled:

> Sharon was sitting on the floor in front of the sofa. Where is an eight-and-a-half-month pregnant woman going to run? She said, "All I want to do is have my baby." Susan Atkins looked at her and said, "Look bitch, I don't care about you or that you're gonna die and you better be ready for it."

When Watson and Krenwinkel finished the butchering outside, they returned to the living room to find Sharon, desperate and hysterical, pleading for her life and the life of her unborn son. Watson, who felt nothing for Sharon, uttered two simple words.

"Kill her," he said.

Having witnessed the horrific slaughter of her dear friends, Sharon suffered the same unspeakable fate—a demise so unbearable that her last words were, "Mother! Mother!"

Baden stated that Sharon Tate was stabbed numerous times about her breasts, had a deep wound to the upper abdominal region, and one stab wound in the right leg. He also confirmed there were no traumatic wounds to the fetus, but it died a slow and tragic death.

"The baby would have survived 10 or 15 minutes after the mother lost consciousness," Baden said.

As the killers made their getaway, Atkins immersed the towel that was used to tie Wojciech's hands into a gaping wound in Sharon's body and used the blood-drenched cloth to smear "PIG" on the front door of the residence, then tossed the towel inside the house where it landed on Jay's head. Once again, the motive of the message was to make it appear that the crimes were committed by the Black Panthers—the same group fingered for killing Gary Hinman weeks earlier. First, POLITICAL PIGGIE. Now PIG. It was later proven in court that the Manson gang intended for law enforcement to connect the Topanga and Cielo crime scenes, thereby increasing heat on their enemy, and convincing the authorities that Robert Beausoleil should be released from jail. It was a copycat motive with numerous intentions:

- Frame the Black Panthers for the murders of Hinman and the Cielo Drive victims.
- Avert retribution from the Black Panthers.

- Exonerate Robert Beausoleil of Gary Hinman's murder.
- Incite "Helter Skelter."
- Send a personal threatening message from Manson to Melcher regarding the music deal rejection.

A coroner's report later provided a tally of the wounds the victims at Cielo Drive suffered: seven gunshots, dozens of lethal blows to the face and head, and 103 stabbings.

Jay's extraordinary final actions to defend himself and his friends, which are confirmed by court testimony and forensics, have not been covered in detail in the decades since these grisly murders took place. But Los Angeles District Attorney Patrick Sequeira, who has presided in dozens of Manson family parole hearings, pointed out Jay's bravery in the face of a dire situation:

> Watson describes a scene in which, even though the intent was to go there and murder everyone to begin with, that became chaotic at a certain point by Jay Sebring rushing Tex Watson, which escalated or changed the dynamics of how they were gonna commit these murders. They were trying to do an orderly round up of everybody, but then somebody doesn't go along with the plan. So that caused a scattering of people. That's why you have such a widespread crime with bodies on the outside, inside.

Jay fighting back made a way for Abigail and Wojciech to attempt to flee for their lives and caused the killers to inadvertently leave behind crucial physical and blood evidence that was later used in court to help convict them.

And Jay went out fighting with all his might.

For most of his life, Jay Sebring's nephew, Anthony DiMaria, has been driven by a quest to know truths about his uncle's final moments. On March 29, 2024, he wrote to Watson at the Richard J. Donovan Correctional Prison near San Diego seeking answers to several nagging questions.

Why did you fire the first shot at Jay?

Did you know Jay before that night?

Did you or Manson ever identify directly or know the Cielo victims by name?

In an email dated April 9, 2024, Watson responded, obliterating more than fifty years of speculation and rumor. In his email, Watson revealed, "I had never met Jay, nor heard of him," and that "[Charles] Manson did not ever mention anyone [at the Cielo residence] before the murders."

Regarding rumors of ulterior motives linking the Manson family and Cielo victims, alleging nefarious activity or drug dealing, Watson dispelled those falsehoods as well. He wrote, "The motives of the crimes are at the beginning of *Helter Skelter* Chapter One. There were no other motives."

There was one more final question DiMaria asked Watson: "At your 10/15/21 parole hearing, you described 'I got scared; I shot him.' You were armed with a gun, knife, and [were] considerably larger than unarmed Jay. What occurred that caused you to feel, as you describe 'scared'?"

Watson responded that in addition to descriptions from his book and contextual testimony, "I shot him because of the danger he posed."

~

PROSECUTOR STEPHEN KAY AGREED THAT JAY NOT ONLY POSED a danger but concluded his actions were heroic and indicative of his true character.

Jay was a very brave man. He loved Sharon. And he was not gonna let anything happen to her if he could at all help it. If something happened to Sharon, it was going to be over his dead body. And that's exactly what happened.

CHAPTER 26
A WEIRD HOMICIDE

The five butchered bodies and an unborn fetus laid lifeless for nearly seven hours through the stillness of night into the breaking of dawn. All the victims—Steven Parent, Jay Sebring, Sharon Tate, Paul Richard Polanski (her unborn child), Abigail Folger, and Wojciech Frykowski—met a brutal and gruesome death, suffering their own unique violent assaults.

The process of rigor mortis begins within thirty minutes of death and yields a series of changes in a body that leave them looking less than human. The vicious wounds inflicted upon these victims suggested someone even less than human did the damage. The amount of time it took for the bodies to be discovered set a scene that was not only horrific but confounding.

At a news conference shortly after the crime scene was established, Los Angeles Police Department Lieutenant Robert Helder stated, "We have a weird homicide," heralding a media frenzy that would follow every move of the investigation and draw audiences that would cling to each piece of evidence, trying to unravel the mystery of this unspeakable, bizarre attack.

The group remained undisturbed for hours, their loved ones unaware of the tragedy that had befallen them, and the trail of the lawless, soulless crew grew colder by the moment. It wasn't until fifty-five-year-old housekeeper Winifred Chapman arrived for work at the Polanski household around 8:30 a.m. on Saturday, August 9, that the grisly scene was discovered. Like every morning, Winifred pushed the gate button at the driveway to let herself in. She noticed a broken telephone wire hanging above the house and assumed it fell because of wind. Winifred then picked up a copy of the *Los Angeles Times* from the red mailbox and walked through the gate.

Winifred was running late and rushed to the house, noting that Steven's vehicle jutted out sideways in the driveway but failing to notice his dead body. Upon arrival at the house, she unlocked the back door, "snapped out" the outside lights, and went inside. There, she stumbled upon the slaughterhouse and the world was soon alerted to the "Bloodbath of the Decade."

Initially paralyzed by fear, Winifred grew faint and weak.... then her heart began to race.

"Murder! Murder!" she screeched.

Adrenaline took over Winifred, and she bolted out of the house, down the driveway, and to the safety of a neighbor's home. Fifteen-year-old Jim Asim was getting ready to leave the house and was standing in the driveway when he heard her cries.

"There's bodies and blood all over the place!" she screamed.

Jim, a member of Law Enforcement Troop 800 of the Boy Scouts, relayed the information to his father, Ray, who summoned the West Los Angeles police. He noted Winifred had arrived at 8:33 a.m., hysterically sobbing and eventually collapsing in a heap.

Within minutes, half a dozen police cars raced up to 10050 Cielo Drive. Patrol officers from the LAPD cautiously entered the property with their pistols and shotguns drawn. They first came upon Steven's car in the driveway and discovered his body slumped in the driver's seat, braced against the arm rest, his head leaning back. A quick examination of the vehicle revealed the engine was cool and approximately half a tank of gas remained. They immediately sent out a call for homicide detectives.

Wojciech was the next body discovered. He was found lying on his right side, his head resting on his right arm. His left arm was at his side, his hand clutching the grass. He wore a purple shirt, multicolored pants, brown high-top shoes, and socks. Both his shirt and pants were drenched in blood. Numerous stab wounds were noted, most of them on the left side of his body. He also had stab wounds on his back and defense wounds to his right hand.

Twenty yards away, on the well-trimmed lawn under a fir tree, was the body of Abigail Folger. She was clad in a white, full-length nightgown and was lying in a supine position. Her nightgown was completely drenched in blood from the breast area downward. She had suffered numerous stab wounds to her torso as well as several severe lacerations on the left side of her face. Defense wounds were noted on both her right and left hands.

In the living room, dressed in bikini panties and a brassiere and lying on her left side directly in front of the sofa was the beautiful Sharon Tate. Her legs were tucked up toward her body in a fetal position. Dried blood was smeared over her entire body. It appeared to investigating officers that someone had handled her body, possibly moving her from one location to another, smearing the blood over her. A bloodied white nylon rope was wrapped around Sharon's neck several times and strung over a ceiling beam, linking her to the noose around Jay's neck—his body sprawled approximately four feet from hers.

Even for a seasoned police force, this scene was shocking. Bob Burbridge was one of the first police officers on the scene. More than a half-century later, he told *60 Minutes Australia* that he could never erase the memories of the horrors he witnessed that early morning on August 9, 1969, nor could he have anticipated such brutality inflicted by young people, particularly the women.

"The Sharon Tate murder with five dead bodies was one of the most horrific things I've ever seen in the whole time I was a police-man," Burbridge said. "Nothing compares to that murder scene."

Despite the lost hours after the bloody chaos, the LAPD was able to collect evidence at the crime scene, including:

- a partial gun grip from a Longhorn model .22-caliber, High Standard revolver;
- bloody footprints and one shoe heel print in the walkway and entry;
- type-O blood smears on the electric button and housing inside the gate separating the Polanski property from Cielo Drive;
- a buck knife in the chair;
- a pair of black-framed glasses[1];
- the word "PIG" on the lower portion of the front door, which was written in blood by one of the murderers.

Police then burst through the doors of the guest house with shotguns aimed at William Etson Garretson, who was wiping the sleep from his eyes. The skinny nineteen-year-old was wearing only pinstriped bell-bottom trousers when they frog-marched him to the mutilated corpses, asking him to identify the bodies strewn in the yard. Either hungover or horrified by the massive amounts of blood, William was confused, and the things he said were nearly incomprehensible, prompting police to cuff him, place him in the back of a squad car, and haul him to the downtown station (known as "The Glass House").

Winifred, who was in shock, was taken to UCLA Medical Center for treatment. Later she was escorted to the West Los Angeles station for questioning. Police discovered the befuddled

---

1. Police could never determine to whom the glasses belonged.

young man was employed by homeowner Rudi Altobelli as a care-taker for his three dogs—a Weimaraner and two poodles.

William told an LAPD detective that he had hitchhiked to the Sunset Strip to pick up a TV dinner, cigarettes, and a bottle of Pepsi, and returned around 10:00 p.m. He said Steven visited him around 11:45 p.m., trying to sell him a radio, which he was not interested in. William said Steven left around 12:15 a.m.

Once alone, William said he wrote a few letters while he listened to music in his stereo headphones until dawn and heard nothing because the music drowned everything else out, which he also testified to later in court.[2] LAPD detectives were skeptical he didn't hear the gunshots or screaming after admitting the dogs had barked several times that night, yet he wasn't alarmed and didn't bother to survey the grounds. They detained him on suspicion of murder.

William Tennant, Roman Polanski's business agent, arrived at the house around noon. Tennant's Saturday morning tennis match was interrupted when he was summoned to the estate. He was still wearing his tennis garb when he arrived. He had the unenviable task of identifying the bodies of Sharon, Abigail, Wojciech, and Jay. He left sobbing, without speaking to reporters waiting at the gate. Later he phoned Roman at his London apartment to inform him of Sharon's death.

"There was a disaster at your house," Tennant said. Polanski assumed it might have been an earthquake, a mudslide, a hill collapsing, or some other natural disaster, but certainly not murder. "Sharon is dead.... and Woj and Jay and Abigail."

"No, no, no, no, no....," Roman beseeched. "How?"

---

2. Decades later, William changed his tune when interviewed for *The Last Days of Sharon Tate*, a 1999 documentary for the E! Network. He revealed that he heard what sounded like firecrackers being thrown from Steven Parent's car and thought it was a prank, not gunshots. He also said he heard a woman scream as she ran by the pool but thought it might have been horseplay from the residents of the main house.

"Roman, they were murdered."

The arrival of reporters was almost instantaneous. From the moment the police dispatcher put out the call to officers about a possible multiple homicide at the Benedict Canyon home—an upscale part of Los Angeles not known for crime, much less murder —the media was on scene and wouldn't leave for days.

Ivor Davis, the West Coast correspondent for London's *Daily Express*, arrived around 11:00 a.m. that day after receiving a call from the London office. Reuters had reported that five people had been murdered in a private Hollywood enclave, and it was somehow drug related. He was told to get to the scene as quickly as possible. Before he did, Davis checked the local City News Service ticker tape for the address and raced the fifteen miles over the canyons from his Studio City residence. By the time he arrived, the street was swarming with journalists and onlookers.

"TV cameras, radio, and print media had set up shop, confined to the road leading up to the front gate," Davis said. "From time to time, LAPD media relations officer Dan Cooke tried to answer questions without giving too much away."

By today's standards, LAPD gave away *a lot*. They not only mentioned how many bodies were discovered and estimated time of death but said that the brutal slayings appeared to be "ritualistic," even mentioning that two bodies were connected by a rope. One LAPD spokesperson added that the men were dressed in "hippie clothes," inferring that lifestyle proclivities or drugs were most likely motives for the killings. There would be a lot more inferences in the days to follow.

The only practical information LAPD withheld was the names of the victims until they notified family members, but even that proved to be a difficult task. Davis recalled bumping into gossip columnist Rona Barrett and being surprised.

"What are *you* doing here?" he inquired. "Have they got you covering the police beat now?"

"Don't you know who lives at this house?" Barrett said knowingly. Then she shared her scoop on the names she had. Davis had interviewed Sharon a few years earlier on the set of *Valley of the Dolls* at the 20th Century-Fox lot. In addition to her stunning beauty, as a person he found her "lovely."

As the two conversed, Tennant walked out of the estate and waded through the throng of reporters. As he made his way to his car, Barrett shouted in his direction.

"Is it Sharon, Bill?" she inquired.

Snapped out of his initial shock, he looked up and caught Barrett's eye.

"Oh, Rona," Tennant angrily retorted, "don't be such an asshole!"[3]

News of the tragedy spread to the Tate and Sebring families almost simultaneously as news of the Benedict Canyon killings exploded like a nuclear bomb in radio and television reports throughout Southern California. In Palos Verdes, Jay's uncle, Lieutenant Colonel Harry Gibb, heard his nephew's name in the reports. He immediately called his sister and the Kummers in Detroit to brace his family for the devastating tragedies.

Peggy and Tony DiMaria were working at a salon in Las Vegas when they were hit with the grim news.

"We were at Caesar's Palace working. Peggy's dad called and said that.... Jay had been murdered," Tony DiMaria said. "I had Peggy come out of the shop and we sat her down on the stairs."

Once he told her, she froze, trying to process the information.

"It was like time stopped," Peggy DiMaria said. "I never felt such helplessness."

Once the victims were positively identified by the Los Angeles

---

3. The murders had a profound impact on Tennant who later became addicted to cocaine, divorced his wife, and was homeless for a few years. He eventually moved to London where he got sober, remarried, had a daughter, and became a born-again Christian. He died in 2012.

Police, the news hit Hollywood like a neutron bomb, and the after-burn was immense and far-reaching.

Friend and protégé Joe Torrenueva said he was at his shop on 9000 Sunset Boulevard when the news came over the radio.

I was cutting hair, and the radio comes on, a bulletin. And the voice said, "Sharon Tate and others murdered.... or dead." I knew. I knew Jay was there. And it bothered me because they said, "and others." He wasn't "and others." He was my friend.

SEBRING stylist Dean McClure was in the marine reserves in August 1969, fulfilling his monthly duty.

I was in a meeting, and someone had said they heard the news that Sharon Tate had been killed. I said, "Oh, wow.... she used to date a friend of mine." Then I went home to pick up my wife. She was staying with her sister for the weekend, and they said, "Did you hear the news?" I said, "Do you mean the news about Sharon Tate being killed?" She said, "Yes, but do you know who else?" Then they told me. And I just lost it. My relationship with him [Jay] was very personal and he was very kind to me. He took me under his wing, gave me a job, taught me to do something extremely well. He didn't have to do that. I don't know why he picked me out, but he did. His death is still painful. Surprisingly, but it is.

Actor and director Warren Beatty, who was a longtime client of Jay's, told *Los Angeles* magazine reporter Steve Oney that Hollywood was never the same after the murders.

This hit the movie community very deeply. On a 10-point scale, it disturbed me around a 27. Jay Sebring, Sharon, Abigail, and Wojciech were friends of mine. It was something that happened, and no one knew why. Everybody was trying to come up with a reason. The collective response to these killings was what you might expect if a small nuclear device had gone off.

Jay's neighbor, actor Stuart Whitman, said he was on a Malibu beach when he got the grim news.

A writer named Gary DeVore[4] came running over and said, "Did you hear about this murder?" I said, "No, I didn't," Whitman recalled. I mean, the whole town just went numb. And everyone was so suspicious of everybody else. It was just.... maddening.

Decades later, Robert Wagner recalled how he was "shattered" when he first heard about the way Jay died.

It was terrible when all that happened; it was just unthinkable. Here was this young man who had this tremendous future and was just obliterated in a second. A man like Jay Sebring does not come along very often into this world. He had a particular gift, and he was taken at a very young age when he didn't have to be. It could have gone on forever. It was a big loss to everyone.

Quincy Jones was skeptical when he received a phone call from

---

4. DeVore's screenwriting credits include *The Dogs of War, Back Roads, Raw Deal* and *Showdown in Little Tokyo.*

actor/comedian Bill Cosby who was in London at the time. He remembers:

Bill Cosby calls me, "Man, did you hear about Jay?" I said, "What about Jay?" He said, "He's dead." I said, "Bullshit man." I called SEBRING International, and I said, "Can I speak to Jay, please?" "Who is this?" someone asked. I said, "Quincy Jones." They said, "Jay Sebring is dead." Bam!

Nancy Sinatra, who knew Jay for almost a decade, said her grief regarding Jay's death was initially delayed because her body shut down. She recalls:

There are times in your life when you just have to bring the wall down between you and the things that are so disturbing because of how your body reacts. And that was one of those times for me. Another time was when my grandmother was killed in an airplane crash. The wall comes down and you must protect yourself.... And when a friend is murdered, you don't want to ever think about it again. Not that I saw the real thing, but the imagined images come to mind.

Others, like Vic Damone, felt a sense of guilt when hearing of Jay's passing.

I felt badly because of what happened to him that day because I'm the guy who kept him there.... the one who talked him into staying [in Los Angeles]. Then he's gone. I thought, *Jesus, what did I do?*

Linda Lee Cadwell said the murders were heartbreaking and confounding to her and her husband, Bruce. Decades later she said:

We talked about it but could never come to any conclusions. We didn't know any details, and it was so terribly shocking and frightening when that happened. We lived just a couple of miles away. It was a terrible time. It hurt Bruce so much because he liked Jay and Sharon so much. He reflected on the fragility of life, how we're just going along and then the next day somebody can just be gone. It made him more aware in his martial arts of things like defense to a gun or a knife.

Actress and former girlfriend BarBara Luna learned about it on the way to an audition for a musical. Sharing that memory wasn't easy for her.

I was walking down to the theater when Fred Amsel, a talent agent I knew, was driving up in a convertible and saw me. He yelled out, "Hey Luna, did you hear?" I had been rehearsing all morning for my audition, so up to that point, I hadn't heard anything. And when he told me, that isn't anything you can absorb. He just threw it at me and told me what happened. Then I had to go and sing, and I couldn't. I got up on the stage and my knees just started to buckle. Then I ran home, turned on the TV and heard all that news, which was just staggering.

Then she did what thousands of Angelenos did that day—went out and purchased a firearm. Gun shops and sporting goods stores saw record numbers of sales. Guard dog rentals zoomed from $500 to $1,500 almost overnight. Celebrities felt they might be in danger and ordered extra protection. Comedian Jerry Lewis had a security system installed at his house, as did many others. Frank Sinatra went into hiding with his bodyguards. Mia Farrow, who starred in *Rosemary's Baby* [directed by Roman Polanski], felt she was next in line. Writer Joan Didion assiduously wrote down the license plate numbers of cars parked outside her 1920s mansion in the heart of Hollywood. Many celebrities holed up at the Beverly Hilton Hotel where they could attain a degree of safety and anonymity with five-star hospitality.[5] Some, like Barbra Streisand, who was terrified the killers were still on the loose, took solace in Steve McQueen's Brentwood home. She knew the movie star kept a cache of weapons, which included pistols, shotguns, and machine guns. Streisand was escorted by her agent, the acid-tongued Sue Mengers, who said dismissively, "Don't worry, honey. Stars aren't being murdered, only featured players."

Perhaps no one in Hollywood was impacted harder or as deeply as Steve McQueen, who was one of Jay's best friends. He started keeping a personal handgun on him at all times, forced his wife Neile to carry one, kept a loaded pump-action shotgun at his production office, and installed a closed-circuit monitor on the front gate of his home so he could keep a watchful eye on intruders. His cocaine habit also increased, and he constantly surveyed the rearview mirror of his car, thinking people were following him.

"He got paranoid as hell. The whole place was locked up tight," said friend and stuntman Bud Ekins. "Sharon Tate and Jay Sebring were close friends. It hit too close to home."

The sanctity of the "charmed life" that was supposed to come with fame and fortune was tarnished irrevocably that day. The painful truth that no amount of status or celebrity made you immune to tragedy was driven home like the daggers that ripped apart Jay and Sharon's bodies. Dominick Dunne said the entire city was terrorized.

---

5. When Roman Polanski returned to Los Angeles, hotels refused to take him. Robert Evans, the head of Paramount Pictures, let him stay in a studio dressing room on the lot.

The main word to describe it was fear.... fear overtook the town. The thing that was said was, "They're after the rich. They're after the famous." People sent their children and their grandchildren to other states. Our children—three of them by that time—went to my mother-in-law's ranch. That goes to show you what this terrible event had done to this town.

But it was nothing compared to what was about to happen to Jay's legacy. In the wake of this panic, Hollywood became the snake eating its own tail. Horror over the crimes inflicted upon their peers was distilled into desperation to distance and insulate themselves from perceived physical harm or victimization by osmosis.... particularly where it concerned their reputations and careers.... even major actors, studio publicists, directors and film executives in Jay's inner circle.

Inconceivably, "but for the grace of God" devolved into "better thee than me," and sympathy immediately gave way to self-preservation.

CHAPTER 27
LIVE FREAKY, DIE FREAKY

The media frenzy surrounding the murders consumed the attention of the entire country, and the news of the bloody massacre sent shockwaves throughout the world. Not only was the notion of this idyllic coastal paradise disrupted, the sense of safety and security average Americans felt in their own communities was challenged. If such horrific crimes could happen in a quiet, exclusive enclave like Benedict Canyon, "Could the same happen to me or my family?"

This question ricocheted through the psyche of the nation, and everyone wanted to make sense of a senseless series of terrifying and violent crimes. It wasn't just the misdirects the Manson Family threw up that made it difficult to understand the motives; there wasn't anything about their actions that was rational or reasonable.... or, for that matter, sane.

As humans, we attempt to explain what we don't understand, particularly the blood-splattered massacre of numerous innocent people including a pregnant woman and her unborn child with no discernable motive. When that isn't possible, we attempt to forget it. When that fails, we try to rationalize it. Across the country, Americans needed to explain how such brutality could exist and to reassure themselves such horrors would never befall them. They need to know that ghoulish fiends would not find their way into the normal, everyday lives of Middle America and mutilate them and their families as they slept. As a result, rumors, inuendoes, and blatant lies circulated in the media and gossip circles, almost every story suggesting deviant behaviors and crimes committed by the victims explained the gruesome fates that befell them.

With no obvious motive, this overkill of violence in one of the safest, most exclusive neighborhoods on the planet prompted a feverish search for answers. Some of the reasons reported were absurd and unfounded—Satanic cult rituals, witchcraft, a drug deal gone bad, infidelity, jealous lovers, an orgy gone awry—and didn't get anyone any closer to understanding how this could happen. That includes law enforcement.

The slaughters were beyond the scope of human comprehension, and a *TIME* magazine piece from August 22, 1969, titled, "The Night of Horror," provided the nation with grisly details of what the victims suffered that defied the most twisted imagination. The piece (which, incidentally, did not carry a byline) quotes Los Angeles County Coroner Thomas Noguchi describing the crimes as "so weird and bizarre," where "a large number of pistol bullets were embedded in the walls and ceiling. Blood was splattered over most of the living room walls."

The article described the excessive violence and even sexual humiliation:

Sebring was wearing only the torn remnants of a pair of boxer shorts.... one of Miss Tate's breasts had been cut off.... there was an X cut on her stomach.... Sebring was sexually mutilated, and his body also bore X marks.... Frykowski's trousers were down around his ankles.

The thinly veiled subtext was that the killers knew their targets and the murders were the result of some form of payback, perhaps for a narcotics deal gone bad, or a comeuppance for illicit, sexually perverse lifestyles.

TIME concluded: "Theories of sex, drug and witchcraft spread quickly in Hollywood, fed by the fact that Sharon and Polanski circulated in one of the film world's more offbeat crowds." London celebrity tailor Douglas Hayward was quoted as saying, "They were both enormously popular in a trendy, fashionable, hippie world."

This reputable news publication engaged in character assassination of all the victims. Though Steven Parent was spared any untoward speculation at the time,[1] *TIME* determined that Abigail Folger had been an "aimless heiress," and her companion, Wojciech Frykowski, "was a free-spending Polish refugee.... and a hanger-on." They claimed the Polanskis "habitually picked up odd and unsavory people indiscriminately.... and had as much idea about security as idiots." Jay Sebring "a diminutive men's hair stylist ($11.50 per haircut), was a health nut with violent convictions (especially anti-Negro).... kept guns in his glove compartment and an assortment of whips handy in his purple and black bedroom. An old girlfriend, who said Sebring often asked to tie her up for whippings, reported that he also smoked marijuana."[2]

---

1. Steven Parent's sexuality was brought into question by a 2024 YouTube clip promoting author Tom O'Neill's follow up to *CHAOS: Charles Manson, the CIA and the Secret History of the Sixties*. The clip speculates about the sex life of the adolescent young man.

2. The source of this accusation was most likely model/actress-turned-columnist Nancy Bacon, whose 2017 book, *Legends and Lipstick: My Scandalous Stories of Hollywood's Golden Era*, detailed her supposed affair with Jay Sebring. In it she portrayed Jay as a hell-bent-for-leather character with a fondness for chemicals, cocaine, and orgies. Bacon also writes that he tied her to a bed with thin white ropes and placed a satin hood over his head while they made love. A week after he bedded her, she wrote that Jay invited her to Sharon Tate's house the night of August 8, 1969. Bacon's reputation has suffered over the decades as accounts throughout her book have been met with skepticism, and her ethics as a journalist have been brought into question. She died in 2018.

Authorities spoke with Roman Polanski in London before he returned to the United States, along with friend Victor Lownes. Lownes was later sent on a thankless but necessary errand. He recalled:

> Roman asked me if I'd go up to the house [Cielo Drive], which by that time had yellow police tape around the property. He asked me to get a dress for Sharon to be buried in. I asked, "How will I know which one to pick?" He said, "Use your best judgment." I don't remember the details, but I picked a dress and brought it back to the mortuary.

Lownes had chosen wisely. Sharon's funeral dress was described by the *Los Angeles Times* as a blue and yellow print mini dress. Her father Paul Tate said it was her favorite.

While Lownes was busy performing errands, Roman Polanski met with Los Angeles police detective Lt. Earl Deemer for a recorded polygraph on August 16, 1969. *TIME's* piece confirmed the presence of narcotics at the crime scene and stated that "Frykowski was not believed to be a confidant of Polanski's, as he had claimed, but rather a hanger-on with sinister connections to which even the tolerant Polanski objected"—details contained in the magazine could only have been acquired from law enforcement or Polanski himself.

The famed director provided several statements—mind-boggling, jaw-dropping, and insensitive moments—that piqued Deemer's interest and probably furrowed a brow at times during their 129-minute conversation.

For the first hour, Deemer conducted a routine, by-the-numbers, interview that sorted through Polanski's background, information on the murder victims, a list of possible suspects, and any potential motives for the deaths at Cielo Drive. At times, Polanski was alternately confused and upset, arrogant and cocky, effervescent and light-hearted. It's possible his altering moods were due to the Valium he admitted taking that morning.

Midway through their conversation, Polanski asked about the accuracy of the polygraph machine and mysteriously lied about smoking cigarettes. Deemer saw the polygraph needle jump and then looked at Polanski for a reaction. Polanski burst out laughing, admitting he was not being truthful. Deemer was not pleased.

"You know what I gotta do if you keep screwing around?" Deemer said. "I'm going to have to start over.... See, this is your blood pressure; it's going up just like a staircase. I tell you if you ever do something, don't take this thing. You're a good reactor."

"I just wanted to know if it really worked," Polanski offered. "I'm sorry. I'll finish up and won't lie to you. Okay?"

The line of questioning eventually switched to Polanski's fidelity to his wife, and Polanski was candid. When Deemer asked Polanski about a sexual interlude with two stewardesses after his wife's murder, Roman's response floored the detective.

Deemer: Have you dated any airline stewardesses since Sharon's death?

Polanski: Yes.... Not dated. I've seen a couple of them. But I wouldn't call it "dating."

Deemer: Took 'em out to lunch or something like that?

Polanski: I *fucked* them.

Deemer: Huh. OK. I don't think I'm gonna put that in there though. I think we'll still say "date." How's that? They might play this for school children one of these days.

The investigators became fairly certain early on that Polanski was not involved in the murders. The filmmaker did, however, add several tidbits of information that appeared to be crucial pieces of the puzzle in relation to motive for the slaughters. Polanski posited to the LAPD that Jay was deep in debt, which made Jay a likely target after involving himself in nefarious affairs or dealing with shady underworld characters, which conveniently took the heat away from Polanski. He told Deemer:

> Oh, from what I've heard. Some money thing, I don't know, I heard a lot about this drug thing and drug delivery; it's difficult for me to say. He must have been in trouble or some peculiar business. A very peculiar thing yesterday, I went to see my dentist who is a very expensive dentist, and he was also Jay's dentist for years and he told me that Jay owed him $5,400 dollars [sic]. He showed me the sheet balance, and there was some up to $6,500, $6,600.... something like that. He received a note, "Thank you for your patience," something like that and "I informed your secretary I will be paying you regularly." Then he would receive like a $100 every month of something like that and it lasted two years. That's quite amazing to me considering he was known as a rather prosperous man, you know.... The indication to me is that he must have been in serious financial trouble, in spite of the appearances that he kept.[3]

Perhaps most compelling to law enforcement was when Polanski went into Jay's rumored sexual proclivities and relationship with his wife. Perhaps this was Polanski's way of belittling Jay and convincing himself that he was the main love of Sharon's life.

> Sharon told me about it, that he tied her once to the bed and asked her (inaudible) she was talking about it making fun of him that he was rather disarming in the way that he was doing it. He was more and more often a guest of ours.

---

3. According to Jay Sebring's probate records, he was worth $339,000 at the time of his death. Adjusted for inflation, that amount would be $3,013,805 in 2025. Polanski's assertion to LAPD in 1969 that Sebring was in financial trouble was patently false.

He was just hanging around, hanging around and sometimes Sharon would resent his staying too long, he was
always the last to leave, you know? I'm sure that at the
beginning of this relationship there was still love from
Sharon etc., but I think that gradually it disappeared, you
know I'm quite sure of it. And you know in my mind when
I learned of this, the tragedy and.... maybe Sharon's being
pregnant brought back in his mind.... but I'm quite positive
there was nothing from his part, not from Sharon's, but
Sharon was as much in love with me as much as a human
could be, you know?

To the police, Polanski's wife and her former fiancé being
bound by a rope in the blood-soaked Cielo crime scene seemed
more than coincidental, given Polanski's characterizations. To them
it signaled potential for "ritualistic" killings. One fact was clear:
significant media outlets were somehow getting inside information,
accurate or otherwise.

Joe Gunn, a former detective and commander with the Los
Angeles Police Department, served on the force from 1959 to 1979.
Even though he did not work the Manson case, he said leaks in the
department were not uncommon.

I had a philosophy, which was a good leak is when I do it. A
bad leak is when somebody does it for me. You use the
media as a law enforcement tool. They are your allies. After
I became a commander, I had a trick where I gave each
reporter a different facet of the story, so they'd all have
something different. You want them to be favorable to you
when they write a story against the department. So that
goes on all the time.

    Reporters have a lot of fast ways to get information.
Sometimes I've had to make deals with them. For example,

on Richard Ramirez, a reporter somehow got clued in on the fact that we had identified him. This was before it went public. And so we made a deal with her and said, "Look, you're going to blow the case if he gets away. How about we make this arrest and you'll be the first reporter to come in and interview him and take his picture?" She accepted.

Because the country was culturally in a time of flux, the Cielo Drive murders quickly spun into a morality tale, and the victims got the bitter end of the poison pen. Los Angeles District Attorney Stephen Kay offered his take on the matter:

> The victims were Hollywood people.... It was a feeding frenzy on the Hollywood people. "This must've been, had something to do with drugs, or a drug rip-off." There was so much speculation that maybe they were having orgies or something.

Journalist Ed Cray describes why he believes the murders were fodder for the media:

> The press went nuts! You had celebrity. You had gory murder, lots of blood. You had no understanding. No motive, discernable motive. So, I think when you had all those ingredients—madman killer running loose, killing Hollywood people, movie star, etc.—you're just pulling the plug for the press.

A perception had been taking shape for months since news of the murders broke on Saturday morning August 9, 1969. There had been no arrests or tangible leads, and *LIFE* magazine sculpted what would become the definitive narrative structure for decades to come. The high-profile story proclaimed, "Their inner circle may have been friendly enough to protect them in their lifetimes, but now, in their posthumous notoriety, rumor had revealed them to all be connoisseurs of depravity, figures torn from a life that was pure De Sade, with videotapes in the bedrooms."

LIFE quoted an anonymous source[4] as saying, "The detective, in fact, could almost find a parable for law and order in the killings: 'If you live like that, what do you expect? Sharon Tate, Jay Sebring, Abigail Folger, Wojciech Frykowski—these were not *people*, these were *weird people*. They were weird cause they used drugs and messed around with sex.'"

The LAPD was so convinced the crimes at Cielo were narcotics or ritual-related that they failed to connect the Topanga Canyon and Benedict Canyon killings—even after an identically horrific slaughter with glaring similarities just two nights later.

On Sunday night, August 10, Leno and Rosemary LaBianca were butchered in their home on Waverly Drive in the Los Feliz neighborhood of Los Angeles. This rampage was committed with egregious brutality. Mutilation and messages smeared in victim's blood at the Waverly residence nearly mirrored that of the scene at Cielo Drive and at Gary Hinman's home in Topanga Canyon. Even blatant similarities in sanguine script at each of the murder cites was obvious:

Topanga crime scene—POLITICAL PIGGIE

Benedict Canyon crime scene—PIG

Los Feliz crime scene—DEATH TO PIGS

Leno LaBianca, owner of the Gateway Ranch Markets and State Wholesale Grocery Company and a WWII veteran, had been stabbed twelve times with his own butcher knife (a few blows were dealt with a separate knife), which was left embedded past the hilt

---

4. Quoting people anonymously had not been a practice that *LIFE* magazine employed often, if ever, prior to this event. As a bastion of journalistic integrity, choosing to engage in slapshot journalistic practices became a stain on their otherwise pristine reputation.

in his thorax. He was stabbed fourteen times with the LaBianca family carving fork, which remained plunged deep in his lower abdomen. Rosemary LaBianca had been stabbed forty-one times— at least sixteen of those stabs came at the hands of Leslie Van Houten. In total, the married couple endured over 67 stabbings and mutilation. The overkill was shockingly identical to the rare, egregious severity at the Cielo crime scene.

Except for a few publications that noted the link—UPI: "PAIR MURDERED IN LOS ANGELES.... There were striking similarities," *Los Angeles Times:* "SECOND RITUAL KILLINGS HERE.... Link to 5-way murder seen," and *TIME:* "SECOND SLAUGHTER.... It's a carbon copy"— detectives remained attached to the notion that the Cielo murders were the result of the victims' involvement with narcotics or deviant behavior.... and so did the media.

News reporting gave way to speculation, speculation gave way to narrative, narrative gave way to salaciousness and titillation, all in an effort to keep up with each other. Even respected news outlets resorted to tabloid-style reporting. Gossip rags were consumed as legitimate journalism.

Coverage varied from staid or sensational to salacious and unintentionally satirical. *The Daily News* proclaimed, "SHARON TATE KILLED AT WEIRDO BASH." Another headline from *Modern Screen* asked, "WHAT WENT ON AT THE 'SWINGING' PARTY THAT LEAD [*sic*]TO *MASS MURDER!*" and *PAGEANT* titillated with "Sex * Sadism * Celebrities—The Sharon Tate Orgies."

One publication described a party at Jay's Easton residence in which Jay and Sharon were dressed in Satanic garb as Jay offered guests a choice of goblets—one of red wine, the other laced with rat poison.

Warren Beatty told *Los Angeles* magazine reporter Steve Oney that Polanski's dark-natured films was low-hanging fruit for imaginative journalists.

In their rush to assess what happened, some of the mainstream press brought the nature of Roman Polanski's movies into the nature of the crime and held the movies responsible. Roman was a total innocent. Neither his life nor his movies had anything to do with this. But because he'd made *Repulsion* and *Rosemary's Baby,* he was made to seem responsible.

PAGEANT wrote of an orgiastic gathering at Jay's home in which guests were dressed as North American Indians. An excerpt from an "eyewitness" relayed to readers:

> They had been turned on by pot and mescaline long before I arrived and were dancing to the beat of a tom-tom (Indian drum) by one of the groups. Finally, the dancers reached a point of ecstasy and rushed to carcasses of meat stacked against a wall and bit out huge chunks. Their mouths and faces were bloody, their eyes wild.

Decades later, Dennis Hopper responded to the portrayal this way: "That's, that's insanity. Come on, man! I mean, if that was really going on, you don't think everyone in town would know about it? I mean, PLEASE! Come on. There would've been no more raw meat in the whole city."[5] Sebring nephew Anthony DiMaria had planned to follow up with Hopper regarding controversial comments Hopper had made to the *Los Angeles Free Press* in 1969

---

5. Hopper claimed in a 1994 interview that Manson wanted him to portray him on screen. Hopper even visited Manson in prison but said it didn't go very well. He told a reporter: "I went to go see him in prison. But he's an unfortunate, sick monster. He killed a lot of my friends. I knew everyone in that house. Sharon Tate was an acquaintance. Jay Sebring was a very close friend of mine. I went to prison to ask him [Manson] questions about why he did it. All I got was a long, deluded, confused and emotional response."

about the victims[6] in a second interview, but the actor died in 2010 of prostate cancer during filming of the SEBRING documentary.

Los Angeles Times columnist Patt Morrison wrote about the impact of the murders, the media narrative, and how many in the public felt about the victims. She quoted an unidentified resident of Benedict Canyon that became a lasting mantra for the era: "LIVE FREAKY, DIE FREAKY."

> It was the dark side of paradise. People could shake their fingers and say, "This is where your high-living, rich, hippie, movie-star lifestyle gets you. This is where the drug culture gets you." It's the boomerang effect, the wages of sin.

As absurd and outlandish as some of these accounts were, a surprising amount of source material came from friendly fire. And it was intentional. After an inexplicable crime when the victims, and Hollywood figures by extension, were put on the stand, foes and friends alike stooped to Judas-like measures to distance themselves from what they perceived would be career suicide. Simply being associated with the crimes and/or any stigmas connected to the killings was sure to be reputation-ending. No celluloid star or movie studio was exempt from such peril when America was in a feverish cultural flux. It could end a career or even bring an established studio to its knees.

Steve McQueen, who stated on his death bed that Jay was his best friend, shied away at the time when asked about him.

"I don't dig that weird scene," *PAGEANT* magazine quoted him as saying in a 1969 article.

McQueen also appeared to distance himself from Jay in an LAPD field interview conducted at his Brentwood home shortly

---

6. In the *Los Angeles Free Press* article, Hopper claimed the victims had fallen into "sadism, masochism and bestiality," and recorded misdeeds on videotape.

after the Cielo murders. Regarding a statement he made to someone about ridding the house of drugs to save "Jay's family and friends from the embarrassment," he admitted to a detective that he made the suggestion but insisted he did not actually act on it himself.

When the detective brought up the subject of Jay's drug habit and possible involvement with sadomasochism and bondage, McQueen threw a rival movie star under the bus.

"Warren Beatty would know more about the sadomasochism side of Jay than anyone else," McQueen said. "And possibly the drug angle."

Sammy Davis, Jr. pegged Jay as a card-carrying, hood-wearing leader of satanic rituals who conducted a session in which a female had simulated human sacrifice.[7] That was rich considering that Davis, at the time, was a casual member of Anton LaVey's Church of Satan, along with several other celebrities.[8] Davis stated that he partook of satanic orgies at the infamous Black House at 6114 California Street in San Francisco, which he openly detailed in his 1989 memoir, *Why Me?*

Perhaps no one person betrayed the memories of Jay and Sharon more than writer Joe Hyams, who recalled introducing the two in 1964 and remained a trusted friend up to their deaths. In his memoir, *Mislaid in Hollywood*, Hyams described the morning after the murders and an overseas phone call he received with a money offer.

---

7. Sebring and Davis had a falling out in the mid-1960s after the entertainer made a play for Jay's wife Cami in Las Vegas. When she turned him down, he asked, "It's because I'm Black, right?" Cami corrected him, "No, it's because I'm married to Jay and you're Jay's friend." Davis, however, did send roses for Jay's funeral.
8. In addition to Davis, other notable people who had associations to the Church of Satan and Anton LaVey include Jayne Mansfield, Liberace, and filmmaker Kenneth Anger.

The telephone rang. It was the editor of *Stern*, a German news magazine I had often written for in the past. He asked if I had known Sharon and Jay. "Yes," I answered. "We want a story quick and will pay you top dollars for it. It's the most spectacular murder in Hollywood history. Give us a series on Sharon and Jay and the atmosphere in Hollywood."

Hyams did just that. But the truth was hard to come by so he based his piece on rumor and innuendo—that Sharon and Jay were offed by hired killers; that the two were victims of a bad narcotics purchase and participated in a sex scene or magic ritual and that the murders were committed by people familiar with Sharon and Jay.

Hyams stated that he knew about the two "more than any reporter could or should know," but surmised Sharon and Jay brought "the tragedy on themselves."

When Hyams finally realized he was wrong, he corrected himself a few years after the murders in his 1973 memoir:

Had I been right, perhaps I would not have been so concerned about the venality of what I had written. But when I discovered I had apparently been wrong, I took a soul-searching look at myself and realized that not only had my conclusions been false, but, more important, my motivation had been faulty. There is no denying that the moment Sharon and Jay hit the headlines, my newspaper and commercial instincts had taken over from my personal loyalties.

It bares noting that despite the columnist's despicable betrayal of his friends, Hyams is the only known journalist who engaged in malicious slander to come clean and fess up to his shameful actions. Despite this revelation, the bloodlust resulting from the slaughters remain as entrenched and pervasive today as when news and rampant speculation spiraled unbridled Saturday morning August 9, 1969. And a significant portion of the public continues to eat it up.

Los Angeles historian Don "D.J." Waldie said the murders were "parable-ized because that's the only way it can enter the industrial complex of the media and be consumed by those who are prepared to only buy the pre-packaged, pre-cooked, pre-portioned meal version of history."

David Milch outlined how the murders were sold to readers as a morality play and consumers voraciously devoured it:

> These murders were experienced by so-called "Middle America" and packaged and sold to the rest of America as a commentary on what lay ahead. And in the engine of commerce, people's lives and reputations are simple grist for the mill.... Hollywood had begun to appropriate and market the so-called new lifestyle. "They're all butt-fucking each other, smokin' dope and doing terrible things." Now when people in Hollywood were suddenly maimed by forces that middle America took to [be] forces in collusion with entertainment people—that was a wonderful fable for the mass marketers. The subtext was, "These fucks got what they deserved."

Forensic expert Dr. Michael Baden said when reviewing the actual autopsies and comparing it to the 1969 *TIME* magazine article, two different realities were at play.

> I remember when I read this material way back when, it looked like the decedents somehow had it coming to them. Because of a drunken, sexual orgy so that as portrayed with

having nude bodies, having drugs. All of which wasn't true at all.[9]

Waldie said the public's processing of the horrific slaughters was made easier because the media at the time viewed Hollywood and its fringes as completely aberrant.

If we make the victims' fates more lurid, their behaviors less explicable, if we make them stranger and stranger in our storytelling, we have less identification with them. If we make them grotesque or bizarre, then that's one more zone of immunity from the same fate happening to me. Narratives surrounding the murders morphed and were rescripted into horror pornography in which "the beautiful people" were punished for all their attractive attributes and success.

Tony Timpone, the former longtime editor of *Fangoria,* said that a portion of society took sadistic pleasure in seeing the rich and famous brought down and completely forgot that human lives were stolen in the middle of the night.

"They want to see people who are 'better than them'—standing in life, bigger than them, more famous—brought down," Timpone said.

David Milch defines the consumer's desires in existential terms.

People love to see others punished for their uncertainties. So, every time somebody decides not to smoke reefer or not get laid, or not do something with their life, and goes to

---

9. Los Angeles Police Department crime scene photos, which can be accessed easily online, plainly show that all the murder victims at Cielo Drive were clothed. The official autopsy report also states that both Jay Sebring and Sharon Tate had no drugs in their systems at the time of their deaths, though a vial of cocaine was on his person and a small packet discovered in the glove compartment of his car.

sleep thinking, "I'm a fuckin' jerk. Not only am I living a life I hate, but I'm not trying to do something else." Now if you turn on the TV and see some people got killed, "Well, maybe I made the right choice. Because if you smoke a joint, you may very well be killed by the Manson Family. If there's any justice in the world."

The public's insatiable hunger for the macabre as the sternest of cautionary tales did not wane in the wake of arrests and faces to put to the perpetrators of these vicious acts; it merely shifted focus.

To appease their need to believe the boogeyman would never come to their door, much of the press and public had vilified the innocent victims, turning them into freaks who died freakish deaths. Once the Manson Family was taken into custody and put themselves on parade through their antics and newfound glory, the rest of America could breathe a sigh of relief that the boogeymen were no longer on the loose. With this exhale, they completely forgot about their righteous indignation over the purported deviant lifestyles of those who were cut down by the marauding maniacs.

Director Quentin Tarantino, who featured Sharon and Jay in his 2019 film *Once Upon a Time in Hollywood*, offered up his take on why these murder victims were dragged through the mud in the press and butchered again as they lay in their graves:

> For a long period of time, the victims basically weren't given their proper respect as people who died violently and viciously before their time from a horrible crime. Without a boogeyman to attach to it, the victims were put on the stand and tried in the court of public opinion, and by the way, the most reputable magazines, and the most reputable newspapers. And then when the Manson Family are discovered, all the people, all the magazines, all the journalists who vilified the victims for a whole year—never turned

around, never apologized for anything they did, never said they were wrong, never went out of their way to return the victims to their proper place and their proper status—and just enjoyed the monkey show that was going on in court.

The public and media had a new place to focus their justifiable outrage. And the Family, poised to bask in their newfound spotlight, were insatiably primed to lap it up with a big spoon, ladles, and buckets.

CHAPTER 28

THE FAMILY SHIT-SHOW

While the case dragged on, so did life for everyone who knew Jay Sebring, particularly his family, friends, and acquaintances. For Bernard and Margarette Kummer, their loss was unimaginable.

The death of a child at any age is devastating, and the pain and anguish is compounded when their demise comes at the hand of someone else. The grief process for a loved one lost through violence involves many facets. Often, victims become dehumanized, especially by police, press, prosecutors, and the public. In the case of the seven Manson victims at Cielo and Waverly drives, their names were dragged through the mud and used as grist for the mill of salacious news and tabloid consumption. Magazine articles, television stories, and tawdry talk at Hollywood parties were laden with insensitivity to the devastation the families and friends were experiencing.

Gwen and Paul Tate could not commiserate with just anyone. Perhaps only the Kummers could understand their deep grief and profound sense of loss during this time. In a November 2, 1969, letter to the Kummers, Gwen reached out to the only other people who could comprehend their agony and shared in it. Though it could only have offered hollow comfort, knowing someone else was struggling along the same road gave each of the parents a place to feel understood and supported.

Dear Peg & Bern,

Please excuse me for not writing sooner. I just have not been able to pull myself together enough to get down and do the things that I must do to make life go on. We just sort of struggle thru each day. Well, you know what I mean. I haven't as yet been able to go to the cemetery. I keep hoping this is not true. Day by day though I realize I have to face the facts. The only thing that holds me together is that I know life on this earth is temporary and that there are better things to come after this life is finished. I just keep wondering if the life to come will hold them for us. I cannot imagine happiness without my family.

You know this is the first time we have been in Los Angeles without Jay or Sharon, and it is a very lost feeling. We have no family here. I was very close to Jay. We miss him so. It seems as though I should be able to call him and to talk to him about this horrible loss. Then I think well, they are together.

Well, I have poured my heart out to you and your feelings are the same I know. Your heartbreak and loss is ours as well. Only God can give you the strength to go on, know the blessed Virgin, I hesitate to say that to people, but you are Catholic, so you know the strength that our blessed Mother can give you.

Be sweet both of you and give the other children our best regards. Let us hear from you soon.

Love,

Gwen & Paul Tate

On December 1, 1969, Los Angeles Police Chief Edward Davis told assembled media at a news conference that members of "the

Family"—a pseudo hippie cult who lived in a desert commune—
were responsible for the seven "ritualistic" slayings in August.

The investigation seemed to be hitting all the roadblocks the
Manson Family had put in place to avoid the attention of police.
The investigation had been largely stifled by the detectives'
presumption that the killings occurred because of the victims' life-
style choices involving illicit drug activity, decadence, and reckless
behavior. Law enforcement was looking in all the wrong places.
Then, out of the blue, authorities suddenly caught a break when
Susan Atkins let a critical detail slip to a cellmate.

Having ended up in the Inyo County Jail, then transferred to
the Sybil Brand Institute for Women in Los Angeles for her involvement in Gary Hinman's murder, Atkins was looking for some street
cred to secure her survival in prison. It's also possible that the killer
who craved feedback and attention was proud of her involvement
in events that were playing out in the press to epic proportions on
television, the radio, and newspapers.

Atkins bragged for a period of a few weeks to fellow inmate
Ronnie Howard, who was in jail for forging a prescription, that she
and others were involved in the Hinman killing. Atkins also hinted
at being responsible for Donald "Shorty" Shea's murder and boasted
about her participation in the five murders committed at Cielo
Drive.

In one forty-five-minute discussion, not only did Atkins provide
a detailed account of the slaughter, but she also admitted to
butchering Sharon Tate and her unborn child. "It felt so good, and
when she screamed, it sent a rush through me, and I stabbed her
again. It's like a sexual release, especially when you see the blood
spurting out. It's better than a climax."

Atkins added that after Sharon perished, she thought about
cutting out the baby.

"I had blood all over my hands, and it was so warm and sticky, and nice, so I tasted it," Atkins said. "Wow, what a trip, to taste death, and yet give life!"[1]

Atkins excitedly continued, confessing she and her friends were also responsible for the deaths of Rosemary and Leo LaBianca. But it didn't end there. In a final salvo, she intimated, "And there's more; there are at least eleven bodies that they'll never find."[2]

Though Atkins inadvertently put herself forward as the tip of the spear, Manson would end up becoming the face of the murders —a face that would become the icon of madness and evil for decades to come, even gracing the cover of *LIFE* magazine, a publication usually dedicated to Americana and celebrations of positive societal contributions. Though Watson committed seven murders,[3] Manson's antics so permeated the courtroom.... and every room thereafter.... that all others faded into the background, including the victims.

Nearly four months after what the media dubbed the "Tate-LaBianca Murders," the Los Angeles Police Department had several people in custody and had issued warrants for the arrest of Charles Manson, Susan Atkins, Charles "Tex" Watson, Patricia Krenwinkel, Leslie Van Houten, and Linda Kasabian.

The world got its first glimpse of the smallish, Messiah-wannabe on December 3, 1969, walking into the Inyo County Courthouse

---

1. Atkins also repeated the same account to Virginia Graham, a cellmate at the Sybil Brand Institute for Women. Graham vaguely knew Jay through a female friend of hers. She said she was horrified by Atkins' confession and lack of remorse and felt compelled to tell authorities. She and Howard were both questioned by LAPD detectives and later testified in court.

2. In another conversation with Virginia Graham, who was flipping through a movie magazine at her bunk, Atkins informed her that the Manson Family had a celebrity hit list and were about the target the world's biggest celebrities. This included Frank Sinatra, Elizabeth Taylor, Richard Burton, Tom Jones, and Steve McQueen, among others.

3. Sharon Tate's unborn child, Paul Richard Polanski, is among Charles Watson's victims for which he never stood trial. Watson was also a possible participant in Donald "Shorty" Shea's murder but was never charged.

in Independence, California, after his arrest at nearby Barker Ranch. An *Associated Press* photo taken that day by Harold Filan showed the long-haired, bearded Manson in a denim prison jump-suit, wrists shackled, accompanied by court appointed public defender Fred Shaefer and three Inyo County law enforcement offi-cers. Hands tucked casually in his pockets and strolling as if he didn't have a care in the world, Manson portrayed the disaffected mantra with which he had infected his conspirators.

Ironically, this perp-walk was not for his most heinous crimes. He was being taken into custody in Inyo County for car theft and damage to government property. Behind the scenes, the Los Angeles Police Department was working its own angles to bring him back to their jurisdiction to face accountability for orchestrating the bloody and senseless violence that befell their city and shook the country.

The quintessential agent of mayhem, thirty-five-year-old Manson, used this opportunity to make a mockery of the court system, and he deployed his Family members and other dead-eyed acolytes to turn the proceedings into a nine-month circus. Some of the outlandish histrionics by the defendants included taunting victims' family members, ridiculing the judge[4] and prosecutors, threatening lawyers, screaming, chanting in the courtroom, shaving their heads, and carving "X"s into their foreheads. Adding insult to injury, Manson selected the most contrarian and obstructive attorney he could find—the annoying Irving Kanarek.

Before Atkins testified in front of a grand jury, she gave her reconstruction of the August 9th and 10th killings to her Beverly Hills attorney, Richard Caballero, a former deputy district attorney. The conversation was recorded by Caballero who was going to plead insanity on her behalf. Before he did, Caballero handed over the transcription of their conversation to photojournalist Lawrence

---

4. During the trial, Manson charged at the presiding judge with a sharpened pencil and shot paper clips at him.

Schiller who enlisted the help of a pair of reporters from *The Los Angeles Times* and ran it in a long-form piece called "Two Nights of Murder." Britain's *News of the World* paid $40,000 for the story, and the content also became a quickie book titled *The Killing of Sharon Tate* (Signet, 1970).

It was an unscrupulous tactic by Caballero to a) exploit a client for cash, and b) get her side of the story out into the public domain and hope to convince the state not to give her the death penalty. Atkins' recounting to her attorney was a radical rewrite of what she told her two Sybil Brand cellmates, minimizing her participation in the murders. She lay the sole blame for Sharon Tate's death at Charles Watson's feet, claiming it was he who savagely butchered the actress. Atkins also informed readers she was under Manson's hypnotic spell and never questioned what he said.

If the purpose for getting her side of the story out was to elicit public sympathy, it failed miserably. She admitted to telling Sharon Tate, moments before her death, "Woman, I have no mercy for you." That revelation was tantamount to a 20th century scarlet letter. Society at large and women in particular reviled Atkins, wondering how anyone could be so inhumane to a mother-to-be eagerly anticipating the birth of her child.

The article also served to reinforce Atkins' lack of self-awareness, unbridled immaturity, and total insensitivity regarding the wreckage she and others caused during those massively publicized two nights of bloodshed. Near the end of the piece, Atkins said the constant media coverage regarding the killings left her emotionally spent. She concluded: "I can't tell about it anymore. Anyway, I haven't time. My lawyer is coming soon, and he's bringing me a dish of vanilla ice cream. Vanilla ice cream really blows my mind." Clearly, Atkins and her cohorts were relishing in their newfound attention and notoriety.

Those who followed the crimes especially despised Atkins, and for good reason. Her participation on any level in these crimes was just cause for anger, but the blasé manner she employed in sharing her story fueled contempt and fanned the flames of outrage.

She didn't have her desired effect on the grand jury either. After two-and-a-half hours of shocking testimony, the jurors were stunned and spellbound. After twenty minutes of deliberation, they handed down seven murder indictments against her, Watson, Kren-winkel, and Kasabian, with Manson being indicted under conspiracy laws for engineering the homicides. Leslie Van Houten was indicted on two counts of murder and one count of conspiracy in the deaths of Leo and Rosemary LaBianca. After the grand jury determined there was more than enough probable cause to move the case forward, attorneys were assigned, deals were cut, alliances were formed, and heroes and villains emerged. And plenty of false starts followed.

Los Angeles County District Attorney Aaron Stovitz, a bright and respected litigator, was originally assigned the Tate-LaBianca case and worked six months collecting evidence. However, he was removed by his boss, Evelle J. Younger, in September 1970 after making an off-the-cuff remark to a reporter about Susan Atkins being too ill to continue with the trial.

"She's putting on an act worthy of Sarah Bernhardt," a United Press International reporter quoted Stovitz as saying.

Stovitz was already on thin ice. Prior to the trial, he had granted an interview to a *Rolling Stone* reporter in which he talked about details of the murder case despite a gag order from a judge. Stovitz said he thought the interview was for background and not for publication. After the piece, titled "The Most Dangerous Man in the World," ran, Younger ordered Stovitz not to say another word to the media.

Stovitz was replaced by his younger colleague, Vincent T. Bugliosi, an ambitious deputy district attorney who always acted self-important and was a legend in his own mind. According to reporter and author Ivor Davis, Bugliosi got the job only because a more seasoned DA, J. Miller Leavy, took a pass. Leavy knew it was going to be a grind, and suggested Bugliosi take the second chair for the trial.

Attorney Paul Fitzgerald of the Public Defender's Office was first assigned Manson's case, but on December 17, days after his indictment, Manson insisted on acting as his own attorney, claiming that "there is no person in the world who could represent me as a person."

William Keene, the presiding judge, had his attorney Joseph Ball, determine if Manson was competent. Ball assessed that Manson was competent, and Keene had no other choice but to approve Manson's request.

Manson used the opportunity to make brash motions and requests of the court while not bothering to mount a viable defense. He demanded that copies of every document regarding the case be delivered to his jail cell. He asked for outside travel privileges and for the court to fork over the names, telephone numbers, and home addresses of every prosecution witness. Three months later, in March, when he asked that the prosecuting attorneys be jailed under conditions similar to his own, Judge Keene had had enough. He revoked Manson's privileges and assigned him a new defense attorney.

His new representation, Charles Hollopeter, didn't last long. Displeased with some of the motions he made, Manson had him replaced with Ronald Hughes, a hefty rookie lawyer who had never tried a case before.

The following month, Manson filed an affidavit of prejudice against Judge Keene, and the case was assigned to Judge Charles H. Older, a former World War II Flying Tigers pilot and Korean War veteran who had been appointed to the bench by Governor Ronald Reagan three years earlier. His ability to keep order in the courtroom would be severely tested and, early into the trial, he ordered a bodyguard to stand next to him. He had dealt with murderers,

rapists, and seasoned criminals throughout his judicial career, but
the Manson bunch, he'd soon discover, were in a league all
their own.

With Manson's legal house in order (for the time being) his
fellow defendants were left to select their attorneys, and they
muddied the legal waters as well. Krenwinkel requested Paul
Fitzgerald as her counsel— the first attorney assigned to Manson.
The Public Defender's Office felt that this new assignment constituted a conflict of interest, but Fitzgerald was anxious to be a part
of the defense team. He surprised everyone by resigning from his
steady day job and going into private practice, taking Krenwinkel
on as his sole client.

Van Houten went through a myriad of attorneys, rivaling
Manson in his revolving door of representation. Donald Barrett was
initially assigned to her, but he drew her ire when he requested a
psychiatric evaluation. She requested his dismissal and got it. Her
case was then forwarded to Marvin Part who repeated the same
mistake as his predecessor. He got dropped, too. Van Houten's case
was transferred to Ira Reiner at Manson's suggestion. But he only
lasted eight months—until jury selection—when he attempted to
separate her defense from the Manson crew. Van Houten replaced
him with Ronald Hughes, another former Manson attorney.

Adding to the chaos was Atkins' move to break away from the
prosecution and align herself with Manson, Krenwinkel, Van
Houten, and Kasabian after a jailhouse visit with Manson in
March. She did it against the wishes of Caballero, who had accompanied his client to the Los Angeles County Jail. Sitting at a table in
the visiting room opposite Manson in his jailhouse blues and
Caballero to her right, Manson stared at Atkins and asked, "Sadie,
are you afraid of the gas chamber?"

"No, I'm not afraid of it now," she said smiling. She remembers
him launching into a diatribe filled with Manson-speak, essentially
telling her to fire Caballero, not to cop to an insanity plea, and to

refuse any possible deals with Bugliosi. After her meeting with Manson, Atkins dropped Caballero and hired Korean-born attorney Daye Shinn. Then she recanted everything she had told the grand jury and quashed her deal with the district attorney's office. Atkins knew she might get the death penalty, but being back in the Family's good graces was far more important to her.

This left an opening for a star witness for the prosecution. Twenty-year-old Linda Kasabian was the one defendant who could fill those shoes. Prodded by her attorney, Gary Fleischman, Kasabian finally made a deal with Bugliosi when it was made clear she could avoid jail time for her part of as driver and being at two scenes of the crime. It was fortuitous for both parties who essentially needed each other. Kasabian could get immunity for her role as the chauffer and lookout at Cielo Drive, and Bugliosi could get someone who didn't have blood on her hands to testify against those who did. Despite threats made to Fleischman by Family members that "if Linda testifies, thirty people are going to do something about it," Kasabian agreed and became the prosecution's star witness.

Two weeks before the trial started, Manson requested Judge Older reassign his case once again, this time to Irving A. Kanarek, a well-known courtroom dissenter who made a name for himself in the legal community for his excessive use of objections, oddball questions, and masterful delay tactics. He was every judge's worst nightmare, and Manson knew it. Older approved the request and Hughes was replaced by Kanarek who, in turn, went on to represent Van Houten. Everything was done at the behest of Manson, convincing his conspirators to entrust their fate to his hands, even if it meant receiving the worst defense possible and going down with the ship alongside him.

On Monday, June 10, 1970, the "Trial of the Century" commenced in Department 104 on the eighth floor of the Hall of Justice in downtown Los Angeles. Manson, Atkins, Krenwinkel, and Van Houten were finally standing trial for the murders of Sharon Tate, Jay Sebring, Wojciech Frykowski, Abigail Folger, Steven Parent, Leno La Bianca, and Rosemary LaBianca. Not present was Charles "Tex" Watson, who had a hand in murdering all seven victims.[5] He was sitting in a Texas jail cell, fighting extradition to California. The defendants' attorneys all claimed they had a right to a speedy trial and forced the district attorney's office to proceed without him. Watson would face his own separate trial later in 1971.

It took five weeks for jury selection, and Bugliosi told prospects, "It is the intent of the prosecution to ask for the death penalty for all of these defendants."

But it would take nine months to reach that decision, and Manson made sure to make it as painful as possible for everyone involved. Throughout the trial, he ranted, raved, shrieked, mocked, and railed at the injustices of every decision made by Older and the entire penal system.

On July 24, 1970, the trial officially got underway. Spectators queued in line by 6:00 a.m. that day for a seat in the courtroom to get a glimpse of the action. Some of the more prominent names included author Joan Didion, journalist Dominick Dunne, and actors Sal Mineo and Dennis Hopper. Also present was writer Curt Gentry who was there to chronicle the case for a book he would pen with Bugliosi—1974's *Helter Skelter*—which eventually became the bestselling true crime book in history, selling more than seven million copies over the years.

Seeing Gentry in the courtroom was initially a surprise to Los Angeles County Deputy District Attorney Stephen Kay, who was twenty-seven and three years out of law school at the time of the

---

5. Surprisingly, California did not have a law covering the murder of Richard Paul Polanski, Roman and Sharon's unborn son. This was corrected in 2004 with the passage of the Unborn Victims of Violence Act, which recognizes "a child in utero" as a legal victim if they are injured or killed during the commission of a violent act.

trial. He said Bugliosi used the case to simultaneously pump up his career and blow up his legend:

> Vince all along knew that this case was gonna be his meal ticket. And he had this guy Curt Gentry sitting in the courtroom. I thought he was just a reporter. I didn't know he was writing the book for Vince. The whole time that Vince was doing the trial, they were writing the book and Vince saw the dollar signs and everything.... To know him (Bugliosi) was *not* to love him. Vince was such an egomaniac.

Kay said *Helter Skelter* was a tough read for him given that he knew all the players and the subject matter intimately. He said he could not finish the book.

> I got about halfway through it and put it down. It was hard to read. Vince treated the police like they were errand boys, and you'd never know that Aaron Stovitz was originally the chief prosecutor. So no, I'm sorry. I haven't read the whole book.

The sidewalk in front of the courthouse became the stage for a spectacle every day. Manson minions who were not arrested or locked up held vigil for him, existing on donated food and cigarettes. By day, they summoned spectators, journalists, and TV cameras to offer up their warped ideology. At night, they slept in vans parked on the street so they could show their support. However, some of the Manson women were repeatedly ejected during the first phase of the trial because of their disruptive conduct. Later, they were altogether banned.

There was also a ban on cameras in the courtroom, which meant Family members such as Sandra Good, Lynette "Squeaky"

Fromme, Kathryn "Kitty" Lutesinger, Catherine "Gypsy" Share, Susan Bartell, Ruth Ann "Ouicsh" Moorehouse, Catherine Gillies, and Nancy "Brenda" Pitman received their fair share of media attention just by being present outside. In addition to their apocalyptic predictions and undying proclamations of love for Manson, cameras caught them inside the courthouse and outside on the streets, ramping up the rhetoric.

Berto Ferreria, who was a lightshow operator at a Southern California rock club, had an encounter with Lynnette Fromme during the Manson trial. He was at L.A.'s Hall of Justice, answering charges after getting beat up by the LAPD at a concert at Olympic Auditorium. He met Fromme on a hallway bench waiting for his trial to get underway. They talked for about forty-five minutes, and he said Fromme left an indelible impression:

> Of course, I'd heard about the Manson murders but didn't know the specifics. I also had no idea I was showing up at the Hall of Justice right in the middle of the Manson trial. I arrive and there's media and TV cameras all over the place. There's also heavy-duty security and screenings to get in and I went, "What the hell?" Then I finally figured it out.
>
> When I gathered my bearings, I was told my courtroom wasn't ready yet. I was directed to a hallway bench and told to wait. There was one other person sitting on the bench, Ms. Lynette "Squeaky" Fromme. I had a wait ahead of me and I sat there for a few minutes. I didn't have anything else to do, so I decided to sit and talk with this other person. I initiated the conversation: "Hi, how are you? Who are you and what are you here for?" That's how it unfolded, and [I] eventually figured out who she was.
>
> I found her to be bright and articulate. I expected to her be a sloppy, drugged-out, crazy hippie. She was communicative and sharp, but her reality was seeded in a place that

I could not comprehend. The more I talked to her the more I saw it. When she explained why she was there and who she was there to support, the goose bumps went up on my arms. She was present and accounted for but was from a planet that I'd never heard of.

The only recorded history of the trial came in the form of transcriptions and illustrations, the latter captured by TV station sketch artists Bill Robles for CBS and Bill Lignante for ABC. What they were able to capture did not quite convey the madness and mayhem that occurred over the next seven months. Ivor Davis said it was the most outrageous trial he had ever witnessed. He wrote in his 2019 memoir, *Manson Exposed: A Reporter's 50-Year Journey into Madness and Murder*:

> Indeed, it was a bad Fellini movie on acid: part theater of the absurd and part Monty Python's Flying Circus without the humor. The four defendants faced the death penalty if convicted, and so comedy had no place there; but, Manson was a classic clown, a natural performer who quickly realized that now he could achieve the notoriety and fame that eluded him as a songwriter. He made the conscious decision to do whatever he could to muck up the proceedings, masterfully doing just that with his maniacal machinations.

Like all clowns, Manson certainly knew how to make an entrance. He breezed into the courtroom on the first day with an X carved into the center of his forehead. A statement signed by Manson was distributed in the hallway by a reporter from *The Free Press*, a weekly underground publication.

In it, Manson was quoted as saying that he made the X in his forehead to express that he had "X'ed" himself from the world because he had not been allowed to speak for himself as his own attorney.

Manson's three co-defendants soon followed suit, as did his acolytes on the street, all sporting an X on their foreheads in allegiance to their long-haired leader, each of them craving their share of the spotlight.

Davis, who covered many famous trials over the course of his decades-long career, including Sirhan Sirhan and Patty Hearst, said he hadn't seen such courtroom antics before or since. Davis reflected:

> As the days turned into weeks and the weeks into months, each day I thought surely nothing would top the previous one. I was wrong. Whatever Manson did, the three girls in court mimicked. When Manson screamed, they screamed. When he turned his back on Judge Older, they followed in puppet-like fashion. They parroted his every disruption until they eventually were forced to watch their own trial from a separate room.

This utter shit-show turned a tragedy into a travesty as it seemed there would be no justice because it's difficult to hold people accountable who have no remorse. Whether the Family was actually crazy, or it was all for show, they demonstrated a cavalier attitude throughout the trial that indicated punishment would simply be another novelty for them.

But the prosecution's case was only strengthened by their behavior. The murders were unfathomable, and the incomprehensible behavior of the defendants only served to make their guilt make sense. Perhaps they were enjoying themselves, but it would backfire, and their warped conduct and stick-it-to-the-man attitude was about to come to an end.

CHAPTER 29

THE SPAGHETTI DEFENSE

When the absurdist performance the Family put on display did nothing but harm their case, their attorneys began pulling out the stops to deflect attention and redirect blame. They adopted a "spaghetti defense," where they would throw any explanation, opinion, tactic, or misdirect to see what might stick.

In early August 1970, Charles Manson attempted to disrupt the proceedings further by pushing for a mistrial when he flashed to the jury a front-page story from the *Los Angeles Times* with the blaring headline: MANSON GUILTY, NIXON DECLARES.

President Richard Nixon had made the remarks at an August 4 press conference briefing with law enforcement in Denver, Colorado. He lamented that the media makes "heroes out of those who engage in criminal activity" and stated that Manson was "guilty, directly or indirectly, of eight murders without reason." Later, he issued a retraction.[1]

---

1. Famed defense attorneys Percy Foreman and Melvin Belli stated Nixon should receive a reprimand or should be disbarred from the American Bar Association for his comments on the Manson case. Belli told a scribe, "If I had done what Nixon did, they'd be heating the oil for me."

Attorneys for the defense seized on the opportunity to call for a mistrial. Manson was quickly removed from the courtroom and Judge Older soon discovered that Atkins' attorney Shinn had slipped him the newspaper. That earned Shinn two weeks in jail, by order of Older.[2] He also rejected the request to declare a mistrial and stated the headline had no influence on the jury, who had already been selected, sequestered, and instructed not to read media accounts of the trial.

Vincent Bugliosi wisely opted to stay above the fray and remain focused on giving the jury witnesses (84 in all) and evidence (297 exhibits), including the gun and knives that killed the Tate-LaBianca victims, to make his case. He let Manson and his tribe of nomads legally hang themselves with their courtroom antics,[3] knowing the perception that they were deranged ruffians would ensure no jury would allow them back into society.

He succinctly summarized the tragedy that had taken place at the Tate and LaBianca residences those two nights in August 1969. He then offered a brief history of the Family and portrayed Manson as its undisputed leader to whom everyone deferred. Bugliosi emphasized that while Manson ordered these killings, Atkins, Krenwinkel, and Van Houten were willing participants in the excessive brutality and bloodshed that befell the victims.

His opening statement was crisp, clear, and unrelenting:

---

2. Shinn had a history of misbehavior and was disbarred in 1992 from the California State Bar for misappropriating client funds in another case.

3. On September 5, 1970, a time bomb ripped out a 9 x 12 concrete wall in a bathroom adjacent to the district attorney's office at the Los Angeles Hall of Justice, two floors below the scene of the trial. Although no one was injured (the blast took place on a Saturday), it shattered a six-inch water main and caused more than $10,000 in damages. Though the Manson Family or his acolytes were never blamed in print, many wondered if it was their handiwork. District Attorney Evelle Younger told the Associated Press, "I would have no more reason to believe it is connected with that Tate case than 40,000 other criminal cases we file during the course of the year, if it is."

The evidence at this trial will show that these seven incredible murders were perhaps the most bizarre, savage, nightmarish murders in the annals of crime. I am, of course, excluding wartime atrocities. What kind of diabolical, satanic mind would contemplate or conceive of these mass murders? We expect the evidence at this trial to show that defendant Charles Manson owned that diabolical mind, who, the evidence will show, at times, had the infinite humility if you will, to call himself Jesus Christ at times. But most of all, the evidence will show him to be a killer who cleverly masqueraded behind the common language of a hippie—that of being peace-loving.

Bugliosi stated that Manson was a fervent follower of The Beatles who claimed he was receiving secret messages from The Fab Four through their music, specifically their November 1968 release titled *The Beatles* (commonly referred to by music fans as *The White Album*). Bugliosi said Manson told his lemmings that the song "Helter Skelter" forecast the rise of the Black man against the Whites, an event he said already started.

Manson's plan, Bugliosi said, was to blame the seven killings on Black people in order to start a war with the White establishment. Once it commenced, he and his followers would head to Death Valley and live in the biblical "bottomless pit" of Revelation IX until Blacks emerged as the victor. However, he said that he would take back the reins of power when Blacks discovered they were too inexperienced to lead.

"In Manson's mind, his family, and particularly he, would be the ultimate beneficiaries of the Black-White civil war," Bugliosi said.

While these statements were central to Manson's manifesto and not taken out of context, many critics of Bugliosi believe he was opportunistic in using the "Helter Skelter" theory as the centerpiece of his case. Instead of addressing the more commonsense motive—which was to frame the Black Panthers and to cover for Bobby Beausoliel in the aftermath of the drug burn/shooting of Bernard Crowe and Gary Hinman's murder—he was seeking to grab sensational headlines.

As expected, Linda Kasabian's seventeen-day testimony proved to be the most fatal blow to the defense, offering a detailed, eyewitness account of the two nights of murder. She was repentant for getting caught up with Manson and sympathetic toward the victims, crying openly in court when shown crime scene photos of their butchered bodies and discussing their demise.

Another who made a deep impact was former Family member Barbara Hoyt who bravely showed up in court despite an attempt by Manson followers to silence her. Hoyt had joined the Family on April Fool's Day in 1969 after getting into an argument with her father. She said life at Spahn Ranch in the beginning was a playground, a "Disneyland existence." Hoyt said things got heavy after Manson shot Bernard Crowe, which set off a chain reaction. Suddenly, armed guards appeared at the ranch and field phones were set up on the grounds. Manson was also putting everyone through "ego-death" exercises.

"He wanted you to forget there was ever a right and wrong," Hoyt said. "And to have no thought in your head. These were deprogramming exercises."

The night after the Cielo Drive murders, she was watching television with Watkins and Atkins when a news broadcast aired. Suddenly, the room grew cold. It was the first time she had heard that Sharon Tate had been killed.

"God, it scared me. And no one said anything for a while," Hoyt recalled. "Now, at this point, I knew about the murders. But I did not know that I was sitting with the murderers themselves. I had no clue."

When Hoyt moved to Death Valley with the Family after the

murders, she overheard Atkins talking about it to Catherine "Gypsy" Share. Her interest was piqued when she heard Sharon Tate's name whispered among them.

> I started listening and she [Atkins] described Sharon's murder; she described Abigail Folger's murder; she described the death of the LaBianca couple. She said that Sharon Tate cried for her mother, that Abigail Folger broke away and ran out on the lawn where Katie tackled her. Then she had called for Tex to help her, and that Tex had gutted her.

The next time Hoyt saw Watson, he noticed a change in her demeanor and pallor.

"Wow, Barb," he said. "Your face is all colors of the desert."

Hoyt did everything she could to hide her knowledge of the crimes. She felt as if her life was in jeopardy and walked twenty-seven miles out of the Panamint Valley to safety and, finally, back to her parents' home. In the intervening months, she said she received daily death threats and noticed strange cars driving by her home. Police began patrolling in the vicinity of the Hoyt home for protection.

Knowing she was going to testify for the prosecution, a few members of the Family—Lynette Fromme, Catherine Share, Clem Grogan, and Ruth Moorehouse—persuaded her to join them on an all-expenses paid trip (gratis thanks to a few stolen credit cards) to Hawaii. Hoyt knew it wasn't a smart move to join them, but she was afraid of putting her actual family in harm's way.

She and Moorehouse checked in under an assumed name at the Hilton Hawaiian Village Hotel, but their stay was short-lived. Her friend abruptly announced her return to California but insisted that Hoyt stay. She accompanied Moorehouse to the Honolulu Airport and they had a final meal together. Moorehouse watched Hoyt eat a hamburger with ketchup. When they finished, Hoyt walked her to the gate to see her off. Moorehouse's farewell was both cryptic and revealing.

"The last thing she says to me was, 'Just imagine if there were ten tabs of acid on it (the hamburger)'" Hoyt said. "Then she told me to go to Waikiki Beach and lay down on the beach."

As Hoyt got on a bus to the beach, she started to trip. What Moorehouse said to her at the airport finally dawned on her—the burger *was* laced with acid. She got off the bus, found a bathroom, stuck her finger down her throat, and emptied the contents of her stomach. A stranger asked Hoyt if she was okay. She asked him to summon a policeman who took her to a local Red Cross. The social worker there specialized in drug cases and immediately put Hoyt on an IV filled with Valium. She recalled:

I remember going to a gray place. I had no body. I had no memory. I had no name. There was just nothing. I think I died. And then I just got thumped back into life. I remember screaming for my mother. The doctor and nurse debated whether or not to put me into the hospital or psych ward. They put me in the psych ward because they didn't want another attempt on my life.

Two weeks later, Hoyt came roaring back and walked into the Hall of Justice to testify against her former friends. She was on the stand for three days and ran the table with all four defense attorneys, especially Kanarek.

Kanarek asked me, "Did you spend a lot of time in a mental hospital?" and I said, "No, but I did spend a night in one two weeks ago," which just opened the door regarding my trip to Hawaii. I found out I could turn 'em—control those attorneys. I could control them, and I was just eighteen.

There was also an attempt to smear Sharon's and Jay's names by attorney Daye Shinn, who represented Susan Atkins. In his cross examination of Paul Tate, he asked about Sharon's involvement with Jay and how well he knew him, and if he attended parties or consumed drugs or alcohol with the couple.

"Never," said Tate, who folded his arms to show his dismay with the question. "You got any snake oil to sell with this load of manure?"

Shinn objected and Older had the answer stricken from the court record. Shinn then asked to approach the bench, so he, Bugliosi, and the other defense attorneys huddled in front of the judge as he asked to proceed with the line of questioning in an attempt to tie Jay to a drug dealer and other undesirables. Shinn was told by Older to proceed but with extreme caution.

"Mr. Tate, did you ever see Jay Sebring use a whip on someone in a sexual—"

Older's gavel slammed hard on his desk from the bench. He looked at Shinn in disgust.

"That question is stricken. Your examination is over, Mr. Shinn," Older said. "You are excused, Mr. Tate, subject to being recalled."

To add insult to injury, when Paul Tate exited the courtroom that day, he was greeted by a throng of reporters who hurled insensitive questions his way.

"Is it true that Sharon and the others used Manson as their drug connection?" Another asked, "Did Manson really attend orgies with Sharon at Cielo Drive?"

Tate justifiably told these jackals to kiss his ass. While Tate was able to keep his temper in check, Manson began to boil over. Four months into the trial, on October 5, Manson interrupted a morning session. Los Angeles Sheriff's Office detective Paul Whitely had finished his testimony, which Manson sensed was being used to destroy his alibi. He was angered when defense attorneys opted not to cross-examine Whitely. Manson asked Older if he could cross-examine the witness himself. He was rebuffed.

"Are you going to use this courtroom to kill me?" Manson asked sarcastically. "I am going to fight for my life one way or another. You should let me do it with words."

Older was not amused and told Manson to remain quiet or he'd have him removed.

"I will have *you* removed if you don't stop," Manson retorted. "I have a little system of my own."

With that, Manson put one foot on the defense table and hurled himself headfirst toward the judge's bench with a sharpened pencil in hand, landing spread-eagle on the floor after the ten-foot leap.

Sheriff's Deputy William Murry dove after Manson and landed on top of him, pinning him to the ground with all his might. Manson was led from the courtroom shrieking, and forced to watch the rest of the day's testimony from a holding cell. Older, clearly shaken by the attack, ordered a driver-bodyguard as well as twenty-four-hour security at his house. He also carried a firearm—a reliable .38 snub nose pistol—under his black robe. War hero or not, he wasn't taking any chances.

Paul Fitzgerald used the frightening occasion to call for a mistrial, citing the judge's state of mind.

"It isn't going to be that easy, Mr. Fitzgerald," Older said in defiance. "They are not going to profit from their own wrong.... Denied."

A few days after the pencil attack, Charles Watson was finally extradited to California, having exhausted his legal maneuvers to block being brought back to the Golden State. On October 7, he appeared before Superior Court Judge George Dell. The emaciated Texan was a shell of himself and stared blankly at the judge. The six-foot-two former athlete had dropped from 160 to 110 pounds and was being force-fed through intravenous tubes. Many felt

Watson was faking some of his symptoms, and his attorney, Sam Bubrick, requested three court-appointed psychiatrists examine him. They reached different diagnoses (schizophrenia, catatonia, and suicidal ideations) but came to consensus on the fact that Watson was reverting to a fetal state and in danger of dying. One went so far as to call him a "vegetable." On October 29, Judge Dell ruled that Watson was incompetent to stand trial at that time and remanded him, as a "life-saving measure," to the Atascadero State Hospital in San Luis Obispo, California.

"He is not capable of understanding at this time the nature of the charges against him," Dell said. "I feel that it is imperative that he be placed in a facility where he may be able to regain his sanity."

After twenty-two grueling weeks, the prosecution rested its case against Manson at 4:27 p.m. on Monday, November 13, 1970. The court was recessed until November 19, and when the defense was asked to proceed with their case, Fitzgerald threw everyone a curve ball.

"Thank you, your honor," Fitzgerald said. "The defense rests."

Atkins, Krenwinkel, and Van Houten simultaneously stood, shouting that they wanted to testify. Judge Older called the defense attorneys to his chambers where they informed him they had rested because Atkins, Krenwinkel, and Van Houten were going to take the stand and cover for Manson, confessing they committed the murders and advocating for his innocence.

Though astonished by this answer, Older ruled that the three should have the opportunity to take the stand. However, before they were given that opportunity, Kanarek made a motion to sever Manson from his three co-defendants to be tried separately. In effect, he was letting the three ladies take the rap so he could skate free.

The following day, Manson said he wanted to testify after all. Older agreed but would not allow it in front of the jury. Rather than be questioned by Kanarek, he asked to make a statement

instead. It was granted by Older, who probably regretted the decision. Manson went on a two-hour rant, going through a full range
of emotions and expressions, displaying his warped but somewhat
effective oratory skills, touching on issues such as his upbringing,
his lack of education, societal ills, and even love. He concluded:

> It's all your fear. You look for something to project it on,
> and you pick out a little old scroungy nobody that eats out
> of a garbage can, and that nobody wants, that was kicked
> out of the penitentiary, that has been dragged through every
> hellhole that you can think of, and you drag him and put
> him in a courtroom. You expect to break me? Impossible!
> You broke me years ago. You killed me years ago.

When court resumed on Monday, November 30, Ronald
Hughes was not present and could not be accounted for. When he
did not return after a few days, Older appointed Maxwell Keith as
Van Houten's co-counsel. The case was getting stranger by the day.[4]

The jury spent the Christmas holidays sequestered at the
Ambassador Hotel but were allowed to have family visits and enjoy
holiday celebrations.

On January 13, 1971, Bugliosi started his final summation but
with plenty of interruptions by Kanarek. Even after a contempt
citation and a $100 fine, Kanarek continued. Older finally had
enough.

"I have come to the regretful conclusion during the course of
the trial that Mr. Kanarek appears to be totally without scruples,
ethics, and professional responsibility," Older said. "So far as the

---

4. Though many have speculated over the decades that Manson had Hughes killed
while on a weekend camping trip to take a break from the trial, an autopsy later
revealed he died of an accident when he was caught in a rainstorm and was swept
away by a flash flood and drowned.

trial of this lawsuit is concerned, and I want the record to reflect that."

Finally on January 15, 1971, Older dismissed the jury of seven men and five women to deliberate the case, asking them for a verdict upon their return. They did so after nine days, and on January 25, they found Manson, Atkins, Krenwinkel, and Van Houten guilty on all counts—twenty-seven separate verdicts in all.

Manson, Atkins, and Krenwinkel learned of their fate on March 29. But, before the hammer came down, Manson usurped the proceedings once again.

"You have no authority over me," Manson told the jurors. "Half of you aren't as good as I am."

Older ordered Manson out of the courtroom, but in his absence, Atkins took up for Manson and began shouting.

"You've all judged yourselves," she said, lunging toward the jury box.

Krenwinkel echoed: "You're removing yourselves from the face of the earth. You're all fools! There has never been any justice in this courtroom."

"Your system is a game. You blind, stupid people," Van Houten screeched, getting in the last word before order was restored.

It took court clerk Gene Darrow almost twenty minutes to read the verdicts and their fate: the four were sentenced to die in the gas chamber.

At the sentencing phase, it wasn't Manson who stole the show on February 11, 1971. That distinction belonged to Susan Atkins, who casually stated for the record that killing Sharon Tate "seemed like a good idea at the time" and still thought it was "the right thing to do." She elaborated to a stunned jury:

I didn't relate to Sharon Tate being anything more than a store mannequin. She sounded like an IBM machine. She kept begging and pleading and I got sick of listening to it,

so I stabbed her.... Jay Sebring reminded me of a Samurai
warrior.

Atkins elaborated that the motives for the murder were nothing
more than to commit a copycat murder in the Gary Hinman case
to free Bobby Beausoleil.

"I would do anything to get Bobby out of jail, short of going to
the police myself," Atkins said. "It seemed like a good idea at the
time. It would have worked if I hadn't talked."

More than a half-century after the murders, Atkins' tone-deaf
and soulless comments still echo in the broken hearts of those
closest to the victims. The inconceivability of the ambivalence with
which each of the Family members recounted their actions is only
outmatched by the lunacy and rage they displayed after being held
accountable.

Charles Watson was also sentenced to die on October 12, 1971,
when a separate jury found him guilty on seven counts of first-
degree murder, though his trial was almost an afterthought—ironic
considering he was the person whose hands were bloodiest when it
came to the Tate-LaBianca killing spree.

None of the seven victims were mentioned by Darrow in
reading the verdicts, a slight that had pervaded the proceedings in
the months that followed their deaths. But, with the spectacle
concluded, there was hope that the dead and the mourners might
have a chance for some peace.

CHAPTER 30
DAMAGED DYNASTY

Those who lost loved ones to the Manson Family violence were forced to put their grief on hold as the horror of the murders, the spectacle of the investigation, and the marathon trial consumed all the air in the room.

Though each victim was laid to rest immediately, those left behind had their process of mourning halted while Manson and his acolytes populated the minds and daily lives of their families and friends with their maniacal behavior.

Jay and Sharon's funerals took place just hours apart on Wednesday, August 13, 1969, four days after their murders. Peter Sellers, Yul Brynner, and Warren Beatty all flew in from London to attend Sharon's service at Good Shepherd Church in Beverly Hills. They were joined by Kirk Douglas, James Coburn, Stuart Whitman, and approximately 150 others. Roman Polanski sat with Paul and Gwen Tate, along with their two teenage daughters—Debra and Patricia—on the front pew on the right side of the chapel. Two bouquets of marguerites were placed to the left and right side of her closed casket.[1] The family held their composure until Reverend

---

1. Sharon Tate was interred, along with her unborn son, at Holy Cross Cemetery in

Peter O'Reilly gave his final blessing: "Goodbye, Sharon, and may the angels welcome you to Heaven and the martyrs guide the way...."

Gwen's body heaved, then broke into deep, inconsolable sobs. Dial Torgeson of the Associated Press was present and reported this:

> As the family stood up to say a last farewell before the closed casket, it was Polanski who comforted Mrs. Tate and helped her to her feet. He stood facing the casket a long moment, blinking, but seemingly composed. Then he kissed the casket. Funeral director Richard Cunningham handed Mrs. Tate five pink roses from the large spray of roses and carnations atop the casket, and the family left the church.

Never letting a good tragedy go to waste, 20th Century-Fox seized the occasion to line their pockets by re-releasing *Valley of the Dolls* nationwide to coincide with Sharon's funeral. The studio honored her in a fashion befitting such a gesture—they generously bumped Sharon to top billing this time around.

Barely two hours after Sharon's funeral, many of the same people, including Roman Polanski and the Tate family, made the hour-long trek to Glendale for Jay's 2:00 p.m. service at the Wee Kirk o' the Heather Chapel at Forest Lawn Memorial Park. It was an overflow crowd of immediate and extended family, friends, customers, and celebrity clients. Some of the famous mourners included Steve McQueen, Paul Newman, Bruce Lee, Henry Fonda, Peter Fonda, James Garner, Dennis Weaver, Alex Cord, George Hamilton, and singer Keely Smith.

Jay's family—the Kummers from Detroit and the DiMarias from Las Vegas—in shock and having just arrived in Los Angeles,

---

Culver City, California. Gwen Tate insisted they be buried together in a single casket.

were driven to the memorial service by Paul Greenwald, Jay's friend and son of his attorney, Alvin Greenwald. Cami Sebring was also with Jay's family in the commute. Greenwald recalled the following:

> It was my responsibility to drive Jay's family to the funeral. So, I went and picked them up. I drove up, and the most unbelievable experience was pulling right up at the family entrance to Wee Kirk O' the Heather Chapel. And there was a cordoned off area about 15 by 15 feet. There were all photographers, and I opened the door to get out of the car, and then I opened the back door because I had Jay's family with me. As we got out, I never heard the sound of a gazillion cameras going off like that. I'll never forget it.

McQueen and attorney Alvin G. Greenwald co-conducted the nonsectarian service. Greenwald eulogized Jay in this way:

> Though this person will leave our community, his genius will always be with us, for he personified the spirit of discovery. His was the eye of intellect on the wing of thought. He was always in advance of his time, a pioneer for the generation which he preceded. A creative, gifted artist who did not have to be taken from us to be appreciated.
>
> Jay Sebring had within himself a driving, impelling perfectionism that was his alone. He sought to and did share it with all. Sebring's genius, Sebring's legacy, Sebring's beautiful faith remains with us—it is only his dust that departs.

When McQueen spoke of his dearly departed friend he was less verbose than Greenwald, but equally poignant. "Most men spend their lives fantasizing about their dreams," McQueen said. "Jay *lived* his dreams."

McQueen's first wife, Neile, who was also present, was shocked to see Jay lying in an open casket considering the gruesome manner of death that befell him. She also noted that the "morticians had done a masterful job." She wrote in her 1986 memoir *My Husband, My Friend*, however, that the memorial was not drama free or without incident.

> As we sat waiting for the service to start, a strange man climbed up to the altar where Jay's body lay and began a bizarre chant. Nobody knew who he was, and it galvanized everyone present to attention. Warren Beatty, who was sitting next to me, was ready to throw me on the floor, fearful that some sort of altercation was about to occur. He was aware that Steve [McQueen] had a gun and was concerned what might happened if anybody open fired. But somebody removed the man who was chanting in front of Jay's body and order was restored.

Joe Torrenueva said Jay's funeral was eerie and devoid of a typical send-off. He remembers how out of sorts everyone was in attendance.

> The whole thing was a blur. I saw a lot of people I knew but it didn't really register. It was so traumatic, and everyone was in a daze or fog. It was as if no one spoke to one another. They couldn't because they were in shock. They were terrorized. At a typical funeral, you see people from the past and smile and catch up because you shared a past with this person, so there's great affection. This wasn't a celebration of life. This was, "Oh my God! Oh my God!" There was no hugging, no greetings, no smil-

ing. You couldn't because everyone was in fear for their lives.

After the funeral service, several of Jay's intimate friends visited with the Kummers and DiMarias at their hotel in Beverly Hills. Jay's brother-in-law Tony DiMaria recalled the following:

When we went to the hotel after the funeral, I remember Steve McQueen couldn't even get three words out of his mouth, he was so shaken up. He was crying. He was trying to be as nice and warm as he could be, but he was just torn up. So was Paul Newman. Both could barely speak. And they were there for quite a while trying to welcome and comfort the family. Ironically, we ended up trying to comfort Steve and Paul. They were just really broken up about the loss of Jay.

Bernard Kummer and his son Fred had flown to Los Angeles to attend Jay's funeral service. Jay's mother, Margarette, was bedridden in Michigan with a severe case of shingles, and her daughter Geraldine cared for her. The DiMarias, Cami Sebring, and Paul Greenwald completed the family in attendance at the service. Jay was ultimately buried at Holy Sepulchre Cemetery in Southfield, Michigan after a second funeral service was observed for family and friends near Detroit.

During that time in Los Angeles, Jay's family visited the Easton residence to sort out inconceivable affairs in Jay's absence. The moment is indelibly etched in Anthony DiMaria's memory. Though only three years old, Jay's nephew recounts the following:

I remember we went to the house. I didn't know why we were there, but this was a place I'd never seen before. There was nothing like this in Las Vegas. For the most part, we all lived in cinderblock houses, at least the home I was raised in. But this was like something out of Disneyland to me. It was magical—stained wood beams, lush steep hillsides, stained glass windows, a chalet steeple. It was like a castle. When my mom and grandfather went upstairs, I was so excited to go with them, but I couldn't. When my dad told me I had to stay downstairs with them, I got upset. Wisely, he distracted me, "You wanna go see the pool?" "Yeah!"

We went into the backyard. The pool was being drained. It was so deep, it scared me and I wanted to go back inside. There was a knock at the front door, and I stood next to my father to see who might be coming to see us. It was a girl in a nice dress, almost like an Easter dress. She was holding a box of pastries. I'm guessing she was the daughter of one of Jay's neighbors. She was several years older than me and very pretty. I have tried to figure out for years who she was, but never had any luck. It was a nice gesture during a devastating time for our family.

Looking back, my parents and grandparents worked hard to protect my sisters and me from the horrors and hell that impacted our family. They did so throughout our lives. They always reminded us that Jay wouldn't want us to suffer any more than what is natural, and that he would remind us to live life with the passion and zeal that he did.

Having said goodbye to his son, Bernard Kummer was left to find a successor to keep Jay's dynasty running, which was no small feat.... perhaps impossible.

In May 1969, while on a trip to Albuquerque, New Mexico, to promote his next franchise, Jay and his self-professed protégé, Jim Markham, said they spent a few days together promoting the salon, drinking, and hitting the clubs. According to Markham, in the haze of activity, they managed to have a private moment in which Markham said Jay made an "eerily prophetic" statement to him.

"He had always told me, if anything ever happens to me, you've got to take over because you're the only one who knows how to do this," Markham told *American Salon* reporter Kristen Heinzinger.

These words immediately came rushing back to him on August 9, 1969, as he was inside his SEBRING International Shop in Albuquerque around ten in the morning, cutting a client's hair. He heard a news bulletin regarding the murders in Benedict Canyon, which specifically mentioned Sharon Tate.

The news saddened Markham, who had seen Sharon with Jay a month before on a trip to Los Angeles. Naturally, Markham grew concerned because whenever he was in California he noted Jay and Sharon were often in close proximity.

"She was a really sweet lady," Markham told the *Hollywood Reporter*, who added that he never saw her with Polanski, only Jay. "She seemed to like Jay a lot. They were always kissing. Lovey-dovey."

Nearly an hour later, he received a phone call from John Madden, vice president of SEBRING, informing him that Jay and Sharon were found murdered, and police were grasping at straws regarding a suspect or motive. After the initial shock wore off, Madden asked Markham if he could fill in for Jay. It remains unclear how, or who might have concurred with, Madden to suddenly decide to promote the New Mexico native to his position at SEBRING in Los Angeles. According to Markham's memoir, *Big Lucky*, John Madden's phone call was made within an hour after news of the murders exploded throughout the media.

The twenty-four-year-old Markham was an unlikely successor to Jay. He had none of Sebring's style, flair, or sophistication, and was admittedly wide-eyed and wet behind the ears when it came to the high-octane Southern California lifestyle. This would be a daunting task for any Hollywood neophyte, but relocating from Albuquerque to Hollywood to become representative, and beneficiary, of the SEBRING Enterprise was the opportunity of a lifetime. It also meant proving himself to Jay's celebrity clientele and gaining the confidence of the existing SEBRING staff who were used to being a part of, and amongst, exclusive Hollywood circles on a daily basis. Equally challenging, the SEBRING staff knew Jay's philosophies and concepts for years and held great loyalty to their mentor. For many of them, the introduction of Markham to fill Jay's shoes in West Hollywood must have seemed abrupt and what appeared to be almost like an out of the blue replacement.

Yet, days before Markham arrived in Los Angeles to take over the operations, he was sent a letter of confidence by Bernard Kummer, dated August 28, 1969. It read:

Dear Mr. Markham,

As I remember and read again, the eulogy of Jay Sebring given by Alvin Greenwald on August 13, the trait of my son's character shone forth as we all knew him. The accolade given in the venture of his enterprise was not for him alone.... but it is also attributable to you. In this we are very proud. One man was the originator, the artist, the spark and driving force; but Thomas [Jay] alone did not fulfill the job.

I say to you that it was also your loyalty and perseverance that made a large contribution. Thence for your benefit and his remembrance, I am sure you will continue with great fortitude.

So, I close with strong feeling from Margarette, his mother, and I, joined by Fred, his brother, Gerry and Peggy, his sisters —to express our heartfelt appreciation to you for the expression of sympathy in the hour of sorrow.

Sincerely,

Bernard J. Kummer

Detroit, Michigan

According to Markham, he didn't just step into Jay's shoes but he also slipped into the position of his mentor. When Markham took over Jay's empire, he used Jay's office at the SEBRING salon, inherited Jay's 400-plus clientele list, drove his Porsche,[2] and even slept in the house on Easton Drive, which was still tastefully decorated and left in immaculate condition. A light sleeper, Markham often would be rousted in the early morning hours by strange noises.

"I'm living in Jay's house with raccoons on the roof—it would sound like somebody walking on the top of the house," Markham told the *Hollywood Reporter* in 2019. "I finally had to move out. I thought I was going to be next. They hadn't caught Manson. Nobody knew why it happened."

He found the Fairfax salon a less frightening place, but the shop held some unexpected surprises he didn't bargain for. When Markham was ushered into Jay's old office by John Madden, he told him the phones were bugged by the FBI and that one of the stylists was a suspect.

In addition to the anxiety around the ongoing investigation, Markham had immense pressure in keeping Jay's empire afloat. Not only did he have to win over and maintain Jay's exclusive clientele, but he also had to oversee the SEBRING product line, set up distributorships, meet with new buyers, and field calls from the press as well.

Certainly, this was an extreme amount of pressure for a young man in his mid-twenties. But it was a golden opportunity to helm an exclusive and thriving institution and take a thrill ride through Candyland, according to Markham. He told reporter Kristine Heinzinger the following:

---

2. As executor of Jay's estate, Bernard Kummer sold his son's 1966 Porsche 911 to Markham for $4,700. But to retrieve the sports car, Markham had to venture to 10050 Cielo Drive, where it had sat since the night of the murders, according to Markham.

Once in California, I had purchased Jay's black Porsche from his father, I was running the salon and the company, while styling Jay's former celebrity clients. I took over his membership at The Candy Store, a private club, and even dated some of his girlfriends [*laughs*]. It was the most exciting time of my life, but also one of the scariest times, that is until they caught Manson.

The salon was always bustling. Phones were ringing off the hook, and there were always celebrities coming and going. The main salon was downstairs, and upstairs was my office. The downstairs salon was where most [of] the action took place with two manicurists, two shoeshine guys, and a parking attendant to bring up the client cars. I mostly worked upstairs where I had a private area where I could cut and style my clients and give them some privacy away from the hustle and bustle.

On December 2, 1969—a day after the Los Angeles Police Department announced arrests for the Tate-LaBianca murders—Bernard and Margarette Kummer attended an exclusive event at Los Angeles' The Factory nightclub hosted by Peter Lawford in which Markham was announced as Sebring business president.

"We are relieved," Bernard told the assembled press before turning the floor over to Markham, who was dressed in a dark striped suit, paisley tie, and a jeweled ankh ring on his left pinky finger. Naturally, some of the assembled press were skeptical about Markham's new role. One of them was Lydia Lane, a syndicated beauty columnist.

"What makes you qualified for this position? Where do you see the company a year from now?" she asked.

Markham deftly sidestepped the first question and only replied to the second. He told her that SEBRING International would continue to advance with their innovative product line, unique cutting method, and first-class treatment in men's hair. The answer seemed to satisfy Lane.

While the press event caused a wave of publicity, things weren't so smooth at the Fairfax shop. Markham recalled the mood as tense, and many of the stylists viewed him as both an outsider and interloper. He'd overhear some of them refer to him as "Mr. Albuquerque." This was one obstacle he could not overcome; however, Markham found others to offer him comfort.

By November 1970, the business was faltering under the new leadership—perhaps a testament to the fact that the company wasn't just built on Jay's blood, sweat, and tears, but that Jay was the lifeblood of the entire operation.

Joe Torrenueva, who had been running his own place for a few years, continued to keep tabs on the Fairfax shop.

I had kept in touch with some of the guys and heard some rumblings about what was happening at the shop—weird things. Factions were starting to form after Jay's death, and no one was happy with the situation at Fairfax. With Jay no longer around to hold it all together, it all eventually fractured and fell apart.

One of Jay's stylists convinced a handful of others to join him in opening a salon down the street. When they opened their doors, four more stylists jumped ship and joined them. That left Markham with less cutters to handle their clients. Because of the level of talent Jay required for SEBRING, it wasn't quick or easy to replace these stylists.

After a year at the helm, Madden and Markham's relationship grew strained. Also, the SEBRING partners defaulted on numerous months of rent, pushing the Kummers to an insurmountable financial position. According to Markham, Jay's father, Bernard Kummer, abruptly filed for bankruptcy in May 1971. But the filing was hardly "abrupt," as Bernard had been reminding the new management team of their financial delinquencies since November of the previous year (1970) through at least a dozen letters.[3]

This was evidenced in an April 13, 1971, letter from Bernard Kummer to the trio of SEBRING managing officers—Helen Nielsen, Jim Markham, and Robert Papin—whom he admonished for failing to pay rent for over three straight months at the Fairfax location. The letter read:

> *J. Markham, H. Nielsen, R. Papin,*
>   *ESTATE OF THOMAS JAY SEBRING*
>   *-Rents-*
>   *Miss Nielsen and Gentlemen:*
>   *You have created and developed an untenable situation.*
>   *Our position on financial requirements relating to the Fairfax property has been clearly set forth to you—in which you have not only clouded the skies but have muddied the waters. Charges are accruing to your detriment.*
>   *Your delinquency in payment of rents and security deposit cannot be condoned: the security deposit of $1,000.00; rents for February, March, and April of $3,000; and totaling $4,000.00—all PAST DUE.*
>   *Your remittance covering the deposit of $1,000.00 and the rents is required within ten (10) days.*
>   *Very truly yours,*
>   *Bernard J. Kummer*

---

3. Bernard Kummer, Jay's father and executor of the Sebring Estate, maintained extensive notes and records pertaining to his son's estate, probate, and business enterprise throughout his life. His documentation is sourced from files of letters and documents exchanged between Kummer, several attorneys, and SEBRING International managers. The correspondence spans several years, and chronicle financial delinquencies and strain caused by the Los Angeles partners.

This was particularly bitter for the Kummers as they had supported their son and his endeavors before Day One. In his son's absence, Bernard Kummer was forced to fly across the country to tend to his son's business situations and probate issues, sometimes monthly. Peggy and Tony DiMaria, whose family now included their son Anthony and newborn daughter Christine, offered to relocate to Los Angeles to work in and oversee Jay's salon to ensure the SEBRING legacy. While Jay's sister and brother-in-law preferred to remain in Las Vegas, they hoped to alleviate any further emotional and financial pain that continued to plague their parents ever since Jay was killed. However, Margarette Kummer, devastated by her eldest son's murder, asked her youngest daughter and her husband to stay away from Los Angeles. No doubt Jay's cautionary words haunted his mother, "L.A. is a dog-eat-dog town." The DiMarias honored the wishes of their parents and remained in Las Vegas.

With heavy hearts, the Kummers placed the assets of their son's salons and the SEBRING product line up for auction. The decision seemed the best possible way forward to legally and fiscally protect the Kummer family and Jay's legacy. Jim Markham, Bob Papin, and Helen Nielsen placed the highest bid and won. But three months into their partnership, Papin and Nielsen filed a lawsuit to oust Markham. They finally settled the lawsuit in 1972, but ultimately Papin and Nielsen ended up with SEBRING International and SEBRING Products. Markham was awarded 33 1/3 percent of SEBRING stock, rights to half of Papin and Nielsen's salaries—$30,000 a year for life—as well as the right to start a competing company, Markham Products. Taking a page out of the SEBRING playbook, Markham began packaging a grooming kit that included shampoo, conditioner, hair spray, a shampoo brush, and a brush comb with long teeth. He also began to certify barbers in the "Markham Method," offered them distributorships, and encouraged others to become a Markham Style Innovator shop. Markham seized a once-in-a-lifetime opportunity to capitalize on the many innovations and clever business strategies he learned from Jay, and he never looked back.

Original SEBRING stylists such as Paul Yamashiro and Bob Cox finally left the Fairfax salon and started their own businesses. A massive number of SEBRING clients left with them, though some celebrities such as Paul Newman, Henry Fonda, James Garner, Dennis Weaver, and Peter Lawford opted to stay with Markham. Original Fairfax customers sought SEBRING alumni throughout Southern California—Joe Torrenueva in West Hollywood, Paul Yamashiro in Beverlywood, Bob Cox in Palm Springs, and Jimmy Silvani in Newport Beach. Within a few short years, amidst infighting at Fairfax and void of Jay's vision, talent, or integrity, the SEBRING salons closed,[4] and his empire eventually dissolved, except for the SEBRING product line. Jay's heirs do not have any ownership in the product line, nor have they ever received a dime of royalties since his untimely death.

Earlier, we noted in this book that Jay Sebring died two times: first, his physical body in his brutal murder, and second, his reputation in how he was characterized in the aftermath of his murders. The death of his business enterprise could be considered a third death—one that added crushing insult to catastrophic injury. His empire was cut into many pieces and claimed by outsiders seeking to line their pockets from his genius and his tireless efforts. This unbearable assassination of his personhood and his legacy were only made worse by what his family endured as the world sought justice for the Manson Family's crimes. Keeping the agony fresh, parole hearings would rear their ugly heads over the next fifty-plus years, reopening the wounds the loved ones of the victims struggled to heal.

---

4. A lone SEBRING International Shop remains standing in Albuquerque, New Mexico, but with the passing of its original owner Armando Medina, the shop has faded.

CHAPTER 31
PAROLE PURGATORY

A February 18, 1972, 6-to-1 decision by the California Supreme Court to abolish the death penalty altered the futures of criminals and their victims in incalculable ways, none more so than the Manson Family and those who suffered losses in the Tate-LaBianca murders. With the revocation of the original death sentences, the Manson killers were sentenced to the next most severe sentence of life *with* the possibility of parole.[1]

The Court determined that the death penalty constituted "cruel and unusual punishment." Five years later, a modified version of the statute was implemented, creating a provision for cases of "exceptional concern" to public safety, such as "those involving the particular brutality, or the homicide of multiple victims."

This five-year window was fortuitous for Charles Manson, Charles Watson, Susan Atkins, Patricia Krenwinkel, Leslie Van Houten, Bruce Davis, and Robert Beausoleil. Their sentences were

---

1. At that time in California law, life without the possibility of parole was not an option. That was reversed along with the 1972 California Supreme Court decision that ruled the death penalty cruel and unusual punishment. This also automatically qualified lifers for automatic parole consideration.

automatically commuted to life imprisonment with the potential of parole after seven years. They were not grandfathered in to the later ruling. This meant that, by 1978, these convicted murderers could be eligible for release.

Not only did this decision chill the nation, it caused additional heartbreak for the victims' families. Each parole board hearing that has come up for the killers and others involved with the Manson Family has put the loved ones in a cycle of reliving the horrors and the pain of the loss over the last half-century. This parole purgatory has made it impossible for there to be any sense of real justice or the chance for the dead to rest in peace. Over fifty years of legal twists, detours, and endless parole hearings of eight Manson Family members has offered an ongoing renewal of the pain of loss.

When the Kummers learned of the states' abolishment of capital punishment, they contacted the California authorities to determine how the ruling would impact justice for their son and the other Manson Family victims. Jay's family was promised by representatives from the Los Angeles County District Attorney's Office and the Los Angeles Police Department that none of the "family" butchers would ever actually be paroled and, in fact, "The possibility of parole or release was purely a technicality." This was a determination that made definitive sense in 1972, but times would change, and with them so would judgments, rulings, and legislation.

The very first Family member to receive parole consideration was Patricia Krenwinkel on July 18, 1978. Original Manson trial co-prosecutor Stephen Kay represented the Los Angeles District Attorney's Office at the initial parole hearing. He said Krenwinkel and the other Manson Family members were there on a fluke.

All these defendants got a big benefit because in 1972 in February, the California Supreme Court held that the death penalty in California was unconstitutional, that it was cruel and unusual punishment. Everyone on Death Row at that time, including Manson, Watson, Van Houten, Atkins and Krenwinkel all had their sentences commuted from death to life. And in those days, a life sentence meant that you were eligible for parole after seven years. I started attending the parole hearings in 1978. Krenwinkel's was the first. I was the first district attorney in California ever to attend a "Lifer hearing." Now they're called Lifer hearings because the defendant is under a life sentence.[2]

Parole hearings take place in a private room at the correctional facility where the inmate is serving time and can last anywhere from three to nine hours. Typically, two parole commissioners preside behind a desk across from the petitioner, his/her attorney, a district attorney, and an armed prison guard. At times, a reporter and a news camera crew are present. For some years, victims' family representatives were not present at parole hearings. That all changed in the 1980s when Gwen Tate devoted her life to fight for victims' rights. After enduring years of mental anguish and family strife, she experienced an epiphany in 1982. That's when she was informed of news that Manson killer Leslie Van Houten was receiving significant public support, including 900 letters advocating for her release. This awakened a beast in Gwen that forever altered the course of her life. She decided to increase public awareness around Van Houten's possible release by giving interviews to newspapers and magazines and appearing on news and daily talk shows. She mounted a potent counter-offensive in which she amassed a staggering 350,000 signatures in opposition to the convicted killer's release.

---

2. Another lifer whose original death sentence was overturned was Sirhan Sirhan, who received a capital sentence for the 1968 assassination of presidential candidate Robert F. Kennedy, Jr.

With her newfound purpose and status as a public figure, Gwen switched her first and middle names and became known as "Doris Tate" to the public to signal her metamorphosis. She became a dedicated and influential advocate for victims' rights and a counselor in the Los Angeles chapter of Parents of Murdered Children. She also spearheaded legislation—Proposition 8, the Victims' Bill of Rights—that would allow the victims' interests to be represented in the parole process, giving family members or the victims themselves the opportunity to deliver an impact statement to be additionally considered by the board to determine the suitability of an inmate's release.

Doris also became a member of the Orange County-based Citizens for Truth, the organization that petitioned to keep assassin Sirhan Sirhan in prison. Also in 1982, Doris helped pass Proposition 89, which gave the governor authority to overturn release decisions reached by the state parole board. Manson prosecutor Stephen Kay recalled when Doris manifested her calling.

> At one point Doris was probably the most powerful woman in the State of California. But she didn't look at it as her having power. She looked at it as a chance to help family members of victims.... and to change the way victims were viewed. And she did a marvelous job.

Manson Family members used a variety of certificates of rehabilitation to tout themselves to the prison board, state officials, and the public at large to demonstrate that they'd drastically changed while behind bars. Anthony DiMaria had a different take:

> It's very surreal and disturbing to sit at a parole hearing year after year and listen to commissioners, attorneys and killers consider how college degrees, self-help certificates, AA/NA

meetings, penitentiary performances with the Actor's Gang, Tai Chi, and the Prison Puppy Program are weighed against the value of my uncle's life. For decades, our families endure how the slaughters of our parents, children, siblings—our flesh and blood—are reduced to a piece of paper. Or a medal. It's a perverse comparison that is deafeningly amplified in that these achievements are presented as extraordinary feats when in fact the inmate's behavior behind bars, at taxpayer dollars, is simply normal in free society.... but it's what the murderers did abnormally that warranted the original death sentences.

Through the years, district attorneys and victims' families provided numerous examples of questionable Manson Family extracurricular activities that was condoned under the California Department of Correction and Rehabilitation's (CDCR's) supervision.

Susan Atkins was married twice while incarcerated. First to Donald Laisure (1981-1982) then to James Whitehouse (1987-2009). Atkins also had a hand in four books written about her over the span of four decades: *The Killing of Sharon Tate* (1970); *Child of Satan, Child of God* (1978); *The Dove's Nest Newsletters: A Collection of Christian Letters* by Susan Atkins (2010); and *The Myth of Helter Skelter* (2012).

Leslie Van Houten married William Syvin in August 1982. Syvin had served time with grand theft auto and drug-related charges. The two fell for each other after a letter writing exchange and were married in a private ceremony behind prison walls. They were granted conjugal visits. The union lasted two months—until it was discovered that Syvin was plotting to break his wife out of prison. Authorities found sets of stolen California Department of Corrections uniforms after a search of his residence. When Syvin's grandiose scheme was revealed, Van Houten claimed to be unaware of the plan and immediately filed for divorce and ceased all communication with him.[3]

Van Houten laid low for the next decade but then made several national television appearances, notably in 1994 on *The Larry King Show* and with Diane Sawyer on ABC to discuss her roles in the murders, the "control" Manson had over her during the murders, and her parole status. These appearances proved to be opportunities for pleading her case to the public, eliciting sympathy and attempting to rehabilitate her image with the parole board. The propaganda campaign continued with her participation in a 2016 book titled *The Long Prison Journey of Leslie Van Houten*, the 2018 feature film *Charlie Says*, and the 2021 podcast Ear Hustle. Through each one of these platforms and in numerous parole hearings, Van Houten minimized her role in the murder of Leno and Rosemary LaBianca ("I stabbed Mrs. LaBianca in the lower back about sixteen times," describing her stab wounds as "superficial" and "post-mortem") and attempted to cast herself as another victim, not a perpetrator.

Patricia Krenwinkel also participated in a 20/20 interview with Diane Sawyer and gave interviews for *The Long Prison Journey of Leslie Van Houten*. She contacted filmmaker Olivia Kraus to produce a short documentary about her called *Life After Manson*. The 2014 op-doc video informs the viewer that Krenwinkel is the longest-serving woman in the California prison system, and "exposes a broken woman struggling with her past, her arduous effort to evaluate the cost of her choices, and the possibility of self-forgiveness," according to a press release. But it's clear this twenty-five-minute short is an overt attempt to help this murderer's chances

---

3. Van Houten began an affair with Peter Chiaramonte in 1977 when a state appellate court overturned her 1971 conviction and ordered her to be retried, largely due to the disappearance of her attorney Ronald Hughes near the end of her trial. Chiaramonte wrote about their year-and-a-half relationship in his 2015 memoir, *No Journey's End: My Tragic Romance with Ex-Manson Girl Leslie Houten*.

for parole. Precisely in lockstep with her female co-killers (Atkins and Van Houten), Krenwinkel's narrative heavily leans on the "girls" as victims of not only Manson, but society at large. On the film's website, director Krause describes the convicted killer of seven as a "woman who society has labeled a 'monster'" that "continues to be demonized by the public."

On January 18, 2024, during a parole hearing for Bruce Davis at San Quentin Prison, Board of Parole Hearings (BPH) Commissioners Julie Garland and Matthew Brueckner probed the inmate about his future plans to write his memoir. Of particular concern to the board was Davis' recent appearance on a podcast titled The Lighter Side of Serial Killers.

Commissioner Garland issued a continuance for the hearing so they could investigate Davis' involvement in the podcast. Before convening for the day, Gary Hinman's next of kin, Kay Martley Hinman and Sheryl Pickford, delivered impact statements. Debra Tate and Anthony DiMaria were also in attendance and delivered statements as Hinman family representatives.

In her statement, Kay Martley Hinman emphasized, "The title of this podcast is The Lighter Side of Serial Killers. I would very much like to know what Davis thinks the lighter side of a serial killer is. I would like him to explain what the lighter side of my cousin Gary's murder is. I very much doubt he has an answer."

On August 8, 2024—exactly 55 years to the day since Steven Parent, Jay Sebring, Abigail Folger, Wojciech Frykowski, Sharon Tate, and her unborn son were slaughtered at Cielo Drive—Bruce Davis' hearing resumed. All participants from the previous January hearing were present. However, less than two days before the hearing, victims' family and representatives were informed by the California Department of Corrections and Rehabilitation (CDCR) that a member of the media would be present to observe the proceedings. She would remain anonymous (due to "protocol") until the observer identified herself in the proceedings as Sophia Arguelles from Smuggler Entertainment.

The hearing proceeded without a hitch. After deliberations, Commissioner Julie Garland issued a three-year denial, citing "minimizing," "lack of self-awareness," "criminal mindset," and lying about "involvement with the media in the past January hearing."

It wasn't until the next morning in an email chain between Shelly Pickford, Kay Martley Hinman, Debra Tate, and Anthony DiMaria it was revealed that the "media observer," Sophia Arguelles, was also Charles Manson's granddaughter through Mary Brunner. Months earlier, both Martley Hinman and DiMaria were approached by a producer requesting interviews for a project that possibly involved a Manson grandchild. Both declined.

This realization was particularly disturbing since victims' families and representatives experience strict time and vetting requirements rigidly enforced by the CDCR. In a *Hollywood Reporter* article dated October 9, 2024, editors Benjamin Svetkey and Julian Sanction noted, "There haven't been reporters at the hearings for years, and they used to be vetted months in advance, but this woman was let in." They also reported, "Shortly after the hearing, Tate discovered that Arguelles was actually the daughter of L.A. realtor Daniel Arguelles, who has been claiming to be Manson's biological son." Tate was profoundly disturbed.

"A grandchild is not responsible for a grandfather's actions, but it's a blood relative in the victims' faces," Tate said. "It's disturbing."

Convicted murderer Robert Beausoliel has a personal website touting himself as an "American musician and multi-disciplined artist who has produced a wide-ranging body of original recorded music, sound design and visual art, most of it over the past five decades while doing time behind bars for a murder he committed in his youth."[4] He also has a social media presence on Facebook, Twitter/X, YouTube, and Soundcloud as well as two websites promoting his drawings and six albums, including a film soundtrack.

When Anthony DiMaria[5] pointed out these violations (prisoners are typically not allowed to profit from their crimes or promote themselves) and Beausoleil's numerous promotional internet platforms in a January 2022 parole board hearing, he was interrupted by attorney Jason Campbell (objecting to Beausoleil's connection to the Tate-LaBianca crimes) and inmate Beausoleil (denying DiMaria's statement that "Mr. Beausoleil's website has five additional links to Facebook, SoundCloud, Instagram, YouTube and Twitter" to which Beausoleil blurted, "No it doesn't").

Campbell also took exception to DiMaria's fourteen-page statement, which he intimated was too long. Commissioner Patricia Casady maintained order and admonished Campbell for attempting to censor DiMaria, who outlined the three days of torture Gary Hinman had to endure at the hands of Beausoleil, Atkins, and Brunner, and how it was the primary catalyst igniting the "most notorious rampage of killing and human destruction in California history." A formal complaint was filed in an email from DiMaria to CDCR regarding the inmate's possible perjury under oath. As a result, the BPH initiated an investigation looking into Beausoliel's online activities, stating that the board's findings would be addressed at his suitability hearing in January 2025. But, before that occurred, Los Angeles Superior Court Judge William Ryan issued a decision on a *habeas corpus* writ regarding Beausoleil's parole hearings—that no victim's family member or representative could address in future hearings that Beausoliel's crimes were directly

---

4. Beausoliel was twenty-one years old when he killed Gary Hinman. In the colloquial sense he might have been a "youth" but, legally, he was very much an adult.
5. DiMaria was asked to speak as a family representative by Gary Hinman's niece, Shelly Pickford.

connected to the Tate-LaBianca murders even though Beausoliel confirmed this fact to writer Truman Capote in a 1972 interview, telling Capote the Tate-LaBianca murders were a ploy to "get me out of jail. None of that came out an any of the trials." Hinman killer and co-defendant Susan Atkins confirms, "It was a plan for copycat murders that would make the police believe they had the wrong man."

Curiously, not one member of the Hinman family was informed of the legal proceedings, and their awareness and involvement was excluded from the process, which worked to Beausoliel's favor. On January 7, 2025, a state parole board panel made every possible effort to underscore Beausoliel's age and health condition, asking if he was wearing his compression stockings, knee brace, orthotics, and his wrist support brace, all supplied by California taxpayers. That was in addition to yoga and art classes and college education courses offered to Beausoliel.

The board also looked into Beausoliel's online activities; his claim being that his social media and two websites were tribute pages run by others who just so happened to be his friends. The inmate claimed to the Board, "When I made that comment to the statement that Mr. DiMaria made in his remarks—I didn't even know it was recorded. I was speaking to myself.... I was speaking specifically of Twitter, which I instructed my agent that she deactivate because I hadn't used it in about ten years or so."

When it came to his involvement with the Manson Family, Beausoleil went into victim mode almost immediately.

"I was actually being manipulated and didn't understand that that's what was going on," Beausoleil said. "I was this young kid and I was being played."

Later in the proceedings, he had the audacity to say he and Gary Hinman shared a commonality.

"I do see he and I both as victims," he said. "I don't see just him as a victim. I see myself as a victim."

After L.A. Deputy District Attorney Julianne Walker[6] concluded her thorough and effective closing argument, the Hinman family and representatives delivered impact statements:

Kay Hinman Martley: "Mr. Beausoleil is an unreliable narrator of his actions who has spent decades lying about his crimes."

Debra Tate: "He negotiates with filmmakers by email for using his music in their show, films…. He has spoken to Academy Award winning filmmaker Errol Morris for his high-profile upcoming Netflix documentary (*CHAOS: The Manson Murders*) about the Manson murders. That shows he is still linking himself to that notoriety."

Anthony DiMaria: "Attorney Campbell took exception to 'Mr. DiMaria's statement is approximately 14 pages long.' First, I'm pretty sure that everyone in this meeting would concur, including petitioner Beausoleil and his attorney, that enduring a 14-page impact statement is preferable to enduring three days of torture, having your face sliced in half, having your ear pierced with a needle and dental floss, and then slowly being stabbed and suffocated to death as you drown in your own blood. Perhaps we all might agree, too, that impact statements, as lengthy as they may be, are a hell of a lot better than laying 55 years in a cold, black coffin."

Shelly Pickford: "My mother was absolutely devastated by Gary's murder. Even as I grew older, she refused to talk about the horror. She was traumatized. I was left with a mother whose life was upended, and I can't even count the ways that this affected my upbringing. My grandmother, Gary's mother, passed away shortly after the murder…. of a broken heart."

The Board deliberated for an hour. When the hearing resumed,

---

6. Walker's involvement in the hearing was the first time in four years that a district attorney was present at a Manson family parole hearing, a direct manifestation of Nathan Hochman's election victory for DA director in 2024.

Commissioner William Muniz revealed the determinate factors in the board's unexpected decision for release.

"In your case today Mr. Beausoleil, we were obligated and did give great weight to your Youth Offender factors[7] when determining your parole suitability today, as well as our obligation to give special consideration to Elderly Parole factors when determining your parole suitability. In light of that, today, this is a grant for parole."

Beausoleil was the second Manson Family killer to be paroled in a period of two years,[8] indicating an alarming trend emerging within the California Department of Corrections and Rehabilitation. Furthering the pattern of revisionist history, Patricia Krenwinkel, who had a hand in killing seven people, was found suitable for release by the parole board on May 30, 2025.

And then there's Charles "Tex" Watson. In 1979, he married Kristin Svege and fathered four children. He wrote several books,[9] participated in two self-aggrandizing documentaries (*Pardoned from Above: The Charles "Tex" Watson Story* and *Forgiven: The Charles Tex Watson Story*), and set up a prison ministry that promotes his activities, religious philosophies, and offers site visitors updates on his life. When DiMaria requested an interview for his documentary,

---

7. Presiding Commissioner William Muniz, who was appointed by California Governor Gavin Newsom in April 2022, made a special point in this hearing of noting that Beausoleil was sexually assaulted at age fourteen. "That can be an extremely traumatic situation. That's not something anyone should have to go through. I'm sorry."

8. Steven "Clem" Grogan was the first Manson Family member to released, which was in 1985. Leslie Van Houten was released on parole supervision in July 2023.

9. Watson has authored *Will You Die for Me?* (1978); *Christianity for Fools: A Simple Understanding of the Christian Faith* (2013); *Manson's Right-Hand Man Speaks Out!* (2013); *Charles Watson Speaks Out* (2013); *Identity: Spirit, Soul and Body* (2013) *Illumination Bible Chart* (2017), and *Cease to Exist: The Firsthand Account of the Journey to Becoming a Killer for Charles Manson* (2019). Many are these titles are available through his ministry website.

JAY SEBRING...CUTTING to the TRUTH, Watson replied in a 2009 letter:

> *Dear Anthony:*
>
> *I was pleasantly surprised to hear from you, and to have received your request for an interview. And yes, it is "sensitive territory", not only for us but also for many relatives of my victims.*
>
> *First of all, let me say how very sorry I am for the loss I have caused your family for all these years. I made terrible choices in the '60s, and I deeply regret the pain I have caused so many.*
>
> *Several production companies have asked me for interviews during the 40th anniversary of the murders, but I turned them all down. It seems their main focus was sensationalism at a profit, which I am not interested in helping to promote.*
>
> *I hope you realize that I am truthful about the murders in my book,* Will You Die for Me?, *which you can read at my website. My word should help you tell Jay's story accurately.*
>
> *For years I have discussed the murders openly with professionals and anyone in authority. One day, a psychologist suggested that I should stop living in the past, since I had made peace with God and myself. I realize how difficult this can be for my victim's family members like you; but I have found it to be very helpful for my health.*
>
> *I hope you will understand my declining to do an interview. If you would like to talk about this more, I'm willing to correspond, but I don't want to build up your hopes. I will be praying for you and your project.*
>
> *Sincerely,*
>
> *Charles D. Watson*

In a change of heart, Watson sent a letter to DiMaria on March

23, 2011, expressing a new willingness to do an interview to describe Jay's last actions before his death for the documentary. Watson's timing of the letter was transparently convenient, sent just months before his next parole hearing on November 19, 2011. Also, in the correspondence, Watson felt it appropriate to probe for what DiMaria intended to do with proceeds from the documentary, inquiring, "How do you plan to distribute your film? Will it be marketed for profit, or non-profit? Or funds from it given to charity?"

DiMaria's perspective on his response is this:

> Watson has written several books, engaged in a documentary, and runs a prison ministry that accepts donations, and he has the audacity to question how the profits for his victim, Jay Sebring's documentary will be used? It blows my mind how he says he's not interested in "sensationalism for profit" yet appears to profit behind bars. He once wrote a book titled *Manson's Right-Hand Man Speaks Out!* and it took a parole board member to point out that his title might be insensitive to the victims' families, and only after that was the title changed.

The hypocrisy of Watson's 2011 letter revealed what can be characterized as narcissistic tactics and a lack of self-awareness that otherwise would have been laughable had the circumstances not been so tragic. After Watson's initial decline to be interviewed, DiMaria uncovered Jay's definitive last actions in direct testimony at the District Attorney's Office with the assistance of Patrick Sequeira and Stephen Kay. At this point there was no further need for correspondence with Watson. However, he did continue to see Watson over the years in subsequent parole hearings.

On October 15, 2021, Charles Watson appeared before California's Parole Board for the eighteenth time. At the time, the inmate was incarcerated at the R. J. Donovan Correctional Facility in San Diego, the same facility where Lyle and Erik Menendez were also serving time for the grisly shotgun murder of their parents, José and Mary Louise "Kitty" Menendez. Victims' family members who delivered impact statements at Watson's 2021 parole hearing included Louis Smaldino, Kay Martley Hinman, Debra Tate, Margaret DiMaria, and Anthony DiMaria. When it came his turn to speak, Anthony DiMaria explained to the parole board his family's position on these heinous crimes:

> I feel profound sadness for all of us impacted by these crimes. I also feel genuine sorrow for Charles Watson. To be clear, our family's involvement in these hearings have nothing to do with anger, "hatred", or vengeance towards the killers of our loved ones. Rather, we speak out of love for those who remain voiceless in their graves.

Watson was found unsuitable for release with a five-year denial. He'll face the parole board again in October 2026.

DiMaria's lifelong urge to learn everything about his uncle was reignited by new questions that arose during research for this book. Fifteen years since his first letter to Watson, DiMaria reached out again to him in a letter dated March 29, 2024. It read:

> *Mr. Watson,*
>
> *As you know, I have been on a lifelong quest to know my uncle [Jay Sebring] as much as I can…. which includes his last moments, etc.*
>
> *This letter finds you as a continuum in this endeavor.*
>
> *I have some questions I'd like to ask you if you are willing to answer.*
>
> *Sincerely, Anthony DiMaria*

On April 3, 2024, Charles Watson responded via email:

Anthony,

I'm so sorry for being such a "continuum" in your life for all these years. I pray that one day you will find a place in your heart to forgive me. Send me your questions about Jay's last moments to this email address. I will see what I can do to help you with your quest in that specific area.

Be loved,

Charles

NOTICEABLE IN MR. WATSON'S EMAIL WAS AN ABSENCE OF agenda, narcissistic demand, or lack of insight as were exhibited in past correspondence. His intentions seemed sincere, unlike any of his other cohorts—Bobby Beausoleil, Bruce Davis and, in particular, Patricia Krenwinkel, Leslie Van Houten, and Susan Atkins—who positioned themselves as victims of Charles Manson in their arguments. Even Watson, who dealt a vast majority of the fatal blows, never spit on the memories of his victims during his trial or taunted their families as the "girls" did. There is a lot to suggest the Manson women were just as cruel and diabolical in their behavior and lack of insight throughout their parole hearings as the men were.... but that's another matter.

After Watsons' 2024 letter, DiMaria felt compelled to consider forgiveness after what genuinely seemed to be an act of sincerity from Watson. There's a Biblical sentiment regarding crimes of extreme nature that DiMaria gave great weight to: "the individual might be forgiven, but not the crime."

DiMaria responded to Watson in a letter, "I genuinely wish I could grant forgiveness (even if just for what was done to me). But until the direct victims arise from their graves and grant their forgiveness, all is moot."

CHAPTER 32

POLITICS, POLICIES, AND PERNICIOUS PRECEDENTS

Throughout the decades, statements and interactions with Manson Family members and their victims' next of kin have provided a plethora of incomprehensible moments, ranging from the Theatre of the Absurd to the heartbreaking to the indelible. Doris Tate, who showed up to Charles Watson's 1984 parole hearing, finally got a chance to confront the butcher of her daughter and look him in the eye.

"What mercy, sir, did you show my daughter when she was begging for her life? What mercy did you show my daughter when she said, 'Give me two weeks to have my baby and then you can kill me'?.... When will Sharon come up for parole? When will these seven victims and possibly more walk out of their graves if you get paroled?"

In the ensuing years, Doris Tate, joined by her youngest daughter, Patricia, Louis Smaldino, Angela Smaldino, Janet Parent, and John DeSantis, carried the torch to represent their flesh and blood. On July 10, 1992, after a brain tumor diagnosis, Doris succumbed to cancer at the age of sixty-eight. Patricia then followed in her mother's footsteps to fight for justice, representing her family at parole hearings and making appearances to increase public awareness. Tragically, just eight years after the passing of her mother, Patricia Tate succumbed to cancer on June 3, 2000, at the age of forty-two. Paul Tate, disgusted by the California Justice system, lived in virtual seclusion, and Debra Tate, the only surviving sibling of Sharon, took the reins for the family, continuing their activism and launching a website: NoParoleForMansonFamily.com.

She continues the fight to this day.

In 2003, Peggy DiMaria grew alarmed after observing news reports indicating her brother's murderers might actually be released in current or subsequent parole hearings despite what the Los Angeles District Attorney and Los Angeles Police Department's offices had originally reassured the Kummer/Sebring family, that parole release was an "impossible technicality." She asked her son, Anthony, to contact the Los Angeles District Attorney's office to determine if justice was, in fact, at stake. Peggy relayed that she was bound and determined to speak out for her brother and fight for justice. On behalf of his mother, Anthony called District Attorney Stephen Kay's office and was surprised to speak to him directly after identifying himself and stating his family's purpose for the call.

"Anthony! Steve Kay. So good to hear from you and the Sebring family," he said. "Yes, it's true. We are in a real fight. Some of these inmates might actually be let go."

On July 7, 2004, at the very next hearing for Patricia Krenwinkel, Jay's family joined the parole proceedings in what would become a decades long fight for justice. Since, then, they have been involved in dozens of hearings, speaking as Jay's next of kin and as representatives for the LaBianca family (at the request of Louis Smaldino and John DeSantis) and the Gary Hinman families (at the request of Shelly Pickford and Kay Hinman Martley).

A few weeks later the DiMarias received a phone call from a producer on ABC's *Good Morning America* (GMA), requesting they be interviewed by Diane Sawyer. It was for a segment on the 35th "anniversary" of the murders. Debra Tate would also be interviewed. Anthony told the producer that he and his family were not interested in being involved in an "anniversary" piece rehashing the crimes. The producer explained this piece was going to focus on the victims, not the crimes. Though very private, the DiMarias decided the national morning show might increase public awareness at a time when justice was at stake.

The following day Debra Tate (from Los Angeles) and Anthony DiMaria (from Las Vegas) were on separate flights bound for New York City. Early that Monday morning, Diane Sawyer introduced herself before they took their seats in the GMA studio. Minutes before the live broadcast, Sawyer said a video lead-in of the segment would be presented before the interview. She asked if they would prefer not to see it in case it might be disturbing. Debra and Anthony said they wanted to see how the lead-in was presented, before the live segment for context.

As the two watched, it followed the predictable narrative—a recap of the murders, Van Houten and Krenwinkel claiming naïveté and being brainwashed while under the influence of drugs and, of course, the ubiquitous crazy Manson tirade.

"I got all the money in the world!" Manson protested to Sawyer. "I'm a gangster, woman!"

As the clip played live on air, Anthony DiMaria observed three cameramen laugh and exchange jokes. It was exactly the kind of circus his family despised and tried hard to avoid. And now he was part of a shit-show for all of America to view.... and then they were live.

Sawyer introduced the panel, said she was grateful to have them on, and then came the left hook.

"Debra, listening to them [Manson, Van Houten, and Krenwinkel], thirty-five years now. Thirty-five years later, is it time to say, 'As awful as it was, they should be released? That they were different people than they were then?'"

Anthony described the surreal and emotionally upsetting experience:

> I felt like a deer in headlights. I had been guarded my entire life from sharing a deeply private, painful family tragedy that had been played out in epic exploitation; but this was a true baptism by fire. Reeling, I wasn't clear if Sawyer was referring to the victims when she asked if "they should be released?" To this day, I regret not responding with this, "Well, Diane, as awful as it was, we should release the killers when each of their victims are released from their graves." But I was still gathering my wits after Sawyer's baffling question under a set of some very powerful and blinding lights. I know Debra felt similarly as she raised up and grabbed both arm rests with her hands. She responded, "I truly don't think so....," and articulately described the complete lack of remorse expressed from the murderers to her or any of our families.

After Debra Tate finished, Sawyer asked Anthony how these murders have impacted me being three years old at the time. I told her:

> These crimes didn't end thirty-five years ago. It's something that becomes who you are. If I consider the nature of these crimes—the heinous nature, how many people's lives were murdered, the hundreds of family members whose lives were destroyed or devastated—the killers sentenced our relatives, our loved ones to death. They sentenced our families to a lifetime of heartbreak and pieces. And that's without parole.

There was no response or clever retort from Sawyer regarding

Anthony's answer, but before the segment's conclusion, Sawyer signed off, "Again, I think that for a lot of people it's hard to imagine that you're living with it, daily, still after all these years later. But Debra, again thanks for being with us. And Anthony. When we come back...."

Anthony was dumbfounded by Sawyer's sensitivity to the murderers and the insensitivity to the victims' family members.

It's hard to imagine that you're living with it, daily, after all these years.

It never occurred to Anthony that the impact and scars of murder had a shelf life. And now a world-renowned, highly respected American journalist is telling the country on national television that the Sebring and Tate families most likely have overstayed the appropriate shelf life of murder.

Years later, former Los Angeles District Attorney Stephen Kay and Anthony discussed the Sawyer interview for the 2020 SEBRING documentary. Kay plainly stated, "She's become an apologist for them."

The victims' families continue to be baffled and outraged by the extensive minimization, deflection, and manipulation employed by inmates and their attorneys at these hearings.

When Kay and Anthony spoke in their initial phone conversation, the prosecutor warned that justice for the mass killings might be thwarted due to the state's changing political climate. There was a growing perception that incarceration was oppressive and inhumane. His concerns regarding California legislation specific to violent crime and victims' rights proved prophetic and accurate. In 2014, the state passed SB-260 titled "Youth Offender Parole." The law creates a special parole process for people who were eighteen or younger at the time of their crimes and received life sentences. In 2016, SB-261 was passed, increasing the age to twenty-three. Two years later, AB-1308 was passed to provide "special consideration of release" for convicted felons whose crimes were committed before the age of twenty-five.

Additionally, California implemented the Statutory Elderly Parole Program (known commonly as Section 3055) which demands the parole panel "must give special consideration for release for the offender when the inmate turns fifty years old and has served twenty years of continued incarceration." The penal codes and programs provide special provisions for violent criminals, yet no comparable regard or consideration for the state's victims of violent crimes. The current laws seem to be designed to empty the state's prisons deemed by a majority of California's politicians and institutions as draconian, "systemically racist," and a massive drain to the California state budget. The first two are simply a smoke-screen for the latter—the current California state prison budget for 2024-25 is nearly $14.5 billion. And it continues to go up every year even though there has been a prison population drop in the last decade.

Susan Atkins' husband/attorney James Whitehouse said as much at a 2009 parole hearing at The Central California Women's Facility. He echoed California's fiscal ideological tactic when Atkins' health took a sudden turn for the worse.

> In March of 2008, my wife suffered a malignant tumor. In the fourteen months California taxpayers have spent $6 to $7 million guarding and caring for her.... It was costing about $17,000 a day to take care of Susan, and this is a time when we're cutting healthcare for kids and Medi-Cal.

Disgusted by Whitehouse's ploy to parole his wife by any means possible, Anthony responded:

> There are many things that are disturbing to hear in these parole hearings, but the mention of cost efficiency strikes to

the core. We are not here to balance the California state budget. We are here because Susan Atkins sent several people to their graves. I find any talk of dollars and cents in this room inappropriate and gut-wrenching.

Even after the state's revocation of the original death sentences and Kay's warning regarding legislative twists and turns, the victims' families had no idea of the detours that lay ahead in the years to come.

With decades of experience and support from Kay, Patrick Sequeira, and Donna Lebowitz of the Los Angeles District Attorney's Office, the victims' families were aware and prepared to address defense attorney arguments and pro-criminal legislation. But a pro-inmate agenda from the CDCR and Parole Board revealed the agencies to be offender advocates once the departments initiated a formal investigation on June 22, 2017, to determine whether convicted killers Krenwinkel and Van Houten were victims in relation to these crimes.

Anthony addressed the anomalies to the CDCR and the Board of Parole Hearings' top authority, Jennifer Schaffer, in a February 1, 2017, letter. He wrote that his family and he had attended seventeen hearings to date and the parole board had functioned by and large with objectivity and fairness. However, at Krenwinkel's December 29, 2016, hearing, the board requested a judgment to initiate an investigation to determine if the petitioner was a victim of "intimate partner abuse" of Charles Manson.

"This development—47 years after the killer, convicted on seven counts of murder and sentenced to death—is mind-boggling and yet another twist of justice by local authorities impacting our families," he wrote. "These endless hearings come at a heavy cost, but we are compelled to be present and speak for those silenced in their graves. For justice."

Anthony also took umbrage at the fact that he was not in full view of the deputy commissioner who sat behind her computer monitor. The only time their eyes met was when he leaned across the table and tried to connect with her. Anthony was also dismayed that Commissioner Ali Zarrinnam, who was there as an observer, was smiling and texting on his cell phone throughout the proceeding. But more troubling were the leading questions Commissioner Nga Lam asked Krenwinkel, such as, "When did he (Manson) start indoctrinating you with his philosophies?"

Anthony wholeheartedly objected to that line of questioning and let it be known he found it troubling in a letter to the parole board.

"This is a vast overreach of authority whose jurisdiction is to determine danger to society and suitability of parole. The word indoctrinate was never even mentioned until Ms. Lam introduced it…. Is this practice of putting words in the inmates' mouths inspired by predetermined assumptions…. or agenda? Neither is acceptable."

Anthony also brought up the investigation to determine whether Krenwinkel was an abuse victim of Manson's. He asked that the board also investigate Krenwinkel and Van Houten's roles as a caretaker of children at the Spahn Ranch and how Krenwinkel knew of several rapes of young girls, ranging in age from 12 to 15. He submitted to Shaffer that Krenwinkel and Van Houten not only should be held accountable but should be investigated as an accessory after the fact.

"Let there be no distraction from who the *actual* victims are with regard to these murders, or the rape of children. When authority and judgment are formed selectively or politically, the scales of justice are thrown in the trash, leaving us all blindfolded. This is madness."

Anthony's request for a formal investigation into the rapes of children at Spahn Ranch was not pursued by Jennifer Schaffer, the CDCR, or the BPH. All three authorities did, however, launch a formal investigation to determine whether Patricia Krenwinkel and Leslie Van Houten were intimate partner abuse victims of Charles Manson. Both women, convicted killers of multiple people, were found to be victims by California Department of Corrections and the BPH.

On December 7, 2020, George Gascón assumed office as the 43rd District Attorney of Los Angeles County (LADA). Under his directive, the lead law enforcement authority for justice and victims' rights, the LADA was prohibited from any involvement or presence at any Los Angeles County Lifer parole hearings. This unprecedented policy left thousands of victims of violent crimes to fend for themselves with no legal representation from the county's highest legal office.

For decades, the prosecutor's office notified victims of crime or next of kin when an upcoming parole hearing was nearing well in advance. They also sent representatives to hearings to vigorously argue against the early release of offenders. But that changed in February 2021 when Gascón quashed the policy. He also disbanded a group of victim advocates and prosecutors (known as the "Lifer Unit") in his office who notify victims, their families, and their representatives about their assailant's parole hearings. A July 2022 statement from his office read:

> After consulting with victim experts, we do not believe this is a trauma-informed approach. Contacting victims and their next of kin can be very triggering, especially if they do not welcome the intrusion. We consulted with the California Department of Corrections and Rehabilitation, and they have advised and confirmed that it is their responsibility to contact victims who have registered for notifications and provide information and support to those victims.

After release dates were granted by the Board to Leslie Van

Houten, Patricia Krenwinkel, and Bruce Davis, Anthony DiMaria described how all the victims' families have been impacted by the parole hearings and ever-changing policies of the BPH, CDCR, and LADA.

> It's incomprehensible to directly witness and cope with mandates and determinations that devote so much care, resource, and consideration to cruel-hearted killers while our loved ones are treated as bygone collateral damage. We are impacted year after year, despite the horrific pain and suffering dealt to the victims and our families—that the world is increasingly turned upside down by authorities that in the past were institutions of victim's rights and justice. These are a travesty of justice.

The futility and outrage amongst the victims' families is expressed in Anthony's impact statement at a Van Houten parole hearing on September 6, 2017.

> *Miss Van Houten's attorney states, "Miss Van Houten is the most modeled prisoner in the system and has been for a long, long time. She cannot change her offenses, but she has changed herself."*
>
> *While the petitioner and her attorneys maintain Leslie Van Houten has changed, Leno and Rosemary LaBianca remain unchanged, unrehabilitated, unparoled. And they will remain so for eternity. They are just as dead today as the night Leslie Van Houten sent them to their graves.*
>
> *From the LA Times article referenced at the beginning of this statement, Parole Executive Officer Jennifer Shaffer describes the changing philosophies in California hearings as a shift from "You did what? Tell me about the crime" to "Who were you then? Who are you today, and what's the difference?"*

These are relevant questions. So, I ask the same to those most impacted by Leslie Van Houten.

Rosemary LaBianca, who were you before August 10, 1969? Who are you today? What's the difference?

What's the difference of spending a peaceful Sunday evening with your husband or being held against your will with a cord thrown around your neck, hood over your head, hearing your husband slaughtered in the next room with a butcher knife? How does it feel to know that you, too, will be restrained and stabbed 41 times?'

Leno, where were you on August 10, 1969? Where are you now? What's the difference? Tell us. How does it feel to have carving instruments shoved into your abdomen, throat over two dozen times? Dozens of times. What's the difference living 50 years with your children, playing with your grandson, Tony, your grandchildren, your nephew, Lou, great-grandchildren or lying mutilated and dead 18,250 days in a cold, black coffin? Who were you then? Who are you today? What's the difference?'

Tell us, Leno. Tell us, Rosemary.

Commissioners, how can we make amends for Leslie Van Houten when none of us can make amends for her dead?

After her conviction in 1971, Petitioner Van Houten defiantly said, "Your whole system is a game, you blind, stupid people." Commissioners, today you will determine how prophetic that statement is.

In a deeply progressive, single party state, the tide had turned. California's budding, permissive approach to dealing with violent criminals—along with their "decarceration" policies— would forge a dangerous, pernicious precedent.[1] And it set the stage for releasing a

---

1. In November 2024, George Gascòn was overwhelmingly defeated by Nathan Hochman for Los Angeles District Attorney. California constituents had grown

Manson Family killer back into the public.

---

weary of the state's pro-criminal policies, manifesting in Proposition 36. However, Gascòn appeared to be leaning for the release of killers Erik and Lyle Menendez in what appeared to a last-ditch momentum grab. Had it not been for Gascòn's directive prohibiting district attorney involvement in all L.A. county lifer hearings, Leslie Van Houten's release would have been less likely.

CHAPTER 33

DISTORTION, DISTRACTION AND DEFLECTION

At about noon on Tuesday May 30, 2023, Anthony DiMaria received an unexpected email from Associated Press reporter Christopher Weber. It read:

Hi again Anthony,
Looks like the appellate court ruled on Van Houten? Could you please call me ASAP so I can get some context and detail from you?
Regards,
Chris W

This was devastating news. The email was the culmination of years of concerned anticipation that began when the California BPH found inmate Leslie Van Houten (CDC# 13378) suitable for release on July 23, 2020. California Governor Gavin Newsom reversed the board's decision in November of that year, and Superior Court Judge Ronald S. Coen later rejected an appeal by Van Houten and her legal team.

Van Houten's attorneys then filed a writ of habeas corpus with

California's Appellate Court, and on January 26, 2023, the appellate panel granted a hearing for Van Houten on March 16, 2023.

Several of the victims' relatives had been in contact with Victims' Services at CDCR and with media relations at the Attorney General's Office. On the day of the hearing, Anthony observed the hearing via live video feed and later that day was told by Rose Robinson, the Attorney General representative, that it usually took three months for the justices to issue an opinion. The AP reporter's email was such a surprise, as an announcement wasn't expected until mid-June based on established protocol.

Anthony immediately informed his family in Las Vegas, and he was troubled to hear that they had learned of the developments from a reporter and not from authorities. For several years, Anthony, and the other victims' family members had aggressively lobbied representatives from the CDCR and the Attorney General's Office to be kept abreast, as did the other victims' families, of any and all developments regarding Leslie Van Houten and the never-ending legal goalpost expansions since the original murder convictions.

Anthony describes the chain of events:

I first called Louis Smaldino, nephew of Leno and perennial LaBianca family representative. He was cheery when he picked up the phone. "How are you?!" Smaldino asked. "Pretty good, Lou, all things considered, I guess. Have you heard the news?" "What news?" The conversation turned somber as I informed him that earlier in the day, the appellate court ruled 2-1 to reject the Governor's parole reversal and we pondered what might be the next steps forward.

Dissenting Judge Frances Rothschild concluded the following:

The record contains some evidence[1] Van Houten lacked insight into the commitment offence. Coupled with the heinous nature or the crime, that is sufficient under LAWRENCE, supra, 44 Cal.4th p.1214, to provide some evidence of current dangerousness and support the Governor's decision. Accordingly, I would deny Van Houten's petition for writ of Habeas Corpus.

With a sense of desperation, Anthony persisted with the authorities. On June 13, 2023, he shared his concerns in a Zoom meeting with Deputy Attorney General Jennifer Cano; legal counsel from the Governor's office, Eliza Hersh; and Jasmine Turner-Bond. Hersh informed Anthony that only 3% of appeal filings from the governor were actually heard by the California Supreme Court, and of those cases, very few reverse the appellate court's ruling. Attorney General Cano added that Youthful Offender Statute weighed in favor of the inmate.

He shared his argument that considering the "unusual extreme nature" of the crimes, the historical impact on American culture, and Van Houten's extensive lack of insight into her offenses throughout her hearings, the California Supreme Court would very likely overturn the appellate court's 2-1 decision. Anthony cited relevant case law (*Lawrence, Shaputis and Rosencrantz*) that would surely be definitive determinants of this argument in the Supreme Court. This is when Eliza Hersh interjected.

"Excuse me, but I would like to chime in here," Hersh said. "Mr. DiMaria…. are you an attorney?"

He was deflated.

"The authorities were generous with their time and input," Anthony said. "But I had a gut instinct that Governor Newsom

---

1. "Some evidence" is significant legal language.

would not file for the appeal as this was a political third rail in many ways for him."

The days that followed included additional follow ups and continued correspondence via email and phone. On July 7, 2023, at 2:14 p.m., Anthony sent an email to Newsom and his representatives:

> *Dear Eliza Hersh, Jasmine Turner-Bond and Governor Newsom,*
>
> *Going over my files last night I came across a recording of Leslie Van Houten (CDC#W-13378) with her then attorney Marvin Part 12/29/69 illustrating damning evidence specific to her sworn statement to BPH on July 23, 2020.*
>
> *At the parole hearing Ms. Van Houten states, "I ran into the doorway, and I called out to Tex and I said, 'We can't kill her!' At that point, he came into the room...." [P.23 ll.23-25] The petitioner describes this [as] if she didn't have the will to kill Rosemary LaBianca.*
>
> *But in Ms. Van Houten's statement December 29, 1969, Leslie describes that when the knife bent after Patricia Krenwinkel was stabbing their victim, Leslie Van Houten called out to Charles Watson, "Tex, we can't kill her! The knife's bent." This complete statement clearly establishes Leslie Van Houten as DIRECTING Watson to finish the kill. This is in complete opposition to the passive portrayal presented by the inmate at her 2020 parole hearing.*

Anthony cited other examples of Van Houten contradicting herself several times in past parole hearings but instinctively felt this communication was likely falling on deaf ears and ended the email this way:

The images of what Leslie Van Houten did to her victims are seared in my soul. I could not sleep with myself at night if I did not give my all to fight so that justice be served for Leslie Van Houten's horrific atrocities. I am certain that this (and past) material shared with you—once considered fairly and rigorously litigated—will reveal Ms. Van Houten not as she and her attorneys portray (as a rehabilitated indoctrinated "follower"), but who Leslie Van Houten was and continues to be—a cunning, narcissistic sociopath.

Within approximately thirty minutes of sending that email, Anthony received a phone call from Hersh informing him that Governor Newsom would *not* be filing an appeal to the California Supreme Court, essentially solidifying Leslie Van Houten's release from prison. At 3:08 p.m., Anthony sent emails to Louis Smaldino, Tony LaMontagne, Debra Tate, and Kay Hinman Martley, all of whom had been past direct participants in the parole hearings. He also reached out to the Folger, Frykowski, and Parent families as well.

On July 11, 2023, Leslie Van Houten was released from prison and the news reverberated across the country instantly. A CNN producer contacted Anthony at work to request a live interview that evening on CNN Primetime to hear a victim's perspective on her release.

Anthony describes his response:

I felt disheartened and diminished by the turn of events that culminated with Van Houten's release. After the initial shock wore off, I asked the producer if I could have some time to think it over. I expressed to the producer that feeling defeated and dejected, I was not feeling up to doing any interviews at the moment. The producer empathized she understood yet reminded me of the timely nature and kindly requested, "Please let me know as soon as you decide. The segment airs 7:00 p.m. Pacific Time. We would like to have you in the studio by 6:30. We can send a driver."

Live interviews are unusually unnerving, particularly when sharing a painful, private family tragedy on national television. So much can go south and be misinterpreted or manipulated. Deflated, I wondered, *What's the point?.... Does anyone even care anymore?*

Also nagging though were the cultural shifts and events that led to Van Houten's release. A twisted perspective had been emerging that made victims of violent crime incidental footnotes as their violent offenders were morphed into victims of circumstance (or even law and penal systems) and propped up as proof of the redeeming nature of the criminal-centric system.

Eventually Anthony decided to participate in the broadcast, if for no other reason than to shed a light on these disturbing realities.

Fifteen minutes before the show went live, Anthony sat alone in an isolated CNN studio room on Sunset Boulevard, viewing the television monitors with the live feed and an additional screen with legal analyst Laura Coates in the New York studio on standby. Waves of anxiety and thoughts on what to say and what not to say consumed Anthony.

Coates was suddenly on the air and introducing Anthony to millions.

Coates: I want to bring in Anthony DiMaria. His uncle Jay Sebring was one of the victims of the Manson family. Anthony, thank you for joining me this evening. Tell me what you are feeling on a day knowing that one more person is now freed.[2]

---

2. Manson Family member Steve "Clem" Grogan was paroled and released on November 11, 1985, after admitting to killing Donald "Shorty" Shea, and showing

DiMaria: The first thing is that my thoughts are with the victims and all our families. But clearly, Leslie Van Houten's release is, it profoundly impacts our families, but I fear a very dangerous, pernicious precedent is established today that will impact millions of victims of violent crime throughout the state of California today and in the years to come.

Coates: What is the precedent you are talking about? Because of course you have been very critical, understandably, of the idea that she could be a victim of Charles Manson. And I wonder, what is the precedent that you are speaking about that the governor has decided not to stop this appeal?

DiMaria: The precedent established now: Leslie Van Houten has always propped herself as a Manson "follower," but she is anything but. She is a cold-blooded killer in one of the most notorious murder rampages in United States history. So, with her release now, any other violent criminal or killer, whose crimes fall beneath the bar of Leslie Van Houten's very extreme [acts] that have historical impact—that opens the door for them. And it is our fear that the floodgates in the California penal system will be unhinged.

Across the country, the interview struck a chord with Andy Ostroy in New York City, and he contacted Anthony to inquire about an interview for his podcast, The Back Room. In their correspondence, he learned Ostroy was extraordinary on several levels. He was also a victim of violent crime, and his perspective was unusually insightful. He shared that his wife, actress/director Adrienne Shelley, was killed in a violent attack. Anthony was taken aback because decades earlier, in 1994, he and Adrienne had been cast in the roles of Janey and Eddie in the New York independent film *Grind*. The film was shelved due to investor conflicts, which was a heart-breaking pill to swallow. During the lengthy casting

---

authorities where he was buried. He also named Manson, Watson, and Bruce Davis in having roles in the ranch hand's death.

process, Anthony had come to know Adrienne as organically spon-
taneous, feisty, uniquely talented, and beautiful.[3]

Anthony was impressed and felt an instant kinship with Ostroy.
They both had family members who were victims of violent crime,
and both had private tragedies played out in sensational narratives
on the global stage. Both Jay Sebring and Adrienne Shelley were
immensely talented, successful forces who were struck down before
the prime of their lives. Ostroy and Anthony had each directed
films to restore the reputations of their loved ones.

In the podcast, Ostroy asked Anthony when he decided to tell
Jay's story. He responded:

> I was living in New York and a book came out, a Greg King
> book [*Sharon Tate and the Manson Murders*], and there was
> a whole chapter titled JAY. I read it, and again, it was
> rehashing the entrenched rumors and mythology about Jay.
> That Jay was disinherited by his family—which is absurdity
> —and I thought, *"Why are people just continuing to perpet-
> uate these myths?"*

The passage from the book claims:

> With Jay, image was everything.... [he] suffered from
> personal insecurity, both from his middle-class background
> and about his height: at five-feet six inches tall, he
> constantly felt overshadowed by others. To compensate for
> his short stature, he indulged in a flashy and extravagant
> lifestyle: driving expensive, trendy cars; attending important
> parties; and moving in elite Hollywood circles. The move

---

3. Months later, the film began pre-production with new investors. One executive
producer wanted Billy Crudup for the role of Eddie. After several readings among
the three actors, Crudup was cast in the lead role. *Grind* was finally released in 1997.

did not sit well with his parents, and they virtually cut off all communication after his success in California.

These characterizations were eerily like Vincent Bugliosi's curious psychological assessment of Jay in his 1974 book, *Helter Skelter*. It purports that, for Jay, "appearances were all-important. He drove an expensive sports car, frequented the 'in' clubs, even had his Levi jackets custom-made. He employed a full-time butler, gave lavish parties, and lived in a 'jinxed' mansion.... [and] he had a blackbelt in karate (he had taken a few lessons from Bruce Lee)."

The obvious sculpted subtext described a troubled, wimpish, pretentious fop, hiding his sordid inadequacies and shortcomings behind a grand façade.

Jay never had a butler[4] and did, in fact, extensively train in the martial arts with Bruce Lee and Ed Parker for several years. He sought to bring out the best in himself and his clients, and he cultivated the finest qualities in life, whether it be in clothing, cars, beautiful women, or in his craft. A few authors might see these qualities as "troubled insecurity," but for the ordinary person, such passion, regard, and achievement are the manifestation of a confident, influential, and powerful man.

When interviewing anyone who knew Jay for the documentary *JAY SEBRING...CUTTING to the TRUTH*, DiMaria would read this description of his uncle from Bugliosi's *Helter Skelter*: "The mundane truth appeared to be that behind the carefully cultivated public image there was a lonely, troubled man so insecure in his role that even in his sex life he had to revert to fantasy."

Reactions varied from disgust to outrage to hysterical laughter.

---

4. This was an errant detective's mischaracterization in the Los Angeles Police Department's report, of Jay's friend, Amos Russell, who was staying at Sebring's Easton residence while he painted the house's exterior.

"Insecure?! He had the all-time most beautiful women," Nancy Sinatra said.

Former wife Cami Sebring, said, "Can I say this? Jay had big balls."

Peggy DiMaria was almost indignant upon hearing Bugliosi's characterization of her brother Jay. Her response was simple and astute, "This from someone who never met my brother?"

Sebring friend, attorney, and Bugliosi colleague Peter Knecht summed it up this way:

> There's nothing wrong with fulfilling your fantasies. It takes a helluva cool guy to be able to fulfill your fantasies. Jay and I fulfilled our fantasies. As far as him being insecure, that's ridiculous. Vince Bugliosi, as long as I've known him, has been married, straight, and never, I believe, had a single life like Jay and I had. He doesn't understand the nature of the beast. I don't think he really knew our world. And when he wrote this, he was thinking like a prosecutor. And like a cop, rather than like one of the guys that's having fun.

It's quite telling that, for several decades, Bugliosi has shared endless interviews about the crimes, the killers, and his involvement in the prosecution of the murderers, but nothing significant in relation to the victims of these events. In his true crime book of nearly 700 pages, only eleven pages (pp. 35-46) are devoted to the victims of the Tate-LaBianca murders, and significant portions of those pages are tabloid in nature.[5]

For several years, Anthony contacted the former prosecutor, requesting an interview for his 2020 documentary. Bugliosi declined but left this message on his voicemail:

---

5. Gary Hinman and Donald Shea are omitted.

I got your message about a Jay Sebring documentary. But I can't tell you about poor Jay, that there's nothing I know about him that is not in the book. But I wish you the best on whatever project you're on. Take care. Thank you. Bye.

Bugliosi's second and final declination was awkwardly delivered, this time by his wife Gail. This was the voicemail she left:

Mr. DiMaria, my name is Gail Bugliosi, and I'm Vincent's wife. He asked me to call you. I guess you're doing a documentary on Jay Sebring. He never really met Jay Sebring and really doesn't know anything about him. So, it wouldn't be a good idea to interview him on Jay Sebring. But thank you for thinking of him. Bye.

Bugliosi's denial to be interviewed for a film on the victim of a crime that generated millions for him in profit through his book, television deals, and lectures[6] was troubling. Why would the extremely successful, high-profile Manson murder *authority* refuse to be involved in a story on Jay Sebring?

For almost 45 years, the district-attorney-turned-author appeared on nearly every American network and/or entertainment platform and was handsomely paid to espouse his opinions on the murders. Yet he would contribute nothing to a project focusing on one of the victims of these killers and their crimes.

DiMaria had a litany of questions for Bugliosi that he never had the opportunity to ask as Vincent Bugliosi died on June 6, 2015, at the age of 80.

So many of Bugliosi's portrayals, characterizations, and omissions, particularly regarding the victims, irked and disturbed Jay's

---

6. Bugliosi's speaking fee was $2,500 an appearance after *Helter Skelter* was released in 1974, equivalent to about $16,000 today.

family. DiMaria revealed one such offensive, deceitful Bugliosi omission to Andy Ostroy in The Back Room podcast in August 2023.

> I needed to know what Jay did in the last moments of his life. And, as I got to know the district attorneys in over two dozen parole hearings over several decades, I became friendly with them. I really appreciated them. I was able to look through the testimony and I found out a story that Bugliosi didn't put in his book. And I thought, "Holy shit! Jay charged Watson when he had his back turned to him with a gun and a bayonet!" And I was like, "Why in the hell didn't you put THAT in your book?!" And I wanted to ask Bugliosi, "You had all these character descriptions of Jay as being insecure—and all these things—and you sweep under the rug that Jay charged a man, and tried to protect himself and his friends?"
>
> For decades, I questioned the glaring omission. My personal perspective is this: behind the carefully sculpted public image as protagonist [Bugliosi] in the most exploited crimes of the century—there was a parasite so insecure in his role as hero—there was an opportunistic, cowardly scribe that even in his grandiose promotional portrayal had to revert to tabloid tactics and revisionist omissions.

Bugliosi's prosecutorial tactics and narrative have been challenged over the years. Many question and scoff at the notion he presented in court—*that a hippie band of followers committed the ghoulish Tate-LaBianca murders in two nights of random violence in order to start a race war that would result in an American apocalypse in which mentally inferior African-Americans could be saved by leadership from said hippies existing in a pit deep in the California desert.*

The mainstream media, by neatly packaging the Manson Family's extensive crimes—from late 1967 to 1975, culminating in the attempted assassination of President Gerald Ford—into two nights of unspeakable violence triggered by a contrived motive, the stage was set for the ultimate sensational shit-show in which killers are followers, true victims are deviant players, a crime group is a hippie cult in which the murderers become victims, all of which hinged on false premises.

Today, the Manson murder cottage industry continues to thrive in epic proportions. The old false premises have spiraled into conspiracy theories and other new dramatic narratives.

In 2019, a book titled *CHAOS: Charles Manson, the CIA, and the Secret History of the Sixties* was published by Little, Brown & Company. In it, author Tom O'Neill concluded early on, "The one thing everyone seemed to agree on—everyone outside the DA's office, that is—is that Bugliosi's *Helter Skelter* motive didn't add up." The writer further speculated, "What could cause these young women to kill strangers in two nights of inexplicable violence?"

Nearly twenty years earlier, O'Neill contacted Peggy DiMaria in Las Vegas, requesting an interview for his book. He expressed special interest to learn more about Jay Sebring and Sharon Tate. His book would be "more focused on the victims." With some prodding, Peggy agreed to meet the author on a Saturday afternoon at a coffee shop in The Hard Rock Hotel and Casino. Her son, Anthony, joined them.

As they sat at the table, O'Neill was quick to mention that he had heard great things about Jay from previous interviews he conducted. He then asked if he could record the conversation, but Peggy politely refused. The meeting lasted approximately ninety minutes as they discussed the Kummer family, Jay, his business, his relationship with Sharon, Jay's future plans, and the murders. In a very emotional, candid moment late in the discussion, Peggy revealed that she was pregnant when her brother was killed. In the distress and trauma after the murders, she had lost that child.

In the weeks following the interview, O'Neill remained in contact with Anthony DiMaria and confided that his mother's interview was one of the most difficult interviews he'd conducted and that among what Peggy shared, the details of her miscarriage after Jay's murder, "altered the direction of my project." In the ensuing twenty years, they have become friendly, even sharing some information with one another for their respective projects.

It would take decades for both O'Neill's book (2019) and Anthony's documentary (2020) to be completed. O'Neill was able to script an extensively researched MK Ultra whodunnit involving the Manson Family, the CIA, the FBI, LSD, and the author's twenty-year exhaustive mission to confirm his hypothesis, which yielded no definitive, concrete evidence that the CIA somehow was involved in the Manson murders. The reader is left to connect a series of titillating dots that are mere speculation. A 2025 Netflix documentary directed by Errol Morris titled *CHAOS: The Manson Murders* also left the director underwhelmed.

"Do I believe that Manson was programmed by MKUltra, by the government—a Manchurian candidate programmed to kill? Not quite," Morris told a reporter for *The Guardian*. "Can it be proven? I don't think so. But can it be disproven? I don't think it can be. One can provide the requisite skepticism."

But certain narratives remain crucial and entrenched in the packaging and selling of these crimes—primarily tabloid-style minimizing and maligning the victims. Even fifty years after the tragedies, O'Neill appeared to utilize victim marginalization, referring to Wojciech Frykowski as leading "an aimless life in America" and referencing "footage, clearly filmed by Polanski, depicting Sharon Tate being forced" into a compromising situation. The entertainment writer goes on to describe the Polanski/Tate footage as the "Seedier side of Cielo."

And then, Jay's turn. Quoting Sebring's protégé and friend "Little" Joe Torrenueva, O'Neill cites Charlie Baron (a SEBRING client) who "was close with a cabal of right-wight military intelligence and Hollywood figures, many of whom had been SEBRING's clients" and alleged that they "did terrible things to Black people." Sebring "was a bad businessman.... the deals kept falling through and Jay's West Hollywood salon a nest of mobsters and criminals."

After the publication of *CHAOS* in 2019, Torrenueva refutes several depictions contained in the book. O'Neill's descriptions of Jay's clients as "right-wing" and the shop as a "nest of mobsters and criminals" was absurd. Torrenueva noted:

> Jay was the best. People from all walks of life sought him out and flocked to the shop for a SEBRING cut. Sure, there were mobsters, there was also Cardinal James McIntyre, Archbishop Timothy Manning, Fletcher Jones, Del Webb, Vin Scully, Sandy Koufax, and Democrat politicians. The author quoted me as saying "The deals kept falling through. He was a bad businessman." I regretfully misspoke. I worked with Jay, and we were close friends but I was not privy to his business dealings.

It is confirmed in Sebring's 1965 appointment book the supposed failed deals were by Jay's choice. Raymond Lee (Rayette Company) and Jerri Redding (Redkin Labs) were interested in the SEBRING product line and forming a partnership. Jay was open to possibilities but ultimately decided against it because partners would dilute the profit margin of the product line that he had been funding and developing for years on his own.

To anyone who knew Jay, or anyone who significantly delved into his true legacy, these tawdry characterizations are laughably outlandish, maliciously slanderous, and sadly predictable.

Anthony was particularly baffled by O'Neill's statement: "I was rebuffed by the intimates of Tate, Polanski, and Sebring—sometimes with vehemence, sometimes with tersely worded emails or phone calls." Anthony witnessed firsthand O'Neill's extensive interview with his mother, and the twenty years of insight and correspondence shared with him and from Sharon Tate's sister, Debra. Anthony personally shared significant information about Jay for nearly two decades since the author first contacted Jay Sebring's family. O'Neill expresses "sincerest gratitude to the survivors of the known victims of the Manson group.... especially, Anthony DiMaria and Debra Tate" in the acknowledgements of his book, but the inclusion, while kind, was unnecessary as nothing he nor his mother shared was included in the book, except buried in footnote #83 on page 449. Why would O'Neill omit all this insight from Sharon's and Jay's families in his book?

O'Neill's appearance on Joe Rogan's podcast in April 2020, may reveal his inclinations in this regard. He described for Rogan alleged events that occurred at Jay's Easton home on Thursday night August 7, 1969. O'Neil sources his allegations from a police report and interview with Jay's friend and electrician, Paul Greenwald.

In his interview for the *SEBRING* documentary, Greenwald stated he received a call from Jay on Thursday night, complaining about electrical issues at his home. After Jay was killed, Paul went to Jay's Easton home to select a suit for his friend to be buried in. During that visit, he found a severed wire between the home and the backyard eave.[7]

Greenwald hypothesized this possible scenario:

If you were, as Manson says, doing your creepy crawler, going around some place where it's pitch black, and you think you're cutting the phone line. Then all of a sudden,

---

7. The wire measured approximately eighteen inches and remained suspended above the ground with little exposure to sunlight or water.

you've got a Christmas tree of light that all the grounds were lit up. You might leave. That's what I suspect happened.

But O'Neill stated to Rogan, "The night before the murders they were gonna watch a movie and, all of a sudden, there was a power surge and the lights went really, really bright and dimmed and they lost the cable. So, Jay called Paul Greenwald.... who had done all the wiring for Jay. And Jay called [Paul] and said, 'Can you come over here? The cable went out and there was power surge.' So, unless those twenty-four [hour]s before, the same four people at a different house had the house wires cut by somebody[8] who might have been spooked by the surge or something, uh, they weren't random. They were being targeted. That undermines the randomness of it—that they were strangers to their killers."

There are only two people on the planet who could possibly describe such an occurrence to Paul Greenwald: Jay Sebring and Amos Russell. In Russell's LAPD polygraph, there is no reference to such a dramatic, alarming power surge. In fact, Russell confirmed the television cable was working perfectly fine that evening and in the future. He stated, "They were looking at a program. TV. In his room." Then on Friday, "I stopped painting, went into the house and looked at the TV."

In an email dated November 21, 2024, Anthony DiMaria asked Greenwald, "Did Jay ever say anything to you about a power surge or that the 'lights went really, really bright and then dimmed' inside the house or anywhere else?" Greenwald responded, "I do not recall Jay saying anything about that. Thus, my answer is.... no."

A recently uncovered letter dated February 21, 1969, from Greenwald to Jay Sebring reveals a definitive alternate reality. The document, which remains in the Sebring family collection, reads:

---

8. Manson was out of town at that time and Watson confirms not knowing Jay Sebring before the murders.

Jay,

Hi, how are you? Hope all is going well.... Thanks so much for calling. Your call was really a morale booster. Working up here can get tiring.

SORRY ABOUT THOSE OUTSIDE LIGHTS. I'LL BE HOME IN TWO WEEKS (CAN'T WAIT) AND REPAIR THEM.

The New York plans sound exciting—good luck.
Your friend,
Paul

Upon this discovery, Anthony scanned and sent the document to Greenwald, who confirmed the note was his. When asked if the wire could have been severed in February of that year, Paul responded, "I cannot say No to that."

"You mentioned in your note that you'd repair the outside lights. Do you recall ever repairing the lights?" Anthony followed up.

"I don't recall doing any repairs to those lights," Greenwald said. "In fact, I didn't remember those issues or even the note until you sent it to me."

As Joe Rogan wrapped up his interview with O'Neill, the host asked, "But there's no conclusive thing that you can point to that says, 'This is why they were targeted'?"

The writer's answer was predictable.

"No," O'Neill said.

It's impossible to overstate what a shock to the conscience the Manson killings were, and continue to be, on the country. Or how irresistible the bloody events were to endless profiteers, consumers, and opportunists seeking money, existential consolation, or relevance. A July 30, 2019, *The Hollywood Reporter* article by Tatiana Siegel titled "Manson Victim's Friend Posits Alternative Motive: 'I Never Bought into the Race War Theory'" is one such example.

In the piece, Siegel describes former SEBRING associate Jim Markham sipping a Perrier on the deck of the Majestic Hotel in Cannes when she met him a day after the world premiere of Quentin Tarantino's magnum opus, *Once Upon a Time in Hollywood* (in which Sharon and Jay were featured as characters). Siegel wrote, "Back in 1969, Sebring was nicknamed 'The Candyman' and was said to have used his salon to peddle drugs to the stars.... Five decades later, Markham floats his own theory...."

Markham alleged in the article that Sebring and Manson had nefarious dealings with each other, and Jay attacked Manson the day before the murders. Siegel quotes Markham as saying:

I believe Manson had gone up to the house and wanted to sell cocaine and marijuana. He showed Jay and Wojciech the product. They were going to buy some of it, but the two beat him up at the gate. The next night, Manson sent his Family up [to kill them].

Anthony was apoplectic. He felt that Markham, Jay Sebring's self-proclaimed successor, disparaged the memory of the very person who elevated his life exponentially with these comments to Siegel. Why make such a public pronouncement, especially when there's documentation and a confession by Manson that he had been in Big Sur from August 3-7, 1969?

Manson related that he had met and picked up seventeen-year-old Stephanie Schram on August 3, 1969, around 3:00 a.m. when they bumped into each other at an out of the way gas station. She had just come back from Reno, Nevada, with a male companion. As Schram came out of the bathroom, she was greeted by a smiling Manson.

"Hi, beautiful."

Schram said that, while her male companion was in the restroom, Manson was able to tell her everything about her life in under two minutes. When Manson promised to show her the sights and sound of Big Sur—a place she had always wanted to visit—she impulsively ditched her ride to hang out with Manson for the next few days.

While driving on Interstate 5, Manson was stopped by California Highway Patrol officer Richard C. Willis, about ten miles south of Oceanside. Willis cited Manson for a mechanical violation and noted on the ticket that he was driving a 1952 cream-colored Ford bakery van, license number K70683. Willis also noted the time and date: 6:15 p.m. on August 7, 1969. Later, Schram told LAPD detectives that after she and Manson collected her things at her parents' place, they parked and slept next to the van in San Diego. She said they returned to Spahn Ranch the following day, arriving around two in the afternoon on August 8.

How or why Markham thinks that Jay and Manson made a drug deal and got into a scuffle is inexplicable, other than it was scuttlebutt swirling around the shop in the aftermath of the murders. Despite this, the damage had been done.[9]

---

9. Another drug burn rumor posted from a public LAPD report claimed Jay allegedly told his receptionist, Karlene Ann McCaffrey, that he had been burned on $2,000 worth of narcotics by Joel J. Rostau on August 7, 1969, the night before the murders. McCaffrey stated in the report that Rostau, a known dealer and mob figure, informed her that he had delivered cocaine and mescaline to the house, but that Frykowski and Sebring wanted some additional narcotics and had gone back down the hill. However, Rostau was unable to procure the drugs and did not return to the Tate residence. McCaffrey opined to the LAPD that Sebring would do almost anything to get back at the person who had burned him. Investigators interviewed Rostau, who stated he had only met Jay Sebring once or twice at the SEBRING salon. Rostau was Wardell Jackson's client at the salon and was on friendly terms with Frykowski. Rostau denied being at the Cielo address prior to the homicide and was never brought up on charges. This rumor was also debunked in a detailed three-part series on The Manson Family Blog, who believe that Rostau concocted the incident to "impress on his friends that he had a brush with death and to gain his fifteen minutes of fame."

A SEBRING staffer who requested to remain anonymous for safety reasons refuted several of these allegations in 2025. She said Jay was "a lovely man and a very good big brother" and "no way Jay was a drug dealer.... don't believe the press." This

Numerous versions of the piece had circulated throughout the world in several languages in various publications and throughout the internet, where it still lingers. Anthony sent an email to Siegel and *The Hollywood Reporter,* questioning where Siegel obtained her unsourced information about Sebring peddling drugs to people at his salon or why she referred to Jay as "Candyman" to the stars. He also questioned Markham's theory that Manson was at the Tate house the day before the murders, and that Jay was a violent man who beat Manson up. The following portion of Anthony's email to *The Hollywood Reporter* makes clear the warranted outrage:

> *In her piece, Ms. Siegel literally twists an innocent murder victim into a violent criminal.... and portrays one of the most notorious killers in United States history as VICTIM. How any reporter or publication could perpetuate such malice and distortion is deplorable. Disgusting. Shameful.... Have you no decency?*
>
> *Sadly, the damage has been done.... as has been the case for nearly 50 years. Your article is yet another example how the victims have been discarded as props in the mass peddling of their own slaughter.... and how these crimes have been used as a cash cow through distorted narratives.*
>
> *I can only imagine that the article's writer, Tatiana Siegel, and her company* The Hollywood Reporter—*might see fit to take the only proper and decent course of action regarding these matters—to set the record straight with a public apology, make the appropriate corrections and present this formal complaint publicly in its entirety.*

---

source went on to describe Rostau as a "flashy man who liked to flaunt his money," causing two men to follow him home and commit a holdup at gunpoint during their "first date from hell." The source also refuted the alleged $2,000 drug burn. "[The receptionist] would have never told anyone this and Jay would have never shared this information with [the receptionist]."

Anthony never received an apology from the publication or its author, and there was no retraction to the article. Anthony also felt that Markham's comments to *The Hollywood Reporter* lingered far beyond its publication date as illustrated on Jay Sebring's Wikipedia page:

> Back in 1969, Sebring was nicknamed "The Candyman" and was said to have used his salon to peddle drugs to the stars. Jim Markham was Sebring's protégé and business partner in a budding franchise of men's hair salons and has made this statement publicly.

Markham's quote to *The Hollywood Reporter* continues to be perpetuated in recurring articles and throughout the internet on web and blogsites dedicated to true crime and the Manson Family. It has now become part of the Jay Sebring narrative.

Former Los Angeles Police Commander Joe Gunn, who oversaw the narcotics division during a stretch in his twenty-year career, said the entertainment industry was rife with drug use at the time of Jay's death. However, he never heard Jay's name connected to these circles. Gunn said in 2023:

> The LAPD had formed the Narcotic Intelligence Network, which is intelligence information from law enforcement agencies such as the L.A. County Sheriff's Office, the Drug Enforcement Agency, Customs, etc. The reason for its formation was not to step on each other's toes. For example, if somebody is an informant and they screwed over police in a jurisdiction, you don't want to move them into another jurisdiction.
>
> I had never heard Jay Sebring's name mentioned in any relation to the Narcotic Intelligence Network. I don't know if he was doing narcotics or not, but I never heard of him

being a dealer. He was so successful, and we'd find successful people who sell dope to others as a side job. He didn't have to because that is usually someone who is on the fringes. If he had dealings with Manson, we would have heard about that, or it would have come out in the investigation.

After more than five-and-a-half decades of negative publicity and dark mythology, Jay's family has been left to wonder why history has been so unkind to their beloved son/brother/uncle. Would he forever remain obscured as he lay in his grave? Or would Jay Sebring, the man who lived life to the fullest and made a positive impact on American culture, ever be known in his true form?

EPILOGUE

As we closed out the writing of this book, we were coming upon what would have been Jay's 91st birthday. While odds are good he would not have been with us to this day had he been allowed to live out his natural life, he could have survived to see the explosion of the men's haircare industry and would, no doubt, have been a continuing force within it for many decades.

If the 1960s were about changing the world, the 1970s were about changing ourselves. In the "Me" decade, self-expression was no longer taboo and was quickly commodified, leading to consumer product lines that were all about feeling good about yourself and knowing you were worth it. Jay was far ahead of the pack with the launch of his haircare products at the time his life was cut short. Seeing the landscape ahead of him where others couldn't was one of Jay's gifts, and we can only imagine what he might have achieved had he been around as the marketplace opened wide for these goods and services.

His British cohort Vidal Sassoon took up the mantle and burst onto the scene in 1973, bringing his "if you don't look good, we don't look good" mantra to households everywhere. Many other brands have come and gone in the decades since, but the desire for salon-style haircare at home has only continued to grow. Today, it's approximately a $100 billion per year industry, but most people don't know who to credit for that.

We Like L.A. covered Anthony DiMaria's documentary on Jay's life and aptly offered this insight:

> Jay Sebring was a pioneer of men's hair, a navy vet who dreamed of elevating utilitarian cuts into iconic styles.... but Jay isn't always associated with his success or cultural legacy. The sum of his life is often overshadowed by its final moments, when he was murdered by the Manson Family.... on August 9, 1969.

Jay's ambitions stretched well beyond his salons and styling techniques. Anyone who knew him saw that he was a visionary who could achieve whatever he set his mind to. As we reflect on the full spectrum of his life, we naturally contemplate what could have been. It isn't unreasonable to suggest he could have expanded his empire to areas of personal expression that were just emerging or hadn't even been conceptualized yet.

Jay's interests were broad and reached into film production, clothing, fragrances, and etiquette, among other things. He dreamed of cultivating and curating style through various avenues and was right on the brink of making all of that happen.

Tragically, Jay's destiny was hijacked in August 1969, if not obliterated. His legacy was obscured by prisms of exploitation, greed, fear, and delusional self-promotion in the aftermath of one of the most notorious murders in history.

In part, his story is the tale of two men: Jay Sebring the living, breathing man, and a perverse facsimile contorted into dramatic narratives. The latter version bears almost no resemblance to the man incarnate.

In a life of such scale and scope as Jay Sebring's, coupled with his untimely demise, a few enigmas will forever remain. But one accurate, indisputable reality about Jay's brief thirty-five-year life is known.

Former *Los Angeles Times* film critic Charles Champlin remembers Jay Sebring this way:

> There are people in this world, in whatever line of work they do, who leave a mark on their time. Whether they're famous or whether they're quiet and private, but they still leave a mark on those around them or maybe the larger world. From inauspicious beginnings in Detroit, Michigan, Jay became a guy who was destined to leave a mark on the world. And he did. Not only in his work but the things that radiated from him.

Though Jay Sebring was taken out of the game too soon, his influence lives on. Too much emphasis has been placed on how Jay died, and our goal is to reveal to new generations how he lived because living well and living with intention was his great purpose and what he wanted to offer the world. Our aim is to bring to light just how great and lasting his impact has been. You may have come to this account of Jay's life only knowing he was a Manson Family victim; perhaps you didn't even know that much. But his legacy has touched everyone and his story, now accurately related, can serve as inspiration for many more generations of dreamers like Jay.

By early 1964, Jay had expanded his business empire by teaching the SEBRING method of hair styling and modern barbering techniques to others. Once they paid the fee and completed the course, they received a plaque bearing the official SEBRING International Registered Seal of Approval to proudly hang on their salon wall. *Courtesy of Jay Sebring Collections/The DiMaria Family.*

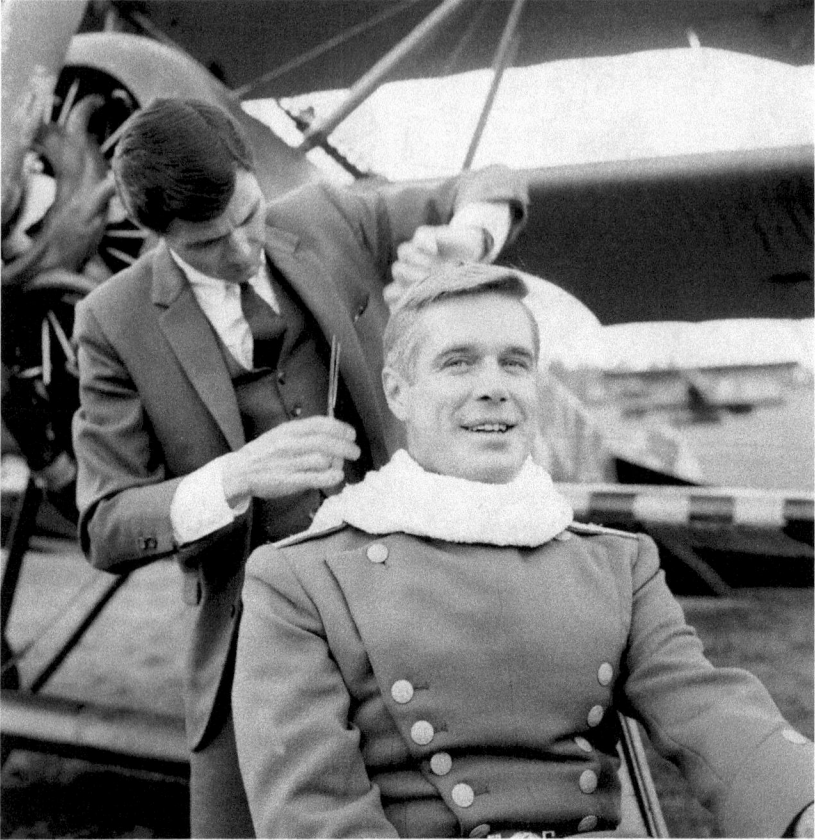

In August 1965, Jay was summoned by actor George Peppard to give him a trim on the set of *The Blue Max* in Ireland. Jay's fee was a history-making $2,500 (the equivalent of $25,000 in 2025) and grabbed headlines around the world. Photo by Alamy.

Jay presenting stylist John F. Media with a SEBRING International Registered Seal of Approval plaque. *Courtesy of Jay Sebring Collections/The DiMaria Family.*

SEBRING International also rolled out in 1966 a hair control spray, shampoo, and cologne for men, prominently featuring an ankh symbol to promote masculinity. Soon thereafter, Jay introduced a conditioner to his product line. *Courtesy of Jay Sebring Collections/The DiMaria Family. Photo by Mishele DiMaria.*

Hired by Elektra Records in late 1966 to create a new image for
The Doors' lead singer Jim Morrison, Jay Sebring designed, cut,
and styled the iconic look that would transcend Morrison from
roadhouse rocker to a rock and roll sex symbol for the ages.
Photo by Alamy.

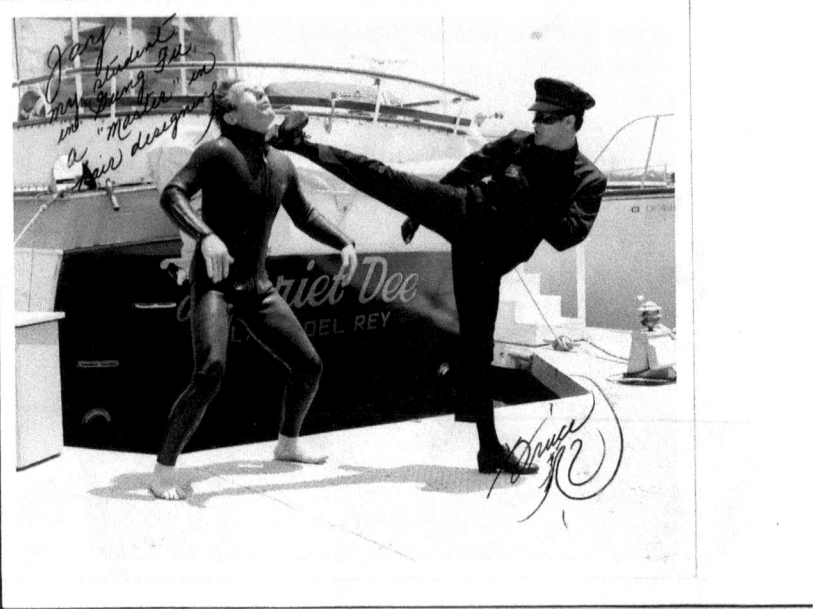

Jay Sebring introduced martial arts legend Bruce Lee to popular culture. Their friendship included elements of self-defense, nutrition, business, and an unstinting affection towards one another. *Courtesy of Jay Sebring Collections/The DiMaria Family.*

KENNEDY *For President* HEADQUARTERS

2000 L Street, Northwest - Washington, D.C. 20036

April 10, 1968

Dear Mr. Sebring:

I'd like to take this opportunity to thank you for supporting the reception at the Sportsman's Lodge.

I was greatly impressed by the warmth and enthusiasm of the people of Los Angeles, and your generosity and efforts meant a great deal to me personally.

I am looking forward to seeing you the next time I am in Southern California.

Best wishes.

Sincerely,

Robert F. Kennedy

Mr. Jay Sebring
725 Fairfax Avenue
Los Angeles, California

A letter from Robert F. Kennedy thanking Jay for his financial support of his 1968 presidential campaign. Jay attended a $250-per-plate fundraiser held at the Sportsmen's Lodge, an iconic Los Angeles gathering spot on Ventura Boulevard. Weeks after Jay received this letter on April 10, 1968, Kennedy was assassinated by twenty-four-year-old Pasadena resident Sirhan Sirhan. *Courtesy of Jay Sebring Collections/The DiMaria Family.*

Jay giving director Roman Polanski a haircut on a trip to Joshua Tree National Forest, July 1968. Even though Sharon Tate broke up with Jay and later married Polanski, the three were friends. It might have seemed strange to outsiders that Jay and Sharon were there together with other people and remained close even in the company of their significant others, but not to those who knew them. *Courtesy of Jay Sebring Collections/The DiMaria Family.*

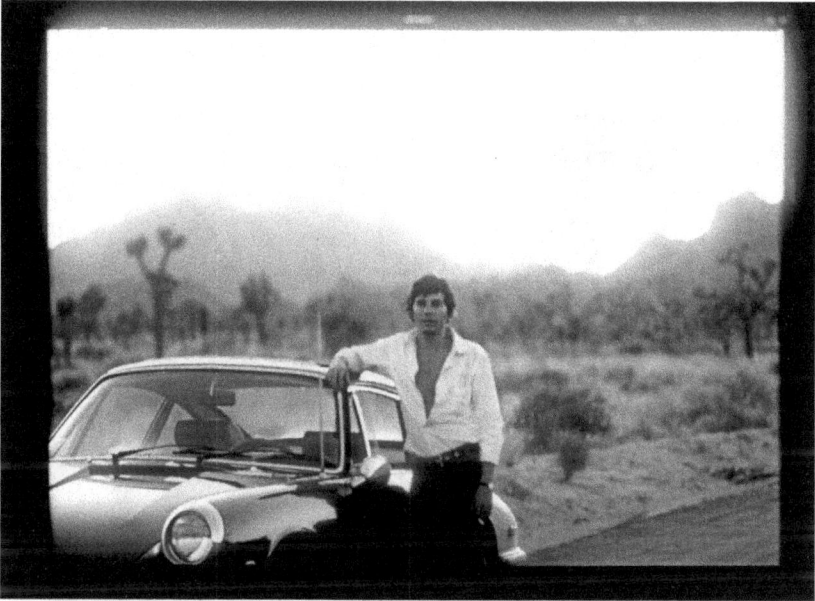

Jay with his black 1968 Porche 911 in Joshua Tree National Park, July 1968. Joshua Tree and its grand boulders, spectacular rock formations, Yucca trees, and 250 different species of birds embodied the mystical elements of Jay's innate sensibilities. Sebring embraced the national park beneath the endless stars as a gateway to cosmic possibilities and the great beyond. *Courtesy of Jay Sebring Collections.*

Photograph taken by Jay Sebring of his two families: the
DiMarias and Kummers in 1968 at the DiMaria Las Vegas
residence. From left to right: Tony (brother in-law), Peggy (sister),
Anthony (nephew), Margarette (mother) and Bernard (father).
Courtesy of the DiMaria Family.

Jay taking a Formula One car for a spin on the
track of the Jim Russell Racing School in England
sometime in the late 1960s. *Courtesy of Jay
Sebring Collections/The DiMaria Family.*

Jay with actor and client Warren Beatty and actress Julie Christie and a few other friends hanging out on his houseboat in Sausalito, which he co-rented with Ron Reynolds, owner of a discotheque in North Beach. *Courtesy of Jay Sebring Collections/The DiMaria Family.*

to

a reception

celebrating the opening

of

Sebring International

(formerly MacBlum's)

Saturday, May 24th, 1969

from 4 p.m. to 5:30 p.m.

629 Commercial Street
San Francisco

on hand will be
Joanne Woodward
&
Paul Newman

R.S.V.P. 981-5204

An invitation to Jay's champagne opening to an exclusive group of influential people and the Bay Area's press of his SEBRING International salon in the heart of San Francisco's financial district. Note the mention of Paul Newman and his wife Joanne Woodward, who were investors in the location. *Courtesy of Jay Sebring Collections/The DiMaria Family.*

Jay and Paul Newman outside of the San Francisco SEBRING International salon, where a crowd quickly assembled at the sight of the blue-eyed movie star. *Courtesy of Jay Sebring Collections.*

A smiling Jay with Paul Newman and Joanne Woodard sipping champagne inside the San Francisco shop. *Courtesy of Jay Sebring Collections.*

Jay and Paul Newman in an intimate moment with investor Abigail Folger (far left) talking to others during the San Francisco shop's gala opening. *Courtesy of Jay Sebring Collections.*

Jay, with a bottled beer in hand, with his arm around a very pregnant Sharon Tate, sharing a lazy day at the pool at 10050 Cielo Drive. This photo was taken days before the murders. Los Angeles Police detectives confiscated Jay's Nikon and had it developed. The photo reveals a definitive intimacy between the two as friends and, as some believe, much more. *Courtesy of Jay Sebring Collections/The DiMaria Family.*

Procession of coroner's vehicles starts out the driveway, carrying the bodies of the five people. The residence at 10500 Cielo Drive is where killers from the Manson family murdered Sharon Tate, Abigail Folger, Jay Sebring, Wojciech Frykowski, and Steven Parent. *Photo by the Herald Examiner Collection.*

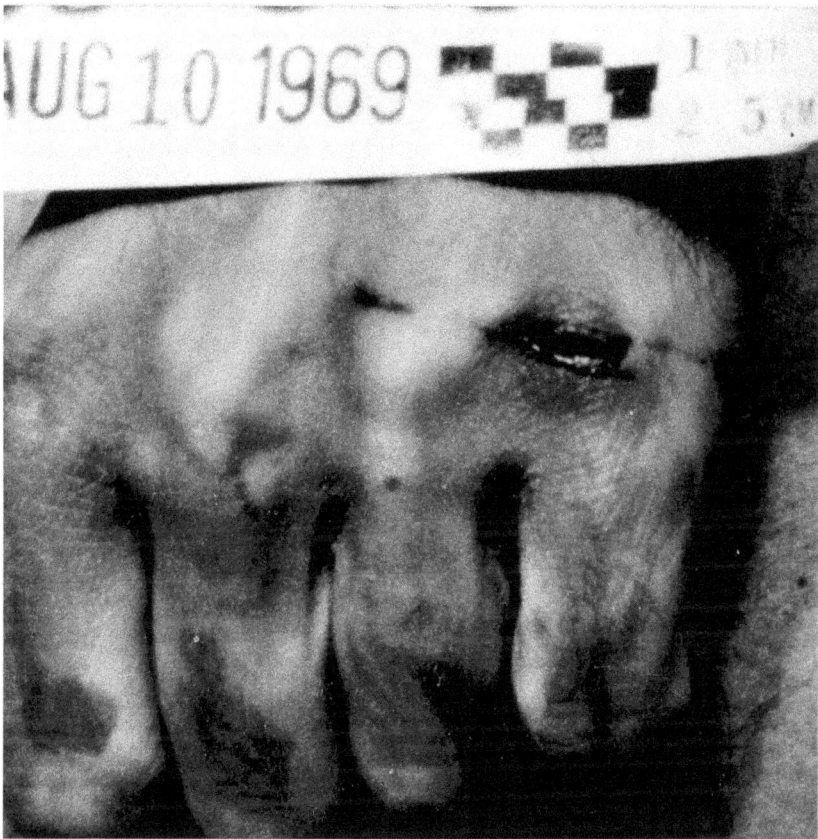

An autopsy photo of Jay Sebring's left hand, which shows multiple defense wounds as he fought to the death in attempt to shield himself, Sharon Tate, Abigail Folger, and Wojciech Frykowski from the Manson family. *Photo courtesy of County of Los Angeles Medical Examiner.*

Charles Manson being led back to his cell following a session in the penalty phase of his trial on March 23, 1971. After heard making death threats to Bugliosi and others if he got the death penalty, the jury was ordered to be sequestered until the end of the penalty trial for their safety. *Photo by the Herald Examiner Collection.*

Manson family killers Patricia Krenwinkel (foreground), Leslie Van Houten (center), and Susan Atkins (rear) during the Tate-LaBianca murder trial. All three were sentenced to the death penalty. *Photo by the Herald Examiner Collection.*

Convicted killer Charles "Tex" Watson being escorted between the jail and court on March 1, 1971. He had a hand in all seven murders, including Jay Sebring and Sharon Tate. His trial began after Manson, Krenwinkel, and Van Houten were convicted and sentenced. He was later found guilty. *Photo by the Herald Examiner Collection.*

CO-273 B (6-64)

OFFICIAL FILE COPY   FILE AUTH._____ CALL UP_____

☐ TEMP.   ☐ FILE CAPTION_____

DATE   May 11, 1971

TO J. Markham, H. Nielsen, R. Papin   C. C.   Edward B. Rasch, Esq.
725 North Fairfax Ave.   Los Angeles
Los Angeles, Calif.   90046   Alvin Greenwald, Esq.
Attn. Miss Helen Nielsen   Los Angeles

ESTATE OF THOMAS JAY SEBRING

- R e n t s -

Miss Helen Nielsen and Gentlemen, et al:

You have continued in your delinquency of rents
and the security deposit. The security deposit
of $1,000.00; rents for February, March, April,
May of $4,000.00; totaling $5,000.00 -
all PAST DUE.

For the Estate and its Administrator,

Bernard Kummer

Bernard J. Kummer
23551 Sutton Drive, Southfield, Mi. 48075
BJK/k

cc: Gerald C. Simon, Esq., Detroit
cc: William R. Power, California
cc: Edward Traubner, Los Angeles

Weeks after Manson, Krenwinkel, Atkins, and Van Houten were
sentenced to death, Bernard Kummer sent a letter dated May 11,
1971, notifying SEBRING managing officers—Helen Nielsen, Jim
Markham, and Robert Papin—they were $5,000 in arrears (almost
$40,000 in 2025) for back rent at the Fairfax location after Jay's
death. *Courtesy of Jay Sebring Collections/The DiMaria Family.*

Mishele, Peggy, and Anthony DiMaria at a 2011 parole board hearing for Charles Watson at Mule Creek State Prison in Ione, California. Photo by Johnny Bishop.

Jay Sebring is credited as the architect of men's hair care, which today is estimated to be around a $100 billion a year industry. Many of his business and hair design concepts are widely emulated in unisex salons and men's hair industries throughout the world. *Courtesy of Jay Sebring Collections/The DiMaria Family.*

AFTERWORD

BY ANTHONY DIMARIA

From the moment I was told I would never see him again, I was pulled into an inexplicable vortex that amplified my desire to be with him, and a need to KNOW everything about my uncle, Jay Sebring.

I was three when he was killed on Friday night August 8, 1969.

It is understandable that some may question the veracity of this "vortex," but then, they never met Jay. They've never lived with the constant reminders that a personal family tragedy would be played out as entertainment on the global stage for over 55 years.

It is also understandable for some to feel that a blood relative might be "too close" to write about a family member. It is equally valid to posit that most are not "close enough" to the realities contained in this book.

From that seminal moment, I was compelled to learn the whole story, whether I liked it or not.

Throughout this lifelong quest, I observed two starkly contrasting Jay Sebrings: the man who existed and a victim portrayed after death.

All that matters is the truth.

CLOSING

Now we have basically covered everything possible. And I'd like to [leave] you with this closing thought. Sometimes when I feel glum and things look pretty dim, I remember this thought myself and that is—for every positive action, there is an equal and positive reaction. And doing everything your best, and to God leave the rest....

Jay Sebring

ACKNOWLEDGMENTS

The scale and scope of Jay Sebring's story required massive research and investigation. The extraordinary blueprint was initiated October 10, 1933, when Bernard and Margarette Kummer started chronicling and saving family collections after the birth of their firstborn, Thomas John Kummer (AKA Jay Sebring), everything throughout his life (which they did with each of their children), and well beyond his death on the night of August 8, 1969. Part of the Kummers' endeavor was necessitated by probate and business developments that emanated after the murder of their son. With the extensive scope (and scale) of material amassed for over ninety years, with additional collections from Jay himself and Peggy and Tony DiMaria—it was as if they had been preparing to tell the Jay Sebring story since its inception.

Formal research for this Jay Sebring story began in 1997 which would culminate in the feature length film documentary *JAY SEBRING....CUTTING to the TRUTH*. This endeavor required the gargantuan dedication, efforts, and talents of Johnny Bishop, Chad Layne, and Voss Boreta.... and is significantly contained in this book.

Our warmest appreciation goes to Joe Torrenueva, who was Jay's true protégé and friend, and one of our guiding lights in the writing of this book.

The authors would like to acknowledge those who either graciously supported or granted interviews for this endeavor or offered valuable insight and support. They appear in alphabetical order: Deana Abell, Noor Ahmed, Paul Anka, Dr. Michael Baden, Max Baer, Jr., Christopher Barson, Rodney Beckwith, Pat Boone, Kim Brake, Linda Lee Cadwell, Charles Champlin, Regina Corrado, Ed Cray, Vic Damone, Ivor Davis, Stephen Davis, Yvonne Depatis-Kupka, Christine DiMaria, Mishele DiMaria, Peggy DiMaria, Tony DiMaria, Dominick Dunne, Griffin Dunne, Bo Edlund (CieloDrive.com), Berto Ferreira, Elle Elliot Fiero, Peter Folger, Patricia Fripp, Larry Geller, Carlos Goodman, Jim Graham, Brian Greenspun, Alvin G. Greenwald, Paul Greenwald, Joe Gunn, Martin Halloran, Laura Hanifin, Pamela Hastings, Frank Hill, Dennis Hopper, Barbara Hoyt, Katie James, Loren Janes, Quincy Jones, Paul R. Kavieff, Stephen Kay, Andy Kimura, Peter Knecht, Fred Kummer, Mike Leavitt, Donna Lebowitz, Barbara Leigh, Deborah Levin, Larry Longlott, Trey Lovell, BarBara Luna, Lance Mazmanian, Ken Mansfield, Dean McClure, Shannon McIntosh, David Milch, Jerry Millen, Jane Ann Morrison, Gordon Mullinger, Andee Nathanson, Andy Ostroy, Valerie Perrine, Jozy Pollock, Amos Russell, Vidal Sassoon, Glenna Schultz, Cami Sebring, Fred Segal, Joe Segal, Patrick Sequeira, Nancy Sinatra, Alisa Statman, Jackie Stewart, David Tadman, Darlene Tafua, Quentin Tarantino, Debra Tate, Terry Thornton, Tito Tiberti, Tony Timpone, Kimberly Valentine, Mamie Van Doren, Gloria Vizer, Robert Wagner, Don "D.J." Waldie, Sheliah Wells, Sandie Wernick, Carrie White, Stuart Whitman, Lauren Wild, Van Williams, Kurt Zacho, and Shane Zade.

Special gratitude is also extended to Manson victim family members who have shared their fight for justice privately and/or in parole hearings throughout the decades: John DeSantis, Corinna LaBianca, Louise LaBianca, Kay Hinman Martley, Gregory Parent, Janet Parent, Shelley Pickford, Angela Smaldino, Lou Smaldino, and Debra Tate.

Thanks to Cara Highsmith for her editorial skills, keen insight, and indefatigable spirit. Cara dedicated three years of her life to this work, and it was great riding shotgun with her.

To Tony Seidl of TD Media for the agenting of this book.

Thanks also goes to Celisia Stanton and Paul Jacobs for their support.

And lastly, thanks go to Steven and Leya Booth of Genius Book Publishing for bringing this work to market and understanding the importance of Jay's role as an American Dreamer, Hollywood revolutionary, and unknown hero, and correcting the record of a historical figure.

SOURCE NOTES

TOM FROM MICHIGAN

1. "You should never be ashamed you're poor," Peggy DiMaria, personal interview, May 2, 2022.
2. "My parents met in New Orleans," Peggy DiMaria, personal interview, May 2, 2022.
3. "He could shoot you down," Peggy DiMaria, personal interview, May 2, 2022.
4. "I think their personalities conflicted," Fred Kummer, personal interview, Aug. 8, 2019.
5. "It doesn't matter to me what you decide," Peggy DiMaria, personal interview, May 2, 2022.
6. "I was one of the four guys painting," Jerry Mullins, personal interview, Aug. 8, 2009.
7. "He was the leader of the pack," Peggy DiMaria, personal interview, May 2, 2022.
8. "He was at his best at night," Peggy DiMaria, personal interview, May 2, 2022.

9. "I heard a stone at my window," Jim Graham, personal interview, Nov. 1, 2008.

10. "He was very friendly," Jim Graham, personal interview, Nov. 1, 2008.

11. "You know, once they lost him," Peggy DiMaria, personal interview, May 2, 2022.

12. "He was very good looking," Jim Graham, personal interview, Nov. 1, 2008.

13. "He was the only CPA that I knew," Peggy DiMaria, personal interview, May 2, 2022.

14. "Instead of being smart and snippy," personal letter from Jay Sebring to Bernard Kummer, February 1949.

15. "He was probably thinking I'm out," Peggy DiMaria, personal interview, May 2, 2022.

OH, A SAILOR'S LIFE IS NOT FOR ME

1. "Disaster. It was disaster," Larry Longlott, personal interview, Jan. 16, 2009.

2. "In the States, there was a Navy yard," Larry Longlott, personal interview, Jan. 16, 2009.

3. "Through the two years we became buddies," Larry Longlott, personal interview, Jan. 16, 2009.

4. "We would sneak out, went to some bars," Larry Longlott, personal interview, Jan. 16, 2009.

5. "My brother, from grade school to high school," Peggy DiMaria, personal interview, May 2, 2022.

6. "He was sharp… real sharp," Larry Longlott, personal interview, Jan. 16, 2009.

7. "He would look for something different," Larry Longlott, personal interview, Jan. 16, 2009.

8. "I wish I could grow as fast as you," personal letter from Jay Sebring to Peggy DiMaria, April 17, 1951.

9. "For you Dad on Father's Day," postcard from Jay Sebring to Bernard Kummer, June 1951.

10. "We never did find the guy," Larry Longlott, personal interview, Jan. 16, 2009.

11. "I told them I'll try it," Larry Longlott, personal interview, Jan. 16, 2009.

12. "My mother was thrilled to death," Peggy DiMaria, personal interview, May 2, 2022.

13. "I never moved so fast in my life," personal letter from Jay Sebring to Kummer family, January 1953.

14. "I just hope they stay back," personal letter from Jay Sebring to his family, January 1953.

15. "I have much reason to believe," personal letter from Jay Sebring to his family, January 1953.

16. "You mentioned the 'September Song,'" personal letter from Jay Sebring to Bernard and Lillian Kummer, October 7, 1953.

17. "I guess you could say I met," personal letter from Jay Sebring to Bernard and Lillian Kummer, October 7, 1953.

18. "Every time I have my hair cut," Cami Sebring, personal interview, October 26, 2008.

19. "Then I know that I can get a good job," personal letter from Jay Sebring to Bernard and Lillian Kummer, October 7, 1953.

A GAP YEAR

1. "The auto companies absolutely refused," Paul R. Kavieff, personal interview, Aug. 16, 2009.

2. "The Purple Gang was a lot of hard guys," Robert A. Rockaway, "The Notorious Purple Gang: Detroit's All-Jewish Prohibition Mob," *Shofar*, Fall 2001.

3. "There were a whole lot of public officials," Paul R. Kavieff, personal interview, Aug. 16, 2009.

4. "I grew up in the east side of Detroit," Tony DiMaria, personal interview, May 2, 2022.

5. "He went to Grinnell's like he was," Peggy DiMaria, personal interview, May 2, 2022.

6. "My mother was really into fashion," Christopher Barson, personal interview, April 4, 2022.

7. "My mom would buy cashmere sweaters," Christopher Barson, personal interview, April 4, 2022.

8. "She loved Chris Connor," Christopher Barson, personal interview, April 4, 2022.

9. "My dad never spoke of Tom Kummer," Christopher Barson, personal interview, April 4, 2022.

10. "One night in the Seventies," Christopher Barson, personal interview, April 4, 2022.

11. "My dad walked off our porch," Peggy DiMaria, personal interview, May 2, 2022.

12. "I remember him telling me," Jim Graham, personal interview, Nov. 1, 2008.

13. "My dad was very strict," Peggy DiMaria, personal interview, May 2, 2022.

14. "Jay said that he had gotten himself," Christopher Barson, personal interview, April 4, 2022.

15. "It was a sensitive subject for my mom," Christopher Barson, personal interview, April 4, 2022.

16. "He was going to California," Martin Halloran, personal interview, Aug. 1, 2009.

THE MIRAGE FACTORY

1. "There is no brighter sun," D.J. Waldie, "Murder in Old Los Angeles," PBS SoCal.org, October 17, 2021.
2. "He was just always his own self," Charles Champlin, personal interview, October 5, 2008.

REINVENTION AND REVOLUTION

1. "You walked into a barbershop," Robert Wagner, personal interview, Oct. 31, 2009.
2. "They weren't exactly putting a bowl," Dennis Hopper, personal interview, Dec. 17, 2008.
3. "Don Buday was driving the car," Peggy DiMaria, personal interview, May 2, 2022.
4. "He was living in the basement," Gloria Vizer, personal interview, April 13, 2022.
5. "He felt that cosmetology school," Peggy DiMaria, personal interview, May 2, 2022.
6. "Comer & Doran was *the* school," Gloria Vizer, personal interview, April 13, 2022.
7. "He loved my car," Gloria Vizer, personal interview, April 13, 2022.
8. "We had a lot of men who attended," Gloria Vizer, personal interview, April 13, 2022.
9. "TJ—as I knew him—was not a normal," Elle Elliot, personal interview, Jan. 24, 2009.
10. "They used to make me nervous," Elle Elliot, personal interview, Jan. 24, 2009.
11. "I took the bus to his apartment," Elle Elliot, personal interview, Jan. 24, 2009.

12. "They put it in a coconut," Elle Elliot, personal interview, Jan. 24, 2009.

13. "Vito was a gypsy sculptor," Elle Elliot, personal interview, Jan. 24, 2009.

14. "Your progress depended on the teacher," Gloria Vizer, personal interview, April 13, 2022.

15. "He told me his plans," Gloria Vizer, personal interview, April 13, 2022.

16. "He drove me around Hollywood," Gloria Vizer, personal interview, April 13, 2022.

17. "It was the last time," Gloria Vizer, personal interview, April 13, 2022.

THE BALL HAS STARTED ITS ROLL

1. "Crenshaw Boulevard is the main street," Hadley Mears, "Crenshaw Boulevard is Rising," *Curbed*, May 17, 2019.

2. "I agree that it is a shame," personal letter from Jay Sebring to Bernard and Lillian Kummer, May 25, 1957.

3. "This is probably the first hands-on," Anthony DiMaria, personal interview, March 26, 2023.

4. "I didn't know where Sunset Boulevard," Quincy Jones, personal interview, Dec. 10, 2013.

5. "One of the quietest gentlemen," Eve Adams, "The Beauty Scene," *Star-News/Vanguard*, Sept. 17, 1968.

6. "Due to the knowledge and artistry," Eve Adams, "The Beauty Scene," *Star-News/Vanguard*, Sept. 17, 1968.

7. "One of my uncles had passed," Peggy DiMaria, personal interview, May 2, 2022.

8. "I've had ample opportunity," Jay Sebring. "Topping Off the Well-Groomed Man," *Playboy*, April 1965.

9. "The family doesn't know what happened," Anthony DiMaria, personal interview, March 26, 2023.

10. "You don't need much to open," Anthony DiMaria, personal interview, March 26, 2023.

11. "Thanks to a few fine people," personal letter from Jay Sebring to Bernard Kummer, March 3, 1959.

12. "The ball has started its roll," personal letter from Jay Sebring to Bernard Kummer, March 3, 1959.

PIECE BY PIECE

1. "People seem to think that," personal letter from Jay Sebring to Bernard Kummer, April 5, 1959.

2. "The only thing wrong is that," personal letter from Jay Sebring to Bernard Kummer, April 5, 1959.

3. "He was the cutest guy," BarBara Luna, personal interview, May 30, 2009.

4. "He was not an outgoing person," BarBara Luna, personal interview, May 30, 2009.

5. "It was a little steakhouse," BarBara Luna, personal interview, May 30, 2009.

6. "Jay wanted to change his name," BarBara Luna, personal interview, May 30, 2009.

7. "I just kept plugging away," *Dateline*, 1963.

8. "I have been sitting here writing," personal letter from Jay Sebring to Bernard Kummer, Aug. 18, 1959.

9. "My dad didn't really understand," Peggy DiMaria, personal interview, May 2, 2022.

10. "When you think about it," Fred Kummer, personal interview, Aug. 8, 2019.

11. "Jay cut my hair like I've never," Vic Damone, personal interview, Nov. 22, 2008.

12. "He cut it in such a way," Vic Damone, personal interview, Nov. 22, 2008.

13. "Jay was a gentleman," Vic Damone, personal interview, Nov. 22, 2008.

14. "Jay deserved success," Vic Damone, personal interview, Nov. 22, 2008.

15. "I had the power of the pencil," Corrine Entratter Sidney, interview with the University of Nevada, Las Vegas, June 5, 2007.

16. "That was the start of the monster," BarBara Luna, personal interview, May 30, 2009.

A JACK IN VEGAS

1. "You want them to come," Corrine Entratter Sidney, interview with the University of Nevada, Las Vegas, June 5, 2007.

2. "This is the first chance that," personal letter from Jay Sebring to Bernard and Lillian Kummer, January 19, 1960.

3. "My dad was in World War II," Brian Greenspun, personal interview, January 26, 2023.

4. "The Sands was the first hotel," Nancy Sinatra, personal interview, Feb. 19, 2009.

5. "It was still very racist," Quincy Jones, personal interview, Dec. 10, 2013.

6. "The Sands was built," Nancy Sinatra, personal interview, Feb. 19, 2009.

7. "Dinah was actually reading," Nancy Sinatra, personal interview, Feb. 19, 2009.

8. "The guys who owned," Nancy Sinatra, personal interview, Feb. 19, 2009.

9. "There was one night," Nancy Sinatra, personal interview, Feb. 19, 2009.
10. "You come into that environment," Paul Anka, personal interview, Jan. 25, 2009.
11. "I'm standing there with this towel," Joe Torrenueva, personal interview, Aug. 3, 2019.

A SLAVE TO FASHION

1. "I wanted everything about *Spartacus*," Kirk Douglas, *The Ragman's Son*: *An Autobiography* (Simon & Schuster, 1988), pg. 288.
2. "When *Spartacus* is released," Sheila Graham, "Hollywood Today," *Los Angeles Evening Citizen News*, June 23, 1959.
3. "For the first time, I managed," Vernon Scott, "Sparta"), *Los Angeles Evening Citizen News*, Aug. 8, 1959.
4. "He wore the same black suit," Loren Janes, personal interview, March 4, 1990.
5. "When I did Alexander Mundy," Robert Wagner, personal interview, Dec. 31, 2009.
6. "One day I walked into the shop," Joe Torrenueva, personal interview, Aug. 3, 2019.

DEMAND AND SUPPLY

1. "Before Jay came along, a barbershop," Charles Champlin, personal interview, Oct. 5, 2008.
2. "French poodles get better clippings," Jay Sebring. "Stylist Hits Neglect of Men's Hair," Associated Press, July 22, 1962.

3. "Jay had a private room," Dominick Dunne, personal interview, Dec. 12, 2009.

4. "We were both in sort of an embryonic," Fred Segal, personal interview, Oct. 31, 2009.

5. "It was really a tough and arduous," Ken Mansfield, personal interview, March 3, 2019.

6. "Jay was not a morning person," Joe Torrenueva, personal interview, Aug. 3, 2019.

7. "It was hard to explain," Robert Wagner, personal interview, Dec. 31, 2009.

8. "Having a new hairstyle for a man," Fred Segal, personal interview, Oct. 31, 2009.

9. "Jay was really good at telling," Joe Torrenueva, personal interview, Aug. 3, 2019.

10. "You bathe and brush your teeth," Larry Geller, personal interview, December 7, 2008.

11. "Henry Fonda came in," Gordon Mullinger, personal interview, Dec. 12, 2008.

12. "I had just got out of cosmetology school," Larry Geller, personal interview, Dec. 7, 2008.

13. "Jay Sebring was so innovative," Larry Geller, personal interview Dec. 7, 2008.

14. "All of Jay's cutters were on a three-year contract," Joe Torrenueva, personal interview, Aug. 3, 2019.

TO HAVE AND TO HOLD ONTO FOR ONE HELL OF A RIDE

1. "My career was taking off," BarBara Luna, personal interview, May 30, 2009.

2. "Cami and I went to Hollywood High," Larry Geller, personal interview, Dec. 7, 2008.

3. "I was sort of twirling around," Cami Sebring, personal interview, Oct. 26, 2008. 10/26/2008.

4. "I flew to Las Vegas separately," Cami Sebring, personal interview, Oct. 26, 2008.

5. "Sammy came in and started handing," Cami Sebring, personal interview, Oct. 26, 2008.

6. "After the wedding I called my mother," Cami Sebring, personal interview, Oct. 26, 2008.

7. "Everybody listened to Johnny Magnus," Joe Torrenueva, personal interview, Aug. 3, 2019.

8. "He loved that xylophone," Cami Sebring, personal interview, Oct. 26, 2008.

9. "We were at PJ's, which was one," Cami Sebring, personal interview, Oct. 26, 2008.

10. "Jay told me at the table," Cami Sebring, personal interview, Oct. 26, 2008.

11. "He (Jay) had that quiet magnetism," Cami Sebring, personal interview, Oct. 26, 2008.

12. "Jay was the first person I knew," Cami Sebring, personal interview, Oct. 26, 2008.

13. "Jay was never the type," Cami Sebring, personal interview, Oct. 26, 2008.

14. "We were driving around on Mulholland," Cami Sebring, personal interview, Oct. 26, 2008.

15. "You didn't usually get people," Dominick Dunne, personal interview, Dec. 12, 2009.

16. "Jay was quite a player," Cami Sebring, personal interview, Oct. 26, 2008.

17. "He told me his dreams," Cami Sebring, personal interview, Oct. 26, 2008.

18. "The house we lived in on Easton," Cami Sebring, personal interview, Oct. 26, 2008.

19. "He used to swim in the pool," Cami Sebring, personal interview, Oct. 26, 2008.
20. "Kind of this crazy guy," Cami Sebring, personal interview, Oct. 26, 2008.
21. "Bobby was crazy about Sandra," Cami Sebring, personal interview, Oct. 26, 2008.
22. "I almost got run over by the Cobra," Stuart Whitman, personal interview, Oct. 4, 2008.
23. "He talked about the day," Cami Sebring, personal interview, Oct. 26, 2008.

THE COST OF SUCCESS

1. "There is an easy casual atmosphere," John Locksher, "How the Hollywood Stars Get Clipped!" *Motion Picture*, July 1963.
2. "You were constantly waiting for Jay," Robert Wagner, personal interview, Oct. 31, 2009.
3. "There was no other place," Gordon Mullinger, personal interview, Dec. 12, 2008.
4. "People would often ask the barbers," Joe Torrenueva, personal interview, Aug. 3, 2019.
5. "The board kept giving us," Gordon Mullinger, personal interview, Dec. 12, 2008.
6. "Jay was the odd man out," Charles Champlin, personal interview, Oct. 5, 2008.
7. "Jay first told me about," Joe Torrenueva, personal interview, Aug. 3, 2019.
8. "The barbers wanted to put us," Joe Torrenueva, personal interview, Aug. 3, 2019.
9. "There was a big resistance," Robert Wagner, personal interview, Oct. 31, 2009.

10. "You know what it costs," Larry Geller, personal interview, Dec. 7, 2008.

11. "Cami would call my mom," Peggy DiMaria, personal interview, May 2, 2022.

12. "I didn't get to see him," Cami Sebring, personal interview, Oct. 26, 2008.

13. "That was a difficult thing," Cami Sebring, personal interview, Oct. 26, 2008.

14. "Jay comes in one day," Joe Torrenueva, personal interview, Aug. 3, 2019.

15. "I had the feeling that," Charles Champlin, personal interview, Oct. 5, 2008.

16. "Jay took it very hard," Peggy DiMaria, personal interview, May 2, 2022.

FRIENDS TO THE END

1. "I'm a hard guy to have for a friend," Marshall Terrill. *Steve McQueen In His Own Words* (Dalton Watson Fine Books, 2020), pg. 107.

2. "I'm glad Dean's dead," Marshall Terrill. *Steve McQueen: The Life and Legend of a Hollywood Icon* (Triumph Books, 2010), pg. 73.

3. "Go ahead, I don't care," John Millranny. "Van Nuys Actor Slain at Girlfriend's Home," *Valley Times*, Oct. 6, 1962.

4. "These iconic images, a lot," Nancy Sinatra, personal interview, Feb. 19, 2009.

5. "I don't know that Steve McQueen," Cami Sebring, personal interview, Oct. 26, 2008.

6. "He knew style. He knew what," Joe Torrenueva, personal interview, Aug. 3, 2019.

7. "McQueen never liked it when," Frank Hill, personal interview, March 20, 2023.

8. "Steve and Jay were very much alike," *Steve McQueen: The Life and Legend of a Hollywood Icon* (Triumph Books, 2010), pg. 215.

9. "Jay was driving like a bat," Gordon Mullinger, personal interview, Dec. 12, 2008.

10. "Laurel Canyon the one we go up," Amos Russell, personal interview, Feb. 15, 2009.

11. "Steve was worse," Quincy Jones, personal interview, Dec. 10, 2013.

12. "Jay was like a magnet," Nancy Sinatra, personal interview, Feb. 19, 2009.

13. "You could get LSD over the counter," *Steve McQueen: The Life and Legend of a Hollywood Icon* (Triumph Books, 2010), pg. 295.

14. "Steve and Jay and I were inseparable," Quincy Jones, personal interview, Dec. 10, 2013.

15. "I'd get these strange phone calls," Joe Torrenueva, personal interview, Aug. 3, 2019.

16. "I asked Jay if there was," Fred Segal, personal interview, Oct. 31, 2009.

17. "No way am I playin' a cop," Neile McQueen Toffel. *My Husband, My Friend* (Atheneum, 1986), pg. 163.

18. "Both men were high as kites," Neile McQueen Toffel. *My Husband, My Friend* (Atheneum, 1986), pg. 163.

19. "Jay Sebring was my best friend," Neile McQueen Toffel. *My Husband, My Friend* (Atheneum, 1986), pg. 163.

ENTER THE DRAGON

1. "Jay did Elvis' hair," Larry Geller, Larry Geller, personal interview, Dec. 7, 2008.

2. "Jay was very strategic," Joe Torrenueva, personal interview, Aug. 3, 2019.

3. "Jay had many sides," Larry Geller, personal interview, Dec. 7, 2008.

4. "My dad was very fond," Darlene Tafua, personal interview, Aug. 5, 2019.

5. "Jay arranges for us to take," Salvatore R. Orefice. *Tripping with the King and Others* (BookSurge Publishing, 2007), pg.77

6. "When this kid punched," Loren Franck. "Full Contact Karate… and Ed Parker," *Black Belt*, November 1985.

7. "Bruce and I were married," Linda Lee Cadwell, personal interview, Sept. 25, 2009.

8. "We're chug-a-lugging," Salvatore R. Orefice. *Tripping with the King and Others* (BookSurge Publishing, 2007), pg. 102

9. "It wasn't until the Ed Parker," David Tadman, personal interview, Sept. 26, 2009.

10. "I took a phone call," Linda Lee Cadwell, personal interview, Sept. 25, 2009.

11. "Per our phone conversation," letter from William Dozier to Bruce Lee, Jan. 25, 1965.

12. "It just happened that," Gordon Mullinger, personal interview, Dec. 12, 2008.

13. "Jay and Bruce had," Linda Lee Cadwell, personal interview, Sept. 25, 2009.

14. "Jay was cutting the hair," Linda Lee Cadwell, personal interview, Sept. 25, 2009.

15. "Bruce didn't only show," Vic Damone, personal interview, Nov. 22, 2008.

16. "When he (Lee) came," Fred Segal, personal interview, Oct. 31, 2009.

17. "Jay had an overall influence," Linda Lee Cadwell, personal interview, Sept. 25, 2009.

18. "Bruce would come in," Joe Torrenueva, personal interview, Aug. 3, 2019.

19. "Well, at one time, Bruce," Loren Franck. "Ed Parker on Bruce Lee, Elvis Presley, Full Contact Karate… and Ed Parker," *Black Belt*, November 1985.

20. "He and our stunt guys," Van Williams, personal interview, May 14, 2009.

21. "When you see all these," David Tadman, personal interview, Sept. 26, 2009.

THE GO-GO GENERATION

1. "The night after that," Matt Keleman. "Q & A with Johnny Rivers," *Las Vegas Magazine*, Feb. 19, 2016.

2. "Well, what do you mean?" "Q & A with Johnny Rivers," *Las Vegas Magazine*, Feb. 19, 2016.

3. "It was a way of life," David Kamp. "Live at the Whisky," *Vanity Fair*, Nov. 10, 2000.

4. "All those guys that owned," Fred Segal, personal interview, Oct. 31, 2009.

5. "The sixties were an interesting," Nancy Sinatra, personal interview, Feb. 19, 2009.

6. "So, I came back to Los Angeles," David Kamp. "Live at the Whisky," *Vanity Fair*, Nov. 10, 2000.

7. "I'd like to sign you," David Kamp. "Live at the Whisky," *Vanity Fair*, Nov. 10, 2000.

8. "I had been to all the other," Joe Torrenueva, personal interview, Aug. 3, 2019.

9. "Steve McQueen had his own," Stephen Davis, personal interview, Dec. 12, 2009.

10. "This unique entertainment phenomenon," Steve McQueen's FBI files.

11. "Everything was so much looser," Joe Torrenueva, personal interview, Aug. 3, 2019.

12. "Brian Epstein called the office," Gordon Mullinger, personal interview, Dec. 12, 2008.

13. "It didn't just happen," Vidal Sassoon, personal interview, Dec. 20, 2008.

14. "We threw a big cocktail party," Gordon Mullinger, personal interview, Dec. 12, 2008.

15. "Jay was a stud, man," Larry Geller, personal interview, Dec. 7, 2008.

16. "There was a time when," Peter Knecht, personal interview, Feb. 19, 2009.

EXQUISITE BEAUTY

1. "We took my show to Italy," Pat Boone, personal interview, May 16, 2022.

2. "I suggested there was a place," Pat Boone, personal interview, May 16, 2022.

3. "College isn't going to help," Alisa Statman with Brie Tate. *Restless Souls: The Sharon Tate Family's Account of Stardom, the Manson Murders, and a Crusade for Justice* (!t Books, 2012), pg. 62.

4. "I came to Los Angeles," Sheila Wells, personal interview, May 24, 2009.

5. "Mrs. Tate, what do you think," Alisa Statman with Brie Tate. *Restless Souls: The Sharon Tate Family's Account of Stardom, the Manson Murders, and a Crusade for Justice* (!t Books, 2012), pg. 63.

6. "Gene says, 'Jay, a new starlet," Larry Geller, personal interview, Dec. 7, 2008.

7. "We lived right up the street," Sheila Wells, personal interview, May 24, 2009.

8. "Jay Sebring looked questioningly," Joe Hyams. *Mislaid in Hollywood: The Autobiography of a Slightly Reformed Columnist Who Knew His Victims All Too Well* (P. H. Wyden, 1973), pg. 126

9. "Although he charged $15 to $500," Joe Hyams. *Mislaid in Hollywood: The Autobiography of a Slightly Reformed Columnist Who Knew His Victims All Too Well* (P. H. Wyden, 1973), pg. 126

10. "Does he know anything," Joe Hyams. *Mislaid in Hollywood: The Autobiography of a Slightly Reformed Columnist Who Knew His Victims All Too Well* (P. H. Wyden, 1973), pg. 127

11. "She was as beautiful," Joe Hyams. *Mislaid in Hollywood: The Autobiography of a Slightly Reformed Columnist Who Knew His Victims All Too Well* (P. H. Wyden, 1973), pg.127

12. "Sharon said, 'Oh I've met,'" Sheila Wells, personal interview, May 24, 2009.

13. "It's been six months," Salvatore R. Orefice. *Tripping with the King and Others* (BookSurge Publishing, 2007), pg. 40)

14. "A girlfriend of mine," Stuart Whitman, personal interview, Oct. 4, 2008.

15. "Sharon and Jay were madly," Dominick Dunne, personal interview, Dec. 12, 2009.

16. "I loved Sharon," Gordon Mullinger, personal interview, Dec. 12, 2008.

17. "I have a friend Betty," Sheila Wells, personal interview, May 24, 2009.

18. "He always dressed so beautifully," Sheila Wells, personal interview, May 24, 2009.

19. "She had on an overcoat," Kurt Zacho, personal interview, March 29, 2009.

20. "He was very charming," Debra Tate, personal interview, Sept. 21, 2008.

21. "I was expecting at the time," Peggy DiMaria, personal interview, May 2, 2022.

22. "Jay was an absolute invite," Debra Tate, personal interview, Sept. 21, 2008.

23. "When Sharon would come," Fred Segal, personal interview, Oct. 31, 2009.

24. "We were all on a boat," Kimberly Valentine, personal interview, March 25, 2023.

25. "One afternoon we saw," Kimberly Valentine, personal interview, March 25, 2023.

26. "Jay had just come back," Tony DiMaria, personal interview, May 2, 2022.

27. "Sharon went and met," Kimberly Valentine, personal interview, March 25, 2023.

28. "Looked like it was written," Stuart Whitman, personal interview, Oct. 4, 2008.

EXPAND THE BRAND

1. "Jay knew he could," Joe Torrenueva, personal interview, Aug. 3, 2019.

2. "His work was very comfortable," Hector Rodriguez, personal interview, March 16, 2009.

3. "I remember Jay spending," Joe Torrenueva, personal interview, Aug. 3, 2019.

4. "I would make Jay's paycheck," Gordon Mullinger, personal interview, Dec. 12, 2008.

5. "Their hair looks like," quote from Jay Sebring. Playboy, Jay Sebring, Topping off the well-groomed man, April 1965

6. "We told people not," Larry Geller, personal interview, Dec. 7, 2008.

7. "He told me his dreams," Cami Sebring, personal interview, Oct. 26, 2008.

8. "In those days I had long hair," Jackie Stewart, personal interview, April 12, 2001.

9. "Just a wee Scottish note," personal letter from Jackie Stewart to Jay Sebring, Oct. 11, 1968.

10. "Jay and I put the school," Gordon Mullinger, personal interview, Dec. 12, 2008.

11. "With such a wide cross-section," "Jay Sebring: Topping off the well-groomed man," *Playboy*, April 1965

12. "Meeting Jay Sebring had," Jim Markham. *Big Lucky* (Jim Markham Enterprises, 2020), pg. 45

THE TASTEMAKER

1. "I remember going to grade," Peggy DiMaria, personal interview, May 2, 2022.

2. "Those were the days," Martin Halloran, personal interview, Aug. 8, 2009.

3. "One of the things," Jerry Millen, personal interview, Aug. 8, 2009.

4. "It's funny. People can," Dennis Hopper, personal interview, Dec. 12, 2008.
5. "Gypsy Rose Lee had," Gordon Mullinger, personal interview, Dec. 12, 2008.
6. "Now, she has him," Gordon Mullinger, personal interview, Dec. 12, 2008.
7. "Jay was upset because," Paul Greenwald, personal interview, Feb. 28, 2010.

BREAKING UP IS HARD TO DO

1. "Fiscally up until the sixties," Vidal Sassoon, personal interview, Dec. 20, 2008.
2. "I think we kind of lost," Dean McClure, personal interview, March 3, 2023.
3. "Jay had a policy," Quentin Tarantino, personal interview, Aug. 7, 2018.
4. "There was a big exodus," Joe Torrenueva, personal interview, Aug. 3, 2019.
5. "There was tension between," Gordon Mullinger, personal interview, Dec. 12, 2008.
6. "It was just a creepy story," Dick Kleiner. "Did Sharon Have a Premonition?" The Tennessean, Dick Kleiner, Sept. 7, 1969.
7. "Sharon was wanting to get," Peggy DiMaria, personal interview, May 2, 2022.
8. "I was up for a TV series," Sharon Tate, "School is Over, So Sharon Sails Out," January 31, 1966.
9. "Jay was a little apprehensive," Debra Tate, personal interview, Sept. 21, 2008.
10. "Sharon got a job," Stuart Whitman, personal interview, Oct. 4, 2008.

11. "What had impressed me," Debra Tate. *Sharon Tate Recollection* (Running Press, 2014), pg. 198.
12. "She told me she had," Sheila Wells, personal interview, May 24, 2009.
13. "That's rare. When you're," BarBara Luna, personal interview, May 30, 2009.
14. "Jay needs to find a woman," Gwen Tate cassette recording, June23, 1966.
15. "Sharon called Jay over," Debra Tate, personal interview, Sept. 21, 2008.
16. "I felt very, you know, uneasy," Los Angeles Police Department polygraph test of Roman Polanski, Aug. 16, 1969.
17. "I don't know what," Fred Segal, personal interview, Oct. 31, 2009.
18. "Sharon was very nice," Andee Nathanson, personal interview, June 13, 2022.
19. "Jay was with Steve McQueen," Jozy Pollack, personal interview, June 16, 2022.
20. "Sharon was one of the most," Debra Tate. *Sharon Tate Recollection* (Running Press, 2014), pg. 215.
21. "There are some guys," Peter Knecht, personal interview, Feb. 19, 2009.
22. "In London, Jay came," Vidal Sassoon, personal interview, Dec. 20, 2008.
23. "It kind of amazed me," Tony DiMaria, May 2, 2022.

THE BEAUTIFUL PEOPLE

1. "I would go on the weekends," Dennis Hopper, personal interview, Dec. 12, 2008.

2. "We'd gone through the Summer," Dennis Hopper, personal interview, Dec. 12, 2008.

3. "So now people my age," David Milch, personal interview, Feb. 1, 2009.

4. "You would hear about picket," Gordon Mullinger, personal interview, Dec. 12, 2008.

5. "We didn't want the old," Stephen Davis, personal interview, Dec. 12, 2009.

6. "He would put us down," Lonnie Frisbee and Roger Sachs. *Not by Might, Nor by Power: The Jesus Revolution Part One* (Freedom Publications, 2017), pg. 49.

7. "San Francisco was the first," David Milch, personal interview, Feb. 1, 2009.

8. "We were nothing of," Vidal Sassoon, personal interview, Dec. 20, 2008.

9. "One night Vadim watched," Patricia Bosworth. *Jane Fonda: The Private Life of a Public Woman* (Houghton Mifflin Harcourt, 2011), pg. 283.

10. "LSD was then the drug," Neile McQueen Toffel. *My Husband, My Friend* (Atheneum, 1986), pg. 130.

11. "We'd go on weekends," Dennis Hopper, personal interview, Dec. 12, 2008.

12. "He actually had his own," Cami Sebring, personal interview, Oct. 26, 2008.

13. "Jay thought very highly," Cami Sebring, personal interview, Oct. 26, 2008.

14. "She had never seen me," Cami Sebring, personal interview, Oct. 26, 2008.

15. "He was protective of Sharon," BarBara Luna, personal interview, May 30, 2009.

16. "Their relationship had switched," Debra Tate, personal interview, Sept. 21, 2008.

17. "I just felt they were together," Fred Segal, personal interview, Oct. 31, 2009.
18. "Did you hear that?!" Ed Sikov. *Mr. Strangelove: A Biography of Peter Sellers* (Hyperion, 2002), pg. 281.
19. "We have written a note," personal letter from R.O. Murphy to Jay Sebring, July 9, 1968.

TRIAL AND ERROR

1. "You are cordially invited," invitation from Congressman Thomas M. Rees to Jay Sebring, March 21, 1968.
2. "I'd like to take this opportunity," personal letter from Robert F. Kennedy to Jay Sebring, April 10, 1968.
3. "I think the dream," Ed Cray, personal interview, Oct. 3, 2009.
4. "If something happened that Jay," Gordon Mullinger, personal interview, Dec. 12, 2008.
5. "I have the pimp show up," Richard Corliss. *The Hollywood Screenwriters: A Film Comment Book* (Avon Books, 1972), pg. 193.
6. "Jane Fonda is absolutely delighted," postcard from James Poe to Jay Sebring, July 18, 1969.
7. "San Francisco wasn't a big city," Sandie Wernick, personal interview, July 6, 2023.
8. "Art was close friends," Sandie Wernick, personal interview, July 6, 2023.
9. "Art was a pig," Sandie Wernick, personal interview, July 6, 2023.
10. "My friend Wendy worked," Patricia Fripp, personal interview, July 8, 2023.

11. "Art contacted Jay and said," Patricia Fripp, personal interview, July 8, 2023.

YOU'VE COME A LONG WAY, BABY

1. "Mainly because I love," Mildred Hamilton. "Stars Fall for His Clips," *San Francisco Examiner*, May 9, 1969.
2. "Thank you for your invitation," personal letter from Bruce Lee to Jay Sebring, 1969.
3. "Anyone who has hair," Mildred Hamilton. "Stars Fall for His Clips," *San Francisco Examiner*, May 9, 1969.
4. "My most expensive haircut," Mildred Hamilton. "Stars Fall for His Clips," *San Francisco Examiner*, May 9, 1969.
5. "I kept the desert boots," Mildred Hamilton. "Stars Fall for His Clips," *San Francisco Examiner*, May 9, 1969.
6. "We extend congratulations," telegram from Bernard and Lillian Kummer to Jay Sebring, May 24, 1969.
7. "Our opening was spectacular," Patricia Fripp, personal interview, July 8, 2023.
8. "Jay inherited me and naturally," Patricia Fripp, personal interview, July 8, 2023.
9. "He was generous and kind," Yvonne Depatis-Kupka, personal interview, July 23, 2023.
10. "Jay was a showman," Patricia Fripp, personal interview, July 8, 2023.
11. "No one ever walked out," Patricia Fripp, personal interview, July 8, 2023.
12. "He'd stay in San Francisco," Patricia Fripp, personal interview, July 8, 2023.
13. "Every Friday evening," Patricia Fripp, personal interview, July 8, 2023.

14. "The walkout from a few," Joe Torrenueva, personal interview, Aug. 3, 2019.
15. "Many up-and-coming barbers," Joe Torrenueva, personal interview, Aug. 3, 2019.
16. "A barber who did 86 haircuts," Dave Larsen. "Barbers Find that Business is Thinning Out," *Los Angeles Times*, March 25, 1968.
17. "The bill basically said," Joe Torrenueva, personal interview, Aug. 3, 2019.
18. "A lot of them passed," Joe Torrenueva, personal interview, Aug. 3, 2019.
19. "I was seriously grieving," Joe Torrenueva, personal interview, Aug. 3, 2019.

THE FAMILY

1. "Every morning I'd drive," Joe Torrenueva, personal interview, Aug. 3, 2019.
2. "Your parents threw you out," Joe Lewis. *Road Trip to Nowhere: Hollywood Encounters the Counterculture* (University of California Press, 2022), pg. 256.
3. "My sister had a friend," Patricia Krenwinkel, State of California Board Parole Hearings transcripts, CieloDrive.com, Dec. 29, 2916.
4. "Prior to leaving with Manson," Patricia Krenwinkel, State of California Board Parole Hearings transcripts, CieloDrive.com, Dec. 29, 2916.
5. "He would tell me," Patricia Krenwinkel, State of California Board Parole Hearings transcripts, CieloDrive.com, Dec. 29, 2916.
6. "We traveled up to," Patricia Krenwinkel, State of

California Board Parole Hearings transcripts, CieloDrive.com, Dec. 29, 2916.

7. "A New Generation has come," David Milch, personal interview, Feb. 1, 2009.

8. "The song that caught," Susan Atkins interview with Richard Caballero and Paul Caruso. CieloDrive.com, Dec. 1, 1969.

9. "San Francisco was the first," David Milch, personal interview, Feb. 1, 2009.

10. "He gave me the loan," Ann Louise Bardach. "Jailhouse Interview: Bobby Beausoleil," *Oui*, November 1981.

11. "I joined a band," Ann Louise Bardach. "Jailhouse Interview: Bobby Beausoleil," *Oui*, November 1981.

12. "I was living on Pacific Coast," Charles Watson, State of California Board Parole Hearings transcripts, CieloDrive.com, Oct. 27, 2016.

13. "I can see these things," Joe Taysom. "The Song Neil Young Wrote About the Infamous Murderer Charles Manson," Far Out, Dec. 24, 2020.

14. "You meet people and audition," Sandy Robertson. "Hi, I'm, umm, TERRY MELCHER," *Sounds*, May 12m 1979.

15. "He did partake of the girls," Ivor Davis. *Manson Exposed: A Reporter's 50-Year Journey into Madness and Murder* (Cockney Kid, 2019), pg. 322.

16. "Manson asked Rosina for money," Charles Watson, State of California Board Parole Hearings transcripts, CieloDrive.com, Oct. 15, 2016.

EXPOSED

1. "Hi, my name is Jay," *Hair Power*, unfinished film, 1969.
2. "Jay got into a very specific," Peggy DiMaria, personal interview, May 2, 2022.
3. "I think Jay wasn't promoting," Anthony DiMaria, personal interview, September 21, 2023.
4. "So far, my greatest contribution," *Hair Power*, unfinished film, 1969.
5. "We don't know how," Anthony DiMaria, personal interview, September 21, 2023.
6. "It was magical," Rudi Altobelli to Martin Bashir, *20/20*, 2011.
7. "He told her how," Ed Sanders. *Sharon Tate: A Life* (Da Capo Press, 2015), pg. 50.
8. "Married? Sharon, he's," Alisa Statman with Brie Tate. *Restless Souls: The Sharon Tate Family's Account of Stardom, the Manson Murders, and a Crusade for Justice* (!t Books, 2012), pg. 28.
9. "It doesn't matter who he's," Alisa Statman with Brie Tate. *Restless Souls: The Sharon Tate Family's Account of Stardom, the Manson Murders, and a Crusade for Justice* (!t Books, 2012), pg. 29.
10. "We have a good arrangement," Ed Sanders. *Sharon Tate: A Life* (Da Capo Press, 2015), pg. 147.
11. "Sharon told me about Roman," Ed Sanders. *Sharon Tate: A Life* (Da Capo Press, 2015), pg. 119.
12. "He's very sympathetic," Debra Tate. *Sharon Tate Recollection* (Running Press, 2014, pg. 212.
13. "He treated her like," Thomas Kiernan. The Roman Polanski Story (Delilah/Grove Press, 1980), pg. 214.

14. "Jay went with Sharon," Kirk Douglas, *The Ragman's Son*: An Autobiography (Simon & Schuster, 1988), pg. 288.

15. "Roman and Sharon sort of," Dominick Dunne, personal interview, Dec. 12, 2009.

16. "I don't know why she," Fred Segal, personal interview, Oct. 31, 2009.

17. "I met them on the street," Kurt Zacho, personal interview, March 29, 2009.

18. "They were in love," Andee Nathanson, personal interview, June 13, 2022.

19. "I do believe, down the road," Debra Tate, personal interview, Sept. 21, 2008.

20. "Later we sat around," Joe Hyams. *Mislaid in Hollywood: The Autobiography of a Slightly Reformed Columnist Who Knew His Victims All Too Well* (P. H. Wyden, 1973), pg. 218

21. "She wasn't devastated," Ed Sanders. *Sharon Tate: A Life* (Da Capo Press, 2015), pg. 169.

22. "When we were in London," Debra Tate. *Sharon Tate Recollection* (Running Press, 2014), pg. 262.

23. "The police were questioning," Jill Sederstrom. "Who Did Roman Polanski First Suspect Who Murdered His Wife Sharon Tate?" Oxygen.com, Aug. 25, 2020.

24. "I see that Jay has this," Paul Greenwald, personal interview, Feb. 28, 2010.

25. "I drew the papers," Alvin Greenwald, personal interview, Feb. 28, 2010.

26. "I can tell you what I know," Peggy Di Maria, personal interview, Dec. 17, 2001.

HOT AUGUST NIGHT

1. "What had been promised," Donald "D.J." Waldie, personal interview, Sept. 20, 2009.

2. "Morally we started to sink," Nancy Sinatra, personal interview, Feb. 19, 2009.

3. "It was awe inspiring," Ed Cray, personal interview, Oct. 3, 2009.

4. "The very last time," Debra Tate, personal interview, Sept. 21, 2008.

5. "It was about three," Stuart Whitman, personal interview, Oct. 4, 2008.

6. "I just felt they were together," Fred Segal, personal interview, Oct. 31, 2009.

7. "Please don't hurt me," Vincent Bugliosi and Curt Gentry. *Helter Skelter: The True Story of the Manson Murders* (W.W. Norton & Company, 1974), pg. 227.

8. "I'm the devil," Vincent Bugliosi and Curt Gentry. *Helter Skelter: The True Story of the Manson Murders* (W.W. Norton & Company, 1974), pg. 228.

9. "Be quite and come with me," Susan Atkins. *Child of Satan, Child of God* (Bantam Books, 1978), pg. 139.

10. "There were practical jokes," Tony DiMaria, May 2, 2022.

11. "Can't you see she's," quote from Jay Sebring (find out where this came from)

12. "The only thing I couldn't," Vic Damone, personal interview, Nov. 22, 2008.

13. "Anybody with a gun," Linda Lee Cadwell, personal interview, Sept. 25, 2009.

14. "Once they realized the events," Debra Tate, personal interview, Sept. 21, 2008.
15. "The girls were bringing," Charles Watson psychiatric evaluation, 1971.
16. "It would have impaired," Michael Baden, personal interview, Dec. 13, 2009.
17. "Frykowski ran out and Susan Atkins," Stephen Kay, personal interview, Oct. 25, 2008.
18. "You've got me," Susan Atkins. "Susan Atkins' Story of 2 Nights of Murder," CieloDrive.com, Dec. 14, 1969.
19. "Sharon was sitting on the floor," Stephen Kay, personal interview, Oct. 25, 2008.
20. "Watson describes a scene," Patrick Sequeira, personal interview, Mar. 16, 2010
21. "The autopsy findings indicate," Michael Baden, personal interview, Dec. 13, 2009.
22. "Jay was a very brave man," Stephen Kay, Oct. 25, 2008.

A WEIRD HOMICIDE

1. "Murder! Murder!" Ivor Davis. Ivor Davis. *Manson Exposed: A Reporter's 50-Year Journey into Madness and Murder* (Cockney Kid, 2019), pg. 5.
2. "The Sharon Tate murder," *60 Minutes Australia*, April 2, 2019.
3. "There was a disaster," Loren Kantor. "Disaster in Hollywood," *Splice Today*, Aug. 26, 2020.
4. "TV cameras, radio, and print," Ivor Davis. *Manson Exposed: A Reporter's 50-Year Journey into Madness and Murder* (Cockney Kid, 2019), pg. 9.

5. "What are *you* doing here?" Ivor Davis. *Manson Exposed: A Reporter's 50-Year Journey into Madness and Murder* (Cockney Kid, 2019), pg. 9.

6. "Is it Sharon, Bill?" Ivor Davis. *Manson Exposed: A Reporter's 50-Year Journey into Madness and Murder* (Cockney Kid, 2019), pg. 10.

7. "Doris, have you talked," Alisa Statman with Brie Tate. *Restless Souls: The Sharon Tate Family's Account of Stardom, the Manson Murders, and a Crusade for Justice* (!t Books, 2012), pg. 2.

8. "My God, Sharon's been murdered," Alisa Statman with Brie Tate. *Restless Souls: The Sharon Tate Family's Account of Stardom, the Manson Murders, and a Crusade for Justice* (!t Books, 2012), pg. 1

9. "We were at Caesar's Palace," Tony DiMaria, personal interview, May 2, 2022.

10. "It was like time stopped," Peggy DiMaria, personal interview, May 2, 2022.

11. "I was cutting hair," Joe Torrenueva, personal interview, Aug. 3, 2019.

12. "A writer named Gary DeVore," Stuart Whitman, personal interview, Oct. 4, 2008.

13. "It was terrible when," Robert Wagner, personal interview, Oct. 31, 2009.

14. "Bill Cosby calls me," Quincy Jones, personal interview, Dec. 10, 2013.

15. "There are times in your life," Nancy Sinatra, personal interview, Feb. 19, 2009.

16. "I felt badly because," Vic Damone, personal interview, Nov. 22, 2008.

17. "We talked about it," Linda Lee Cadwell, personal interview, Sept. 25, 2009.

18. "I was walking down," BarBara Luna, personal interview, May 30, 2009.

19. "Don't worry honey," *Steve McQueen: The Life and Legend of a Hollywood Icon* (Triumph Books, 2010), pg. 296.

20. "He got paranoid as hell," *Steve McQueen: The Life and Legend of a Hollywood Icon* (Triumph Books, 2010), pg. 297.

21. "The main word to describe," Dominick Dunne, personal interview, Dec. 12, 2009.

LIVE FREAKY, DIE FREAKY

1. "Sebring was wearing only," "A Night of Horror," TIME, Aug. 22, 1969.

2. "Theories of sex, drug and witchcraft." "A Night of Horror," *TIME*, Aug. 22, 1969.

3. "You know what I gotta do," Los Angeles Police Department polygraph of Roman Polanski, Aug. 16, 1969.

4. "I just wanted to know," Los Angeles Police Department polygraph of Roman Polanski, Aug. 16, 1969.

5. "Oh, from what I've heard," Los Angeles Police Department polygraph of Roman Polanski, Aug. 16, 1969.

6. "Sharon told me about it," Los Angeles Police Department polygraph of Roman Polanski, Aug. 16, 1969.

7. "The victims were Hollywood people," Stephen Kay, personal interview, Oct. 25, 2008.

8. "The press went nuts," Ed Cray, personal interview, Oct. 3, 2009.

9. "The detective, in fact," Barry Farrell. "In Hollywood, the Dead Keep Right on Dying," *LIFE*, Nov. 7, 1969.

10. "They had been turned on." "The Sharon Tate Orgies," PAGEANT, November, 1969.

11. "That's, that's insanity," Dennis Hopper, personal interview, Dec. 12, 2008.

12. "It was the dark side," Ann O'Neill. "Manson's Lasting Legacy: 'Live Freaky, Die Freaky,'" CNN, Aug. 10, 2009.

13. "I don't dig that weird," Steve McQueen. "Those Sharon Tate Orgies," PAGEANT magazine, November 1969.

14. "Warren Beatty would know," Kelsey Norman. "The Truth About Helter Skelter," *Speeding Bullitt*, Nov. 18, 2021.

15. "That chick was happy," Jake Austen. "Sammy Devil Jr.," *VICE*, May 1, 2008.

16. "The telephone rang," Joe Hyams book. (Find page number)

17. "Parable-ized because that's," Donald "D.J." Waldie, personal interview, Sept. 20, 2009.

18. "These murders were experienced," David Milch, personal interview, Feb. 1, 2009.

19. "I remember when I read," Michael Baden, personal interview, Dec. 13, 2009.

20. "If we make the victims' fates," Donald "D.J." Waldie, personal interview, Sept. 20, 2009.

21. "They want to see people," Tony Timpone, personal interview, May 14, 2009.

22. "People love to see others," David Milch, personal interview, Feb. 1, 2009.

23. "For a long period," Quentin Tarantino, personal interview, July 7, 2018.

THE FAMILY SHIT-SHOW

1. "I had blood all over," Alisa Statman with Brie Tate. *Restless Souls: The Sharon Tate Family's Account of Stardom, the Manson Murders, and a Crusade for Justice* (!t Books, 2012), pg. 12.
2. "I can't tell about it," Susan Denise Atkins, "The Slayings of Leno and Rosemary La Bianca," The Capital Times, Dec. 18, 1969.
3. "Sadie, are you afraid," Susan Atkins. *Child of Satan, Child of God* (Bantam Books, 1978), pg. 163.
4. "To know him was," Stephen Kay, personal interview, Oct. 25, 2008.
5. "I got about halfway," Stephen Kay, personal interview, Oct. 25, 2008.
6. "Of course, I'd heard," Berto Ferreria, personal interview, July 9, 2023.
7. "Indeed, it was a bad," Ivor Davis. *Manson Exposed: A Reporter's 50-Year Journey into Madness and Murder* (Cockney Kid, 2019), pg. 164.
8. "As the days turned," Ivor Davis. *Manson Exposed: A Reporter's 50-Year Journey into Madness and Murder* (Cockney Kid, 2019), pg. 166.

THE SPAGHETTI DEFENSE

1. "The evidence at this trial," Vincent Bugliosi with Curt Gentry. *Helter Skelter: The True Story of the Manson Murders* (W. W. Norton & Co., 1974), pg. 411.
2. "In Manson's mind," Vincent Bugliosi with Curt Gentry. *Helter Skelter: The True Story of the Manson Murders* (W. W. Norton & Co., 1974), pg. 410.

3. "He wanted you to forget," Barbara Hoyt, personal interview, April 10, 2009.

4. "God, it scared me," Barbara Hoyt, personal interview, April 10, 2009.

5. "I started listening," Barbara Hoyt, personal interview, April 10, 2009.

6. "The last thing she says," Barbara Hoyt, personal interview, April 10, 2009.

7. "I remember going to," Barbara Hoyt, personal interview, April 10, 2009.

8. "Kanarek asked me," Barbara Hoyt, personal interview, April 10, 2009.

9. "Never… You got any," Alisa Statman with Brie Tate. *Restless Souls: The Sharon Tate Family's Account of Stardom, the Manson Murders, and a Crusade for Justice* (!t Books, 2012), pg. 127.

10. "Mr. Tate, did you ever," Alisa Statman with Brie Tate. *Restless Souls: The Sharon Tate Family's Account of Stardom, the Manson Murders, and a Crusade for Justice* (!t Books, 2012), pg. 128.

11. "That question is stricken," Alisa Statman with Brie Tate. *Restless Souls: The Sharon Tate Family's Account of Stardom, the Manson Murders, and a Crusade for Justice* (!t Books, 2012), pg. 128.

12. "Is it true that Sharon," Alisa Statman with Brie Tate. *Restless Souls: The Sharon Tate Family's Account of Stardom, the Manson Murders, and a Crusade for Justice* (!t Books, 2012), pg. 128.

13. "Are you going to use," Alisa Statman with Brie Tate. *Restless Souls: The Sharon Tate Family's Account of Stardom, the Manson Murders, and a Crusade for Justice* (!t Books, 2012), pg. 135.

14. "I will have *you* removed," Vincent Bugliosi with Curt Gentry. *Helter Skelter: The True Story of the Manson Murders* (W. W. Norton & Co., 1974), pg. 482.

15. "It isn't going to be," Vincent Bugliosi with Curt Gentry. *Helter Skelter: The True Story of the Manson Murders* (W. W. Norton & Co., 1974), pg. 482.

16. "He is not capable," Linda Deutsch. "Judge Finds Accused Leader of Tate Murder Mission, Tex Watson, Insane," Associated Press, Oct. 31, 1970.

17. "Thank you, your honor," Vincent Bugliosi with Curt Gentry. *Helter Skelter: The True Story of the Manson Murders* (W. W. Norton & Co., 1974), pg. 500.

18. "It's all your fear," "Thank you, your honor," Vincent Bugliosi with Curt Gentry. *Helter Skelter: The True Story of the Manson Murders* (W. W. Norton & Co., 1974), pg. 506.

19. "I have come to the," Vincent Bugliosi with Curt Gentry. *Helter Skelter: The True Story of the Manson Murders* (W. W. Norton & Co., 1974), pg. 529.

20. "You have no authority." "Death Sentence Decreed for Manson, 3 Women," United Press International, March 30, 1971.

21. "You've all judged." "Death Sentence Decreed for Manson, 3 Women," United Press International, March 30, 1971.

22. "You're removing yourselves." "Death Sentence Decreed for Manson, 3 Women," United Press International, March 30, 1971.

DAMAGED DYNASTY

1. "Goodbye Sharon, and may," Dial Torgeson, Associated Press, Aug. 14, 1969.
2. "As the family stood up," Dial Torgeson, Associated Press, Aug. 14, 1969.
3. "Though this person will," Alvin Greenwald, Jay Sebring eulogy, Aug. 13, 1969.
4. "Most men spend their lives," Steve Queen, Jay Sebring eulogy, Aug. 13, 1969.
5. "As we sat waiting," Neile McQueen Toffel. *My Husband, My Friend* (Atheneum, 1986), pg. 199.
6. "The whole thing was," Joe Torrenueva, personal interview, Aug. 3, 2019.
7. "I remember we went," Anthony DiMaria, personal interview, September 21, 2023.
8. "If anything were to ever," Jim Markham. *Big Lucky* (Jim Markham Enterprises, 2020), pg. 44.
9. "I was in my SEBRING," Jim Markham. *Big Lucky* (Jim Markham Enterprises, 2020), pg. 57.
10. "We've got all of his," Jim Markham. *Big Lucky* (Jim Markham Enterprises, 2020), pg. 58.
11. "The only way to deal," Jim Markham. *Big Lucky* (Jim Markham Enterprises, 2020), pg. 60
12. "As I remember and read," personal letter from Bernard Kummer to Jim Markham, Aug. 28, 1969.
13. "I'm living in Jay's house," Tatiana Siegel. "Manson Victim's Friend Posits Alternative Motive: 'I Never Bought into the Race War Theory," *The Hollywood Reporter*, July 30, 2019.
14. "The FBI has our lines," Jim Markham. *Big Lucky* (Jim Markham Enterprises, 2020), pg. 62.

15. "I was caught in the middle," Jim Markham. *Big Lucky* (Jim Markham Enterprises, 2020), pg. 62.

16. "Once in California, I had," Kristen Heinzinger. "Jim Markham Reflects on Jay Sebring and His Hollywood Life," *American Salon*, Aug. 22, 2019.

17. "We are relieved," Joan Kaber. *Women's World*, "Tate, Sebring Parents Help Launch Successor," Dec. 4, 1969.

18. "What makes you qualified," Joan Kaber. *Women's World*, "Tate, Sebring Parents Help Launch Successor," Dec. 4, 1969.

19. "She treated me like," Jim Markham. *Big Lucky* (Jim Markham Enterprises, 2020), pg. 69.

20. "Jay was excited too," Jim Markham. *Big Lucky* (Jim Markham Enterprises, 2020), pg. 69.

21. "Gwen's assumption seemed," Jim Markham. *Big Lucky* (Jim Markham Enterprises, 2020), pg. 69.

22. "The department store business," Jim Markham. *Big Lucky* (Jim Markham Enterprises, 2020), pg. 74.

23. "I had kept in touch," Joe Torrenueva, personal interview, Aug. 3, 2019.

24. "We need to talk about," Jim Markham. *Big Lucky* (Jim Markham Enterprises, 2020), pg. 84.

25. "I was thinking more," Jim Markham. *Big Lucky* (Jim Markham Enterprises, 2020), pg. 85.

26. "Well, take it or leave it," Jim Markham. *Big Lucky* (Jim Markham Enterprises, 2020), pg. 85.

27. "I was shocked and disappointed," Jim Markham. *Big Lucky* (Jim Markham Enterprises, 2020), pg. 86.

28. "You have created and developed," personal letter from Bernard Kummer to Jim Markham, Helen Nielsen, and Robert Papin, April 13, 1971.

PAROLE PURGATORY

1. "All these defendants got," Stephen Kay, personal interview, Oct. 25, 2008.
2. "At one point Doris," Stephen Kay, personal interview, Oct. 25, 2008.
3. "It's very surreal and disturbing," Anthony DiMaria, personal interview, September 21, 2023.
4. "I was pleasantly surprised," personal letter from Charles "Tex" Watson to Anthony DiMaria, Oct. 17, 2009.
5. "What mercy, sir, did," Charles Watson, State of California Board Parole Hearings transcripts, YouTube.com, May 1, 1984.
6. "Anthony! Steve Kay," Anthony DiMaria, personal interview, September 21, 2023.
7. "I got all the money," Charles Manson to Dianne Sawyer, "Good Morning America," Aug. 9, 2004
8. "Debra, listening to them," Diane Sawyer, "Good Morning America," Aug. 9, 2004
9. "These crimes didn't end," Anthony DiMaria to Dianne Sawyer, Good Morning America/ABC News, Aug. 9, 2004
10. "Again, I think that," Dianne Sawyer, "Good Morning America," Aug. 9, 2004
11. "The laws are designed," Anthony DiMaria, personal interview, September 21, 2023.
12. "In March of 2008," James Whitehouse, California Department of Corrections and Rehabilitation parole board hearing for Susan Atkins, July 16, 2008.
13. "There are many things," Anthony DiMaria, California

Department of Corrections and Rehabilitation parole board hearing for Susan Atkins, July 16, 2008.

14. "This development—47 years," Anthony DiMaria, California Department of Corrections and Rehabilitation parole board hearing for Patricia Krenwinkel, Dec. 30, 2016.

15. "This is a vast overreach," DiMaria letter to California Department of Corrections and Rehabilitation parole board members, Jan. 30, 2017.

16. "Let there be no distraction," DiMaria letter to California Department of Corrections and Rehabilitation parole board members, Jan. 30, 2017.

17. "After consulting with victim," George Gascón statement from the Los Angeles Police Department District Attorney's Office, July 13, 2022

18. "It's incomprehensible to directly," Anthony DiMaria, personal interview September 21, 2023

19. "Miss Van Houten's attorney states," Anthony DiMaria impact statement to California Department of Corrections and Rehabilitation parole board, Sept. 6, 2017.

DISTORTION, DISTRACTION AND DEFLECTION

1. "Looks like the appellate court," personal email from Christopher Weber to Anthony DiMaria, May 30, 2023.

2. "The record contains some evidence," Judge Frances Rothschild (need to source this)

3. "Going over my files," personal email from Anthony

DiMaria to California Gov. Gavin Newsom, July 7, 2023.

4. "The images of what Leslie," personal email from Anthony DiMaria to California Gov. Gavin Newsom, July 7, 2023.

5. "I was living in New York," Andy Ostroy. *The Back Room*, Aug. 19, 2023

6. "With Jay, image was everything," Greg King, *Sharon Tate and the Manson Murders* (Barricade Books, 2016), pg. 52.

7. "Insecure?! He had the all-time," Nancy Sinatra, personal interview, Feb. 19, 2009.

8. "Can I say this?" Cami Sebring, personal interview, Oct. 26, 2008.

9. "This from someone who," Peggy DiMaria, personal interview, May 2, 2022.

10. "There's nothing wrong with," Peter Knecht, personal interview, Feb. 19, 2009.

11. "I got your message," voicemail left by Vincent Bugliosi to Anthony DiMaria, Dec. 10, 2013.

12. "Mr. DiMaria, my name," voicemail left by Gail Bugliosi to Anthony DiMaria, Dec. 10, 2013.

13. "I needed to know what," Andy Ostroy. *The Back Room*, Aug. 19, 2023.

14. "The mundane truth reveals," Anthony DiMaria, personal interview, September 21, 2023.

15. "The one thing everyone," Tom O'Neill, *CHAOS: Charles Manson, the CIA, and the Secret History of the Sixties,* (Little, Brown and Company, 2019), pg. 46.

16. "An aimless life in America," Tom O'Neill, *CHAOS: Charles Manson, the CIA, and the Secret History of the Sixties,* Little, Brown and Company, 2019, pg. 18.

17. "Footage, clearly filmed by Polanski," Tom O'Neill, *CHAOS: Charles Manson, the CIA, and the Secret History of the Sixties*, (Little, Brown and Company, 2019), pg. 54.

18. "He was close with a cabal," Tom O'Neill, *CHAOS: Charles Manson, the CIA, and the Secret History of the Sixties*, (Little, Brown and Company, 2019), pg. 82.

19. "I was rebuffed by the intimates," Tom O'Neill, *CHAOS: Charles Manson, the CIA, and the Secret History of the Sixties*, (Little, Brown and Company, 2019), pg. 49.

20. "Sincerest gratitude to the survivors," Tom O'Neill, *CHAOS: Charles Manson, the CIA, and the Secret History of the Sixties*, (Little, Brown and Company, 2019), pg. 442.

21. "I believe Manson had," Tatiana Siegel, "Manson Victim's Friend Posits Alternative Motive: 'I Never Bought into the Race War Theory,'" *The Hollywood Reporter*, July 30, 2019.

22. "In her piece, Ms. Siegel," email from Anthony DiMaria to *The Hollywood Reporter* editor, August 2019.

23. "Jay Sebring was a pioneer," Juliet Bennett Rylah. "Documentary Shows Jay Sebring More Than a Manson Victim," *We Like L.A.*, Sept. 20, 2020.

SELECTED BIBLIOGRAPHY

Amburn, Ellis. *The Sexiest Man Alive: A Biography of Warren Beatty*. Harper Collins, 2002.

Angelo. Frank. *Yesterday's Detroit*. E.A. Seeman Publishing, 1974.

Bacon, Nancy. *Legends and Lipstick: My Scandalous Stories of Hollywood's Golden Era*. Excessive Nuance, 2017.

Biskind, Peter. *Easy Riders, Raging Bulls*. Bloomsbury Publishing, 1998.

Bosworth, Patricia. *Jane Fonda: The Private Life of a Public Woman*. Houghton Mifflin Harcourt, *2011*.

Corliss, Richard. *The Hollywood Screenwriters: A Film Comment Book*. Avon, 1972.

Dawes, Amy. *Sunset Boulevard: Cruising the Heart of Los Angeles*. Los Angeles Times Books, 2002.

Douglas, Kirk. *The Ragman's Son*. Pocket Books, 1988.

Eubanks, Bob with Matthew Scott Hansen. *It's in the Book, Bob!* BenBella, 2004.

Faith, Karlene. *The Long Prison Journey of Leslie Van Houten: Life Beyond the Cult*. Northeastern University Press, 2001.

Feinstein, Barry. *Unseen McQueen*. Reel Art Press, 2013.

Frisbee, Lonnie with Roger Sachs. *Not By Might, Nor By Power: The Jesus Revolution*. Freedom Publications, 2017.

Kavieff, Paul R. *The Purple Gang: Organized Crime in Detroit*. Barricade Books, 2000.

Kiernan, Thomas. *The Roman Polanski Story*. Delilah Grove Press, 1980.

King, Greg. *Sharon Tate and the Manson Murders*. Barricade Books, 2000.

Krist, Gary. *The Mirage Factory: Illusion, Imagination, and the Invention of Los Angeles*. Crown, 2018.

McKeen, William. *Everybody Had an Ocean: Music and Mayhem in 1960s Los Angeles*. Chicago Review Press, 2017.

McQueen, Neile. *My Husband, My Friend*. Atheneum, 1986.

Orefice, Salvatore R. *Tripping with the King and Others*. BookSurge Publishing, 2007.

Phillips, John with Jim Jerome. *Papa John: A Music Legend's Shattering Journey Through Sex, Drugs and Rock 'n' Roll*. Dolphin Books, 1986.

Phillips, Michelle. *California Dreamin': The True Story of the Mamas and Papas*. Warner Books, 1986.

Phoenix, Charles. *Southern California in the '50s*. Angel City Press, 2001.

Pollock, Jozy. *Backstage Pass to Heaven*. CreateSpace, 2017.

Polly, Matthew. *Bruce Lee: A Life*. Simon & Schuster, 2018.

Priore, Domenic. *Riot on Sunset Strip: Rock 'n' Roll's Last Stand in Hollywood.* Jawbone Press, 2007.

Sanders, Ed. *Sharon Tate: A Life.* Da Capo Press, 2015.

Sanford, Christopher. *Polanski.* Palgrave Macmillan, 2008.

Sikov, Ed. *Mr. Strangelove: A Biography of Peter Sellers.* Hyperion, 2002.

Statman, Alisa with Brie Tate. *Restless Souls: The Sharon Tate Family's Account of Stardom, the Manson Murders, and a Crusade for Justice.* It Books, 2012.

Tate, Debra. *Sharon Tate: Recollection.* Running Press, 2014.

Terrill, Marshall. *Steve McQueen: The Life and Legend of a Hollywood Icon.* Triumph Publishing, 2010.

www.ingramcontent.com/pod-product-compliance
Lightning Source LLC
Chambersburg PA
CBHW070047030426
42335CB00016B/1820